Modern Rice Technology and Income Distribution in Asia

Modern Rice Technology and Income Distribution in Asia

■

edited by
Cristina C. David
Keijiro Otsuka

Lynne Rienner Publishers ■ Boulder & London
International Rice Research Institute ■ Manila

Published in the United States of America in 1994 by
Lynne Rienner Publishers, Inc.
1800 30th Street, Boulder, Colorado 80301

and in the United Kingdom by
Lynne Rienner Publishers, Inc.
3 Henrietta Street, Covent Garden, London WC2E 8LU

Published in the Philippines by the
International Rice Research Institute
P.O. Box 993, 1099 Manila
Philippine ISBN 971-22-0043-4 (pb)

Library of Congress Cataloging-in-Publication Data
Modern rice technology and income distribution in Asia / edited by
    Cristina C. David, Keijiro Otsuka.
        p. cm.
    Includes bibliographical references (p.   ) and index.
    ISBN 1-55587-404-5 (hc : alk. paper)
    ISBN 1-55587-431-2 (pb : alk. paper)
    1. Rice—Asia.   2. Rice—Economic aspects—Asia.   3. Rice—Asia—
Varieties.   4. Farm income—Asia.   5. Green Revolution—Asia.
6. Agricultural innovations—Asia.   I. David, Cristina C.
II. Otsuka, Keijiro.
SB191.R5M555   1993
338.1'3318—dc20   93-28584
                                                          CIP

British Cataloguing in Publication Data
A Cataloguing in Publication record for this book
is available from the British Library.

Printed and bound in the United States of America

⊖∞ The paper used in this publication meets the requirements
     of the American National Standard for Permanence of
     Paper for Printed Library Materials Z39.48-1984.

To
Randolph Barker,
Yujiro Hayami,
and Robert W. Herdt

Contents

Tables

Figures

Preface

The spread of modern rice varieties and the accompanying technology in Asia has been dubbed the "Green Revolution." There has been no significant literature that empirically analyzes the impact of differential adoption of that modern rice technology across production environments. Yet fears are widely expressed that limited adoption of the modern rice technology in the irrigated and favorable rainfed lowland areas has exacerbated inequalities in the distribution of income. It is generally believed that by allocating greater rice research resources to unfavorable rice-growing regions, overall distribution of income will be improved.

The goals of the studies we report herein are to understand the impact of technological change in favorable rice-growing regions on incomes of people in the unfavorable rice-growing areas—those bypassed by the new technology—and to shed light on the trade-off between efficiency and equity objectives in rice research allocation across production environments.

Two decades have passed since the introduction of the modern rice varieties and their accompanying technology in Asia. It is now possible to examine not only the direct effects of technology on productivity, factor use, and income but also its indirect effects through labor, land, and commodity market adjustments. But because the ultimate outcome of the adjustment processes involved in adoption of the technology depends crucially on the characteristics of the production environment and on the institutional and policy framework governing the functioning of factor and commodity markets, an international collaborative research effort was required to develop a comprehensive understanding of technological impact. This volume represents the final report of such an effort by economists in seven Asian countries—the Philippines, Indonesia, Thailand, Bangladesh, Nepal, India, and China—with widely diverse production environments and agrarian and policy structures.

A common methodological framework in examining the question was agreed upon by the collaborators during a 1987 planning workshop at the International Rice Research Institute (IRRI). Although a Philippine study initiated in 1985 served as a prototype, the collaborators were encouraged to adopt modifications suited to each country's circumstances as well as the

xxi

capability for data collection. Participants in subsequent workshops and field visits to Thailand, Bangladesh, Indonesia, and Nepal reviewed progress of the work, exchanged experiences and observations, and jointly resolved methodological problems encountered during the analysis. In 1990, the results of the country studies were presented in a workshop at IRRI and reviewed and discussed with leading agricultural economists concerned with technology impact.

The idea for this research originated with Yujiro Hayami. His guidance and technical advice was invaluable in shaping the methodological approach adopted for the project.

Many individuals contributed critical comments to various papers written by collaborators and added greatly to the quality of this report. Randolph Barker, Robert Evenson, and Ammar Siamwalla participated in all workshops and provided valuable support during the evolution of our project.

We also benefited from comments and suggestions from Arsenio Balisacan, Cynthia Bautista, Ernesto Bautista, Jere Behrman, Dante Canlas, Gelia Castillo, Luzviminda Cornista, Ian Coxhead, Bart Duff, Emmanuel Esguerra, Artemia Ferrer, John Flinn, Wojcieck Florkowski, Sagrario Floro, Sam Fujisaka, Dennis Garrity, Leonardo Gonzales, Cielito Habito, Alejandro Herrin, Mukarram Hossain, Ponciano Intal, Zenaida Kenmore, Gurdev Khush, Masao Kikuchi, Mario Lamberte, Leonardo Lanzona, Antonio Ledesma, Abraham Mandac, Mahar Mangahas, Jerry McIntosh, Shen Minggao, Excelsis Orden, Alastair Orr, Weera Pakuthai, K. Palanisami, Thelma Paris, Tirso Paris, Jr., Prabhu Pingali, Jaime Quizon, V. Rajagopalan, Hanumantha Rao, Mitch Renkow, Fermina Rivera, Mark Rosegrant, Scott Rozell, Nicholas Stern, Peter Warr, Ram Yadav, and Hubert Zandstra.

We are deeply indebted to IRRI's highly competent staff, who worked tirelessly and unselfishly. Esther B. Marciano, Cristina Carpio, Luisa Bambo, Divah Cecilia Depositario, and Alice Laborte performed a whole range of research tasks from field surveys to computer analysis.

The secretarial staff—Mirla Domingo, Veronica Gonzalvo, Yolanda Aranguren, Jocelyn Reyes, and Hedda Rada—not only typed manuscripts but also assisted in administrative matters and organizational work.

We are grateful to Walt Rockwood, who patiently edited our manuscript and guided us through the final process of publication.

The Rockefeller Foundation provided generous financial support to the country studies and to network activities. Robert W. Herdt, director for agricultural sciences, recognized the value of this research not only for the knowledge to be gained but also for its implications to research prioritization and for the strengthening of national research institutions. This collaborative research was led by Cristina C. David and Keijiro Otsuka, who were formerly senior scientist and visiting scientist, respectively, at IRRI.

Our sixteen collaborators enthusiastically conducted the country studies and patiently revised estimates and drafts to provide a consistent analytical framework and coherent analysis of the impact of modern rice technology on income distribution.

All of us gained an intercountry perspective on agricultural development that will ultimately enrich our professional contributions to our respective countries.

This book is dedicated to Randolph Barker, Yujiro Hayami, and Robert W. Herdt, three former agricultural economists at IRRI. Without their insight and research on the rice economy of Asia, this study would not have been possible. We acknowledge our debt to them.

Cristina C. David
Keijiro Otsuka

Modern Rice
Technology and
Income Distribution in Asia

■

PART 1

■

Scope, Focus, and Methodology

1
Introduction

■

CRISTINA C. DAVID AND KEIJIRO OTSUKA

The Green Revolution that developed in Asia during the 1960s had a dramatic and pervasive impact on the tropical Asian rice economy. The cultivation frontier—the limit of new land available foʀ rice production—was reached in most countries by 1965. Despite that, annual growth in rice production in South and Southeast Asia, which was 3.3% for the decade prior to 1965, remained at 3.0% from 1966 to 1987. The major source of growth shifted from crop area expansion to increases in yields per hectare, ranging from 1.8 to 2.3% per year after 1965. Those yield increases were made possible by the widespread adoption of fertilizer-responsive, high-yielding modern rice varieties introduced in 1966. By 1970, the modern varieties had been adopted in 50% of the rice areas in the Philippines. In South and Southeast Asia as a whole, the adoption rate of modern varieties was 40% by the end of the 1970s and reached 60% by the end of the 1980s.

The term "modern variety" refers to the short-statured, stiff-strawed, fertilizer-responsive, nonphotoperiod-sensitive Indica rice varieties, as exemplified by IR8, which were developed at the International Rice Research Institute (IRRI) during 1962–1966 (Chandler 1982). Modern varieties that followed IR8 incorporated new traits—improved grain quality, greater pest resistance, and shorter growth duration—that further promoted their diffusion.

The modern varieties were fertilizer-responsive, a marked difference from the traditional Indica varieties, which had tall, weak stems and lodged easily in fields where high rates of fertilizer were applied. Thus, the modern varieties increased demand for fertilizer (David 1976). Public investment in irrigation also accelerated, as modern varieties increased the profitability of irrigated rice culture (Hayami and Kikuchi 1978). Nationwide production programs to disseminate the new technology and provide credit to farmers were instituted in many countries.

Adoption of the new technology lowered the unit cost of rice production and provided countries with an opportunity to reconcile the inherently conflicting food policy objectives of providing low and stable prices to consumers, increasing farm income, and achieving rice self-sufficiency. Without the remarkable productivity growth that the modern varieties brought to Asian rice farming, either the cost of rice production and hence the

3

price of rice to consumers would have increased significantly or food self-sufficiency ratios in most Asian countries would have declined. In fact, several countries that were traditionally major rice importers—Indonesia, India, and the Philippines—rapidly adopted modern varieties and achieved self-sufficiency, which sharply reduced the Asian share in total world rice imports, from about 60% in the 1960s to 20% in the late 1980s. In the Philippines and India, real rice price has declined significantly since the 1970s. Because of the broad impact of modern varieties and their associated inputs on production, income, prices, and consumption, the phenomenon became popularly known as the Green Revolution.

THE EQUITY ISSUE

Although there is little dispute about the productivity effects of modern varieties, questions continue to be raised about their impact on income distribution. There is widespread belief, particularly in the early Green Revolution literature, that the modern varieties may have made income distribution less equitable (Wharton 1969; Johnston and Cownie 1969; Frankel 1971; Cleaver 1972; Griffin 1974).

Early researchers often argued that although the modern variety itself was scale-neutral, the larger and more commercialized farms had a higher rate of adoption, mainly because they had better access to information and formal credit markets and better ability to provide the cash requirements of modern variety adoption. It was further argued that small-scale farmers and tenant farmers either did not adopt or were late adopters and thus may even have been hurt when real rice price declined. It was also believed that as large farms became more profitable, landowners consolidated landholdings through tenant eviction and land purchase, exacerbating the problem of landlessness. Furthermore, increases in farm size and income of large farmers may have promoted mechanization, further reducing employment opportunities and wage rates for landless households and small-scale farmers.

Comprehensive, rigorous empirical studies do not generally support those arguments. There were a few cases where adoption rates by large and owner-operated farms may have initially been more rapid (Hazell and Ramasamy 1991). That trend, however, was soon mitigated by government credit programs and by induced institutional innovations, such as the interlinking of credit with product and input markets, which lowered the cost of credit to small-scale and tenant farmers. Accumulated empirical evidence indicates that farm size, tenure, and other social and institutional factors did not significantly affect the diffusion rate of modern varieties (Ruttan 1977; Barker and Herdt 1985).

The distribution of productivity gains among landholders and landless households depends directly on the factor-use bias of the new technology and indirectly on its growth effects on the nonfarm sector and on the supply elasticities of labor and land. Studies have generally shown that adoption of modern varieties increases labor demand, particularly when the effects on cropping intensity and its effects on growth of nonfarm sector are taken into account (Barker and Cordova 1978; Ishikawa 1978; Bell, Hazell, and Slade 1982; Hazell and Ramasamy 1991; Heytens 1991c). Much less is known, however, about the relative income gains among landlords, owner and tenant cultivators, and agricultural laborers.

From the equity point of view, the extent to which adoption of new rice technology increases demand for hired labor is critically important, because poor landless laborers and marginal farmers depend on employment opportunities in agriculture. Theoretically, landholders are expected to receive relatively more of the direct income benefits—in the form of increased returns to land—than landless households as long as the supply of land is more inelastic than the supply of labor (Binswanger and Quizon 1989; Quizon and Binswanger 1983; Evenson 1975). Empirically, however, these distributional issues have seldom been analyzed.

The positive distributional effects of lower rice prices resulting from technological change are often ignored. Studies in the Philippines and India show that poor consumers receive most of the benefits of the new rice technology through lower rice prices (Hayami and Herdt 1977; Quizon and Binswanger 1986; Coxhead and Warr 1991). Declining real rice prices have a favorable effect on income distribution, nutrition, and health, because rural and urban poor households—landless agricultural laborers, small-scale farmers, and urban unskilled workers—are principally net buyers of rice and spend a greater proportion of their income on rice than do the rich.

Our review of the literature on the Green Revolution indicates that the main empirically unresolved distributional issue is the regional distribution (see Lipton and Longhurst 1989). Agricultural technologies are highly location-specific, and the scope for the direct transfer of technology across regions is inherently limited. In particular, adoption of modern varieties has been constrained by environmental conditions, especially degree of water control, and thus diffusion of modern varieties has been limited to irrigated and favorable rainfed areas (Barker and Herdt 1985). Nearly 40% of the rice areas in South and Southeast Asia, particularly the unfavorable rainfed lowland, upland, deepwater, and tidal wetland areas, were still planted to traditional varieties by the late 1980s (IRRI 1991). Concern has been expressed that the widening productivity gap between favorable and unfavorable rice-production environments not only accentuates relative income disparities but also exacerbates the absolute poverty of the farmers and the landless in the unfavorable environments (Falcon 1970; Ruttan 1977; Lipton and Longhurst 1989; Vyas 1992).

Renkow (1993) recently developed a general equilibrium model that demonstrated that a conflict between the goals of improving agricultural productivity and enhancing income distributional equity does not appear to exist in the case of the wheat Green Revolution in Pakistan. This conclusion, however, depends on the untested assumption that regional wage differential does not arise due to efficient interregional migration of labor.

Modern varieties suited to irrigated and favorable rainfed environments were developed because the research cost of producing new technologies for these areas was lower than for less favorable rainfed environments. A large amount of basic research knowledge already existed for irrigated rice, and the probability of success for applied research in that environment was higher. Most major research stations, including IRRI, were in or near irrigated or favorable rainfed rice-growing environments. Moreover, the homogeneous character of irrigated areas across regions widened the scope of technology transfer and increased the total benefit to be derived from a new variety or improved cultural practice.

The people living in the rainfed areas within a country, however, are generally poor. Asian countries with a high proportion of unfavorable rice-growing environments (such as those in South Asia) are, to a large extent, poorer than other rice-growing countries. The research cost of increasing rice productivity for those environments is high. The problems are widely different and much more difficult to solve across diverse types of unfavorable environments. In these areas, not only are the degree of water control lower, the soil quality poorer, and the climatic conditions harsher, but also the marketing and social infrastructure are much less developed.

There is, therefore, a common belief that a sharp trade-off exists between efficiency and equity in allocating rice research investments among different production environments or regions. There has been, however, no major empirical research to examine whether and to what extent differential technology adoption across production environments adversely affects income distribution. Moreover, not enough attention has been given to the proposal that areas not well suited to intensive rice cultivation, such as the uplands, may be better suited for crops that will better enhance agricultural sustainability in those areas. Yet national and international rice research institutions have been under pressure to shift allocation of resources toward the unfavorable environments.

Allocation of rice research across production environments must consider more than the trade-off between efficiency and equity impacts. It is equally important to evaluate the probability of scientific success of rice research in the unfavorable rice-production environment vis-à-vis crops better suited to those environments. Economic returns of investments in land development in those environments must also be evaluated.

FOCUS

What effect has technological change in the favorable rice-growing areas had on the welfare of people in the unfavorable areas bypassed by the new technology? Technology affects the income of the rural population not only directly by influencing productivity and factor use but also indirectly by influencing output and factor prices. The manner in which the indirect benefits are distributed across different production environments depends on how output and factor markets adjust to changes in the supply of output and on changes in demand for inputs triggered by the technological change in favorable areas.

Because labor is a mobile factor of production and the main resource of the majority of the poor rural population, the ultimate distributional impact of the modern rice technology will critically depend on the nature of labor market adjustment. If the higher demand for labor resulting from modern variety adoption in the favorable areas induces migration—permanent, seasonal, or both—from unfavorable to favorable areas, the gains from increased labor income will be shared across production environments. However, if labor markets are imperfect or labor migration costs are high, labor-saving technology, such as tractors, threshers, and direct seeding, may instead be adopted in favorable areas. This will also equalize wages regionally but at a lower level of employment and wages, which will reduce incomes of the landless or near-landless households whose livelihood depends mainly on labor earnings.

The effect of differential technology adoption and the subsequent labor market adjustments on returns to land in favorable and unfavorable areas is another important issue, particularly because land is distributed less equally than labor among rural households. Because the supply of land is much more inelastic than the labor supply, unequal access to new, profitable technology will widen the difference in returns to land between favorable and unfavorable production areas. However, if labor migration reduces farm size in favorable areas and increases farm size in unfavorable areas, the potential inequities may be partly mitigated. Also, gains from higher returns to land in the favorable areas could be shared with tenants or leaseholders through land reform or other institutional changes.

Even if market prices of rice decline in response to increased output in favorable production environments, the potentially adverse effects on rice farm incomes in the unfavorable production environments may be alleviated by reallocating land use to other crops and family labor time toward nonfarm employment. In fact, the cultivation of perennial tree crops instead of rice in ecologically fragile environments, such as the sloping uplands, will improve agricultural sustainability. Similarly, if nonfarm employment opportunities exist, a decrease in labor income from rice farming in unfavorable areas can be offset by increases in nonfarm income.

Greater public investment in market infrastructure and agricultural research for the unfavorable areas, as well as policies to promote production of nonrice crops, can also mitigate adverse effects.

APPROACH

Proper evaluation of the trade-off between efficiency and equity effects of differential technology adoption across production environments requires quantification of the direct and indirect effects on income of the various earners from rice production.

This book comprises an analysis of the factors affecting adoption of modern varieties and a quantification of the direct impact of modern variety adoption on fertilizer and labor use as well as on yield and rice cropping intensity. The indirect effects of differential technology adoption are evaluated by examination of:

- Regional migration patterns based on village-level population growth,
- Regional factor-price (wage and land rent) differentials, and
- Determinants of rural household incomes by source.

Because of limited data availability, however, population and land rent analyses were not made for all countries studied. Finally, the overall distributional consequences of the differential technology adoption is evaluated by applying Gini decomposition analysis.

The following chapters report the results of an international collaborative work among seven Asian countries to examine the impact on income distribution of differential technology adoption across production environments. The countries covered are Bangladesh, China, India, Indonesia, Nepal, the Philippines, and Thailand. They represent a wide variety of conditions in terms of production environments, agrarian structure, policy framework, and overall performance of the economy that ultimately condition the distributional effects of differential technology adoption.

China is unique among the countries studied for several reasons. The impact of differential adoption of hybrid rice, instead of conventional modern varieties, is examined. Hybrid rice, which has a 15 to 20% higher yield potential than conventional modern varieties, was introduced in 1974 and is now grown on almost 40% of China's rice crop area. Nearly all rice is grown in irrigated fields. China is the most densely populated country and has the smallest farm size and most intensively cultivated rice farms. Its average fertilizer use and crop yields are highest among the countries studied. China's agrarian structure and characteristics of factor markets are uniquely different. Operational landholding is equally distributed because farm size is determined by equity considerations. Land market transactions among households are not allowed, although rental of land is occasionally observed. There are no landless households in the rural sector. Use of hired labor in rice production is extremely limited, and interregional migration is restricted.

Although government market interventions are pervasive in varying degrees in the other six countries, output and factor markets function more freely there than in China. Thailand, traditionally a major rice exporter, has the largest endowment of land relative to population. Bangladesh, Indonesia, and Nepal have the lowest ratio of arable land to agricultural population. Issues of tenancy and land reform are important in the Philippines and the South Asian countries, where tenancy is more common than in Indonesia and Thailand.

The specific modern varieties adopted differ among the six countries. Following the release of IR8 in 1966, a series of modern varieties was developed and released by IRRI and national institutions. Those new varieties incorporated characteristics such as better grain quality, greater resistance to insects and diseases, shorter growth duration, and greater tolerance for adverse environments. As new varieties suited to local conditions were developed through national programs, modern varieties spread widely.

In the Philippines, only IRRI-bred modern varieties are grown. In Thailand, where high grain quality is necessary for the export market, only locally bred modern varieties with suitable grain quality are grown. Some IRRI varieties have been adopted in Indonesia, but modern varieties developed by the national program are now more popular.

In India, Nepal, and Bangladesh, where rice-growing environments are least favorable among the seven countries, adoption of IRRI-bred varieties is usually limited to the irrigated areas, and varieties developed in national programs are more widely employed. Mahsuri, an intermediate-statured, high-yielding variety developed by Japanese scientists in Malaysia in 1965, is particularly popular in many areas in South Asia. The effects of different types or generations of modern varieties are distinguished in the Indonesia and Nepal studies.

ORGANIZATION OF THE BOOK

In Chapter 2 we examine broadly the characteristics of the production environments and the determinants of modern variety adoption and demonstrate how differential technology adoption widened the productivity gap across environments in six Asian countries from 1960 to 1987.

In Chapter 3 we present the analytical framework and methodological approach generally adopted by the country studies to analyze the direct and indirect effects of differential technology adoption on household income distribution.

Although a common conceptual framework and methodological approach generally underlie each of the country studies (Chapters 4–11), differences in coverage of issues, data used, and analytical emphasis exist. For India and China, the analysis is limited to a province or state—Hunan in central China, Tamil Nadu in southern India. For other countries, the data collected cover most major rice-growing regions.

In general, each country analysis is based on cross-section data from the late 1980s, two decades after the first modern variety was introduced. Two sets of data are used:

• The first set is from an extensive survey of forty to sixty villages representing different production environments. Village-level data on the characteristics of the production environments, technology adoption, factor markets, migration, and other demographic factors were collected.

• The second set is from an intensive survey of farm and landless households in selected villages to obtain detailed information on labor and other input use, rice output, and income from all sources. In the cases of Bangladesh and China, intensive survey information was collected from selected households in all of the villages covered in the extensive survey. Although some retrospective data on technology adoption were obtained in the extensive survey, only the case study of Lampung, Indonesia, gathered detailed retrospective data on land prices, technology adoption, and other factors, which enabled the unique analysis of the impact of technological change on land prices.

The Indonesia analysis is presented in two chapters. The study by Sudaryanto and Kasryno (Chapter 5) focuses on determinants of technology adoption, productivity impact, and labor market adjustments using only the extensive survey. The study of Lampung by Jatileksono (Chapter 6) focuses on the effects of differential technology adoption on land values and on household income distribution based on farm household data.

In Chapter 12 we summarize the major findings of the various country studies and examine implications for rice research priorities and agricultural policy.

2
Differential Impact of Modern Rice Varieties in Asia: An Overview
■

CRISTINA C. DAVID AND KEIJIRO OTSUKA

In this chapter we demonstrate how the productivity gap has widened between favorable and unfavorable rice-growing environments in Asia. We do so to gain a perspective of the importance of the distributional consequence of differential technology adoption across production environments. Our analysis is limited to Bangladesh, India, Indonesia, Nepal, the Philippines, and Thailand. China is not included because the major technological change in its rice farming was the introduction of hybrid rice rather than semidwarf modern rice varieties.

PRODUCTION ENVIRONMENTS AND MODERN RICE TECHNOLOGY

Rice is grown in widely diverse production environments. Five major rice-growing environments can be broadly identified based on water regime: irrigated, rainfed lowland, tidal wetland, deepwater, and upland (Khush 1984). The distribution of crop area planted to rice by type of production environment in the six countries is presented in Table 2.1. The irrigated areas, which are most favorable for rice production, produce the highest yields and allow a second or third rice crop during the dry season. For the six countries as a whole, only 40% of rice crop area is irrigated, but this segment accounts for nearly 60% of total rice production.

Although the irrigated production environment is essentially homogeneous, the nonirrigated rice areas have vastly diverse conditions that affect the performance of the new rice technology. The rainfed lowlands, where rice is grown in bunded fields with water depth not exceeding 50 cm, are at least as important as the irrigated rice areas in terms of size. The rainfed lowlands, however, contribute less than half of total rice production.

Portions of the rainfed lowlands, mostly those in the Philippines and

Indonesia, have adequate wet-season rainfall and water control, and modern varieties perform almost as well in those regions as in irrigated areas (see Chapters 4, 5, and 6). Most of the rainfed lowlands, however, particularly those in eastern India, northeastern Thailand, Nepal, and Bangladesh, are either drought- or flood-prone (or both), and farmers continue to grow low-yielding but stable traditional varieties (see Chapters 7 through 9).

The rainfed lowlands also include tidal wetlands near seacoasts and in inland estuaries, which typically suffer from salinity and other adverse soil stresses that make them unsuitable for modern varieties. Large tracts of tidal swamps are found in Kalimantan and Sumatra in Indonesia and in southern Bangladesh.

Deepwater rice areas, where standing water from 50 cm to more than 3 m deep accumulates during the growing season, are exclusively planted with traditional varieties. Nearly all of the deepwater areas are in low-lying tracts on the river deltas—Chao Phraya in Thailand and the Ganges Brahmaputra in Bangladesh and eastern India. In Bangladesh, 24% of rice crop area is planted with deepwater rice; in Thailand, India, and Nepal, from 6 to 8%.

Upland rice is grown in nonbunded fields with naturally well-drained soils and no surface water accumulation. Significant upland areas are still found in the outer islands of Indonesia and in India and Bangladesh.

In the upland, deepwater, tidal wetland, and unfavorable rainfed areas, only traditional varieties that yield from 1 to 2 t/ha are grown. An exception is the Philippines, where farmers grow a few improved upland varieties.

The modern varieties developed so far have been best suited to irrigated and favorable rainfed lowland environments. Thus, differences in modern variety adoption rates and associated fertilizer use across countries are positively related to the percentage of area irrigated (Table 2.2). Countries with low adoption rates—Thailand, Bangladesh, and Nepal—are those where less than 30% of rice area is irrigated. In Thailand and Bangladesh, rice is cultivated in large deltaic regions where the cost of developing effective water control is high. In Nepal, about 20% of rice area is in the hills and mountainous regions; even in the lowland (*tarai*) areas, almost 70% of rice area is rainfed.

The higher ratio of modern variety adoption (as compared to irrigation ratio) in Bangladesh and Nepal reflects the fact that modern varieties have been adopted in the favorable rainfed areas. The opposite is seen for Thailand, where the export market confers a price advantage to the higher grain quality of traditional varieties.

Countries with relatively high modern variety adoption are those where the cost of irrigation is lower and, therefore, the ratio of irrigated to total rice area is higher. The Philippines has a high rate of modern variety adoption because a large part of the Philippine rainfed areas is favorable and the modern varieties provide a yield advantage. In India, particularly eastern India, a high proportion of rainfed areas is drought- or flood-prone, and modern varieties do not provide significant economic advantage over traditional varieties (Chattopadhyay 1986).

Fertilizer use and rice yield per hectare are highest in Indonesia and lowest in Thailand, reflecting differences in modern variety adoption rates and irrigation ratio. Fertilizer use and crop yield are relatively low in the Philippines despite its having the highest rate of modern variety adoption, which suggests that factors other than rice varieties and irrigation ratio significantly affect input use and land productivity.

DIFFERENTIAL IMPACT ON PRODUCTIVITY GROWTH

Table 2.3 compares production and yield performance across countries. The new rice technology not only has shifted the comparative advantage to irrigated areas within a country, it also has shifted the international comparative advantage to countries with relatively higher proportions of irrigated areas—mainly traditional importers—and against countries with low rates of irrigated areas, including Thailand and Nepal, which were traditional exporters (Siamwalla and Haykins 1983).

In Thailand, Bangladesh, and Nepal (where modern variety adoption is lowest), growth performance of either rice production or yields, or both, have declined markedly. The declining growth of the rice sector in Thailand did not severely affect rural incomes because the nonrice agriculture and industrial sectors grew rapidly. In Bangladesh and Nepal, limited (or lack of) productivity growth in the rice sector, which provides the livelihood for most of the population, is an important factor to the stagnation of their economies. From 1965 to 1984, per capita gross national product (GNP) grew 0.6%/yr in Bangladesh and 0.2%/yr in Nepal. Such slow growth hampered the development of infrastructure, research, and extension, which adversely affected the performance of the rice sector.

In contrast, the rice sector performed remarkably well in the other countries after 1965, particularly in Indonesia. Its output and yields grew most rapidly, and its crop area planted to rice continued to increase over the two decades, mainly through higher cropping intensity. Growth in rice output accelerated in the Philippines despite the slowdown in crop area expansion. Nearly all the growth in Philippine rice output was from yield increases.

Such diverse growth performance can be largely explained by the differential adoption of modern variety technology across different environments. However, data on the historical trends of modern variety adoption and rice yields according to the classification of production environments shown in Table 2.1 are not available. Nonetheless, to illustrate the relationship between production environments and modern variety adoption within each of the six countries, trends based on broadly classified production environments are presented in Figure 2.1. The India data in Figure

2.1 are across regions instead of production environments: North and South regions, where 80% of rice area is irrigated, versus the other regions, where irrigation reaches less than 30% of rice area. In Bangladesh, modern variety adoption is classified by crop season. The main-season *amon* and *aus* crops are largely rainfed, and the dry-season *boro* crop is irrigated by tubewells. *Amon* rice accounts for 50% of total rice crop area, *aus* for 27%, and *boro* for 23%.

In Nepal, the low-lying *tarai* region is separated from the hills and mountain regions. In Indonesia, the irrigated and rainfed lowland areas, including tidal swampy areas, are combined.

The difference in adoption rates across countries basically indicates the degree to which the nonirrigated areas are favorable for growing modern varieties:

- In Thailand, adoption is limited to irrigated areas.
- In Nepal, adoption is in the irrigated and favorable rainfed areas of the *tarai* region.
- In Bangladesh, traditional varieties are still widely planted during the *amon* and *aus* crop seasons. All *aus* rice is broadcast seeded, and about 20% of *amon* rice is broadcast seeded in deepwater areas without adequate water control. Only traditional varieties are grown as broadcasted *amon* rice. However, the *boro* (dry-season) crop is dominated by modern varieties. In many deepwater areas, farmers have actually shifted rice cultivation out of the flooded period to the *boro* season and use modern varieties (Warr, Quayum, and Orr 1988).
- In India, adoption of modern varieties has been concentrated in the North and South, which are almost totally irrigated but account for only 26% of total rice area.
- In the Philippines, modern variety adoption in irrigated and rainfed lowland areas is high and remarkably similar. Traditional varieties are grown mainly in upland areas, which currently constitute less than 5% of total rice area.
- In Indonesia, as in the Philippines, modern variety adoption is high in irrigated and rainfed lowland areas.

Differential adoption of modern varieties has widened disparities in yields between irrigated and nonirrigated regions since the mid-1960s (Figure 2.2). Although yields have remained essentially stagnant at 1 to 1.5 t/ha in the unfavorable areas, where traditional varieties continue to be grown, average yields are now 3 to 4 t/ha or higher in the irrigated areas of India, Bangladesh, Indonesia, and the Philippines. In Thailand, productivity increase in the irrigated areas is comparatively lower because of the lower yield of locally improved varieties, which were bred for grain quality.

It is clear that differential adoption of modern varieties has created significant differences in productivity between favorable and unfavorable rice-growing areas. It is also clear that the differences in modern variety adoption and the production environments they are grown in are primarily responsible for the different growth rates of the rice sectors in the six Asian countries.

A CROSS-COUNTRY REGRESSION ANALYSIS

To quantify the impact of differential modern variety adoption on rice production, a system of equations was estimated based on the pooled cross-country and time-series data from 1966 to 1987. The system consisted of modern variety adoption, fertilizer, and yield response functions, wherein a pair—modern variety adoption and one of the other functions—was assumed to form a recursive system of equations. A common set of explanatory variables was specified in all equations, including variables representing production environments (ratio of irrigated area, IRGR), technology (ratio of modern variety area, MVR), price effects (price ratio of paddy to fertilizer lagged one year, PFPRICE1), factor endowment (proxied by the ratio of the sum of arable land and land for permanent crops to agricultural labor force, LANDLAB), human capital (adult literacy rate, LITERACY), and general economic conditions (per capita GNP in real terms converted by purchasing power parity index, GNPCAP).

Data from the IRRI database on paddy-fertilizer price ratio, land-labor ratio, literacy rate, and GNP per capita pertaining to 1987 are shown in Table 2.4. Fertilizer prices, measured by retail price of nitrogen from urea, are similar in all countries except Indonesia, where fertilizer prices have been heavily subsidized by the government (Jatileksono 1987). Paddy prices are somewhat higher in South Asian countries than in Southeast Asian countries because of stricter control of rice imports in the former. Although Nepal is a net rice exporter, its domestic price has been influenced by the declining price trend in its neighboring country, India (David 1990). As a result, the paddy-fertilizer price ratio, which was shown to significantly affect fertilizer use and rice yield in Asia (David 1976), is highest in Indonesia and also relatively high in South Asian countries.

Boserup (1965) hypothesized that population pressure promotes land intensification, reduces unit cost of infrastructure, and increases efficiency through specialization. According to the theory of induced innovation (Hayami and Ruttan 1985; Binswanger and Ruttan 1978), scarcity of land relative to labor is conducive to the adoption of land-saving technologies such as modern varieties and fertilizer. Consistent with these hypotheses, the land-labor ratio is highest in Thailand, where modern variety adoption, fertilizer use, and rice yield are lowest. Yet in Bangladesh, Nepal, and the Philippines, where land-labor ratios are among the lowest, intensity of land use in terms of fertilizer application and rice yield is not the highest.

Literacy rate represents the human capital of farm operators, which is considered the key to transforming less developed agriculture (Schultz 1964). GNP per capita is assumed to reflect the availability of social infrastructure, including public services such as extension and market facilities (Binswanger et al. 1986). These two variables are positively correlated and generally higher in Southeast Asia than in South Asia.

Except for adoption rate of modern varieties, irrigation ratio, and literacy rate, all the variables have been expressed in logarithms. For estimation, the error components model, widely used for pooled time-series and cross-section data in recent years, was applied (Fuller and Battese 1974). This procedure assumes that country- and time-specific effects are randomly distributed with zero means and positive variances.

The estimation results presented in Table 2.5 show a remarkably good fit. The estimated coefficients in the modern variety adoption function are all statistically significant, and the signs are consistent with a priori expectations. Irrigation ratio has a positive and significant coefficient; its estimated coefficient suggests that an increase in irrigation ratio from zero to 100% results in a 62% increase in modern variety adoption. The fact that modern varieties are more fertilizer-responsive than traditional varieties explains why a more favorable paddy-fertilizer price ratio will promote the spread of modern varieties.

The negative and significant coefficient of land-labor ratio in modern variety adoption is consistent with the induced innovation and Boserup (1965) hypotheses—i.e., countries with scarce land resources, relative to labor or population, will tend to adopt land-saving technologies, or technologies that intensify the use of land. Education as measured by literacy ratio appears to facilitate adoption of modern varieties as well as fertilizer use. The positive and significant coefficient of per capita GNP is consistent with the interpretation that this variable captures the availability of, or access to, more working capital, extension, and market infrastructure.

The estimated fertilizer response function confirms expectations that adoption of modern varieties induces greater fertilizer application. Because of high correlation between irrigation and modern varieties, however, the separate effect of irrigation on fertilizer use is not significant. The insignificant coefficient of paddy-fertilizer price ratio is inconsistent with theoretical expectations as well as the results of past studies (David 1976). It may well be that fertilizer price affected fertilizer use primarily through its effect on modern variety adoption.

In the yield function, the estimated coefficient of modern variety ratio is most significant statistically and economically; it implies that the 100% adoption of modern varieties increases yield by 75%. This result confirms our hypothesis that differential modern variety adoption is the single most important factor explaining the widening yield gap across production environments observed within and across countries over nearly three decades.

Irrigation ratio also shows a significantly positive and separate effect on yield; the estimated coefficient indicates that irrigation increases yield by 46%. The paddy-fertilizer price ratio, however, is not significant. Although the level of market infrastructure and public support to the sector as measured by GNP per capita and land-labor ratio significantly affect yield, education, proxied by the literacy rate, does not exert an appreciable positive influence on yield.

SOME UNANSWERED QUESTIONS

Since the mid-1960s, remarkable growth in rice productivity has been achieved in South and Southeast Asia through the diffusion of modern rice varieties. Our analysis of cross-country data clearly indicates the critical importance of irrigation in modern variety adoption and, furthermore, the significant impact of modern variety adoption and irrigation on yield growth. These findings suggest that productivity differentials have widened not only across production environments within a country but also between countries with different endowments of favorable and unfavorable production environments.

Has differential technology adoption adversely affected absolute income levels of farmers and landless households in the unfavorable environments and worsened relative income distribution across production environments? If so, to what extent? These are the main unanswered questions in the Green Revolution literature on rice. How does modern variety adoption affect demand for labor, capital, and land? What are the effects of modern variety adoption on wages and rental value of land? In relation to regional equity issues, has wage differential emerged between favorable and unfavorable areas, or was labor sufficiently mobile to mitigate the wage differential through interregional migration? Similarly, has regional land rent differential emerged? If so, are there mechanisms that prevent the potential income gap between landed and landless people from emerging? Finally, what are the overall effects of the Green Revolution on the absolute poverty and personal income distribution in rural areas?

Until we have a clearer understanding of these issues, the economic analysis of the Green Revolution remains incomplete.

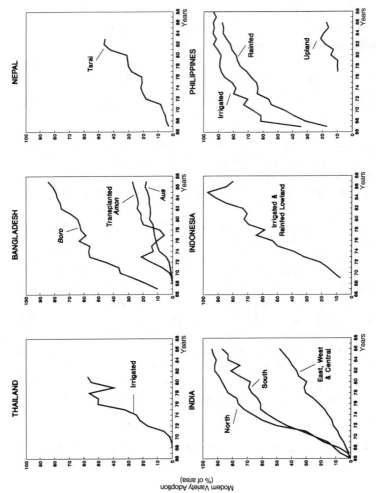

Figure 2.1   Trends in adoption rate of modern rice varieties in six Asian countries by production environments, 1966-1988. *Source:* IRRI, 1991

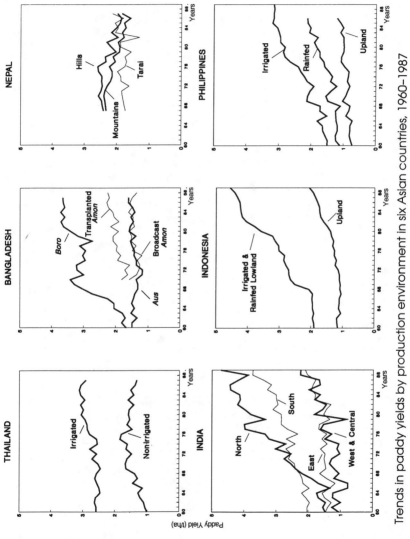

Figure 2.2   Trends in paddy yields by production environment in six Asian countries, 1960–1987

Table 2.1   Distribution of rice crop area by production environment, 1987. Source: IRRI (1991).

	Rice area (thou ha)	Area (%) grown as			
		Irrigated	Rainfed[a]	Deepwater	Upland
Thailand	9,147	27	62	8	3
Bangladesh	10,322	19	49	24	8
Nepal	1,423	23	66	8	3
India	38,806	44	35	6	15
Indonesia	9,923	73	16	0	11
Philippines	3,256	58	37	0	5

a. Includes tidal wetlands.

Table 2.2   Patterns of modern variety adoption, irrigation ratio, fertilizer (NPK) use, and yield in six Asian countries, 1987. Source: IRRI (1991).

	MV adoption (%)	Irrigation ratio (%)	NPK use (kg/ha)	Yield (t/ha)
Thailand	24	27	20	2.0
Bangladesh	32	19	56	2.2
Nepal	36	23	28	2.1
India	69	44	77	2.2
Indonesia	76	73	137	4.0
Philippines	85	58	39	2.6

Table 2.3   Growth rates (%/year) of rice output, area, and yield in six Asian countries, 1955–1987. Source: IRRI (1991).

	1955–1965			1965–1987		
	Output	Area	Yield	Output	Area	Yield
Thailand	6.7	2.8	3.9	2.5	2.0	0.5
Bangladesh	4.5	1.7	2.8	2.0	0.4	1.6
Nepal	-1.9	-2.3	0.4	1.0	1.0	0.0
India	2.9	1.4	1.5	2.8	0.6	2.2
Indonesia	1.5	0.7	0.8	5.3	1.3	4.0
Philippines	2.3	0.9	1.4	3.8	0.2	3.6

Table 2.4   Paddy-fertilizer price ratio, land-labor ratio, literacy rate, and GNP per capita in selected Asian countries, 1987. Sources: IRRI (1991); World Bank (1989).

	Paddy-fertilizer price ratio[a]	Land-labor ratio[b]	Literacy rate (%)	GNP per capita (US$)
Thailand	0.47	1.08	91	850
Bangladesh	0.58	0.43	33	160
Nepal	0.52	0.34	25	160
India	0.47	0.82	43	310
Indonesia	0.79	0.62	74	440
Philippines	0.44	0.38	86	570

a. Ratio of paddy price to retail price of nitrogen from urea.
b. Ratio of the sum of arable land and land for permanent crops to agricultural labor force.

Table 2.5   Regression results of modern variety adoption, fertilizer, and yield response functions.[a]

	MVR	Ln Fertilizer	Ln Yield
Intercept	−2.23** (−6.45)	1.29 (1.00)	−1.61** (−4.50)
IRGR	0.62** (2.58)	0.44 (0.58)	0.38* (1.75)
Ln PFPRICE1	0.06** (2.46)	0.01 (0.07)	−0.00 (−0.12)
MVR	—	1.94** (6.80)	0.56** (7.00)
Ln LANDLAB	−0.34** (−3.83)	-0.32 (−1.04)	−0.18* (−2.15)
LITERACY	1.65** (6.37)	5.30** (5.86)	−0.46* (−1.74)
Ln GNPCAP	0.21** (3.66)	−0.28 (−1.41)	0.33** (5.96)
Mean squared errors	0.007	0.076	0.006

a. Numbers in parentheses are t-statistics.
** Indicates significance at 1% level; * at 5% level.

3
An Integrated
Analytical Framework
■

CRISTINA C. DAVID AND KEIJIRO OTSUKA

In this chapter we provide an integrated theoretical framework for the analysis of the distributional consequences of the Green Revolution in rice-growing rural areas. We start with a basic utility maximization model of a farm household. Modern variety adoption, rice productivity (as measured by rice yield per hectare), and labor demand functions are specified, based directly on that model. Those functions can identify the determinants of modern variety adoption and its direct impacts on factor use and productivity.

We then extend the basic model to present a demand-supply model of labor and land in regional markets to derive the migration function and the wage and land rent determination functions. Finally, we derive household income determination functions by factor components (land, labor, and capital) and by source (rice, nonrice crop, and nonfarm) to identify the direct and indirect impacts of modern rice technology on household income.

We also propose Gini decomposition analysis to identify major income sources contributing to the inequitable distribution of household income in village economies.

THE BASIC UTILITY MAXIMIZATION MODEL

We formulate a simple utility maximization model of a farm household to derive the input demand functions, which provide the basis for various functional relations to be specified in subsequent sections.

First, we define the aggregate utility function of a farm household (U) as

$$U = U(Y, L_e), \tag{1}$$

where Y represents household income and L_e is leisure time. The utility function U is assumed to be a well-behaved concave function with the usual properties of U_y, $U_{Le} > 0$. We note that income in the utility function can be replaced by goods and services to be purchased and consumed without affecting the substance of our analysis on the factor demand.

The farm household produces rice output (Q) using labor (L) and land (A) given technology (T) and physical environmental conditions (E):

$$Q = F (L, A; T, E),   (2)$$

where F is a well-behaved concave production function with positive and decreasing marginal products of labor and land inputs, i.e., $F_1, F_2 > 0$ and $F_{11}, F_{22} < 0$.

We assume that T can be represented by the adoption rate of modern varieties. On the other hand, E is defined such that a larger number corresponds to a better production environment, i.e., $\partial Q/\partial E > 0$.

Whereas modern varieties are higher yielding in favorable production environments, the productivity effect of traditional varieties is less sensitive to environment. Thus, we assume that the relative advantage of modern varieties over traditional varieties increases with E, i.e., $(\partial^2 Q/\partial T \partial E) > 0$. Note that the adoption of modern varieties may not necessarily result in productivity improvement in unfavorable areas; thus, the sign of $(\partial Q/\partial T)$ is uncertain.

We also assume that E is purely exogenous to individual farmers, whereas T is partly endogenous and partly exogenous. We do so because the choice of varieties represented by T is ultimately determined by farmers, whereas the availability of modern varieties suitable for a specific production environment is determined by the results of research activities, which are not within the farmers' control.

Labor input (L) consists of hired labor (L_H) and family labor (L_F). For the sake of simplicity, we assume in the formal model that they are perfect substitutes, even though in reality their substitutability is limited. Family labor tends to specialize in those farm tasks requiring care and judgment, such as land preparation, water control, and chemical application, whereas hired labor is mainly engaged for simple activities such as transplanting and harvesting (Hayami and Otsuka 1993). Similarly, land input (A) consists of rented area (A_H) and family-owned area (A_F), which are assumed to be homogeneous.

The income of farm household from rice production (Y) is defined as

$$\begin{aligned} Y &= PQ - WL_H - RA_H \\ &= PQ - W (L - L_F) - R(A - A_F) \\ &= \pi + WL_F + RA_F, \end{aligned}   (3)$$

where P is output price, W is the prevailing competitive wage rate, R is land rent, and π represents profit from rice farming. The amount of hired labor and the rented area can be negative if the household is a net supplier of labor and land. The last relation in equation (3) states that the household income consists of profit from rice farming and the sum of the returns to owned inputs.

The supply of owned inputs is constrained by the endowments of total time (L′) and owned land (A′) in the following manner:

$$L' = L_F + L_e \tag{4}$$
$$c\,(T, E)A' = A_F, \tag{5}$$

where c represents rice cropping intensity, which is assumed to be a positive function of technology and production environment because the shorter growth duration of modern varieties and the availability of irrigation water are key factors conducive to multiple cropping. Equation (5) shows that given A′, A_F is determined once the choice of technology is made. Note that in a broader theoretical framework, in which the choice of crops other than rice is allowed, area planted to rice as well as to other crops can be treated as a farmer's choice variable.

Assuming that T is predetermined for the time being, the maximization of utility with respect to time and land allocation subject to income (equation [3]) and factor endowment constraints (equations [4] and [5]) results in

$$PF_1 = W \tag{6}$$
$$PF_2 = R \tag{7}$$
$$(U_1/U_2) = W. \tag{8}$$

Equations (6) and (7) correspond to the familiar profit-maximizing conditions of the competitive firm; equation (8) shows the optimum condition for the leisure-labor choice.

Solving equations (6) and (7), total labor and land demand functions can be derived as a function of output price, factor prices, technology, and production environment:

$$L = L\,(P, W, R, T, E) \tag{9}$$
$$A = A\,(P, W, R, T, E). \tag{10}$$

As is clear from equation (8), the supply of family labor depends not only on the variables affecting L and A but also on the labor and land endowments

$$L_F = L_F\,(P, W, R, L', cA', T, E). \tag{11}$$

Based directly on these basic functional relations, we specify the estimable functions for input use, yield, and modern variety adoption in the next section. Income determination functions are specified in a following section (pages 37–43) on income distribution. Elaborating further on these relations, we formulate the village-level (or small regional–level) factor-market model to derive the factor-price determination functions in the section on factor-market adjustments (pages 29–37).

DIRECT IMPACTS

As a first step toward gaining a fuller understanding of the distributional consequences of modern rice technology, we identify factors affecting modern variety adoption and assess their direct impacts on factor demands and productivity. For simplicity, we assume that the production function specified in equation (2) is subject to constant returns to scale with respect to L and A. Then, because there is no optimum farm size under the assumption of perfect competition, we focus on the functional relations per unit of land.

Labor Demand and Supply Functions

Total labor demand function and family labor supply function can both be expressed on a per hectare basis as

$$l = l \ (P, W, R, T, E) \tag{12}$$
$$l_F = l_F \ (P, W, R, L', cA', T, E), \tag{13}$$

where $l = (L/A)$ and $l_F = (L_F/A)$. Although we could estimate equations (12) and (13) simultaneously, we decided to estimate the family labor supply function (equation [13]) and the hired labor demand function per hectare, i.e.,

$$l_H = l - l_F = l_H \ (P, W, R, L', cA', T, E), \tag{14}$$

which is the excess labor demand function derived from equations (12) and (13) under the assumption of perfect substitutability of family and hired labor.

Note, however, that the estimation of equation (14) has a couple of advantages over the estimation of equation (12). First, although equation (12) holds only under the assumption of perfect labor substitutability between family and hired labor, the functional relations shown in equation (14) hold even if the two types of labor are imperfect substitutes. Second, because the major source of the supply of hired labor is landless agricultural laborers, who belong to the poorest segment of rural society, we are particularly interested in the impact of modern variety adoption on hired labor demand vis-à-vis the demand for family labor. We use the intensive household survey data to estimate the hired labor demand and family labor supply functions.

Yield and Fertilizer Use Functions

Under the assumption of a constant-returns-to-scale production function, the yield function, or output supply function per hectare, can be derived by substituting the optimum labor input per hectare to the production function

$$q = f (P, W, R, T, E), \qquad (15)$$

where $q = Q/A$.

To evaluate the direct productivity impacts of modern variety technology across diverse production environments, we estimate the yield function using the extensive survey data. The major advantage of estimating the yield function over the production function is the less rigorous data requirement, as complete data of inputs are not necessary. This approach is also desirable from the econometrics point of view: Because factor quantities are endogenous, the estimated coefficients are biased if we directly estimate the production function.

Although we did not explicitly specify inputs other than land and labor in the basic model, it is straightforward to include other factors. In particular, it is appropriate to consider fertilizer because modern varieties and fertilizer application are strongly complementary. We expect that the lower the fertilizer price, the higher the yield and the profitability of modern variety adoption will be.

SPECIFICATION OF ESTIMATED FUNCTIONS

There is a disadvantage in estimating equations (13) to (15) from cross-section data: Variations in output and input prices are often so small that it is not possible to identify the price effects on the input demand and yield. Moreover, wage rate and land rent should be treated as endogenous variables in a broader analytical framework, as we will discuss in the next subsection. Thus, we do not always use input prices in estimating those functions in this study, but we control price effects by using regional and village dummies. The estimated functions without factor-price variables are called input use functions rather than input demand and supply functions.

In actual estimation, we also consider the effect of farm size and land tenure. In the literature on the Green Revolution, it is assumed that because modern varieties require farmers to have greater liquidity for the purchase of fertilizer and other inputs, the new technology favors large farmers who have better access to credit markets (e.g., Frankel 1971; Bhalla 1979). This belief implies that even if nominal factor prices are the same among farmers, the effective prices, including interest costs, are lower for larger farmers. Similarly, tenants are poorer than owner-cultivators and may have less access to credit markets. Thus, in order to control the differential access of farmers to credit markets, we consistently use farm size and tenure variables. Furthermore, it is widely believed that share tenants tend to undersupply labor and other inputs because of the disincentive effect of output sharing (see Otsuka and Hayami [1988] and Otsuka, Chuma, and Hayami [1992] for recent surveys of the tenancy literature). Therefore, we try to distinguish share tenancy from other tenure categories as much as possible.

As mentioned above, the technology variable (T) is not totally exogenous. However, it is usually not feasible to apply instrumental variable methods (or two-stage estimation procedures) in village studies because of the lack of exogenous variables. We thus estimate the reduced form equations by omitting the technology (or modern variety) variable. Except for the Philippine study, in which the two-stage estimation method is applied, we also estimate equations (13) to (15) directly by assuming the recursive system, in which T is determined by market prices and E in the first stage, and labor use and yield are determined by market prices, E, and T in the second stage. If error terms between the first- and second-stage regression equations are correlated, the use of the single-equation method results in estimation bias. Judging from the Philippine study, such estimation bias seems small.

Modern Variety Adoption Function

By using equations (12) and (15), the profit per hectare (π) can be shown to be a function of P, W, R, T, and E:

$$\pi = \pi \ (P, W, R, T, E). \tag{16}$$

Whether new technology is introduced depends on the sign of $\partial\pi/\partial T$. Because the productivity effect of modern varieties depends on a favorable physical environment, it is reasonable to postulate that the more favorable the production environment is, the larger the profit gain associated with the introduction of modern variety technology will be. It is, however, difficult to predict the effect of P on technology adoption, because profit will change more or less in proportion to changes in P, regardless of the type of technology adopted.

Several remarks are in order about the estimation of the modern variety adoption function. First, because we use the village-level extensive survey data, the adoption rates take values from zero to one. Thus, we apply the two-limit Tobit regression methods developed by Rosett and Nelson (1975). Second, we also use the farm size and tenure variables in this equation because these variables may affect the optimum quantity of factor inputs and, hence, profits. Third, as much as possible we examine the impact of share tenancy on modern variety technology adoption, because some theoretical studies (Bhaduri 1973; Newbery 1975; Braverman and Stiglitz 1986) view share tenancy as deterring the adoption of innovation. Fourth, our empirical analysis of technology adoption is primarily concerned with long-run equilibrium adoption behavior, as the dynamic diffusion process has largely ended. In Griliches' (1957) terms, we may be explaining differences in "ceilings" of adoption. Although we have no data on farmers' education and access to extension service at the village level, the lack of those data may not cause a serious omitted-variable problem because farmers' abilities and their exposures to extension services are important mainly in a dynamic disequilibrium process (Schultz 1975). Fifth, we estimate the modern variety adoption function using only wet-season data. Rice can be grown during the dry season in an irrigated environment and sometimes in favorable rainfed environments that have a prolonged rainy season. Modern varieties are particularly suitable as a dry-season crop because, unlike traditional varieties, they are not photoperiod-sensitive. Therefore, modern varieties are grown in virtually all rice fields during the dry season. Thus, it does not make sense to estimate the modern variety adoption function using dry-season data. Instead, we estimate rice cropping or total cropping intensity function to test the hypothesis that because of modern varieties' shorter growth duration and nonsensitivity to photoperiod, modern variety adoption increases rice as well as total cropping intensity. Barker and Herdt (1985) state, "The impact of reduced growth duration on crop production has probably been as significant as the impact of higher yields."

Aside from the modern variety adoption function, we also estimate adoption functions of labor-saving technology, such as tractors, threshers, and direct seeding. The theory behind those functions is essentially the same as for modern variety adoption function. The difference is that the modern variety adoption rate is included as an explanatory variable in the labor-saving technology adoption functions because the purpose here is to test the validity of the common wisdom that the spread of modern varieties caused the adoption of labor-saving technology (Jayasuriya and Shand 1985). We expect that the adoption of modern varieties in favorable production environments caused the adoption of labor-saving technologies to the extent that modern varieties increased labor demand and wage rates in those environments. Wage rates in favorable production environments, however, may not increase relative to those in unfavorable environments, where technological change did not take place, if interregional migration effectively equalizes the regional wage rates. Thus, the adoption analysis of labor-saving technologies is closely related to the analysis of interregional labor market adjustment.

FACTOR-MARKET ADJUSTMENTS

Changes in factor prices, in both favorable and unfavorable production environments, arising from technological change in the favorable environment are considered here. Competitive output and factor markets are assumed.

Because we use extensive survey data to examine the effect of modern variety technology on factor prices, the observation unit is a village, or a relatively small area with a similar environment surrounding the village. Thus, paddy price and purchased input prices can be assumed as exogenously determined. Because land is an immobile factor of production, it is assumed that land rent is endogenously determined in each village. Wage rate can be regarded as exogenous if labor markets are well integrated over wide areas and as endogenous if they are geographically segmented because of the high cost of migration from low-wage to high-wage areas.

We first develop a dynamic model of factor-price changes resulting from technological change. Then, to facilitate intuitive understanding of the implications of the model, we present its major results using supply and demand diagrams. Finally, we specify appropriate regression models to identify the impacts of differential adoption of modern rice technology on regional factor-price differentials.

The Supply-Demand Model

Our model is based on the model Floyd (1965) developed for the analysis of the effect of government intervention on factor prices. The model was extended by Evenson (1975) and Quizon and Binswanger (1983) for the analysis of technological change. Unlike those previous authors, we specifically attempt to derive the testable implications of the differential technology adoption for interregional labor market adjustments and the regional wage and land rent differentials.

Following the basic model, we assume that there are only two factors of production—labor and land; an extension to more than a three-input case is straightforward but highly tedious. The model, assuming the competitive factor market equilibria, attempts to trace the effects of technological change on the rate of change in factor prices and quantities determined in a local market.

For ease of derivation, we assume the constant-returns-to-scale production function and specialize the technological change to the factor-augmenting type. Thus, equation (2) is rewritten as

$$Q = F(E_L L, E_A A), \tag{17}$$

where E_L and E_A are factor-augmenting coefficients of labor and land, respectively, that are functionally dependent on T and E. Under the assumption of perfect competition in output and factor markets, the equality of the value of marginal product and factor price holds

$$PF_1 = (W/E_L) \tag{18a}$$
$$PF_2 = (R/E_A). \tag{18b}$$

On the right-hand side of the above equations, the factor prices are divided by the corresponding factor-augmenting coefficients because a proportional increase in the factor-augmenting coefficient has the same effect as a proportional decrease in the factor price on the "effective" price of input.

From the first-order optimality conditions, we derive the cost function that relates production cost (C) to output and real factor prices:

$$C = QH\ (W/PE_L,\ R/PE_A), \tag{19}$$

where H is the unit cost function. From Shepherd's lemma we obtain

$$\partial C/\partial(W/P) = L = (Q/E_L)H_1 \tag{20a}$$
$$\partial C/\partial(R/P) = A = (Q/E_A)H_2. \tag{20b}$$

Equation (20a) corresponds to the total labor demand function (equation [9]), and equation (20b) corresponds to the total land demand function (equation [10]) in the basic model.

The unit cost function is related to the elasticity of substitution (σ) in the following way (Uzawa 1962):

$$\sigma = H_{12}H/H_1H_2.$$

With the use of the above relation, following Kawagoe, Otsuka, and Hayami (1986), we obtain the factor-demand functions in the growth equation form by differentiating equation (20) with respect to time (t)

$$L^* = Q^* - E_L^* - s_A\ \sigma\ [(W^* - E_L^*) - (R^* - E_A^*)] \tag{21a}$$
$$A^* = Q^* - E_A^* + s_L\ \sigma\ [(W^* - E_L^*) - (R^* - E_A^*)], \tag{21b}$$

where asterisk (*) denotes the growth rate (e.g., $L^* = (dL/dt)/L$) and s_i (i=L, A) stands for the factor share of input. For notational convenience, we regard equations (21a) and (21b) as the market demand functions for labor and land, even though they are derived from the profit-maximizing behavior of a single farmer.

Corresponding to the market demand functions, we define the factor-supply functions in the growth equation form

$$L^* = \varepsilon_L W^* + \mu\ (W^* - \overline{W}^*) \tag{22a}$$
$$A^* = \varepsilon_A R^*, \tag{22b}$$

where ε_L is the "short-run" supply elasticity of labor, ε_A denotes the supply elasticity of land, $\overline{W}^*$ represents the growth rate of wages in other regions, and μ captures the impact of interregional labor market adjustments induced by the regional wage differential on the long-run labor supply. The supply elasticity of labor in the long run is defined as $(\varepsilon_L + \mu)$. The longer the period and the lower the cost of migration across regions, the larger the coefficient μ. Unlike labor, land is an immobile factor of production, so its markets are not directly linked across regions.

Note that the total supply of labor includes not only the supply of family labor by farm households but also the labor supplied by the landless agricultural labor households. As equation (11) demonstrates, the family labor supply depends not only on the wage rate but also on the whole set of exogenous variables. Equation (22a) assumes away such complications without changing the major qualitative conclusions. Similarly, note that the total supply of land consists of the supply from owner-cultivators as well as from other landowners.

We hypothesize that growth rate of the labor force (N*), which consists of the sum of the natural rate of labor force growth and the rate of net in-migration, is determined by the changes in regional wage differentials, i.e.,

$$N^* = \mu (W^* - \overline{W}^*). \tag{23}$$

If the area under consideration is favorable for rice production, technological change will occur more rapidly than in other areas, which tends to create positive wage differentials in the short run and induce in-migration in the long run. However, if the natural rate of population growth is higher in more favorable environments, the interregional labor market adjustment requires less interregional migration.

Because we assume competitive market equilibrium and linear homogeneous production function, the equilibrium requires that the profit be zero:

$$PQ = WL + RA. \tag{24}$$

Taking the growth rate, we obtain the following zero-profit condition:

$$Q^* - s_L L^* - s_A A^* = s_L W^* + s_A R^* - P^*. \tag{25}$$

Equations (21a) to (22b) and (25) constitute the complete linear supply and demand equation systems, in which exogenous variables are E_L^*, E_A^*, P^*, and $\overline{W}^*$ and the endogenous variables are W^*, R^*, L^*, A^*, and Q^*. We can solve those equations to derive five reduced-form equilibrium price and quantity equations.

Of particular interest for our purpose are the factor-price equations, which can be shown as

$$W^* = 1/D \left[(\sigma - 1) E_L^* + (1 + \varepsilon_A) Z^* + (\varepsilon_A + \sigma) P^* + s_A \mu \overline{W}^* \right] \tag{26a}$$
$$R^* = 1/D \left[(\sigma - 1) E_A^* + (1 + \varepsilon_L + \mu) Z^* + (\varepsilon_L + \mu + \sigma) P^* - s_L \mu \overline{W}^* \right] \tag{26b}$$

where $D = \sigma + s_L \varepsilon_A + s_A(\varepsilon_L + \mu) > 0$ and Z^* stands for the growth rate of total factor productivity (i.e., $Z^* = s_L E_L^* + s_A E_A^*$).

The first term in both equations shows the effects of absolute factor-use bias on factor price; its effect is negative only if the elasticity of substitution is less than unity, because this is the condition for absolute saving of i-th factor by an increase in E_i.

The second term measures the output expansion effect of productivity growth on factor prices, whereas the third term reflects the output expansion effect associated with output price change. The last term represents the factor-price effect of interregional labor market adjustments induced by $\overline{W}$; its effect on wage rate (W^*) is positive, as it induces out-migration from the region under consideration, and negative on land rent (R^*), because labor and land are complementary.

Several testable implications can be derived from equations (26a) and (26b). First, factor prices tend to be positively associated with technological change, unless technology is extremely labor-saving or land-saving such that the first term is negative and absolutely larger than the second term. In the case of modern rice technology, represented by fertilizer-responsive, high-yielding varieties, accumulated evidence indicates that the demand for labor and land increased in absolute terms (Barker and Cordova 1978; Barker and Herdt 1985; Otsuka, Gascom, and Asano 1994b). Thus, a positive effect of modern rice technology on factor prices should be observed.

Second, the effect of technology on land rent tends to be larger than that on wage rate, because the supply elasticity of land (ε_A) is likely to be smaller than the long-run supply elasticity of labor ($\varepsilon_L + \mu$); few crops other than rice can be grown in a wet paddy, whereas labor can be more easily transferred to other jobs.

Third, an increase in wage rate in another region will raise the wage rate and reduce the land rent in the region under consideration by inducing out-migration. In other words, the migration will mitigate the regional wage differential created by the differential adoption of modern rice technology but accentuate the regional land rent differential. In an extreme case, where the migration cost is zero and hence μ becomes infinite, changes in wage rate are equalized across favorable and unfavorable environments.

Diagrammatic Exposition

We use supply-demand diagrams to illustrate the major implications of the theoretical model developed in the previous subsection. Further, we discuss additional considerations relevant to the issue of regional factor-price differentials, which are not explicitly incorporated into the theoretical model.

Figure 3.1 shows how wage rates tend to be equalized between favorable and unfavorable rice-production environments through interregional migration. For simplicity, we assume initially that the migration cost is zero and that output price and input prices other than wage and land rent are given. The initial equilibrium is established at point E_0 with the wage rate of W_0 in the favorable environment, where the demand curve D_0 and the supply curve S_0 intersect. Similarly, the wage rate in the unfavorable environment is determined at W_0, given the supply curve of s_0 and the demand curve of d_0. The technological change takes place in the favorable environment, which shifts the demand curve to D_1, leading to the new short-run equilibrium of E_1 with the wage rate of W_1. An increase in wage rate in the favorable environment induces the migration from unfavorable to favorable in the long run, which shifts the supply curve from S_0 to S_1 in the favorable environment and from s_0 to s_1 in the unfavorable environment so as to equate the wage rates.

If migration cost is substantial or the interregional labor market adjustment takes time, regional wage differentials will be observed. In this situation, the adoption of labor-saving technology may be induced in the favorable environment, which shifts the demand curve from D_1 to D_M. Again, the regional wage rates tend to equalize, but they do so at a lower level of employment and wages in the rural labor markets as a whole. In the formal model, we do not explicitly consider these induced, labor-saving technology effects.

The situation in the land markets is depicted in Figure 3.2. For simplicity, the initial equilibria are assumed to be attained at E_0 in a favorable environment and e_0 in an unfavorable environment with the common land rent of R_0 and r_0. The technological change shifts the demand curve from D_0 to D_1 in the favorable environment, which results in higher land rent of R_1. Although the relative rates of shift of the land and labor demand curves depend on the bias of technological change, land rent tends to increase faster than wages because of the lower elasticity of the supply of land. Furthermore, the labor migration has the effect of widening the land rent differential, because the increased labor force in the favorable environment increases the demand for land (e.g., a shift from D_1 to D_2), whereas the decreased labor force in the unfavorable environment decreases the demand (e.g., a shift from d_0 to d_1). As a result, the land rent differential in the long-run equilibrium will become larger, as indicated by the difference between R_2 and r_1. Thus, the interregional labor market adjustment increases the land rent differential, even though it contributes to the equalization of wage rates.

As Figures 3.1 and 3.2 show, the impact of technological change on factor prices critically depends on the elasticity of the supply of inputs for rice production. The supply elasticity, in turn, depends on the profitability of alternative use of resources. For example, in deepwater rice environments the supply of land for rice production will be inelastic because crops other than rice cannot be grown during the wet season. In upland environments, rice is one of several competing crops; hence, the supply of land for rice production will be relatively elastic. Similarly, the supply elasticity of labor for rice production depends on the availability of lucrative nonfarm job opportunities.

To the extent that the supply of inputs is elastic, the emergence of factor-price differentials between favorable and unfavorable production environments will be mitigated by reallocation of resources within each area.

Note that so far we have implicitly assumed that output price is fixed. Assuming a closed economy, technological change in favorable environments as a whole will decrease rice price through its effect on the domestic rice supply. The impact of the differential adoption of new technology on the economic welfare of rice producers in favorable and unfavorable production environments can be most clearly seen in the supply and demand diagram of a rice market (Figure 3.3). The initial market equilibrium is attained at point E_0, where the demand (D) is equated with the total supply, which consists of the sum of the supply from an unfavorable environment (S_U) and a favorable environment (S_F). When technological change occurs in a favorable environment, the total supply shifts to $S_U + S_F{}'$, which results in the reduction of rice price from P_0 to P_1. In consequence, the producer surplus in the unfavorable environment decreases by the amount represented by the shaded area. Whether the surplus in the favorable environment decreases or not depends on the relative magnitude of the loss indicated by the area marked with a minus (-) sign and the gain indicated by the area with a plus (+) sign. It is clear from this figure that the net gain of producers in the favorable area becomes larger, the larger the elasticity of demand.

We are concerned not only with the welfare of rice farmers but also with that of landless laborers, who belong to the poorest segment of the society. For our purpose, the surplus analysis shown in Figure 3.3 is not, by itself, adequate because the income of landless laborers is regarded as a cost of farming.

Because the technological change taking place in favorable production environments results in a lower output price, the demand for all inputs declines in unfavorable environments. In a favorable environment, the factor demand may or may not decrease because of the offsetting effects of output expansion and the factor-saving effects of technological change. Our formal model does not take into account such output-price effect, partly because output price can be legitimately considered exogenous for a village and, more important, because output prices are practically the same across wide areas. Thus, output price effect cannot be identified from cross-section data. It must be clearly recognized that our study focuses on the relative factor-price changes between favorable and unfavorable environments but not on the absolute factor-price changes common to all areas.

Specification of Regression Models

In this subsection we first discuss how to test the hypothesis that the differential adoption of modern rice technology induces interregional labor market adjustments toward the equalization of wage rates across production environments.

Ideally, we should estimate the labor force growth rate function shown in equation (23). Village-level data on labor force, however, are not available, and data on permanent and seasonal migration are difficult to obtain from farmers' recall. An alternative—use of population data as a proxy for labor force—is used as the best option.

In formulating the empirically estimable labor force growth function, it is important to recognize that the growth rate of the labor force proxied by the population growth rate, or the rate of in-migration, represents a dynamic adjustment process. It is not the current level of technology but the change it induces that causes migration and population change. Because changes in output and purchased input prices are considered largely common across areas, it is reasonable to hypothesize that a major factor that would increase the wage rate in a favorable production environment relative to an unfavorable one is the change in technology. Thus, $(W^* - \overline{W}^*)$ in equation (23) can be replaced by the rate of change in technology adoption in actual estimation.

In the absence of population data, one may be tempted to use the cross-sectional data of man-land ratio or ratio of landless laborers, who are geographically more mobile than farmers, as a proxy for the cumulated result of population adjustments. However, because of the lack of knowledge and the paucity of data on the whole set of variables that would affect the village population, it may be difficult to identify a pure technology effect on population change from cross-section data. In contrast, the use of population growth rate as a dependent variable has the advantage of purging the effects of historical or other structural factors, which are fixed over time.

Unlike the population growth equation, the factor-price equations are reduced-form market equilibrium relations, which are concerned with the result of factor-market adjustments. Ideally, we would estimate directly equations (26a) and (26b). It is, however, not possible to obtain past wage and land rent data. Thus, we assume that E_i^* is linearly related with change in modern variety adoption ratio (ΔMVR) and irrigation ratio ($\Delta IRGR$):

$$E_L^* = \alpha_L + \beta_L (\Delta MVR) + \gamma_L (\Delta IRGR) \qquad (27a)$$
$$E_A^* = \alpha_L + \beta_A (\Delta MVR) + \gamma_A (\Delta IRGR), \qquad (27b)$$

where α_i, β_i, and γ_i are the parameters. Substituting the above relation to equations (26a) and (26b), the following linear relation can be obtained:

$$W^* = a_L + b_L (\Delta MVR) + c_L (\Delta IRGR) \qquad (28a)$$
$$R^* = a_A + b_A (\Delta MVR) + c_A (\Delta IRGR), \qquad (28b)$$

where a_i, b_i, and c_i reflect composite effects of β_i's, μ, ε_i's and s_i's. By integration with approximation, we obtain the following linear equations:

$$\ln W = d_L + b_L \text{ (MVR)} + c_L \text{ (IRGR)} \tag{29a}$$
$$\ln R = d_A + b_A \text{ (MVR)} + c_L \text{ (IRGR)}, \tag{29b}$$

where d_i's are fixed terms of integration. Thus, we regress the level of factor prices on the level of technology and irrigation, controlling the structural differences in regional factor markets by regional dummies, man-land ratio before modern variety technology was adopted, and the access to urban labor markets proxied by distance to regional centers.

Because wage rates are substantially different in different tasks, we estimate wage functions by task. For the sake of comparison, wherever reliable data are available we also estimate rental cost functions of draft animals, which are geographically immobile, and those of tractors and threshers, which are distinctly more mobile.

INCOME DISTRIBUTION

Although the extensive survey is concerned with the factor-price differentials between favorable and unfavorable environments, it is often difficult to obtain reliable data on land rent because land rental markets are often inactive or distorted by land reform regulations. In addition, prevailing rent in a village may be hard to define because land rents vary within a village depending on contracts (e.g., share versus leasehold) and location. In contrast, casual labor markets are usually active, and a unique prevailing wage rate exists for each activity in a village. A sufficiently accurate estimation of the return to land can be made only by estimating the residual return to land (revenue minus actual and imputed costs of all nonland inputs) by use of intensive household survey data.

Our major focus in the intensive survey study is on the personal (or household) income differentials between favorable and unfavorable production environments as well as among households within a village. We are concerned not only with the factor incomes from rice production, including the return to land, but also with the total income of rural households. Thus, income from nonrice production and nonfarm activities is analyzed along with rice income.

Factor-Share Analysis

The first step in assessing the impact of technological change on personal income distribution is the factor-share and earner-share analysis of rice production. This analysis divides total output into the portions going to various categories of inputs provided by landlords, farmers, laborers, and so forth (Herdt 1978; Ranade and Herdt 1978). A simple descriptive analysis provides useful insights into how increased output per hectare of rice production is shared among factors of production and their owners. If factor prices are the same, the comparison of relative factor shares, with and without technological change, indicates the factor-use bias of technology (Kawagoe, Otsuka, and Hayami 1986). If factor prices change before and after the adoption of technology or differ across locations with different technologies, the factor-share analysis indicates the distributional consequences of the composite effects of technology and factor prices.

Because rice output should increase following technological change, it is expected that the absolute amount of all factor incomes per hectare tends to be larger in a favorable production environment than in an unfavorable one. But the income distribution is concerned with relative changes in income, and hence it is more appropriate to examine which factors gain more relative to others. Factor-share and earner-share analysis indicates the magnitude of such changes.

Given that substantial regional differences exist in the factor incomes from rice production, an important question to explore is the extent to which the smaller income from rice production in a less favorable environment is compensated for by the larger production of nonrice crops and more active participation in nonfarm jobs. For this purpose, descriptive analysis of the difference in household income by source, region, and farmer and laborer classes is conducted to supplement the factor-share analysis before undertaking statistical analysis of income determination.

Income Determination Function Approach

Previous analyses of the impact of technological change on personal income in developing-country agriculture have simply compared the income of farm households before and after technological change occurred or in areas with and without technological change (see Bardhan 1974; Chinn 1979; Goldman and Squire 1982; Junankar 1975; Raju 1976; Shand 1987; and Singh 1973). However, because factors other than technology that could affect household income also change over time or differ between areas, simple comparison is at best suggestive. In order to derive the income determination function, which is designed to sort out the influence of various factors on the household income formation, we extend the basic model of labor time and land resource allocations developed in the section on the basic utility maximization model.

We consider three sources of income: rice farming (Y_1), nonrice farming (Y_2), and nonfarm activity (Y_3). Correspondingly, a farm household allocates family labor time to three activities (L_1, L_2, L_3) given wage rates of W_1, W_2, and W_3, and total planted area to rice and nonrice production (A_1, A_2) given equilibrium land rent of R. An implicit assumption here is that L_1, L_2, and L_3 enter into the household utility function as separate variables because of the difference in the nature of the work. Otherwise, the household will allocate all labor time to the job with the highest wage rate. It is also assumed that the equilibrium rental values of land are identical for rice and nonrice production to avoid the complete specialization in the production of a single crop.

Analogous to equation (11), the following optimum land and labor allocation functions result:

$$L_i = L_i (P_1, P_2, W_1, W_2, W_3, R, L', cA', T, E), \quad (30a)$$
$$(i = 1,2,3)$$
$$A_i = A_i (P_1, P_2, W_1, W_2, W_3, R, L', cA', T, E), \quad (30b)$$
$$(i = 1, 2),$$

where P_1 represents the price of the rice crop and P_2 the price of nonrice crops. As before, L' stands for the total endowment of time, A' for owned area, T for rice technology, and E for production environment. Note, however, that c now shows total cropping intensity rather than rice cropping intensity.

The above equations show how changes in factor prices, technology, total cropped area, and the potential availability of labor time affect the allocation of time to various activities and the allocation of land to production of different crops.

Given the diversity of nonrice crop production and nonfarm activities, accurate data on L_2 and L_3 are hard to obtain from the ordinary household survey. A more serious problem in estimating these equations lies in the choice of appropriate factor-price variables. As Deaton (1988) has convincingly demonstrated, dividing total labor earnings by total work days is not an appropriate method of estimating wage rate, because such estimates reflect the difference in the quality of labor inputs—more educated, more motivated, and more skilled labor will earn higher wages. Our analysis, however, is concerned with wage rates for a single quality of labor. Because only one wage rate essentially prevails for the same labor service in rice farming within each village and because there are a relatively small number of villages in the intensive survey, the wage effect predicted by theory cannot be identified from the intensive-survey data.

Land rent is often distorted by land reform, as in the cases of the Philippines and Nepal. Moreover, the opportunity cost of land for owner-cultivators is not easily observed, particularly where the land rental market is inactive. Further, as we argued in the previous section, the land rent, or the return to land, is endogenous in our framework. Thus, we may replace R by a technology variable and directly estimate the effect of technology on land and labor allocations.

Cropping intensity is also affected by technology, particularly by irrigation and by the adoption of short-growth-duration modern varieties. All these considerations point to the use of technology cum environmental variables (e.g., modern variety adoption rate and the ratio of irrigation) in the regression, replacing R, W_i, and c.

Thus, although the basic structure of our model is essentially the same as that of agricultural household models (Singh, Squire, and Strauss 1986), practical considerations prompt us not to estimate factor-price functions. It is reasonable to assume, however, that factor prices depend on variables similar to those that affect L_i and A_i, such as technology, land quality, and labor quality. Thus, rather than separately estimating the factor-quantity and factor-price equations, we simply estimate the functions determining each component of income, which is defined as the product of factor price and quantity. The functional relations may therefore be specified as

$$Y_i = Y_i \, (S, \, AGE, \, MVR, \, IRGR, \, N, \, A', \, TEN), \qquad (31)$$

where S equals schooling (e.g., household head or average of all working members), AGE equals age (e.g., household head or average of all working members), MVR equals ratio of modern variety adoption, IRGR equals ratio of irrigated area, N equals number of working members, A' equals owned area, and TEN equals tenure status dummy.

The major advantage of estimating the income determination functions over estimating factor-quantity and factor-price equations separately lies in the ease of obtaining the data.

For rice production, we have obtained enough information to classify total income as accruing to labor, land, or capital. Because we hypothesize that wages and land rents are affected by technology in different ways, we estimate the rice income determination functions by factor component and examine whether the estimated coefficients of technology and other variables are significantly different across component income equations.

A simple and reasonable specification of equation (31) and component income equations for rice production may be in double logarithmic form except for ratio variables. This specification, however, is inapplicable to many cases, because there are households that have no income from certain sources (e.g., nonfarm wage income among farm households). Unless the number of those households is small, the log-linear specification should not be applied. Simple linear specification of all explanatory variables, however, is untenable, because an implicit assumption of such specification is that the effect of increases in the rate of modern variety adoption and irrigation ratio on absolute income is independent of cultivation area. In order to avoid such misspecification, we apply the interaction terms between the technology and farm size. To show the justification for this specification, consider the land income from rice production (Y_A), which can be expressed as a product of land's marginal value productivity and land input:

$$Y_A = P_1(\partial Q_1/\partial A_1)A_1. \qquad (32)$$

Suppose now that the value of marginal product of land linearly depends on modern variety adoption rate and irrigation ratio, i.e.,

$$(\partial Q_1/\partial A_1) = \alpha_0 + \alpha_1 \, MVR + \alpha_2 \, IRGR, \tag{33}$$

where α_0 shows the return to land without modern varieties and irrigation and α_1 and α_2, respectively, represent the contribution of modern varieties and irrigation to the marginal product of land. Substitution of equation (32) into equation (33) results in

$$Y_A = \alpha_0 \, A_1 + \alpha_1(MVR)A_1 + \alpha_2(IRGR)A_1. \tag{34}$$

Note that in equation (34), A_1 refers to area planted to rice, rather than owned area (A') as specified in equation (31). Because planted area is an endogenous variable, it can be replaced by owned area. Alternatively, farm size, which includes both owned and tenanted areas, can be substituted if it can legitimately be assumed to be fixed, at least in the short run. If we use farm size, coefficients of interaction terms between farm size and modern variety adoption rate or irrigation ratio will reflect not only the productivity-enhancing effects of modern variety adoption and irrigation during a crop season but also their effects on rice cropping intensity. We will make extensive use of a variant of equation (34) in actual estimation.

Decomposition Analysis of Income Inequality

Because adoption of modern varieties affects the various income components differently, a decomposition analysis of the Gini measure of inequality as developed by Fei, Ranis, and Kuo (1978) and Pyatt, Chen, and Fei (1980) is applied to quantify the relative importance of the various income components in accounting for the overall income inequality. It must be pointed out, however, that the inequality contribution assigned to any income source can vary depending on the choice of inequality measures (Shorrocks 1983). In other words, the computed percentage contribution of overall inequality by factor component under the Gini decomposition rule may be substantially different from the decomposition of an alternative measure of inequality.

The Gini decomposition formula is as follows:

$$G(Y) = \Sigma s_i R(Y,Y_i) \, G \, (Y_i), \tag{35}$$

where $G(Y)$ equals Gini ratio of total income, Y_i equals income from i-th source, s_i equals average income share of i-th source, $R(Y,Y_i)$ equals rank correlation ratio, and $G(Y_i)$ equals Gini ratio of i-th income.

The rank correlation ratio is defined as

$$R(Y,Y_i) = Cov\{Y_i,r(Y)\}/Cov\{Y_i,r(Y_i)\}, \qquad (36)$$

where $r(Y)$ and $r(Y_i)$ denote ranking of households in terms of Y and Y_i, respectively. It is clear that R is unity if

$$r(Y) = r(Y_i). \qquad (37)$$

Otherwise, R is shown to be less than unity. In general, the larger R is, the larger the correlation between Y and Y_i.

In the computation of $G(Y)$, households are ranked in accordance with Y, but in the case of G (Y_i) they are ranked in accordance with Y_i. In order to adjust this difference, the rank correlation ratio appears in the formula. In fact, $R(Y,Y_i)G(Y_i)$ is equal to the pseudo–Gini coefficient defined by Fei, Ranis, and Kuo (1978), which is obtained if we use the ranking of household in accordance with total income Y in the computation of factor Gini for Y_i.

Thus, the formula in equation (35) decomposes the Gini ratio of income inequality into income shares, correlation effects, and the Gini ratio for each factor component. It is important to note here that in assessing the contribution of various income sources to overall income inequality, we consider not only the Gini ratio of component income but also the income share and the rank correlation.

To illustrate the problem of interpreting the Gini ratio of component income, let us suppose that the land income of all farm households increases proportionally. Obviously, income distribution becomes less equitable, because the income of landless-labor households does not change. Nevertheless, the Lorenz curve for land income remains unchanged, and thus the Gini ratio remains the same. In this case, the inequities are reflected in increases in the land income share and the rank correlation ratio.

Using equation (35) we can assess, for example, the contribution of land income distribution to overall income inequality. The main desirable feature of this formula is its clear link with conventional economic analysis. In particular, income shares are closely related with technology bias in production and factor prices, which affect factor shares as well as earner shares. Thus, the conventional factor-share and earner-share analysis (see, e.g., Ranade and Herdt [1978]) and the analysis of technology bias (see, e.g., Binswanger [1974] and Kawagoe, Otsuka, and Hayami [1986]) are directly relevant for this decomposition analysis. Moreover, the rank-correlation ratio broadly indicates how various sources of income are substituted as a result of time and land allocation decisions by agricultural households.

Our income distribution analysis has several limitations. First, we are unable to include noncultivating landlords in the survey because they typically reside outside the village. Such landlords belong to the wealthiest class in rural societies, so our analysis, by ignoring them, underestimates the income inequality in the rural sector as a whole. Second, to the extent that modern variety adoption contributes to overall increases in wage rates, our analysis, which does not take into account such an effect, underestimates the equitable effect of modern variety adoption, because wage earnings are a major component of the income of the poor. Third, our analysis often fails to evaluate the separate effects of modern variety adoption and production environment on the household income distribution. Modern varieties are planted in virtually all favorable production environments, and cross-section data can be used to estimate only the combined effect of modern variety adoption and favorable environment. Thus, we tend to overestimate the contribution of modern varieties to income inequality.

CONCLUSION: COMPLEX ANALYTICAL ISSUES

The analytical issues of income distribution within the context of the differential adoption of modern rice technology between favorable and unfavorable production environments are highly complex:

- The determinants and the direct impacts of the adoption of modern rice technology must be examined.
- One must then examine whether and to what extent the interregional labor market adjustment took place toward the equalization of the wage rates between favorable and unfavorable production environments, particularly during the period in which modern rice technology was rapidly disseminated.
- In order to test the significance of interregional labor market adjustments, the regional wage and land rent differentials in the current period must be analyzed.
- Descriptive analysis of factor share and earner share must be carefully performed to link the analyses of the direct impacts of technology and its indirect impacts on the factor-market adjustments with the analysis of factor incomes.
- Finally, it must be determined whether and to what extent the income differential between favorable and unfavorable environments arising from rice production is compensated for by offsetting income differentials from production of nonrice crops and nonfarm activities.

We caution readers to remember that our analysis is concerned with the factor-price and household-income differentials between regions and among farmers, not with the absolute changes in factor prices and household income due to the technological change. The latter analysis requires an estimate of the effect of technological change on absolute levels of rice prices and factor prices based on a nationwide market model and the use of time-series data.

Our analysis does provide, however, an appropriate basis for such a market analysis by showing how factor markets adjust to the differential adoption of modern rice technology between favorable and unfavorable environments.

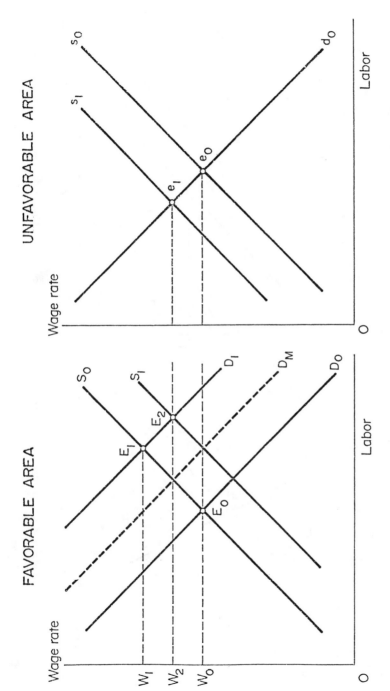

Figure 3.1 Differential technology adoption and interregional wage equalization through labor migration and mechanization

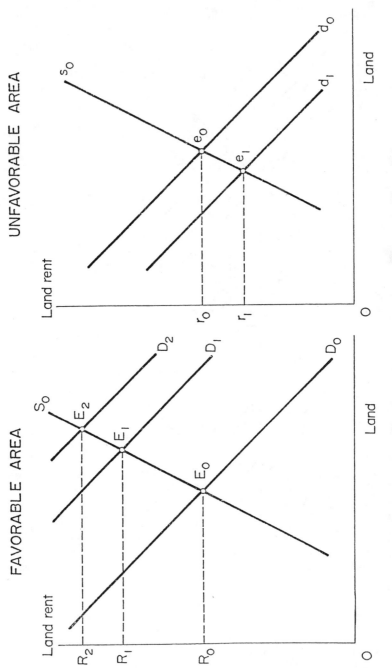

Figure 3.2   Differential technology adoption and interregional land rent differential

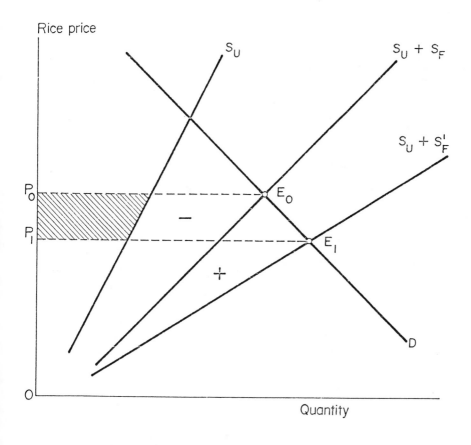

Figure 3.3   Differential technology adoption and changes in rice
price and producer surplus

PART 2
■
Country Studies

4
Technological Change, Land Reform, and Income Distribution in the Philippines

■

CRISTINA C. DAVID, VIOLETA G. CORDOVA, AND KEIJIRO OTSUKA

Fertilizer-responsive, high-yielding modern rice varieties were introduced in the Philippines in the late 1960s. They were rapidly adopted and are now planted on more than 80% of that nation's rice crop area. Fertilizer use increased from an average of 10 kg to nearly 50 kg NPK/ha. Investments in irrigation accelerated in the 1970s, increasing the proportion of irrigated area from 30% to 50% of the rice crop area. As a result, the annual growth rate of rice production increased from 2.3% before 1965 to 4.5% between 1965 and 1980, and the major source of growth shifted from crop area expansion to increases in yields.

Though there is little dispute about the productivity impact of modern varieties, questions continue to be raised about their impact on income distribution. Modern varieties released to date have been best suited to irrigated and favorable rainfed environments with adequate water control (Barker and Herdt 1985). As a consequence, the productivity gap between favorable and unfavorable rice production environments has widened in the Philippines and in other Asian countries (Chapter 2). Fears have been expressed that the modern varieties created large disparities in regional income distribution (Falcon 1970; Ruttan 1977; Lipton and Longhurst 1989).

Although adoption of modern varieties is scale-neutral, tapping their yield potential requires increased liquidity to buy fertilizers and other purchased inputs, which may favor large-scale farmers and owner-operators, who have better access to credit markets than small-scale farmers (Frankel 1971; Bhalla 1979). Moreover, it is often observed that the spread of modern varieties was followed by wider adoption of labor-saving technologies—i.e.,

---

This chapter is based on David and Otsuka (1990); and Otsuka, Cordova, and David (1990, 1992).

tractors, threshers, and direct seeding (Jayasuriya and Shand 1985). Thus, even though modern variety adoption increases labor use per hectare by increasing labor requirements for crop care and harvesting (Barker and Cordova 1978; Otsuka, Gascon, and Asano 1994b), mechanization and direct seeding may well save labor, thereby hurting poor landless households.

The objective of the Philippine study is to analyze the income distributional effects of differential modern rice technology adoption in favorable and unfavorable production environments. Technology affects income of producers directly through its effects on productivity and factor use and indirectly through its effects on output and factor prices. Although differential adoption of new technology may result in the uneven distribution of direct benefits across production environments, the manner in which the indirect effects are distributed will depend on how labor, land, and output markets adjust to changes in the supply of output and demand for inputs.

Labor is a mobile factor and the main resource of the poorest segment of the rural population. As a result, the impact of modern rice technology on the distribution of income critically depends on adjustments in the labor market—specifically interregional migration caused by regional wage differentials, which are in turn created by differential technology adoption.

Conversely, land is an immobile factor of production, and thus its supply is relatively inelastic. Therefore, the differential productivity growth is expected to widen returns to land from rice production across production environments. This effect can be mitigated by adjustments in farm size, shifts to alternative crops, or institutional changes that alter the distribution of returns to land.

VILLAGE SURVEYS

Two sets of data were collected. The first set was based on an extensive survey of fifty villages from representative irrigated and rainfed lowland rice areas encompassing Northern, Central, and Southern Luzon, plus Panay Island (Figure 4.1). The rainfed lowland villages were located in favorable rainfed areas—defined as shallow rainfed regions with no major problem in water control during the wet season—and unfavorable rainfed areas, which are prone to severe flooding, drought, or both. The irrigated villages were served by gravity irrigation systems constructed and operated by the National Irrigation Administration. Provincial and municipal government officials assisted in identifying the environmental characteristics in their areas. The villages were then selected randomly from representative production environments in thirteen provinces.

The second set was taken from an intensive survey of five villages in the extensive survey and included detailed information on rice production and income at the household level. Two villages (CL1 and CL2) are in the

Central Luzon plain, considered the rice bowl of the Philippines. The other three villages (P1, P2, and P3) are on Panay (Figure 4.2).

CL1 and P1 are fully irrigated by well-maintained gravity irrigation systems and are representative of the most favorable production environment. CL2 and P2 are characterized by a shallow, favorable rainfed environment commonly found in the country. P3 is also rainfed but is located in an unfavorable mountainous production environment and has a poorly developed market infrastructure.

The Extensive Survey

The extensive survey provided a broad picture of production environments, factor markets, and changes in rice farming. The distribution of the sample villages was predetermined to be roughly equal among the three production environments. The number of sample villages in the unfavorable areas was more than proportional to their actual share in the total rice crop area to take account of the greater heterogeneity of environmental characteristics in these areas. Upland rice was not included in the survey because it constitutes less than 5% of total rice crop area.

In each village, a couple of interviews were conducted with different groups of knowledgeable farmers to obtain data relating to demographic factors, production environments, cropping patterns, technology adoption, rice yields, labor, and land market characteristics pertaining to the 1986 wet season. We also gathered information on technology adoption in 1970 and 1980, which provided a historical perspective on the state of current technology adoption, although such recall data may be less reliable. This data was supplemented by official census figures on population for 1970 and 1980 and unpublished region-specific data on prices of fertilizer and herbicides from the Bureau of Agricultural Statistics.

Table 4.1 shows the number of sample villages and selected socioeconomic characteristics of villages in the different production environments. Farm size is slightly smaller in drought-prone villages but generally similar across production environments. Man-land ratio, defined as the ratio of the village population to cultivated area, is highest in the irrigated area and lowest in drought-prone areas. The ratio of agricultural landless households is significantly higher in the irrigated than in the rainfed areas. Owner-cultivation is pervasive only in drought-prone areas. Tenure distribution indicates that the ratio of share tenants, who are supposed to be converted to leaseholders and CLT (Certificate of Land Transfer) owners by land reform, is higher in the unfavorable areas. In irrigated and favorable rainfed villages, nearly 70 percent of households are already beneficiaries of land reform.

The cropping pattern is clearly conditioned by environmental factors (Table 4.2). Nearly all irrigated villages are able to plant two or even three crops of rice. In favorable rainfed areas, most of which are on Panay (where rainfall distribution is relatively even), 25% of cultivated area is planted to two rice crops. More than 50% of favorable rainfed areas, however, grow rice only in the wet season, leaving the land fallow after harvest. In submergence-prone areas, only rice can be grown during the wet season. In drought-prone areas, more than 70% of cultivated area is fallow in the dry season and the remainder is planted to other crops.

The Intensive Survey

The intensive survey involved two levels of data collection. A complete census was initially conducted to obtain basic farm and household characteristics, demographic data, history of migration, and changes in tenancy and landownership patterns. A sample survey of farm and landless households was then conducted twice, pertaining to the dry (January to May) and wet (June to December) seasons of 1985. The households were randomly selected from the population stratified by farm size for the farm households and by family size for the landless households. The questionnaire covered detailed information on technology adoption, input use, yields, prices, wages and labor contracts, tenure pattern, assets, and income from all sources.

The number of sample households and selected socioeconomic characteristics are presented in Table 4.3. Farm size is largest in CL1, the most favorable village in rice production, and smallest in P3, the village with the most unfavorable rice-growing environment. The villages in Central Luzon generally have larger farms than those on Panay. Therefore, Panay villages are more densely populated, as evidenced by the pattern of man-land ratios. Within each region, man-land ratio tends to be larger in the more favorable villages. The ratio of landless households is highest in P1 and lowest in P3. The landless are geographically more mobile than farmers, and many of the landless in the favorable villages are migrants from less favorable areas, which suggests that interregional labor markets are linked by labor migration.

Regional difference in tenure patterns can also be observed between the two regions. The smaller proportion of owner-cultivators in Central Luzon reflects the history of the hacienda system that prevailed prior to the implementation of land reform. As in the extensive survey, favorable rice-production environments tend to have a lower rate of share tenancy.

Table 4.4 presents the cropping patterns in the five villages. Almost all of the farms in CL1 plant two consecutive rice crops between late May and February. Unlike CL1, P1 is not constrained by a rotation schedule of irrigation water; hence, rice cropping intensity is even higher, with 25% of the rice area growing three rice crops per year. In CL2, two rice crops are planted only in the area irrigated by pumps, and rice-fallow is the dominant cropping pattern. P2, because of even rainfall distribution, has sufficient moisture after the wet season so that only 12% of crop areas lie fallow during the dry season. The introduction of early-maturing modern varieties, together with associated cultural practices (direct seeding, mechanical threshers) in the mid-1970s, induced higher cropping intensity in many P2 farms. Although P3 is essentially rainfed, 23% of rice fields grow two crops of rice because some farms are located close to a creek or an underground water source.

MODERN VARIETY ADOPTION AND
ITS IMPACT ON LAND PRODUCTIVITY

Most previous studies on modern variety adoption were done prior to the 1980s (Feder, Just, and Zilberman 1985). At that time, the dynamic processes involved in dissemination of information, learning by doing, and adjustments in the various factor and product markets had not been completed.

We analyzed the determinants of modern variety adoption and its impact on land productivity using our extensive survey data from the wet season of 1986. Because the dynamic diffusion process had largely ended by 1986, our analysis is concerned with long-run equilibrium adoption behavior. In Griliches' (1957) terms, we explain differences in "ceilings" of adoption.

Production Environments, Modern
Variety Adoption, and Productivity

Table 4.5 presents the ratio of irrigated area, modern variety adoption, fertilizer use, yields, and cropping intensity by production environment. About 60% of the sample of irrigated villages had irrigation by 1970; the other 40% became irrigated as a result of the higher irrigation investments during the 1970s (Hayami and Kikuchi 1978). A small portion of paddy fields in the rainfed areas are irrigated by water pumps and natural creeks.

Although modern varieties were most rapidly adopted in the irrigated areas, hardly any difference in adoption rate among favorable rainfed and irrigated areas could be observed by the 1980s. Degree of water control is not significantly different between the two areas during the wet season. Moreover, modern varieties have become more widely adaptable as stronger disease and insect resistance, greater tolerance for physical stress, and earlier maturity were bred into newer varieties. In contrast, adoption of modern varieties in the drought- and flood-prone rainfed villages was slower and much less complete. In all areas, the rate of modern variety adoption has essentially leveled off since 1980.

Fertilizer use per hectare has increased over time, closely following the pattern of modern variety adoption across production environments, as yield response is much higher with modern varieties. Unlike the tall, weak-strawed traditional varieties, modern varieties are semidwarf and stiff-strawed, permitting higher fertilizer application without the danger of lodging. Fertilizer application in terms of the sum of NPK was about 90 kg/ha in the irrigated and favorable rainfed areas but less than 40 kg/ha in the drought-prone areas and about 60 kg/ha in the submergence-prone villages in 1986.

Modern varieties increase land productivity by raising yield per hectare per season and by increasing cropping intensity as a result of shorter growth duration and photoperiod-insensitivity. As a consequence of differential adoption of the modern variety–fertilizer technology, significant yield differential between traditional and modern varieties emerged across production environments (Table 4.5). In 1970, there was no significant difference in yields of traditional varieties among favorable and unfavorable rice-growing areas. By 1986, yields of modern varieties ranged from 2.4 t/ha in the submergence-prone areas to 3.6 t/ha in the irrigated villages. Traditional varieties still grown in the unfavorable rainfed areas yielded only half as much as the modern varieties grown in the irrigated areas.

Despite widespread adoption of modern varieties, rice cropping intensity rose markedly only in the irrigated villages, following the increase in the proportion of irrigated area. Between 1970 and 1980, the small increase in cropping intensity in the favorable rainfed areas was influenced most by the Panay villages. Owing to the more even rainfall distribution on Panay, adoption of early-maturing modern varieties, coupled with direct seeding, made it possible to increase cropping intensity.

Determinants of Modern Variety Adoption and Fertilizer Use

The modern variety adoption function was estimated to analyze the effects of village-specific environmental and market factors on the new technology's profitability—i.e., the productivity advantage of a new technology as indicated by environmental factors, economic conditions as reflected in relative prices of inputs and outputs, and institutional structure manifested in farm size and land tenure patterns. The two-limit probit regression method developed by Rosett and Nelson (1975) is used to explain rates of modern variety adoption (MVR), defined as the percentage of total area planted to modern varieties.

Two types of regression equations were estimated for the fertilizer demand function. The first regression was a reduced-form equation in which only exogenous variables were included as explanatory variables, namely:

- environmental variables representing the degree of water control—i.e., an irrigated village dummy (IRG), a favorable rainfed village dummy (RFAV), and a drought-prone village dummy (DPRONE), with submergence-prone area as control;
- socioeconomic variables, i.e., farm size in hectares (FSIZE),

percentage of area under share tenancy (SHARER) and owner-cultivation (OWNERR);

- ratio of the price of nitrogen contained in urea to paddy price (FERTPP); and
- a Panay dummy (PANAY) in order to control for region-specific environmental difference, particularly in rainfall pattern.

In a strict sense, these regression equations are not truly reduced-form equations, because only the few most relevant factor-price variables for each equation were selected because of the limitation of the sample size. Aside from these variables, we also employed the soil texture variables, represented by clay and sandy-soil dummies. These variables, however, were insignificant in these and the productivity regressions.

The second regression was a two-stage simultaneous regression in which the predicted value of modern variety adoption ratio (PMVR) derived from the first-stage two-limit probit regression was used for the second-stage regression. In the second-stage regression of fertilizer-demand function, irrigated village dummy (IRG) was inserted in addition to PMVR in order to separate the impact of irrigation from modern varieties.

Regression results of the modern variety adoption and fertilizer demand functions are presented in Table 4.6. Environmental factors related to degree of water control are the only significant variables explaining variations in modern variety adoption across villages. It is interesting to note that modern varieties are equally likely to be adopted in the irrigated and the favorable rainfed villages, judging from the similarity of the estimated coefficients of IRG and RFAV. The coefficient of fertilizer-paddy price ratio (FERTPP) is not significant.

As with many other studies, neither farm size nor tenure variables significantly affects the adoption rate of modern varieties. These findings suggest that modern variety adoption is neutral to scale and that credit is probably not a major constraint to adoption. Even during the early stages of introduction of modern varieties, tenancy and smallness of farm size, ordinarily associated with low income levels, did not seriously impede adoption in the Philippines (Mangahas 1970; Liao 1968).

In the reduced-form fertilizer demand regression equation (2), two of the environmental variables (IRG and RFAV) are highly significant. Moreover, fertilizer application in irrigated areas is not significantly higher than in favorable rainfed areas during the wet season. Indeed, equation (3) indicates that modern variety adoption is the most significant variable accounting for intervillage differences in fertilizer use and that irrigation does not have any significant additional effect.

It is also remarkable to note that when the PMVR is included in equation (3), the coefficient of FERTPP has the expected negative sign and is significantly different from zero, despite the relatively small interregional variation in the price ratio of fertilizer to paddy. As in the modern variety adoption function, farm size and tenure are not significant in the fertilizer demand function, implying that, at least in the long-run equilibrium, imperfections in the credit market do not seem to significantly affect farmers' demand for fertilizer.

Determinants of Land Productivity

Modern varieties increase land productivity in rice production by increasing yields per hectare per season. Because they are not photoperiod-sensitive and mature earlier than traditional varieties, the modern varieties may also increase rice productivity per hectare per year by promoting double cropping of rice or allowing another crop to be grown after the wet-season rice crop.

We analyzed the impact of the modern rice technology on productivity by estimating wet-season yield and cropping intensity functions. As with the estimation of fertilizer demand function, reduced-form and two-stage simultaneous regression equations were used.

Table 4.7 shows the estimation results of yield, rice cropping intensity, and total cropping intensity functions. The coefficients of irrigated village dummy (IRG) and favorable rainfed dummy (RFAV) are positive and significant in equation (1), implying that there is a clear productivity difference between favorable and unfavorable areas. More important is the finding that the predicted value of modern variety adoption ratio (PMVR) has a positive and highly significant coefficient in equation (2). The implication is that the differential adoption of modern varieties between favorable and unfavorable areas has significantly widened the regional yield differential. Such an observation is consistent with the earlier finding that adoption of modern varieties significantly increases fertilizer application per hectare.

The ratio of share-tenanted area (SHARER) has unexpected negative and significant coefficients in equations (1) and (2). This result appears consistent with the familiar Marshallian argument that share tenants do not work as hard as leasehold tenants and owner-cultivators because of the disincentive of output sharing. However, because share tenancy is still practiced in less favorable areas, the SHARER variable may capture not only the effect of contract per se but also the effects of environmental and technology factors affecting the implementation of land reform. The latter interpretation is supported by the finding of Otsuka (1991) that the implementation of land reform, as measured by declining incidence of share tenancy, is positively affected by the growth of yield. Ideally, we should estimate the simultaneous equation systems in which SHARER is also an endogenous variable. However, because of the lack of exogenous variables, such an estimation was not feasible.

According to equation (3) in Table 4.7, rice cropping intensity in irrigated areas is higher than in unfavorable areas by about 100%. The inclusion of PMVR in equation (4) suggests that the introduction of modern varieties contributes to the increase in rice cropping intensity, as evidenced by the positive and significant coefficient. However, in terms of total cropping intensity, the coefficient of PMVR, although positive, is insignificant according to equation (6). However, the positive and significant coefficients of the regional dummy in equations (5) and (6) indicate that on Panay, where rainfall distribution is more even, total cropping intensity is higher.

This analysis of determinants of technology adoption confirms accumulated evidence that farm size, tenure, and other social and institutional factors have not significantly affected adoption of modern varieties and the associated increase in fertilizer use in the Philippines (Lipton and Longhurst 1989; Barker and Herdt 1985; David 1976; Ruttan 1977). As in other studies, environmental factors, especially the degree of water control and modern variety adoption, are the most important variables in explaining the productivity gap between favorable and unfavorable areas.

We conclude that the differential adoption of modern variety technology has inequitable direct effects on regional income distribution.

IMPACTS ON LABOR DEMAND

The manner in which benefits from productivity gain in the favorable areas are shared among production factors critically depends on the shifts of factor-demand functions. Here we focus on labor demand, as labor is the major resource of the rural poor, particularly the landless. Labor demand depends not only on modern variety adoption and environmental factors but also on adoption of labor-saving technologies—i.e., tractors, threshers, and direct seeding. Because the spread of modern varieties was followed by a wider use of labor-saving technologies (Jayasuriya and Shand 1985), the net effect may well be adverse to the well-being of the poor landless, among whom labor is the primary resource.

We first estimated labor-saving technology adoption functions, based on the extensive survey data, to identify the extent to which the modern varieties induced adoption of labor-saving technologies. We then used the intensive-survey data to estimate labor use functions per hectare by activity and evaluate the direct impacts of various technologies on labor demand.

Modern Varieties and Labor-Saving Technologies

We emphasize at the outset that tractors, threshers, and direct seeding were adopted in the Philippines prior to the advent of modern varieties. At least 10% of overall rice area in the wet season and about 50% in the dry season were already worked by tractors before the mid-1960s (Herdt 1987). Use of big mechanical threshers was also popular in Central Luzon prior to the introduction of modern varieties. The big threshers gave landlords improved control over the sharing of the crop at the time of harvest under a share tenancy arrangement (Hayami and Kikuchi 1982).

The use of the big threshers gradually diminished in the 1970s as land reform was implemented and double cropping expanded in many rice areas. Double cropping made it difficult to use threshers because they had to traverse wet fields during the wet season. The introduction of small portable threshers in the mid-1970s, however, led to even more widespread mechanization of threshing throughout the country (Duff 1978).

Direct seeding had been practiced in rainfed lowland areas well before transplanting became widely adopted as a way to address weed problems (Imperial 1980). The resurgence of direct seeding in lowland rice areas was first observed on Panay in the mid-1970s, when the technology package that combined early-maturing modern varieties and direct seeding was introduced to increase cropping intensity (Barlow, Jayasuriya, and Price 1983). It can also be attributed to the introduction of herbicides, which are effective for weed control (Moody and Cordova 1983), and to the decline in herbicide prices relative to wage rates (Jayasuriya and Shand 1985). In the late 1970s, direct seeding spread in some parts of Central Luzon simply to reduce labor inputs (Coxhead 1984).

The extensive-survey data show an increase in the adoption rate of tractors, threshers, and direct seeding between 1970 and 1986 (Table 4.8). In the case of tractors, adoption rates are markedly lower than the corresponding rates of modern variety adoption (Table 4.5). The exception is in the submergence-prone areas, where the adoption rate of tractors and modern varieties are about the same. Farm size is relatively larger in the submergence-prone areas, which may confer scale advantage to the use of tractors (Table 4.3). Adoption rate of tractors is lowest in the drought-prone areas, where farm size is smallest and transportation of machines across sloping and mountainous terrain is more difficult.

The declining use of big threshers in the 1970s and widespread adoption of small threshers in the 1980s can also be confirmed from this data set. By 1986, adoption of the small threshers was nearly complete except in the drought-prone areas, where the small size of farms and topography of the village makes mechanization uneconomical. Direct seeding was not as widely adopted as the yield-increasing and mechanical technologies; neither was it adopted most intensively in the irrigated areas. It is interesting to observe that in the submergence-prone areas, the shift from traditional to modern varieties accompanied a decline in the rate of adoption of direct seeding.

Although the spread of modern varieties broadly coincided with the increased adoption of labor-saving technologies, detailed examination of the historical pattern of adoption and comparisons of adoption levels by production environments do not strongly indicate that modern varieties caused the wider adoption of tractors, threshers, and direct seeding. We hypothesize that modern variety adoption is not a major cause of adoption of labor-saving technology; instead, economic and social factors are relatively more important in explaining cross-sectional differences in tractor and thresher adoption.

Because tractors and threshers are substitutes for labor and draft animals (Binswanger 1978), profitability of mechanization depends critically on the relative prices of machine service, draft animals, and labor. Machines are, in general, lumpy inputs, and thus efficiency gains accrue to large farmers from higher capacity utilization, although the contract hiring of machines now commonly practiced may help neutralize the scale advantage. Savings on the cost of supervising casual laborers will be also greater for large than for small farms. In addition, imperfections in the credit market may favor adoption of mechanical technology by larger farmers.

Direct seeding involves less time and labor for crop establishment and seedbed preparation than does transplanting, but use of herbicides for weed control and higher seeding rate per hectare are required to obtain yields comparable to those of transplanted rice. This suggests that differences in the relative prices of herbicides and wages affect the adoption rate of direct seeding. However, the choice of seeding method is highly dependent on surface drainage and rainfall patterns (Garrity et al. 1986). In fact, adoption of direct seeding is not feasible in flooded fields, where the germination rate is low and young seedlings can be easily washed away. Direct seeding is also not widely adopted in drought-prone areas, because the farmer is reluctant to drain excess water for broadcasted pregerminated seeds when the possibility of drought occurring at a critical growth stage is high (Moody 1982).

Conversely, because of their excellent seedling vigor and good tillering capacity, the modern varieties are preferred for direct-seeded rice in rainfed lowland fields (De Datta 1980). In favorable rainfed areas, with their more even rainfall distribution, or in areas with year-round irrigation, the time saved from direct seeding in combination with early maturation of modern varieties may also increase cropping intensity. Cross-sectional differences in adoption of direct seeding, therefore, may be influenced not only by relative prices but also by the physical environment and the adoption of modern varieties.

Determinants of Adoption of Labor-Saving Technologies

Table 4.9 presents the estimates of adoption functions of tractors, threshers, and direct seeding as estimated by the two-limit probit regression. In addition to variables indicating environmental factors, modern variety adoption, farm size, and tenure, the following variables were included to examine the effect of relative prices: land preparation wage (WGPLP), threshing wage (WGPTH), transplanting wage (WGPTP), and herbicide price (HERBPP), deflated by paddy price. Actual rental costs of tractors, threshers, and draft animals were not specified directly, because machines are not used in some villages and the tasks performed by draft animals vary across regions (see the following section, "Technology and Labor Use"). Instead we used predicted rice cropping intensity (PRCI), obtained from the regression estimate shown in Table 4.7, to denote the rental cost of draft animals and the machine utilization rate, because increased cropping intensity reduces the amount of land available for grazing draft animals. Also, we used distance from Manila (DISTMLA) as a proxy for price and maintenance costs of machinery, because Manila is an industrial center for the supply of agricultural machinery.

It is not surprising that the estimation results of the tractor and direct-seeding adoption functions show a better fit than those for threshers. Because adoption of threshers in the total sample of villages is already almost complete (95%), the factors affecting adoption of threshers cannot be effectively analyzed in our data set. Nonetheless, it is clear that determinants of adoption for these three labor-saving technologies are markedly different.

Irrigation significantly affects only tractor adoption (equation [1]). The positive and significant coefficient of irrigation in the tractor regression is consistent with our hypothesis that tractors will be adopted where the rental cost of draft animals is high. This interpretation is reinforced by the positive and significant coefficient of the rice cropping intensity (PRCI) variable in equation (2). Adoption of modern varieties does not increase adoption of any of these labor-saving technologies, as evidenced by the insignificant coefficients of the predicted modern variety adoption ratio (PMVR). Wider adoption of tractors coincided with the spread of modern varieties because both are positively influenced by irrigation, although for different reasons. Widespread use of mechanical threshers and significant adoption of direct seeding occurred only about a decade after the introduction of modern varieties. These findings are consistent with recent analysis of changes in labor demand in Central Luzon over the last two decades by Otsuka, Gascon, and Asano (1994b).

The changing price of labor relative to paddy and to capital inputs must be a major reason for the increase in adoption of these labor-saving technologies. However, because of a lack of significant regional wage variation, as will be shown later, their effects cannot be identified in these regressions.

The fact that none of the variables indicating degree of water control in equations (5) and (6) is significant suggests that different measures of degree of water control, such as ease of drainage, are needed to determine the effect of environmental variables. The importance of environmental factors in the adoption of direct seeding is suggested by the significant coefficient of the Panay dummy, which represents the condition of relatively even rainfall.

Farm size is found to be significant in the adoption of tractors but not of threshers or direct seeding, which suggests that economies of scale exist only in tractor technology. Such scale advantage does not lie in the favorable access of larger farmers to cheap credit because contract hiring of machines, which lessens the scale advantage of lumpy inputs, is much more common than individual ownership for tractor and thresher operations. The insignificant coefficients of tenure variables also indicate that credit rationing in favor of wealthier owner-farmers does not affect adoption of labor-saving technologies.

The major reason for the economies of scale in tractor use should be sought in the saving of supervision costs for land preparation. Plowing and harrowing with draft animals require care and judgment, which are not amenable to easy supervision, so that larger farmers tend to incur higher costs of supervision (Otsuka, Chuma, and Hayami 1992). It is likely that such high supervision costs induce large farmers to use tractors.

Technology and Labor Use

Because it was not feasible to obtain accurate information on labor use by a brief visit to villages for the extensive survey, we used intensive-survey data for the labor demand analysis.

Table 4.10 shows adoption patterns of modern varieties and other technology indicators across the intensive-survey villages. Modern varieties have been fully adopted in CL1, P1, and CL2, whereas traditional varieties are planted in the hilly part of P2 and the mountainous portion of P3 during the wet season. Except in P3, all farms use fertilizer. Fertilizer use is generally higher in favorable production environments and in Central Luzon compared to Panay villages. Differential adoption of modern varieties and fertilizer use is reflected in the different production performance among environments; average yield per hectare is higher in the irrigated than in rainfed villages.

Overall, there is no notable difference in patterns of modern variety and fertilizer adoption, yield, and cropping intensities between extensive- and intensive-survey villages.

Table 4.11 compares labor use per hectare, adoption rate of labor-saving technology, and proportion of hired labor by activity. Substantial variability in labor use per hectare can be observed across activities and across villages. In land preparation, differences in labor use are directly related to adoption of hand tractors. Hand tractors are not used in P3 because of the difficulty of moving the machine in the mountainous terrain of the village.

For crop establishment, labor use depends on whether rice is direct seeded or transplanted. Direct seeding can save nearly twenty days per hectare, or 80% of the total labor typically required for transplanting. About 90% of rice area in P1 and P2 is now direct seeded; about half of the rice area in the other villages is transplanted.

In crop care activity (i.e., fertilizer and chemical applications, weeding, and water control), the much higher labor input in P1 results mainly from greater need for weeding. In the case of harvesting and threshing, it is clear that labor use per hectare tends to be higher in the favorable areas with complete adoption of modern varieties.

Despite adoption of hand tractors, total labor use per hectare in the irrigated villages is generally higher than in the rainfed villages. The exception is P3, where complete reliance on work animals for land preparation, a lower rate of mechanical threshing, and less frequent use of direct seeding result in the highest labor use.

A tendency to use relatively more hired labor in the more favorable production environments can also be observed. This trend may be explained by the sharper peak-season labor demand in areas growing modern varieties and by the income effect on family labor use in farm households, which have higher incomes because of the modern variety technology. Also, average farm size in the favorable areas is somewhat higher than in the unfavorable areas.

Determinants of Labor Use

To separate the impact of modern varieties from that of labor-saving technologies, we estimated labor use functions disaggregated by task and specified them in log-linear form. Because wages and paddy prices are largely similar across locations, labor input per hectare is specified as a function of variables representing technology, production environment, farm size, and farmer characteristics. We also note that there is almost no variation in wages and paddy prices within each village. Therefore, it is not possible to use intensive-survey data to statistically identify effects of wages and paddy prices.

It was also very difficult to identify the separate effects of modern varieties and production environments on labor use from our cross-sectional data, primarily because modern varieties are planted throughout the favorable areas in the survey villages. Thus, technology factors have been specified as interaction terms between adoption rate of modern varieties and production environments—i.e., between the ratios of modern varieties and irrigated area (MVR*IRGR) to represent irrigated conditions in CL1 and P1, and between the ratios of modern variety and rainfed area (MVR*RFAVR) to represent favorable rainfed farming conditions in CL2 and some parts of P2 and P3. The omitted technology variable, which serves as a control, pertains to unfavorable rainfed areas planted to traditional varieties in P2 and P3. Besides PANAY, P3U (sloped, upper portions of P3) is included as an environmental factor to distinguish the sloping from the flat terrain within the village P3.

The results shown in Table 4.12 indicate somewhat low goodness of fit (R^2) because of the per hectare specification. However, most of the technology variables, including the interaction terms, have significant coefficients with the correct sign in relation to the appropriate task. For example, the coefficient of tractor use dummy (TRUSER) is negative and significant in land preparation, as is the dummy variable for direct seeding (DSEED) in crop establishment. As expected, the interaction terms between modern varieties and irrigated and favorable rainfed environments have positive and significant coefficients for crop care, harvest, and postharvest labor use. Other environmental factors, as represented by location dummy variables for villages, are important, especially in the labor use in crop establishment. In general, farmer characteristics, such as age and schooling of household head, do not seem to have a statistically significant effect on labor use per hectare.

Given the importance of crop care and harvest and postharvest activities, there is no doubt that irrigation and adoption of modern varieties have had a significant impact on total labor demand per hectare. Total labor demand per year is still higher in irrigated areas planted to modern varieties, where double cropping of rice is commonly practiced. We note that technological change in rice farming has also been reported to increase employment in the nonfarm sector through the intersectoral growth linkage effects (Hazell and Roelle 1983; Hazell and Ramasamy 1991; Gibbs 1974; Wangwacharakul 1984).

Thus, other things being the same, we expect that wage rates, particularly for crop care, harvest, and threshing activities, will tend to be higher in more favorable areas. Also, increased adoption of labor-saving technologies for land preparation, crop establishment, and threshing may offset the positive effect of modern variety technology on labor demand. As we have shown, however, there is no strong indication that modern variety technology causes the adoption of labor-saving technologies. A relevant question is whether and to what extent differential adoption of modern varieties in the Philippines induces labor migration from less favorable areas, where technological change has not taken place, to favorable areas, where technological change has brought about increased labor demand.

LABOR MARKET ADJUSTMENTS
AND REGIONAL WAGE DIFFERENTIALS

The greater demand for labor resulting from modern variety adoption is expected to increase wage rates in the favorable areas, at least in the short run. In this section, we explore whether interregional labor migration from unfavorable to favorable areas occurs to equalize wages and whether any observed difference in the wage rates across the study villages can be explained by differential technology adoption. Specifically, we use extensive-survey data to examine the impact of differential adoption of modern variety technology on changes in village population as a proxy for permanent migration. In practice, permanent and seasonal migration both seem to play significant roles in equalizing wage rates across regions. However, the extensive survey failed to obtain reliable information on seasonal labor migration.

Technology Adoption and Demographic Changes

As in other countries, the dominant migration flow in the Philippines has been from rural to urban areas. Its average annual population growth rate in urban areas (4.4%) was much higher than in rural areas (1.9%) during the 1970s, mainly because of the migration from rural to urban settings.

Under such circumstances, an important part of interregional labor market adjustments is accomplished by the differential rates of rural-to-urban migration from different production environments. Moreover, the systematic difference, if any, in the natural rate of population growth between favorable and unfavorable areas may accentuate or lessen the labor market adjustments by migration.

Although it is obviously desirable to analyze migration data, there are no such data at a disaggregated level classified by rice-production environments and technology. We used the changes in village population between census years 1970 and 1980 and between 1980 and our survey year (1986) as an indicator of the long-run labor supply adjustments. Because there was more rapid adoption of modern rice technology in the 1970s than in the 1980s, labor supply adjustments manifested in the changes in the population are hypothesized to be more pronounced in the 1970s.

In Table 4.13, the pattern of population growth, changes in man-land ratio, and ratio of agricultural landless households are presented. It is remarkable that during the 1970s, when modern varieties were rapidly disseminated and irrigation investments accelerated, population growth rate was highest in the irrigated villages and lowest in the unfavorable rainfed villages. In the 1980s, as adoption of modern varieties tapered off, average population growth rates among the three production environments became more comparable. The higher growth in population in the unfavorable rainfed areas in the 1980s, as compared with the 1970s, is consistent with the reported migration to the upland areas induced by population pressure in the lowlands and the general contraction of the Philippine economy (Cruz, Feranil, and Goce 1986).

Trends in man-land ratio, defined as the population per hectare of cultivated area, followed the pattern of population growth—i.e., increasing most rapidly in the irrigated area and least rapidly in the unfavorable rainfed area. By 1986, the man-land ratio had become highest in the irrigated area and lowest in the unfavorable rainfed area, though they had similar man-land ratios in 1970. There was no significant difference in farm size among the three different production environments, but the ratio of landless households was highest in the irrigated area in 1986. The majority of rural-to-rural migrants were reported to be landless, not only in the Philippines (Kikuchi et al. 1983; Bautista 1988) but also in other countries, such as India (Lal 1976; Dhar 1984). These trends in population and its composition suggest that permanent migration from unfavorable to favorable rice production areas took place.

In order to statistically confirm the impact of modern variety adoption and irrigation on demographic changes at the village level, we estimated the average annual population growth rate functions. Two alternative specifications were employed.

First, because the natural environments and the presence of gravity irrigation can be considered exogenous, we regressed the average annual rate of population growth (POPN) directly on the irrigated (IRG) and favorable rainfed (RFAV) village dummies and the change in the ratio of irrigated areas (ΔIRGR). If the more rapid spread of modern varieties in the irrigated and favorable rainfed areas raised labor demand and subsequently induced interregional migration, positive coefficients of the two environment dummies would be obtained. Similarly, an increase in the ratio of irrigated area, which increases cropping intensity, would affect population growth rate positively.

Second, we estimated a two-stage least squares (TSLS) regression in which changes in the ratio of modern variety adoption (ΔMVR) were regressed on IRG, RFAV, and ΔIRGR in the first stage and population growth rate was regressed on ΔIRGR and the predicted value of ΔMVR in the second stage. If modern variety cum irrigation technology induces mechanization or direct seeding, which would reduce labor demand, the coefficients of ΔIRGR and ΔMVR should capture the net effects on population changes.

In addition, man-land ratio (MLR) in the initial year (i.e., 1970 and 1980), and three regional dummies—Northern Luzon (NORTH), Southern Luzon (SOUTH), and Panay (PANAY)—were included to control possible effects of initial conditions and various region-specific factors.

As expected, the fit of the regression equations is better for the 1970–1980 than for the 1980–1986 equations (Table 4.14), because technology was more stagnant in the latter period. In the 1970–1980 regression, we employed the adoption rate of modern varieties in 1970 rather than the change between 1970 and 1980 because modern varieties were newly introduced immediately before 1970.

It is remarkable to observe in equation (1) that the coefficients of ΔIRGR, IRG, and RFAV are positive and highly significant. Because modern varieties were adopted mainly in the irrigated and favorable rainfed areas and the cropping intensities rose in the irrigated villages as the ratio of irrigated areas expanded, these results strongly indicate the pervasive effect of modern rice technology on population growth through interregional migration. This interpretation is supported by the results of the two-stage regressions shown in equations (2) and (3). According to equation (3), modern varieties were introduced to irrigated and favorable rainfed villages almost equally rapidly regardless of the difference in irrigation. Equation (2) shows the highly significant effect of change in modern variety adoption and irrigation expansion on the growth rate of population. These findings are consistent with historical comparisons of migration patterns of favorable and unfavorable rice villages in the Philippines (Kikuchi et al. 1983; Bautista 1988).

For 1980–1986, as shown in equations (4) and (5), no estimated coefficient except for regional dummies is significant in the population growth rate equations. During this period, however, the adoption rate of modern varieties increased only slightly, and the irrigated area expanded only in three locations. It seems that the interregional labor supply adjustments occurred mainly in the 1970s.

Regional Wage Differentials

Although population changes are observed to be consistent with the hypothesis of interregional labor market adjustments, the extent to which such adjustments lead to equalization of wages across regions needs to be explored. Table 4.15 shows paddy prices, task-specific daily wages, and rental of carabao (draft animals) in irrigated, favorable rainfed, and unfavorable rainfed areas. Because labor contracts are often on a piece-rate or output-sharing basis rather than on a daily basis, imputed daily wages under piece-rate and output-sharing contracts were calculated by dividing total wage payments by the number of workdays. In villages where different contracts coexist for the same task, the wage of the dominant mode of contract was selected.

Paddy prices and wages are generally similar across environments. The exception is the daily wage for transplanting, which is lowest in the most favorable area. Because wage rates generally differ by activity, wage rate functions were estimated separately for land preparation, transplanting, harvesting, and threshing.

The daily rental of carabao also differs across production environments, being highest in the most favorable area. Using the same set of independent variables, a carabao rental equation was estimated to compare the determinants of wages and carabao rental. The rental market for draft animals is known to be imperfect even within a village, because it is costly for the owner to supervise the proper care of the draft animal by a renter (Bliss and Stern 1982; Binswanger and Rosenzweig 1986). Such a market imperfection, coupled with high relocation costs, will lead to low geographic mobility of carabao, and hence their rental will be largely determined by local supply and demand. Wage rates, however, will not be affected by local labor market conditions if labor is sufficiently mobile.

Considering the endogenous nature of modern variety adoption, we applied the two-stage least squares method, in which the adoption rate of modern varieties in 1986 was regressed on village environment dummies in the first stage and the logarithm of task-specific daily wage earning and carabao rental were regressed on predicted modern variety adoption rate (PMVR) and irrigation ratio in 1986 (IRGR) in the second stage.

In addition to the technology variables, we included the logarithms of average farm size (FSIZE) and paddy price of modern varieties (PADDYP) as variables reflecting village characteristics. Other things being equal, the higher the average farm size, the higher the demand for hired labor, which in turn results in higher wages. To distinguish the skill-intensive and laborious work of plowing and harrowing under the *dukit* contract, where use of carabao is limited to the sides of rice fields after tractor operation, the dummy variable (CONT1) was included in land preparation wage and carabao rental regression.

The piece-rate contract dummy (CONT2) was inserted in the transplanting wage regressions, and the output-sharing contract dummy (CONT3) was added in harvesting wage regressions. As is well known in the theory of contract (Stiglitz 1975; Roumasset and Uy 1980; Hayami and Otsuka 1993), daily wage workers are less motivated to work because wage payment is fixed regardless of their real efforts. The more able workers prefer piece-rate or output-sharing contracts because they provide higher remuneration at higher levels of labor. For these reasons, daily labor income will be higher for non–daily wage workers, and thus the contract dummy variables are expected to have positive coefficients.

The logarithms of the distance in kilometers between village and large city (DISTCT)—i.e., Manila for Luzon and Iloilo City for Panay—were included among the independent variables to capture, at least partially, the cost of migration between rural labor markets. Regional dummies were also included to take account of all other environmental variables not explicitly specified in the equation.

Table 4.16 presents the results of the wage and carabao rental regressions. The modern variety adoption function shown in Table 4.6 was used as a first-stage regression. Adoption of modern varieties does not have any significant effect in any of the equations. With the exception of the transplanting wage, irrigation and favorable rainfed ratios do not have any significant coefficients either, suggesting that wage rates are largely equalized between favorable and unfavorable rice-production environments.

In irrigated and favorable areas, transplanting dates are staggered. However, in the unfavorable environment, where traditional varieties are still grown, many farmers transplant on the same day immediately after rain because of poor control of water. Therefore, the demand for transplanters has a higher seasonal peak in the unfavorable areas. Because transplanting in neighboring villages is also done synchronously, short-distance migration does not occur. Seasonal migration from remote areas with a different environment will not occur either, because transplanting dates in the unfavorable areas are unpredictable. Moreover, the expected daily wage will be lower than the actual wage in such a situation, because transplanting jobs are not always available during the transplanting season. Therefore, it is not surprising to find negative and significant coefficients for IRGR and RFAV in the transplanting wage equation.

For carabao rental (equation [5]), the positive and significant coefficient of irrigation is due not so much to higher demand for carabao services as to the higher cost of maintaining draft animals as grazing land declines in an irrigated area. The facts that wage rates are equalized, carabao rentals are significantly higher, and tractors are adopted mainly in irrigated areas strongly support the hypothesis advanced by Rao (1975), Day and Singh (1977), and Roumasset and Smith (1981)—that the tractor is adopted more widely in irrigated areas not necessarily because wage rates are relatively higher but because draft animal service is more expensive.

Farm size and paddy price do not affect regional wage patterns significantly. The significant coefficient of CONT1 in land preparation wage and carabao rental indicates the skill-intensive nature of plowing only the sides of rice fields by carabao, whereas the highly significant coefficient for piece-rate contract in harvesting (CONT3) suggests that daily wage laborers shirk more often or are of lower quality.

The significant coefficient of distance variable in equation (3) and its uniformly negative coefficients in all regressions conform with expectations that wages may be higher near large cities. As long as large cities are centers of gravity in labor markets, these results can be explained by costs of information and transportation involved in interregional migration.

Thus, there is evidence that differential adoption of modern varieties in the Philippines between favorable and unfavorable areas induces interregional migration, which tends to equalize wage rates across different production environments, supporting the hypothesis that rural labor markets are relatively well integrated. As far as labor income is concerned, therefore, there is little indication that the location specificity of modern varieties has significantly worsened regional income distribution. Considering the positive effect of modern rice technology on labor demand, landless laborers in both favorable and unfavorable areas would have benefited from technological progress in the favorable production areas.

MODERN RICE TECHNOLOGY
AND HOUSEHOLD INCOME DISTRIBUTION

Income of agricultural households consists of returns to labor, capital, and land, supplemented mainly by labor earnings from nonfarm sources. Agricultural technology affects farmers' income through its effect on factor demands and factor prices, which in turn induce changes in allocation of farmers' own resources to different uses. Income from farming is also affected by village institutions such as land tenure, which govern the distribution of income between landlords and tenants and affect resource allocations.

The impact of differential technology adoption on regional factor prices and factor incomes depends critically on the mobility of factors. As was shown in the previous section, differential adoption of modern varieties was followed by interregional labor migration from unfavorable to favorable areas, which significantly contributed to the equalization of agricultural wages across production environments. Conversely, land is an immobile factor of production, so productivity growth in the favorable rice-growing areas will be expected to widen returns to land from rice production across production environments. This effect can be mitigated by a shift to alternative crops or institutional changes that alter distribution of returns to land.

In the Philippines, a land reform program was instituted in the early 1970s, soon after adoption of modern varieties started. Share tenants became leaseholders and amortizing owners, with rents and amortization fees fixed at about 25% of yield realized in the early 1970s. That enabled the former tenant farmers to receive the major part of the benefits from the technological change.

Below we explore the differential impact of modern varieties on factor incomes of rice farmers and identify the extent to which land reform redistributed the returns to land in favor of tenants. Our analysis is based on the intensive survey of farm and landless agricultural households in five selected villages.

Land Market Adjustments

There are at least three types of land market adjustments that can mitigate the inequitable income effects arising from increased returns to land in favorable areas—changes in farm size, farming systems, and tenancy relations.

The scope for farm size adjustment as a means of mitigating direct inequitable effects of differential technological change on regional difference in land rental has been limited by land reform laws, which prohibit tenancy and land sale transactions. Thus, labor migration that could have brought about an increase in farm size in unfavorable areas and a decrease in farm size in favorable areas may have exacerbated the income gap between those with access to land and those without. The more numerous the migrants from unfavorable to favorable areas, the greater the demand for land; hence, the landowners in favorable areas enjoy higher land values and lower wages.

That such farm size adjustments either have not occurred or have been limited is suggested by the generally smaller farm size in the intensive-survey villages with less favorable environments (Table 4.3). In the extensive-survey data set, no significant difference in farm size was found across production environments (Table 4.1).

However, the lower profitability of rice farming in the unfavorable areas may induce farmers to cultivate other crops. If alternative crops or livestock can be profitably raised in the unfavorable rice-production environments, the potential decline in land values will be reduced. Our data did not permit us to examine the extent to which this happened because of limited coverage of unfavorable areas, especially the uplands.

A shift away from rice in the unfavorable areas would not only reduce the adjustment cost of differential technical change in these areas but also promote more optimal use of land resources from the standpoint of conservation. There is some evidence that crop area planted to rice in the rainfed and upland areas has declined substantially since the mid-1970s.

The main instrument minimizing the potentially inequitable effects of differential technical change on return to land was the implementation of land reform in the early 1970s, soon after the widespread adoption of modern varieties started. Before the land reform was initiated in 1972, the majority of farmers were share tenants, particularly in the Central Luzon villages, where there were large haciendas, consisting of hundreds of hectares of rice lands. Almost without exception, tenants received half of the rice output after the harvesters' share, and costs of purchased inputs supplied by landlords were deducted. The share of output that accrued to tenants amounted to about one-third of the gross.

Under the land reform program, share tenants were supposed to be converted either to leaseholders when the landlord owned less than 7 ha of land or to amortizing owners when the landlord owned more than 7 ha (Hayami, Quisumbing, and Adriano 1990). A Certificate of Land Transfer (CLT) was issued to amortizing owners, which promised them the right to purchase the land by paying amortization fees to the Land Bank for fifteen years.

The leasehold rents and the annual amortization fees were fixed at about 25% of yield for the three normal crop years preceding 1972. Since then, yields have nearly doubled in villages where modern varieties have been adopted, increasing the divergence between the rental value of the land and the fixed leasehold rents and amortization fees prescribed by law over time. According to Otsuka (1991), land reform was particularly well implemented in favorable rice-growing areas, where returns to land significantly increased because of modern variety adoption.

We attempt to quantify the extent to which land reform redistributed the higher returns to land in favor of ex–share tenants by estimating the factor shares in rice production.

Factor Income in Rice Production

How output is distributed among factor inputs and factor owners depends on relative factor prices and factor-using or factor-saving characteristics of technology. Table 4.17 compares paddy prices, fertilizer prices, wage rates in selected farm tasks, and custom rates of carabao, tractor, and thresher rental across the five selected villages during the 1985 wet season. As may be expected, there are no significant differences in fertilizer and paddy prices among the survey villages. The difference in wage rates is relatively small, despite the wide locational difference and diverse production environments across the study villages. The relatively similarity in wages is consistent with our earlier findings that differential adoption of modern rice technology induces permanent migration from unfavorable to favorable production environments so as to equalize wage rates across different environments.

Custom rates of carabao operation, however, tend to be lower on Panay compared to the Central Luzon villages, where grazing land is limited. On the other hand, the custom rates of hand tractor and thresher operations are largely equalized. Such regional difference in capital costs of carabao and tractor operations may explain, at least partly, why hand tractors are widely adopted in the Central Luzon villages, even though wage rates are not significantly higher (see Table 4.11).

Under competitive factor-market equilibrium, relative factor shares can be shown to be determined by the relative factor prices and the factor-using bias of technology (Kawagoe, Otsuka, and Hayami 1986). Factor-market equilibrium cannot be assumed in this study because land markets are distorted by the land reform program. However, if the production function is subject to constant returns to scale, the competitive factor payment to land can be estimated as a residual, after the actual and imputed cost of current inputs, capital, and labor are deducted from the value of production. The assumption of constant returns to scale is supported by Cordova's estimation results of Cobb-Douglas production function (1987).

In order to estimate the residual, the cost of family and exchange labor was imputed by applying the appropriate market wage rates for different tasks and the prevailing custom rates for family-owned capital such as carabao, tractors, and threshers.

Table 4.18 shows the average factor payments and relative factor shares per hectare per season, estimated as the average of wet- and dry-season values, with the ratios of cultivated areas in the two seasons used as weights. It is clear that the gross value of output per hectare is largest in the most favorable village (CL1) and lowest in the most unfavorable village (P3). Accordingly, the absolute factor payments in each category of inputs tend to be higher in villages with better production environments, which suggests that modern variety adoption in the irrigated areas results in higher returns to all factor inputs. Despite the higher rate of mechanization in the irrigated areas, absolute payments to labor are higher by 30 to 40% when compared to the rainfed villages. Moreover, two-thirds of those payments accrue to hired labor, providing relatively more income to landless households in irrigated villages. Relative labor share, however, is much higher in P3, where adoption of modern varieties, direct seeding, and mechanical technology is lowest.

Returns to land, denoted by the residual, tend to be higher in the irrigated areas than in rainfed villages. This figure is especially low in P3, reflecting the lower productivity of rice cultivation in this most remote village in an unfavorable environment. The difference between the returns to land and leasehold rental, which is subject to land reform regulations, essentially represents the income gained by beneficiaries of land reform from technology. In areas where modern variety adoption and hence yield increases occurred before implementation of land reform, landlords share in the benefits of the new technology, as leasehold rent was prescribed to be 25% of the past average yields. Thus, in P1, where modern varieties were largely adopted by 1970, the leasehold rent is relatively high. In contrast, in CL1, where the construction of irrigation facilities and modern variety adoption occurred after 1972, the gain to tenant households equals nearly two-thirds of the estimated returns to land. In CL2, where modern variety adoption is complete but the increase in productivity is not as great as in CL1 and P1, the gain represents 55% of the estimated returns to land. In P2, the surplus is large primarily because of unusually good harvest in the survey year, as can be inferred from low application of current inputs compared with value of output. Where technology has not changed significantly and share tenancy still widely prevails, such as in P3, the estimated return to land has remained close to the leasehold rent.

It is clear that substantial amounts of income are being redistributed from landlords to tenants because of land reform in favorable areas. We note, however, that the lower value of returns to land in P3 compared to prevailing leasehold rent may be partly due to unusually low yields during that year. But the riskiness of income is precisely a reason why share tenancy is still popular in this village. (See Otsuka and Hayami [1988]; Hayami and Otsuka [1993] for the importance of production risk in the choice of share tenancy.)

It is evident from the factor-share analysis that employment opportunities for hired labor in rice production are relatively limited, as income accruing to it is, at most, 20% of gross revenue. In contrast, the income accruing to land accounts for as much as 30 to 50% of gross revenue, except in P3. As a result, the total income share of a farm operator—defined as the sum of incomes that accrue to owned capital, family labor, and land or tenancy right—is far greater than that of hired labor, despite the lower factor share of family labor compared to hired labor in rice cultivation. This clearly indicates that farmers are much better off than landless workers, unless lucrative job opportunities outside rice production are available.

Determinants of Household Income

Household income is determined not only by technology and factor prices but also by the ownership of productive resources, such as land, human capital, and capital assets, as well as market and institutional factors, such as access to nonfarm employment opportunities and land tenure. In order to identify the impact of modern rice technology and land reform on household income, we estimated income determination functions by income component.

Average annual incomes of farm households and agricultural landless households by source and by village are shown in Tables 4.19 and 4.20. Although our survey villages are essentially rice-dependent, nonrice farm income and nonfarm income account for significant shares of the total of these households.

Rice income derived from operating an owned or rented farm is decomposed according to imputed returns to the family labor and owned capital, and income from land. For owner-operators, income from land is the residual, whereas for tenant operators it is the residual minus rent payments or amortization fees. It should be noted that the residual actually reflects not only the returns to land but also returns to management and errors in imputing income of family labor and family-owned capital. Nonrice farm income includes income from production of agricultural products other than rice, earnings from work as a hired agricultural laborer, and money earned by renting out owned capital to other farms. Nonfarm income includes labor earnings from nonfarm employment, rental or sales of other assets, pensions, and remittances.

Income of farm households from their own rice production is by far the highest in the most favorable village (CL1 in Table 4.19). This village has the largest average cultivation size (2.1 ha), the highest yield and rice cropping intensity, and the lowest proportion of share tenancy. The meager rice income in the unfavorable rainfed village (P3) is in sharp contrast. For P3, cultivation size is smallest (0.9 ha), yield is lowest, rice is generally produced only once a year, and share tenancy is prevalent. Furthermore, because of the drought during the year of the survey, the average land income for P3 is negative.

Rice income in irrigated village P1 is not much larger than in the favorable rainfed villages CL2 and P2, primarily because of P1's smaller farm size. The relatively small rice income in P1, however, is compensated for by large income from other sources. In the other villages, nonrice farm and nonfarm incomes are about the same. As a result, the total income of farm households, both on a per-household and per-person basis, is highest in the irrigated villages, second-highest in the favorable rainfed villages, and lowest in the unfavorable rainfed village.

The average income of agricultural landless households, which originates mostly from labor earnings, is much lower than that of farm households, primarily because of the difference in land income in rice production (compare data in Tables 4.19 and 4.20). As might be expected, landless households depend relatively more on nonrice income than do farm households. There is, however, considerable variation in the level of nonrice income of landless households among the five villages. The total landless household income in P1 and P2 exceeds the total in CL1 even though income from rice production in the Panay villages is only 20 to 40% of the corresponding income in CL1. This may suggest that more favorable nonfarm employment opportunities exist on Panay than in Central Luzon, which, together with the smaller farm size on Panay, leads landless workers to allocate more time to nonfarm jobs. However, P3 landless households have relatively low income from nonfarm work. Therefore, it appears that outside job opportunities alone cannot adequately explain the difference in nonfarm income among the five villages.

In order to identify the determinants of household income, each income component was regressed on technology factors (i.e., adoption of modern varieties and production environments); farm size and tenure; ownership of capital (i.e., tractors, threshers, and carabao); number of working members aged between fifteen and sixty; proxies for the quality of labor (i.e., schooling, age, and sex of household head); and other factors represented by village dummy variables that would affect factor returns and allocations.

Another approach to the income determination analysis would be to explore the determinants of factor returns and allocations of labor time for various activities and of cultivable land for various crops. This approach, however, could not be applied in this study because separate data on quantities and prices of household-supplied factors are required. Moreover, factor prices are quite uniform within each village, and only five villages are covered. The similarity of wages across our survey villages, as seen in Table 4.17, also limited our ability to analyze the effects of technology on income through its indirect effects on wages.

However, it was difficult to identify separately the effects of modern varieties and production environments on household income from our cross-sectional data, primarily because modern varieties are planted throughout the favorable areas in the survey villages. In this study, technology factors have been specified as interaction terms between the adoption rates of modern varieties and production environments—i.e., between the ratios of modern variety and irrigated area (MVR*IRGR) to represent irrigated conditions in CL1 and P1 and between the ratios of modern variety and rainfed area (MVR*RFAVR) to represent favorable rainfed farming conditions in CL2 and some parts of P2 and P3. The omitted technology variable, which serves as a control, pertains to unfavorable rainfed areas planted to traditional varieties in P2 and P3. Thus, the interaction variables between modern varieties and production environments will capture the combined effects of modern variety adoption and favorable production environments. Note here that their estimated coefficients may be biased upward to the extent that irrigated and favorable rainfed production environments positively affect both factor returns and modern variety adoption. For estimation of income determination functions, the log-linear form was adopted except in the case of ratio and dummy variables. We note that because of log-linear specification, some observations with negative values of land income and zero labor earnings from nonrice sources were discarded. There was no significant difference in the results, however, when the functions were estimated in linear form with interaction terms. The log-linear form was chosen mainly because of the robustness and ease of interpretation of the estimated coefficients.

The regression results of farm household income determination functions by income component shown in Table 4.21 are remarkably consistent with a priori expectations. Land income is significantly affected by technology, farm size, and tenure: The estimated coefficients of (MVR*IRGR) and (MVR*RFAVR)—1.61 and 0.97, respectively—indicate that the returns to irrigated areas and favorable rainfed areas planted to modern varieties are, respectively, 5 and 2.5 times higher relative to unfavorable rainfed land planted to traditional varieties. The coefficient of farm size (FSIZE) is significantly greater than zero but not significantly less than unity, suggesting the absence of scale economies in rice production. The significantly negative coefficient of ratio of leasehold and Certificate of Land Transfer area to total farm area (designated as LEASER in Table 4.21) is simply due to rent payments to landlords.

More interesting is the finding that, in absolute terms, the coefficient of the ratio of share tenancy area (designated as SHARER) is significantly larger than the coefficient of leasehold tenancy; the difference suggests that the land income under share tenancy is less than half of that under leasehold tenancy. According to a survey of the tenancy literature by Otsuka and Hayami (1988), income of share tenants tends to be lower than that of leasehold tenants by 20 to 30% because of the larger production risk incurred by the latter even in the absence of rent regulations. Our finding supports our hypothesis that the land reform program redistributed a sizable amount of income from landlords to former share tenants. Because landlords are not included in our sample, an increase in the income of tenants, who are wealthier than the landless, might have worsened the income distribution within our sample households.

Modern variety adoption significantly increases labor use. Although the share of hired labor income is higher in villages widely adopting modern varieties, family labor inputs—mostly used for land preparation, care of crop, and other farm management activities—also increase in absolute terms according to the labor income regression. The fact that capital income is not significantly affected by modern variety adoption supports the hypothesis that it does not encourage the use of capital-intensive production methods. It is interesting to note, however, that modern variety adoption in favorable rainfed areas has a significant, positive effect on the level of nonfarm income. It has such an effect because farm households in rainfed areas that generally grow only one rice crop per year allocate more time for nonfarm employment.

As in the case of land income, farm size is also positively correlated with labor and capital income from rice production and other farm activities but not with nonfarm income. Because labor incomes from rice and all other sources represent returns to labor, the coefficients of the characteristics of labor supply, represented by the number of working household members (designated as WORKER), and of labor quality, represented by schooling, age, and gender dummy of household head (FEMALE), are significant in many cases. It is particularly interesting to observe that although the coefficient of schooling is not significant in the regression equation for labor income from rice, it is an important explanatory variable for capital and nonfarm income. Capital seems to have been substituted for skilled labor, which has a high opportunity cost.

Ownership of tractors (TROWNER) has positive and significant effects on labor and capital income but not on other agricultural income, indicating that tractors owned by farm households are generally used on owned farms operated by family members. Ownership of threshers (THOWNER), which are mostly rented out, is significant only in the other farm income regression. Ownership of carabao (ANOWNER), which are used mainly on the owned farm, increases labor income but does not significantly affect capital income.

Some of the estimated coefficients of village dummies are significant in the regression of component income from rice production. The land income equation indicates that the productivity of land appears to be higher in CL2 and P2 for reasons other than irrigation and modern variety adoption. However, there appears to be a higher propensity to hire labor or use labor-saving technology in P2 compared to the other villages, as evidenced by its significantly negative coefficients in the labor and capital income equations.

In the capital income regression, negative and significant coefficients for P1, CL2, and P2 indicate that tractors and other capital equipment tend to be rented rather than owned in these villages.

With respect to the income of landless households (Table 4.22), village-specific technology variables represented by the interaction terms (MVR*IRGR and MVR*RFAV) did not show any significant effects in both equations (1) and (3). The average farm size in the village has a significant and positive coefficient in the rice income equation (1) but a negative coefficient in the nonrice income equation (3). Alternatively, village dummies are used in equations (2) and (4) to represent environmental, technological, and socioeconomic characteristics of sample villages. The estimated coefficients of these dummies, however, are not significant except that of CL1 in equation (2), where farm size is largest. As in the case of farm households, village characteristics do not seem to be critical determinants of labor income of landless households from either rice or nonrice sources.

Income from rice for landless households is significantly affected by ownership of carabao (ANOWNER), which can be rented out, and by being a permanent laborer (PLABOR), earning a share of the crop or a fixed amount of rice per season under assured employment conditions. (See Otsuka, Chuma, and Hayami [1993] and Hayami and Otsuka [1993] for a theoretical and empirical analysis of permanent labor contract.)

Landless households with no permanent labor contract in rice farming depend largely on other sources of income. Schooling, number of workers, and gender are the important determinants of differences in nonrice income but not in rice income. Thus, the difference in human capital seems important for explaining the intervillage differences in labor income from nonrice sources.

Household Income Distribution

As we have shown, adoption of modern varieties affects the various income components differently. In order to gain insight into the effects of modern variety adoption on household income distribution, a decomposition analysis of the Gini measure of income inequality as developed by Fei, Ranis, and Kuo (1978) and Pyatt, Chen, and Fei (1980) was applied (see the section on "Decomposition Analysis of Income Inequality" in Chapter 3 for methodology). It quantifies the relative importance of the various income components in accounting for the overall income inequality.

Table 4.23 shows the estimated overall Gini ratios and the absolute contributions of factor components measured by the product of income share, rank correlation ratio, and component Gini ratio. To account for differences in family size, household and average per capita incomes were used alternatively. Although the overall Gini coefficients for household income tend to be generally lower than for per capita income, major qualitative results are largely similar. The Gini ratios are highest in P1 and CL2 and lowest in P2 and P3. The most important income source contributing to the overall income inequality in these four villages is nonrice income, especially nonfarm income. Because of the importance of income from nonrice sources (which accounts for 40 to 65% of total household income), its relative contribution to the overall Gini ratio amounts to 45 to 70%, even though the component Gini ratio and the rank correlation ratios of nonrice income are low compared with other income sources in these villages. In contrast, in CL1, the most favorable village for rice production, the combined income share of nonrice income sources is as low as 25%, and the most important contributor to the overall income inequality is land income, whose component Gini ratio and rank correlation ratio tend to be highest among five income sources not only in this village but also in other villages.

Overall, the importance of labor and capital income from rice farming in income distribution is relatively minor. These observations suggest that, given the unequal distribution of ownership of or access to land, or both, land income is a significant income-skewing factor, particularly in favorable rice-growing villages. Nonrice income is a more important factor in villages where farm size is small (i.e., P1 and P3) and where double cropping of rice is not practiced because of the lack of irrigation (i.e., CL2, P2, and P3).

In the environments less favorable for rice production, more resources are allocated to the production of nonrice crops and nonfarm jobs. Such substitution relationships between incomes from rice farming and nonrice sources, as well as the relative importance of nonrice income, suggest that the impacts of the differential adoption of modern varieties on overall income inequality would have been relatively limited.

Our analysis does not take into account the dynamic impacts of modern variety adoption, such as interregional migration, which significantly change the composition of farm and landless households because migrants are mostly landless laborers. To check the possible bias of our analysis using individual village data, we also computed the Gini ratio and the income inequality contributions by factor component using the pooled data of five villages. The overall Gini ratio based on all village data is about equal to the average of village-level overall Gini ratios. The contribution of land income tends to be greater than in the individual villages, reflecting the substantial gap in returns to land across production environments.

In order to illustrate the size distribution of household income in five villages, we present data on the frequency distribution of overall household income of both farm and landless households in Table 4.24 and show the density functions in Figure 4.3 by location (i.e., Central Luzon and Panay). The income distributions are highly skewed to the right, particularly in CL1 and P1. The highly skewed distribution of operational holdings and high returns to land in these villages largely explain such wide income variability. The peaks of the density functions cluster at the income level less than P15,000 ($750), and the landless laborer households generally belong to the income class lower than that level.

Given the significant effect of the modern rice technology on returns to land, we believe it is correct to state that if there had been no technological change, the income distribution in the Philippines would have been less skewed. It must be realized, however, that in the absence of technological change, the density function as a whole would shift to the left, particularly because the labor income of poor farmers and the landless would decrease. Furthermore, given the importance of nonrice income and substitutability between rice and nonrice income, the impacts of the differential adoption of modern rice technology on total household income and its distribution would not significantly alter the dispersion of density functions. This conclusion is supported by the counterfactual analysis of income distribution by Otsuka,

Cordova, and David (1992), which indicates what the Gini ratio would have been if there had been no modern variety adoption, based on the coefficients of modern variety variables in income determination regressions.

KEY POINTS FOR CONSIDERATION

Cross-sectional differences in adoption of modern varieties in the Philippines are explained mainly by environmental rather than socioeconomic factors. Although irrigation was an important determinant of modern variety and fertilizer adoption in the early Green Revolution period, modern variety and fertilizer technology are now equally conducive in favorable rainfed environments. Greater resistance to various pests, better tolerance for less favorable environments, shorter growth duration, and other improvements in the later generations of modern varieties undoubtedly have promoted their wider adoption (Otsuka, Gascon, and Asano 1994a). As a result, a large gap in land productivity has emerged between favorable areas, represented by irrigated and shallow rainfed environments, and unfavorable areas, represented by drought- and submergence-prone environments.

With modern varieties and double cropping in irrigated areas, labor use per hectare per year has increased even though tractors are used. Use of modern varieties with direct seeding has also increased cropping intensity in certain regions. By increasing the labor demand per season and per year, the modern rice technology positively contributes to the welfare of marginal farmers and the landless in favorable areas.

The welfare of the poor in unfavorable areas has also been improved by adoption of modern rice technology in favorable areas. Differential adoption of modern rice technology between favorable and unfavorable areas induces interregional labor market adjustments through migration, equalizing wage rates across different production environments. As far as wage income is concerned, therefore, there is no evidence that the location specificity of modern rice technology has worsened regional income distribution to a significant extent.

The ultimate consequences for income distribution of differential adoption of modern varieties has not been significantly adverse. This is so in part because the inequitable effect of modern variety adoption in favorable areas on regional income distribution is mitigated by the implementation of land reform and reallocation of resources to nonrice production activities in the unfavorable areas.

We note, however, that our analysis on household income distribution is likely to overestimate the inequitable effect of the differential adoption of modern varieties, because the positive effect of modern varieties on wages, through their effects on labor demand (which is obviously equitable), was not explicitly taken into account. If such an effect could have been properly assessed, the inequitable impact of modern variety adoption would have been shown to be more limited.

Our income determination analysis reveals the importance of human capital in the determination of income of the landless laborers, in particular the importance of nonrice labor earnings. This implies that an appropriate means to improve the well-being of the poor laborer class is to invest in their human capital.

Investment in agricultural research for the development of rice technology suitable for unfavorable production environments is likely to be of secondary importance for the regional income differential of the poor; they are geographically mobile, and their relative incomes are thus not significantly affected by differential modern variety adoption or by production environment, at least in the long run. However, greater public investment in research for more suitable crops for the unfavorable areas may be desirable to share the cost of factor market adjustments to differential adoption of modern rice technology in the short run.

Figure 4.1   Location of study areas, extensive survey, Philippines, 1985

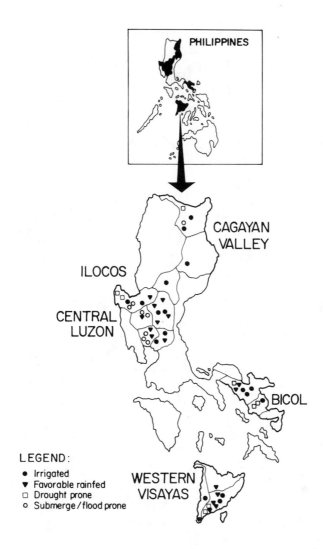

LEGEND:
- ● Irrigated
- ▼ Favorable rainfed
- ☐ Drought prone
- ○ Submerge / flood prone

Figure 4.2 Location of study areas, intensive survey, Philippines, 1986

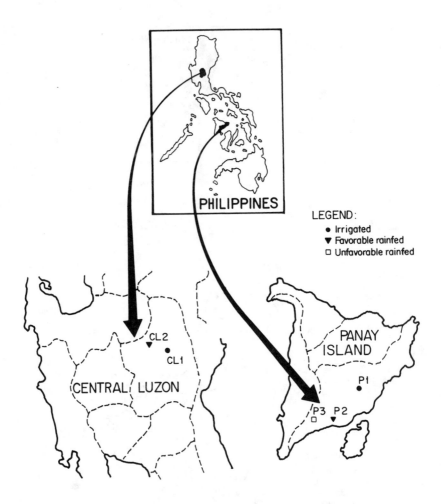

Figure 4.3   Density functions for household income, intensive survey, Philippines, 1985

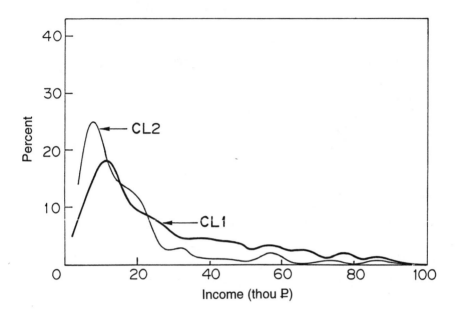

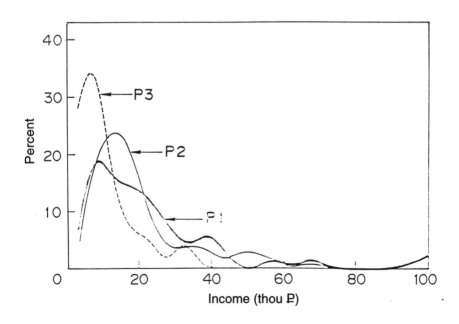

Table 4.1   Selected socioeconomic characteristics of sample villages by production environment, extensive survey, Philippines, 1986.

	Irrigated	Favorable rainfed	Unfavorable rainfed	
			Drought-prone	Submergence-prone
Villages (no)	17	17	9	7
Farm size (ha)	1.7	1.7	1.4	1.9
Man-land ratio (person/ha)	6.3	5.1	3.7	6.0
Ratio of landless households (%)	31	18	9	19
Tenure (% of area)				
Owner-cultivator	22	19	68	18
CLT[a]	34	34	9	31
Leasehold	35	34	5	18
Share tenancy	9	13	18	32
Distance to town (km)	4	4	8	5

a. Holders of Certificate of Land Transfer.

Table 4.2   Cropping patterns (% of area) by production environment, extensive survey, Philippines, 1986.

Cropping pattern	Irrigated	Favorable rainfed	Unfavorable rainfed	
			Drought-prone	Submergence-prone
Rice-rice	82	25	6	3
Rice-rice-rice	11	0	0	0
Rice-fallow	2	57	72	83
Rice–nonrice crop	5	18	22	14

Table 4.3   Selected socioeconomic characteristics of five sample villages, intensive survey, Philippines, 1985.

	Irrigated		Favorable rainfed		Unfavorable rainfed
	CL1	P1	CL2	P2	P3
Sample households (no)	112	60	73	78	54
Farm size (ha)	2.1	1.1	1.8	1.5	0.9
Man-land ratio (person/ha)	2.5	4.4	2.1	2.9	3.1
Ratio of landless households (%)	18	38	26	19	7
Tenure (% of area)					
Owner-cultivator	9	27	18	47	33
Leasehold/CLT[a]	80	38	76	32	8
Share tenancy	6	34	0	17	58
Pawn	6	2	6	5	1

a. Holders of Certificate of Land Transfer.

Table 4.4   Cropping patterns (% of area) by village, intensive survey of five villages, Philippines, 1985.

	Irrigated		Favorable rainfed		Unfavorable rainfed
Cropping Pattern	CL1	P1	CL2	P2	P3
Rice-rice	98	72	14	31	23
Rice-rice-rice	0	25	0	0	0
Rice-fallow	0	1	68	12	8
Rice–nonrice crop[a]	2	2	18	57	69

a. Nonrice crops include maize, mungbeans, cowpeas, vegetables, groundnuts, garlic, and onions.

Table 4.5   Technology adoption, paddy yields, and cropping intensities by production environment, extensive survey, Philippines, 1986.

	Irrigated	Favorable rainfed	Unfavorable rainfed Drought-prone	Submergence-prone
Ratio of irrigated area (%)				
1970	58	4	0	1
1980	84	7	1	3
1986	97	8	1	3
Modern variety adoption (% of area)[a]				
1970	38	29	9	25
1980	89	95	38	39
1986	97	99	33	50
Fertilizer use (kg NPK/ha)[a]				
1970	29	27	7	29
1980	88	68	23	57
1986	87	92	34	63
Yield (t/ha)[a]				
Traditional varieties				
1970	2.4	2.2	2.3	2.1
1980	b	b	2.4	1.7
1986	b	b	2.1	1.8
Modern varieties				
1970	4.1	3.4	2.3	2.5
1980	3.6	3.5	2.6	2.7
1986	3.6	3.3	2.8	2.4
Rice cropping intensity (%)				
1970	148	108	94	100
1980	183	121	95	101
1986	195	123	96	101
Total cropping intensity (%)				
1970	164	130	118	106
1980	192	137	120	114
1986	199	141	118	118

a. Data refer to the wet season.
b. Too few observations.

Table 4.6   Regression results of modern variety adoption and fertilizer demand functions, extensive survey, Philippines, 1986.[a]

	MVR	Ln Fertilizer	
	(1)	(2)	(3)
Intercept	0.38	4.09**	3.24**
	(1.32)	(4.90)	(3.72)
IRG	0.47**	1.14**	0.13
	(3.67)	(3.28)	(0.57)
RFAV	0.48**	1.05**	—
	(3.37)	(3.22)	
DPRONE	−0.23*	−0.74*	—
	(−1.81)	(−1.69)	
PMVR	—	—	2.42**
			(5.35)
Ln FERTPP	0.14	−1.84	−2.43*
	(0.28)	(−1.42)	(−2.10)
Ln FSIZE	0.01	0.33	0.31
	(0.16)	(1.20)	(1.15)
SHARER	0.09	0.41	0.23
	(0.73)	(0.95)	(0.58)
OWNERR	0.06	0.77*	0.58
	(0.47)	(1.72)	(1.41)
PANAY	0.04	0.31	0.21
	(0.42)	(1.19)	(0.79)
R^2	—	0.59	0.59
F-value	—	7.12	8.27
Log-likelihood	−200.77	—	—
(Chi-square)	75.59	—	—

a. Numbers in parentheses are t-statistics.
** Indicates significance at 1% level; * at 5% level.

Table 4.7   Regression results of yield, rice cropping intensity, and total cropping intensity functions, extensive survey, Philippines, 1986.[a]

	Ln Yield		Rice cropping intensity		Total cropping intensity	
	(1)	(2)	(3)	(4)	(5)	(6)
Intercept	4.22** (15.99)	4.05** (14.61)	1.23** (3.37)	1.09** (2.85)	1.53** (4.49)	1.45** (4.06)
IRG	0.33** (2.96)	0.13* (1.71)	0.97** (6.18)	0.79** (7.62)	0.81** (5.54)	0.70** (7.25)
RFAV	0.21* (2.02)	—	0.18 (1.24)	—	0.11 (0.79)	—
DPRONE	−0.14 (−1.00)	—	−0.04 (−0.23)	—	0.02 (0.09)	—
PMVR	—	0.48** (3.29)	—	0.34* (1.69)	—	0.16 (0.85)
Ln FERTPP	−0.19 (−0.45)	−0.29 (−0.78)	−0.33 (−0.59)	−0.34 (−0.67)	−0.55 (−1.04)	−0.51 (−1.06)
Ln FSIZE	−0.02 (−0.25)	−0.02 (−0.29)	−0.11 (−0.91)	−0.12 (−0.97)	−0.05 (−0.47)	−0.06 (−0.52)
SHARER	−0.26* (−1.86)	−0.30* (−2.28)	0.16 (0.81)	0.12 (0.64)	0.09 (0.49)	0.06 (0.35)
OWNERR	−0.01 (−0.08)	−0.05 (−0.37)	−0.04 (−0.19)	−0.04 (−0.25)	−0.09 (−0.51)	−0.08 (−0.51)
PANAY	0.05 (0.59)	0.03 (0.36)	0.18 (1.56)	0.17 (1.44)	0.44** (4.02)	0.43** (3.91)
R^2	0.54	0.54	0.73	0.72	0.72	0.72
F-value	5.95	6.95	13.58	15.89	12.92	15.08

a. Numbers in parentheses are t-statistics.
** Indicates significance at 1% level; * at 5% level.

Table 4.8   Adoption of labor-saving technologies (% of farmers) by production environment, extensive survey, Philippines, 1970–1986.

	Irrigated	Favorable rainfed	Unfavorable rainfed	
			Drought-prone	Submergence-prone
Tractor				
1970	37	24	2	18
1980	63	43	15	59
1986	76	56	16	67
Thresher				
1970	28	37	0	64
1980	66	75	14	81
1986	94	95	47	97
Direct seeding				
1970	2	3	23	32
1980	24	33	19	25
1986	33	51	18	21

Table 4.9   Regression results of tractor, thresher, and direct-seeding adoption functions, extensive survey, Philippines, 1986.[a]

	Tractor		Thresher		Direct seeding	
	(1)	(2)	(3)	(4)	(5)	(6)
Intercept	0.95 (1.11)	0.34 (0.37)	0.95 (0.72)	1.01 (1.49)	0.50 (0.22)	0.66 (0.32)
IRG	0.57* (2.24)	—	-0.02 (-0.05)	—	-0.03 (-0.13)	—
RFAV	0.29 (1.31)	—	-0.04 (-0.12)	—	0.10 (0.48)	—
DPRONE	0.04 (0.19)	—	-0.48 (-1.46)	—	-0.34 (-1.10)	—
PMVR	—	0.36 (1.24)	—	0.004 (1.19)	—	0.47 (1.48)
PRCI	—	0.34* (1.97)	—	0.0003 (0.12)	—	-0.13 (-0.73)
Ln FSIZE	0.49** (3.38)	0.52** (3.32)	0.05 (0.45)	0.07 (0.54)	0.10 (0.47)	0.13 (0.69)
SHARER	0.19 (0.84)	0.08 (0.42)	0.11 (0.39)	0.21 (0.70)	-0.26 (-0.95)	-0.23 (-0.91)
OWNERR	0.08 (0.36)	0.14 (0.62)	-0.01 (-0.05)	-0.13 (-0.63)	0.13 (0.38)	-0.003 (-0.01)
Ln HERBPP	—	—	—	—	-0.18 (-0.27)	-0.31 (-0.50)
Ln DISTMLA	-0.25** (-2.52)	-0.21** (-2.33)	-0.03 (-0.13)	-0.12 (-1.02)	—	—
Ln WGPLP	0.14 (0.65)	0.13 (0.63)	—	—	—	—
Ln WGPTP	—	—	—	—	0.11 (0.30)	0.14 (0.42)
Ln WGPTH	—	—	0.28 (0.95)	0.15 (0.74)	—	—
PANAY	0.12 (0.92)	-0.0004 (-0.003)	0.11 (0.76)	0.15 (1.18)	0.68** (3.07)	0.70** (3.05)
Log-likelihood (Chi-square)	-208.05 55.40	-208.40 54.14	-218.56 26.04	-221.18 21.23	-182.96 35.56	-183.93 34.89

a. Numbers in parentheses are t-statistics.
** Indicates significance at 1% level; * at 5% level.

Table 4.10 Technology adoption, paddy yields, and cropping intensities, intensive survey, Philippines, average of wet and dry season, 1985.

	Irrigated		Favorable rainfed		Unfavorable rainfed
	CL1	P1	CL2	P2	P3
Ratio of irrigated area (%)	100	100	16	0	21
Modern variety adoption	100	100	100	79	59
Fertilizer use (kg NPK/ha)	114	74	100	89	69
Yield (t/ha)	4.7	3.6	4.0	3.0	1.9
Traditional varieties[a]	—	—	—	3.2[b]	1.2
Modern varieties	4.7	3.6	4.0	3.0	2.1
Rice cropping intensity (%)	209	228	118	128	115
Total cropping intensity (%)	210	237	137	164	163

a. Refers to wet season only.
b. Mostly BE 3, an improved local variety.

Table 4.11 Labor use (man-days/ha) and adoption of labor-saving technology, intensive survey, Philippines, average of wet and dry season, 1985.[a]

	Irrigated		Favorable rainfed		Unfavorable rainfed
	CL1	P1	CL2	P2	P3
Land preparation	14	13	16	17	30
(% area tractor)	(92)	(85)	(76)	(32)	(0)
Crop establishment	23	5	17	5	22
(% area direct seeding)	(57)	(91)	(48)	(87)	(47)
Care of crop	8	27	8	8	11
Harvesting & threshing	35	32	36	30	27
(% area thresher)	(100)	(100)	(99)	(99)	(86)
Others	2	4	2	2	1
Total labor	83	81	79	62	91
(% hired labor)	(66)	(80)	(53)	(64)	(37)

a. Figures in parentheses indicate the adoption rates of respective technologies.

Table 4.12   Regression results of labor use functions in rice production by activity, intensive survey, Philippines, wet season, 1985.[a]

	Land preparation	Crop establishment	Crop care	Harvest/ postharvest
Intercept	2.72** (6.09)	3.42** (5.42)	−0.52 (−0.54)	3.37** (8.13)
MVR*IRGR	−0.16 (−1.13)	−0.55** (−2.77)	1.51** (4.84)	0.25* (2.01)
MVR*RFAVR	−0.09 (−0.69)	−0.44* (−2.19)	1.11** (3.63)	0.22* (1.80)
Ln FSIZE	−0.09** (−2.41)	0.07 (1.38)	−0.22** (−2.98)	−0.03 (−1.02)
TRUSER	−0.38** (−4.59)	—	—	—
DSEED	—	−3.09** (−30.31)	—	—
Ln AGE	0.09 (0.92)	0.06 (0.41)	0.35* (1.65)	−0.08 (−0.82)
Ln SCHOOL	0.003 (0.07)	0.06 (0.97)	0.16* (1.77)	0.07* (1.78)
PANAY	0.08 (1.15)	0.44** (4.15)	−0.66** (−4.84)	0.07 (1.15)
P3U	0.31** (2.61)	0.34* (2.03)	−0.31 (−1.20)	−0.14 (−1.23)
R^2	0.33	0.88	0.24	0.12
F-value	17.81	264.5	12.4	5.5

a. Numbers in parentheses are t-statistics.
** Indicates significance at 1% level; * at 5% level.

Table 4.13   Population growth rate, changes in man-land ratio, farm size, and ratio of landless households by production environment, extensive survey, Philippines, 1970–1986.

	Irrigated	Favorable rainfed	Unfavorable rainfed
Average annual population growth rate (%)[a]			
1970–1980	2.9	2.0	1.1
1980–1986	1.7	1.6	2.1
1970–1986	2.5	1.9	1.5
Man-land ratio (persons/ha)			
1970	4.3	4.0	3.7
1980	5.6	4.9	4.1
1986	6.3	5.1	4.7
Farm size (ha)			
1986	1.7	1.7	1.7
Ratio of agricultural landless households (%)[b]			
1986	31	18	15

a. Population data in 1970 and 1980 are taken from the Census of Population.
b. Ratio of the number of agricultural landless households to the total number of farming households.

Table 4.14   Regression results of population growth rate and changes in rate of modern variety adoption, extensive survey, Philippines, 1970–1980 and 1980–1986.[a]

	Population growth rate 1970–1980		ΔMVR	Population growth rate 1980–1986		ΔMVR
	(1)	(2)	(3)	(4)	(5)	(6)
Intercept	1.04*	−0.09	0.44**	4.06**	3.53*	0.07
	(2.31)	(−0.01)	(4.31)	(3.89)	(2.64)	(0.76)
IRG	1.30**	—	0.45**	0.26	—	0.07
	(3.09)		(4.78)	(0.29)		(0.81)
RFAV	0.98**	—	0.52**	−0.30	—	0.02
	(2.63)		(6.19)	(−0.33)		(0.26)
ΔMVR	—	2.15**	—	—	5.08	—
		(3.10)			(0.42)	
ΔIRGR	1.97**	2.01**	0.13	2.18	−0.66	0.56**
	(3.06)	(3.20)	(0.88)	(1.02)	(−0.09)	(2.84)
MLR	−0.01	0.03	−0.01	−0.23	−0.17	−0.01
	(−0.07)	(0.35)	(−0.39)	(−1.27)	(−0.88)	(−0.72)
NORTH	0.27	0.70	−0.11	−2.70*	−1.79	−0.16
	(0.53)	(1.42)	(−0.97)	(−2.13)	(−0.86)	(−1.37)
SOUTH	0.08	0.08	0.06	−1.45	−0.97	−0.09
	(0.19)	(0.18)	(0.65)	(−1.39)	(−0.71)	(−0.96)
PANAY	−0.13	−0.15	0.02	−2.18**	−2.33**	0.01
	(−0.33)	(−0.35)	(0.25)	(−2.41)	(−2.82)	(0.14)
R^2	0.47	0.45	0.57	0.22	0.24	0.21
F-value	5.43	5.77	7.81	1.52	2.09	1.45

a. Numbers in parentheses are t-statistics.
** Indicates significance at 1% level; * at 5% level.

Table 4.15   Paddy price, wage and rental rates by production environment, extensive survey, Philippines, wet season, 1986.[a]

	Irrigated	Favorable rainfed	Unfavorable rainfed
Paddy price (P/kg)			
Traditional varieties	—	3.08 (5)	2.84 (16)
Modern varieties	2.63 (17)	2.58 (17)	2.65 (13)
Wage rates (P/day)			
Land preparation[b]	36 (17)	35 (17)	34 (16)
Transplanting			
Daily wage	22 (12)	25 (12)	29 (16)
Imputed wage[c]	26 (5)	21 (5)	—
Harvesting			
Daily wage	25 (2)	25 (2)	35 (8)
Imputed wage[d]	54 (15)	57 (15)	50 (8)
Threshing			
Imputed wage[e]	54 (17)	56 (17)	50 (16)
Custom rental			
Rental of carabao (P/day)	32 (17)	24 (17)	26 (16)

a. Numbers in parentheses are sample sizes.
b. Wage payment with carabao.
c. Total wage payment divided by workdays under piece-rate contract based on area transplanted.
d. Total wage payment divided by workdays under output-sharing contract.
e. Price of paddy times share of output accruing to labor divided by workdays.

Table 4.16   Regression results of wage rates and rental of carabao, extensive survey, Philippines, 1986.[a]

	Ln Land prep. (1)	Ln Transplanting (2)	Ln Harvesting (3)	Ln Threshing (4)	Ln Carabao rental (5)
Intercept	4.22** (7.74)	3.71** (7.35)	4.42** (7.65)	4.36** (8.39)	3.84** (9.02)
IRG	−0.05 (−0.35)	−0.34** (−2.49)	−0.07 (−0.41)	0.11 (0.80)	0.20* (1.96)
RFAV	0.002 (0.02)	−0.35** (−2.57)	−0.03 (−0.21)	0.17 (1.18)	0.03 (0.29)
DPRONE	−0.16 (−1.35)	−0.17 (−1.37)	−0.09 (−0.57)	−0.12 (−0.91)	0.04 (0.44)
PMVR	0.00 (0.00)	−0.01 (−0.06)	0.10 (0.44)	−0.21 (−0.98)	−0.21 (−1.37)
Ln FSIZE	−0.11 (−1.24)	−0.10 (−1.10)	0.01 (0.10)	0.21* (2.27)	0.04 (0.64)
Ln PADDYP	−0.21 (−0.70)	0.10 (0.32)	−0.21 (−0.59)	−0.26 (−0.83)	−0.02 (−0.07)
Ln DISTCT	−0.08 (−1.21)	−0.05 (−0.97)	−0.15* (−2.32)	−0.03 (−0.54)	−0.11* (−2.17)
CONT 1	0.24** (2.44)	—	—	—	0.44** (5.75)
CONT 2	—	0.02 (0.26)	—	—	—
CONT 3	—	—	0.51** (4.78)	—	—
PANAY	−0.30** (3.14)	0.04 (0.38)	0.07 (0.56)	0.08 (0.74)	0.01 (0.17)
R^2	0.60	0.36	0.59	0.26	0.79
F-value	6.63	2.49	6.42	1.84	16.57

a. Numbers in parentheses are t-statistics.
** Indicates significance at 1% level; * at 5% level.

Table 4.17   Comparison of output and factor prices by production environment, intensive survey, Philippines, wet season, 1985.

	Irrigated		Favorable rainfed		Unfavorable rainfed
	CL1	P1	CL2	P2	P3
Paddy price (P/kg)	2.78	2.86	2.78	2.97	2.79
Nitrogen price (P/kg)	11.3	11.5	11.2	11.6	12.0
Wage rates (P/day)					
Land preparation[a]	29	29	28	25	24
Repair of dikes	33	26	27	21	28
Transplanting	18	20	19	19	20
Fertilizer application	30	36	28	33	n.a.
Harvesting[b]	59	66	49	56	48
Custom rental					
Carabao (P/day)	54	49	53	47	37
Tractor (P/ha)	1,030	947	1,082	995	n.a.
Thresher (P/t)	101	96	99	100	99

a. Wage payment to operator of carabao.
b. Imputed daily earnings under output-sharing contract. Dry season data are shown because harvesting wage rates were unusually low in villages CL1 and CL2 because of severe typhoon damage on yield.

Table 4.18   Factor payments (thou P/ha) and factor shares (%) in rice farming by production environment, intensive survey, Philippines, 1985.[a]

	Irrigated		Favorable rainfed		Unfavorable rainfed
	CL1	P1	CL2	P2	P3
Gross value of output	14.0 (100)	11.1 (100)	10.1 (100)	9.5 (100)	5.4 (100)
Current inputs	3.6 (26)	2.6 (23)	2.9 (29)	1.7 (18)	1.2 (22)
Capital	2.1 (15)	1.6 (14)	1.3 (13)	0.8 (8)	0.7 (13)
Owned[b]	0.6	0.2	0.4	0.2	0.3
Hired	1.5	1.4	0.9	0.6	0.4
Labor	3.6 (26)	3.3 (30)	2.6 (26)	2.5 (26)	2.5 (46)
Family[c]	1.5	1.0	1.3	0.8	1.4
Hired	2.1	2.3	1.3	1.7	1.1
Residual	4.7 (34)	3.6 (32)	3.3 (33)	4.5 (47)	1.0 (19)
Leasehold rent[d]	1.7	2.2	1.5	1.5	1.3
Surplus[e]	3.0	1.4	1.8	3.0	-0.3

a. Weighted average of dry and wet seasons, weights being the ratios of planted areas. Figures in parentheses are factor shares (%).
b. Imputed cost using average machinery rentals in each village.
c. Imputed labor cost using average daily earnings under piece-rate contracts in various tasks.
d. Average leasehold rent.
e. Residual minus leasehold rent.

Table 4.19   Average annual income (thouP) of farm households by source and production environment, intensive survey, Philippines, 1985.

	Irrigated		Favorable rainfed		Unfavorable rainfed
	CL1	P1	CL2	P2	P3
Own rice production	20.6	10.3	8.3	8.9	1.4
Labor[a]	6.4	2.7	2.6	1.5	1.5
Capital[b]	2.3	0.4	0.9	0.4	0.4
Land[c]	11.9	7.2	4.8	7.0	-0.5
Nonrice production	10.0	17.8	11.2	11.0	8.3
Farm[d]	5.5	7.3	8.3	5.6	4.7
Nonfarm[e]	4.5	10.5	2.9	5.4	3.6
Total income	30.6	28.1	19.5	19.9	9.7
Household size	6.0	6.3	5.0	5.5	6.1
(no of working members)[f]	(3.4)	(3.8)	(2.6)	(3.2)	(3.3)
Income per person	5.1	4.5	3.9	3.6	1.6
(per working member)	(9.0)	(7.4)	(7.5)	(6.2)	(2.9)

a. Imputed family labor income in owned farm.
b. Imputed return to owned machineries and carabao.
c. Residual for owner-cultivators; residual minus actual rent payments for tenants.
d. Includes nonrice crops, livestock, poultry raising, fishing, actual labor earnings, and actual rental earnings outside owned farm.
e. Includes labor earnings from nonfarm employment, other assets, pensions, and remittances.
f. Household members between fifteen and sixty years old.

Table 4.20 Average annual income (thou P) of agricultural landless households by source and production environment, intensive survey, Philippines, 1985.

	Irrigated		Favorable rainfed		Unfavorable rainfed
	CL1	P1	CL2	P2	P3
Rice production[a]	6.3	1.2	3.2	2.7	2.9
Nonrice production	5.1	12.6	4.2	11.0	2.7
Farm[b]	1.9	1.2	1.0	1.0	0.9
Nonfarm[c]	2.8	6.9	2.4	7.7	1.0
Remittances and pensions	0.4	4.6	0.8	2.3	0.8
Total income	11.4	13.9	7.4	13.7	5.6
Household size (no of (working members)[d]	5.4 (3.4)	5.3 (3.8)	4.8 (2.6)	4.5 (3.2)	4.0 (3.3)
Income per person (per working member)	2.1 (3.4)	2.6 (3.7)	1.5 (2.8)	3.0 (4.3)	1.4 (1.7)

a. Labor earnings from rice production and rental earnings of carabao.
b. Includes labor earnings from nonrice crop production, livestock and poultry raising, and fishing.
c. Labor earnings from nonfarm employment, remittances, and pensions.
d. Over fifteen and below sixty years old.

Table 4.21   Regression results of farm household income determination functions, intensive survey, Philippines, 1985.[a]

	Ln Rice income (owned farms)			Ln Nonrice farm income	Ln Nonfarm income
	Land	Labor	Capital		
Intercept	−0.84	0.70	−1.49	−1.45	−4.48*
	(−0.67)	(1.45)	(−1.10)	(−1.43)	(−2.20)
MVR*IRGR	1.61**	0.76**	0.72	0.48	1.31
	(2.88)	(3.17)	(1.12)	(0.97)	(1.28)
MVR*RFAVR	0.97**	0.32**	0.10	0.15	0.82*
	(2.58)	(2.72)	(0.32)	(0.62)	(1.74)
Ln FSIZE	0.84**	0.63**	0.62**	0.24**	0.23
	(7.63)	(15.24)	(5.09)	(2.75)	(1.39)
LEASER	−0.42**	−0.05	0.29	−0.22	−0.38
	(−2.44)	(−0.69)	(1.40)	(−1.44)	(−1.24)
SHARER	−1.16**	−0.16*	0.06	−0.37*	−0.46
	(−4.37)	(−1.82)	(0.23)	(−2.01)	(−1.25)
TROWNER	0.25	0.25**	1.57**	0.13	−0.01
	(1.41)	(3.37)	(7.61)	(0.82)	(−0.02)
THOWNER	−0.07	−0.09	0.30	0.42*	−0.10
	(−0.33)	(−1.03)	(1.24)	(2.22)	(−0.11)
ANOWNER	0.15	0.12*	0.05	0.10	−0.34
	(1.00)	(2.10)	(0.27)	(0.83)	(−1.38)
FEMALE	−0.18	−0.38**	0.19	−0.06	−0.07
	(−0.62)	(−3.27)	(0.57)	(−0.24)	(−0.15)
Ln AGE	0.04	−0.17	−0.02	−0.07	1.16**
	(0.14)	(−1.52)	(−0.05)	(−0.28)	(2.43)
Ln SCHOOL	−0.002	−0.05	0.29*	−0.06	0.34*
	(−0.15)	(−1.11)	(2.19)	(−0.64)	(1.74)
Ln WORKER	0.12	0.27**	0.02	0.31**	0.27
	(0.90)	(4.76)	(0.14)	(2.65)	(1.18)
CL1	1.04*	0.22	−0.90	−0.67	−1.16
	(1.88)	(0.93)	(−1.41)	(−1.37)	(−1.16)
P1	0.85	−0.16	−1.45*	−0.29	−0.37
	(1.58)	(−0.67)	(−2.21)	(−0.59)	(−0.37)
CL2	0.74*	−0.15	−0.76*	−0.14	−0.70
	(1.91)	(−1.22)	(−2.19)	(−0.55)	(−1.36)
P2	1.44**	−0.41**	−0.47*	−0.14	−0.25
	(4.39)	(−4.26)	(−1.71)	(−0.69)	(−0.67)
R^2	0.54	0.80	0.49	0.17	0.50
F-value	15.36	70.46	13.93	3.63	2.24

a. Numbers in parentheses are t-statistics.
** Indicates significance at 1% level; * at 5% level.

Table 4.22   Regression results of landless household income determination functions, intensive survey, Philippines, 1985.[a]

	Ln Rice income		Ln Nonrice income	
	(1)	(2)	(3)	(4)
Intercept	0.59	−1.01	−3.75	−2.09
	(0.35)	(−0.71)	(−1.53)	(−1.02)
Ln SCHOOL	0.09	0.06	1.25**	1.28**
	(0.49)	(0.30)	(4.73)	(4.60)
Ln AGE	0.31	0.32	0.11	0.11
	(0.89)	(0.90)	(0.23)	(0.22)
Ln WORKER	0.18	0.20	0.61*	0.60*
	(0.78)	(0.84)	(1.81)	(1.77)
FEMALE	−0.34	−0.42	0.91*	0.97**
	(−1.11)	(−1.25)	(2.24)	(2.34)
ANOWNER	0.66*	0.64*	−0.32	−0.32
	(2.22)	(2.17)	(−0.72)	(−0.72)
PLABOR	0.66*	0.69**	−1.15**	−1.18**
	(2.30)	(2.35)	(−2.60)	(−2.62)
Village–specific variables:				
Ln FSIZE	1.86**	—	−0.84	—
	(3.98)		(−1.29)	
MVR*IRGR	−0.02	—	0.03	—
	(−1.64)		(1.58)	
MVR*RFAV	−0.02*	—	0.02	—
	(−1.89)		(1.37)	
CL1	—	1.12*	—	0.25
		(2.18)		(0.32)
P1	—	−0.04	—	0.74
		(−0.09)		(1.05)
CL2	—	0.41	—	0.35
		(0.88)		(0.48)
P2	—	0.66	—	−0.19
		(1.41)		(−0.26)
R^2	0.43	0.43	0.46	0.46
F-value	4.94	4.43	6.73	6.00

a. Numbers in parentheses are t-statistics
** Indicates significance at 1% level; * at 5% level

Table 4.23 Overall Gini ratios of household and per capita income and contributions by income component, intensive survey, Philippines, 1985.[a]

Villages	Overall Gini coefficient	Contribution by				
		Rice income (own farm)			Nonrice farm income	Nonfarm income
		Land	Labor	Capital		
CL1	0.42	0.21	0.06	0.03	0.03	0.08
	(0.46)	(0.24)	(0.06)	(0.03)	0.03)	(0.10)
P1	0.46	0.11	0.02	0.01	0.09	0.22
	(0.50)	(0.08)	(0.01)	(0.02)	(0.06)	(0.34)
CL2	0.44	0.13	0.05	0.02	0.17	0.07
	(0.53)	(0.17)	(0.04)	(0.01)	(0.20)	(0.10)
P2	0.37	0.15	0.02	0.01	0.05	0.14
	(0.42)	(0.16)	(0.02)	(0.01)	(0.09)	(0.15)
P3	0.39	0.02	0.04	0.01	0.16	0.16
	(0.35)	(0.02)	(0.04)	(0.01)	(0.14)	(0.15)
All	0.44	0.17	0.05	0.02	0.07	0.12
	(0.48)	(0.18)	(0.05)	(0.02)	(0.08)	(0.15)

a. Figures in parentheses are estimates based on per capita income.

Table 4.24   Size distribution of household income, intensive survey, Philippines, 1985.

Income class (thou P)	Irrigated		Favorable rainfed		Unfavorable rainfed
	CL1	P1	CL2	P2	P3
	(% of households)				
< 5	5	7	14	5	28
5–10	17	23	32	19	43
10–15	21	15	15	26	13
15–20	10	15	14	22	6
20–25	9	12	11	9	6
25–30	7	8	1	3	0
30–35	4	3	4	4	6
35–40	5	7	1	4	0
40–45	4	3	1	1	0
45–50	4	0	1	3	0
50 >	15	7	5	5	0
Households (no)	112	60	73	78	54
Average household income (thou P)	30	24	15	19	10

5

Modern Rice Variety Adoption and Factor-Market Adjustments in Indonesia

■

TAHLIM SUDARYANTO AND FAISAL KASRYNO

Remarkable progress has been achieved in the Indonesian rice economy during the past two decades. The country changed from being the world's major importer of rice in the late 1970s, accounting for about 20% of internationally traded rice, to being self-sufficient in the mid-1980s.

Indonesia's rice production grew 4.5% annually from 1965 to 1989. Average rice yields nearly doubled, as the yield increase rate rose from less than 1% per year prior to 1970 to more than 3% per year after 1970. The growth rate of crop area planted to rice increased from about 0.7% to 1.3% per year, mainly because of increases in rice cropping intensity. This extraordinary performance has been attributed to the widespread diffusion of modern varieties and public investment in irrigation, as well as improvements in market infrastructure, nationwide extension and credit programs, and pricing policies (Pearson et al. 1991). Although there is little dispute about the productivity impact of modern rice technology in Indonesia, concern for its distributional impact was expressed from the early stage of its introduction. Because Java is one of the world's most densely populated regions, the impact of new rice technology on employment is of central concern to Indonesia.

A shift from the use of the *ani-ani* (hand knife) to the labor-saving sickle in harvesting was a unique factor in the Indonesian experience with modern rice technology. The *ani-ani* is used to harvest only the panicles, whereas the sickle is used to harvest the entire rice stalk. Because modern varieties have shorter stalks and are more susceptible to shattering than traditional varieties, threshing results are best when a crop is harvested by sickle (Hayami and Kikuchi 1982). Thus, sickle use, which reduces harvesting labor by 25 to 35%, is technically superior to the *ani-ani* where modern varieties are grown.

Collier et al. (1973, 1974), Utami and Ihalauw (1973), and Sinaga and Sinaga (1978) examine changes in labor use per hectare and factor shares and argue that the new technology worsened inequities in income distribution by

107

reducing the welfare of landless households. Subsequent studies on the income distributional implications of modern rice technology in Indonesia focus on the employment impact. By separating the effects of population growth from those of modern variety adoption and considering the effect of the latter on increasing cropping intensity, Hayami and Kikuchi (1982) conclude that the modern rice technology heightened labor demand. Studies in the late 1980s and early 1990s measure the impact of the Green Revolution on overall farm and nonfarm employment and wages (Manning 1988; Naylor 1991a, b; Heytens 1991c). Because Indonesia's farm size distribution is not as skewed as elsewhere in Asia and tenancy ratio is relatively low, there is less concern about differential technology impact between large- and small-scale farmers and between landlords and tenants. In any case, studies from the early 1970s (Ihalauw and Utami 1975; Prabowo and Sajogyo 1975) show that, at least in Java, modern rice technology was broadly accepted, regardless of farm size and tenancy.

We examine the causes of differential adoption of modern varieties in Indonesia and their impacts on regional income distribution. Rice is grown in diverse production environments. Bernsten, Siwi, and Beachell (1981) report that early adoption of modern varieties took place mostly in irrigated and favorable rainfed lowland areas. Irrigation investments accelerated after 1970, and the modern varieties subsequently released were more tolerant of adverse production environments; thus, modern varieties were grown on 80% of total rice crop area and almost 90% of wetland rice area by the late 1980s.

Regional income distribution is a long-standing issue in Indonesian economic development. Java, which occupies only 7% of the total land area, accounts for more than 60% of Indonesia's population. Java also has the most favorable rice production environment, the most developed market and social infrastructure, and the greatest proportion of industry—and therefore the highest level of average per capita income. Whether and to what extent modern rice technology exacerbated regional inequities between Java and the outer islands is of major interest.

The ultimate distributional effects of differential technology adoption across production environments will depend critically on how factor and product markets adjust to changing demand and supply conditions. We examine the effects of modern rice technology on regional patterns of wages and returns to land. We focus specifically on the role of interregional labor migration in equalizing wages and thus in mitigating the potentially inequitable effects of technology adoption in the favorable region on the welfare of people in the less favored region. Because labor is a mobile factor of production and the major resource of the rural poor, the ultimate distributional effects of differential technology adoption hinge on the extent to which labor markets adjust to equalize wages across regions.

We describe the rice-production environments in Indonesia and the study villages, examine factors affecting modern variety adoption as well as the impact of technology adoption on fertilizer use and land productivity, analyze the relation between technology adoption and demographic changes, and explore the extent to which market adjustments lead to equalization of wages and returns to land across regions.

PRODUCTION ENVIRONMENTS AND STUDY VILLAGES

The major rice-production environments in Indonesia are irrigated, rainfed lowland, tidal swamp, and upland. Irrigated and rainfed lowland rice is planted in bunded, floodable land called *sawah*. Irrigated areas range from those with good water control, where three crops of rice, or at least two rice crops in combination with a *palawija* (upland or dryland) crop, can be grown, to those with relatively poor water control, where less rice and more *palawija* crops are grown. Because of sufficient rainfall in many parts of Indonesia, a *palawija* crop can be grown after the wet season rice crop in rainfed lowlands (Heytens 1991b).

The main distinguishing feature of upland and tidal swamp areas, where rice is grown in nonbunded fields, is the total lack of water control. Tidal swamp fields are directly or indirectly influenced by the tide, and waterlogging, salinity, and acidity are major constraints to rice production. Only traditional varieties are grown in the tidal swamp and upland areas. Rice is grown with other crops in a multiple-cropping system in upland areas. In tidal swamp areas, a nine-month rice crop is grown because seedlings have to be transplanted three times to let their stems grow strong enough to survive in the tidal environment. Rice yields are much lower in the tidal swamp and upland areas than in the *sawah* areas. Moreover, these production environments are located mostly in remote areas of the outer islands, which have a poorly developed market infrastructure and have received lower priority in government production programs.

Table 5.1 shows the distribution of rice-production environments and total production in Indonesia by environment. Almost 60% of cultivated area is irrigated. The rainfed lowlands, constituting 20% of the cultivated area, are also generally favorable to rice production in the wet season. There are equal proportions (11% each) of tidal swamp and upland areas, unevenly distributed between Java and the outer islands. Whereas irrigated and rainfed *sawah* systems account for about 94% of the cultivated area in Java, almost 40% of the cultivated area in the outer islands consists of tidal swamp and upland areas. In Kalimantan, for example, 34% of the rice crop area is tidal swamp and 44% is rainfed lowland. In Lampung, Sumatra, at least one-third of rice land is upland. If South Sulawesi, where rice is mostly grown in *sawah*, were excluded, the proportion of unfavorable rice-growing areas would be much higher in the outer islands.

Survey Villages

We did an extensive survey of forty-seven villages representing irrigated, rainfed, and tidal swamp production environments in five provinces—West Java, Central Java, East Java, Lampung, and South Kalimantan (Figure 5.1 and Table 5.2). Major districts representing each type of production environment in each province were first identified. A predetermined number of village samples were then randomly chosen from selected districts.

The survey, taken from January to September 1988, included interviews with the village leader and two to three other knowledgeable farmers in each village. Information obtained included the current socioeconomic and demographic characteristics of the village and historical changes in irrigation, technology adoption, input use, productivity, and population growth since 1970. Input, output, wage, and price data pertained to the wet season of 1987.

Table 5.3 presents socioeconomic characteristics of the survey villages. Average farm size in the irrigated and rainfed areas are about the same (0.5 ha), much smaller than in tidal swamp villages (2.4 ha). The ratio of village population to cultivated area (the man-land ratio) is much higher in irrigated areas than in rainfed and tidal swamp villages. Consistent with those figures, the ratio of landless households is highest in the irrigated villages (26%) and lowest in the tidal swamp areas (8%). Owner cultivation is more commonly observed in rainfed areas. Conversely, the extent of leasehold and share tenancy is relatively high in irrigated and tidal swamp villages. Rice is the major crop grown in all three types of production environments. In irrigated areas, cropping intensity of rice is almost 200%, whereas in most rainfed and tidal swamp villages rice is planted once a year. Other crops, such as maize, soybean, and mungbean, are typically grown as *palawija* crops in the rainfed areas.

TECHNOLOGY ADOPTION AND LAND PRODUCTIVITY

We analyzed trends in modern variety adoption across production environments and determined the factors affecting differential technology adoption. We also analyzed the impact of modern variety adoption on fertilizer use and land productivity.

Environment, Technology Adoption, and Productivity

Technology adoption is determined by socioeconomic and environmental factors. Table 5.4 reports the changes in ratio of irrigated area, modern variety adoption, fertilizer use, paddy yields, and rice cropping intensity across production environments between 1970 and 1987. In the irrigated villages, the ratio of irrigated area increased significantly, from 76% in 1970 to 93%

in 1987, reflecting the acceleration of irrigation development in Indonesia during that period. In 1987, a handful of rainfed villages were irrigated by water pump or natural creeks, but tidal swamp villages relied totally on rainfall.

Modern varieties were more rapidly adopted in earlier years in the irrigated areas. As newer modern varieties—with greater pest resistance, shorter growth duration, and more tolerance for adverse environments—were introduced, adoption reached 80% in the rainfed areas, not much below the rate of modern variety adoption in irrigated areas. The rainfed areas still growing traditional varieties are found in districts that are either drought-prone or affected by salinity. However, in tidal swamp villages, where waterlogging, acidity, salinity, and other soil fertility problems are prevalent, only traditional rice varieties are grown.

As expected, the difference in fertilizer use per hectare is consistent with the cross-sectional pattern of modern variety adoption—i.e., highest in the irrigated villages because of high adoption of modern varieties. Lower risks involved in rice production in the irrigated areas would also stimulate application of fertilizer. It should be noted that fertilizer use per hectare in tidal swamp villages, although lower than in other environments, is still substantial.

It is interesting to note that average yields of traditional varieties did not differ greatly among irrigated and nonirrigated villages in 1970 and 1980 and that yields in tidal swamp villages rose. Average yields of modern varieties were higher than traditional varieties by 1.5 to 3 t/ha. Although yields of traditional varieties increased in irrigated and rainfed areas over time, mainly because of greater use of fertilizer, yield increases of modern varieties were greater, particularly in the irrigated areas. In tidal swamp areas where only traditional varieties were grown, yields had declined by 1987.

Rice cropping intensity clearly increased as a result of growth in the ratio of irrigated land. The increase, however, is higher than the change in irrigation ratio, suggesting that the spread of short-growth-duration modern varieties contributed to the increase in rice cropping intensity. Although no data on total cropping intensity were collected, there could be additional growth from the area planted to *palawija* crops, which require less water than rice during the dry season.

Determinants of Modern Variety Adoption, Fertilizer Use, and Land Productivity

In this section, we first analyze the factors affecting adoption of modern varieties. Assuming a recursive system, we estimate fertilizer use, yield, and rice cropping intensity functions where the independent variables are measures of environmental factors, modern variety adoption ratio, farm size, ratio of tenancy, fertilizer-paddy price ratio, and regional dummy variables.

The equations, estimated by ordinary least squares (OLS), were specified in log-linear form except for ratio and dummy variables.

Table 5.5 reports the regression results of the modern variety adoption and fertilizer use functions. Consistent with general observations, environmental factors represented by irrigation ratio (IRGR) and tidal swamp village dummy (SWAMPY) significantly explain patterns of modern variety adoption. Although the coefficient of IRGR indicates that adoption rate of modern varieties in irrigated areas is significantly higher than in other environments, the difference between it and the rate for rainfed areas is rather small because modern varieties are also widely adopted in the latter environment. The highly significant and negative coefficient of tidal swamp villages, where only traditional varieties are grown, is to be expected. Farm size (FSIZE) and tenancy (TENANCY) do not have any significant effects on modern variety adoption. The lack of statistical significance of fertilizer-paddy price ratio (FPPRICE), however, does not imply the nonimportance of prices but rather the lack of sufficient price variation, particularly of fertilizer, across villages as a result of government marketing policies.

Regional dummy variables are statistically significant, as Java and Lampung generally have more favorable production environments than other regions. This implies that in Kalimantan (the control area), even irrigated and rainfed areas suffer from salinity and other adverse environmental problems.

In the fertilizer use functions, only the ratio of irrigated area in equation (2) and the ratio of modern variety adoption in equation (3) have significant and positive coefficients. Contrary to expectations, the coefficient of tidal swamp is not significant. When IRGR and MVR are both included (equation 3), only the coefficient of MVR is significant. These results imply that modern variety adoption primarily affects the use of fertilizer.

Table 5.6 presents the estimation results of the yield and rice cropping intensity functions. Equations (1) and (2) show similar results—i.e., environmental variables, including the regional dummies, seem to explain more than 70% of variations of yields across villages. Because of the high correlation between modern varieties and production environments, the effect of modern varieties on yield cannot be separated from the effect of production environment. This explains why MVR is not significant in equation (2) despite the clearly higher yields of modern varieties compared to traditional varieties in irrigated and rainfed environments reported in Table 5.4. It was only when the dummy variables SWAMPY and LAMPUNG were deleted that MVR had a significant coefficient, and one larger than IRGR.

In the rice cropping intensity functions, irrigation and farm size are the significant explanatory variables. The coefficient of irrigation ratio suggests that the presence of irrigation increases rice cropping intensity by 60%. The negative and significant coefficient of farm size indicates that smaller farms tend to be more intensively cultivated. There is no evidence that the adoption of modern varieties increases rice cropping intensity.

TECHNOLOGY ADOPTION
AND FACTOR-MARKET ADJUSTMENT

The previous section showed that the concentrated adoption of modern varieties in irrigated and favorable rainfed areas widened productivity differential across production environments.

Although the less favorable environments constitute only a small part of cultivated rice area, the regional income distributional effects of differential technology adoption are of major interest, particularly because most of the unfavorable areas are on the outer islands, which historically have lagged behind Java in economic development. In order to analyze regional distributional effects, however, we must consider not only direct effects on factor use and productivity but also indirect effects through labor and land market adjustments.

The upland areas are covered in the next chapter, which focuses on Lampung, where traditional varieties continue to be grown in upland areas and where yields continue to stagnate.

Technology Adoption and Labor Demand

There have been many studies of the impact of the Green Revolution on the employment and welfare of landless Indonesians. As mentioned earlier, the shift from the *ani-ani* to the sickle induced by adoption of modern varieties sharply reduced labor requirements. Although labor use increased in other tasks following adoption of modern varieties, Heytens (1991b, c) reports that labor use per hectare for modern varieties is still lower than for traditional varieties. However, Heytens assumed that mechanical threshers are used only for modern varieties and not for traditional varieties.

In the study reported in the next chapter, no such difference is observed for Lampung, where threshing is now mechanized for both traditional and modern varieties. It should be noted that the spread of mechanical threshers occurred in the late 1970s, much later than the diffusion of modern varieties. Moreover, the use of tractors for land preparation has also been quite limited. According to the Indonesian Central Bureau of Statistics (1989), tractors were used for land preparation on only about 7% of total cultivated area as late as 1987.

Because of the increases in cropping intensity that expanded the area planted to rice by 35%, total demand for labor in rice must have at least remained the same, and it probably increased to the extent that labor use per hectare did not decline with modern variety adoption. According to the estimation results of labor use functions shown in the next chapter, labor demand, particularly for hired labor, significantly increased with modern variety adoption.

If the growth linkage effects on employment in the nonfarm sector resulting from higher farm income are considered, the adoption of modern varieties was more likely to have resulted in increased total labor demand. Such effects have been documented by other studies in Indonesia (Manning 1988; Collier 1978; Naylor 1991b). Also, studies in India, Nigeria, Malaysia, and the Philippines provide estimates that each unit increase of value added in agriculture stimulates an additional 0.83 unit increase in value added in the nonfarm sector (Hazell and Ramasamy 1991; Hazell and Roell 1983; Bell et al. 1982; Gibbs 1974). Given recent evidence that modern variety adoption has tripled Indonesian rice farm income (Heytens 1991c), significant indirect employment effects on the nonfarm sector must have been generated.

Although rapid growth of the overall economy will largely explain the trend of increasing real rural wages, modern rice technology also has contributed to such a trend. It should be emphasized that increases in labor demand resulting from higher cropping intensity have been concentrated in irrigated areas. Hence, it is important to investigate whether and to what extent labor markets adjust so that benefits of greater employment opportunities in the favorable areas are shared with less favored regions through interregional migration and equalization of wages.

Technology Adoption and Demographic Change

To investigate the patterns of migration across study villages, we examined the rate of population growth between 1980 and 1987 as a proxy for net migration rates, implicitly assuming a constant natural rate of population growth across villages. Official records of migration rates by village were limited, and ad hoc estimates by village leaders were unreliable. Lack of village-level population data prior to 1980 made it impossible to derive population growth rates for the years between 1965 and 1980—the period of most rapid diffusion of modern varieties. Difficulty was also encountered in computing village-level population growth rates for the period after 1980 because of changes in geographic boundaries.

Such data limitations notwithstanding, comparison of population growth rates from 1980 to 1987 across production environments is presented in Table 5.7. Population growth rates are generally lower for the sample villages than for Indonesia as a whole, suggesting net migration from rural to urban areas. However, population growth is clearly highest in the irrigated areas, followed by rainfed areas, with lowest growth rate in tidal swamp areas.

The higher population growth in irrigated villages is consistent with the corresponding figures on man-land ratio, average farm size, and percentage of landless households. Man-land ratio and percentage of landless households are substantially higher in the irrigated than in the rainfed and tidal swamp villages. Because migration studies have shown that landless families and small-scale farmers have a higher probability of migrating than owner-farmers (Anitawati and Rasahan 1986), demographic patterns across production environments indicate a higher net out-migration rate from villages with an unfavorable production environment. The smaller farm size in the irrigated areas reflects the greater population pressure and higher demand for land in the villages with a more favorable environment.

To test our hypothesis that permanent migration from unfavorable to favorable rice-production areas or to urban areas took place in response to widening productivity differentials across production environments, we estimated population growth rate functions. The change in the ratios of irrigated area and modern variety adoption for the 1980–1987 period (ΔIRGR, ΔMVR), man-land ratio in 1980 (MLR80), distance from market center (DISTM), and regional dummy variables (JAVA, LAMPUNG) were specified as independent variables.

Regression results by the OLS method are reported in Table 5.8. Production environments, specifically ΔIRGR and regional dummy variables, significantly explain differences in population growth rate. Villages that have higher increases in the ratio of irrigated area tend to have higher growth rates of population. Java and Lampung's higher rate of industrialization, more favorable agricultural characteristics, and more developed market and social infrastructure, as compared to Kalimantan, seem to have attracted inmigration or deterred out-migration. The fact that ΔMVR did not show significant coefficients may be due in part to the tapering off of modern variety adoption by the 1980s in the irrigated area.

Modern variety adoption did continue to increase in the 1980s but mostly in the rainfed area. Effects of modern variety adoption might have been partly captured, however, by the positive coefficients of Java and Lampung, where most of the rainfed villages are located.

It is interesting to note the negative and significant coefficient of MLR80, which suggests that land-abundant villages are likely to be major destinations of migration. The positive coefficient of distance from the nearest town implies a somewhat surprising result that migration to the remote villages is greater than to the more industrialized town center—or, alternatively, that natural population growth rate is higher in those villages.

Technology and Factor Price Differential

Rural labor market studies conducted in the 1970s in Java suggested the existence of monopolistic behavior on the part of employers that led to labor market segmentation according to age, sex group, and season (White 1976, 1979; Hart and Sisler 1978). More recent studies by Manning (1988), Collier et al. (1988), and Naylor (1991b), however, found evidence of an increasingly well-integrated market for unskilled labor in Java. Wages in agriculture during the peak work season are comparable with wages for unskilled workers in the urban areas. Most rural laborers pursue multiple income-earning activities and migrate seasonally, not only within islands but also across islands.

Having shown that patterns of population growth are consistent with the hypothesis of interregional labor market adjustments, we explored the extent to which such adjustments equalize wages across regions. If a labor market adjusts perfectly, then the wage differentials should reflect no more than the cost of migration. However, because the supply of land is less elastic than the supply of labor, an increase in the demand for land associated with the adoption of new technology and an increase in labor supply in the favorable areas will increase returns to land, thereby widening the income gap accruing from land across production environments. Thus, we also examined the relationship between technology adoption, production environment, and returns to land.

Table 5.9 shows the structure of paddy prices, task-specific wages, land price, and land rental across production environments. In addition to daily wage, imputed wages for certain tasks under custom-rate or piece-rate contract are also presented, computed as wage payment divided by average man-days worked.

In general, wage rates are similar among irrigated and rainfed villages. One exception is the higher wage for plowing (which includes the cost of animal service) in the irrigated villages. However, this is likely due to the higher cost of maintaining work animals in irrigated areas, where the supply of grazing land is limited.

Wage rates in tidal swamp villages tend to be higher. As shown in Figure 5.1, the tidal swamp villages sampled were all in Kalimantan. Cost of living outside Java is typically higher because most consumer goods originate in Java. Rice is also exported to Kalimantan, which is reflected in higher paddy prices in the tidal swamp area. Moreover, labor is scarce relative to land outside Java. The higher wages in tidal swamp areas may also reflect the greater difficulty, and therefore greater effort, involved in performing the work in that environment. And because wages in Kalimantan and Lampung are similar, another plausible explanation may be the greater total employment opportunities throughout the year in Java, so that annual income may be equalized across regions even though peak-season wages differ.

As expected, the wage rate imputed for piece-rate or custom-rate contracts is higher than the average daily wage. Workers under a daily wage arrangement will be less motivated to work because payment is fixed regardless of their effort. Furthermore, more able workers are likely to choose work under an output-sharing contract offering higher remuneration at a higher level of work effort (Roumasset and Uy 1980).

Land price and land rent are clearly highest in the irrigated villages and lowest in tidal swamp areas. We expect that differential technology adoption and production environment should be more closely related to differences in land rent than in land prices. We do so because land prices are affected not only by the marginal productivity of land in rice production but also by its proximity to an urban center, expected increases in future returns to land, profitability of nonrice crops, and so forth. Land price also ought to reflect the effect of higher cropping intensity induced by modern varieties in irrigated areas, whereas rent refers only to returns per hectare per season. It is not surprising, therefore, that the variation in land price across production environments is much greater than the variation in land rent.

In Tables 5.10 and 5.11, we estimate wage, land rent, and land price functions using basically the same specifications. Aside from the modern variety adoption ratio (MVR), the independent variables include environmental factors (IRGR, SWAMPY) and regional dummy variables (JAVA, LAMPUNG), the ratio of fertilizer to paddy prices (FPPRICE), man-land ratio in 1987 (MLR87), and distance from the market center (DISTM). In the wage function, a dummy variable to distinguish piece-rate contracts (CONT2) has been added in the relevant wage equation.

The results of the wage regressions estimated by task are reported in Table 5.10. Without exception, neither irrigation nor modern variety adoption is significant in explaining variations in wages across villages. In three of the four wage regressions, the coefficient of the SWAMPY dummy variable is not significant. The negative and significant coefficient of SWAMPY in weeding can be explained by the fact that in tidal swamp areas, unlike in other production environments, weeding is not widely practiced, and therefore there is not a peak demand season for labor.

The negative and significant coefficient of JAVA in most of the regressions is consistent with the lower cost of living and relatively more abundant labor supply in this region compared to the outer islands. Coefficients of LAMPUNG are not significant except for that of transplanting, suggesting that wages among the outer islands are similar. The existence of significant wage differences between Java and the outer islands has been reported in many other studies, with respect not only to rural but also to urban wages (Kasryno 1988; Naylor 1991b; Manning 1988).

Consistent with theory, the coefficients of dummy variables for contract arrangement are positive and significant because workers receiving contract payments are more motivated to work. Except for distance in the case of transplanting, the other variables do not significantly affect intervillage wage patterns.

Whereas production environments and adoption of modern varieties do not show any significant effect on wage differentials, the ratio of irrigated area is highly significant in the land rent and land price regressions (Table 5.11). In fact, irrigation is the only significant variable in the land rent equation, suggesting that higher production efficiency in irrigated land per season is most important factor determining land rental. Although the coefficient of tidal swamp villages has the expected negative sign, it is not significant, which implies that land rental for rainfed land is not significantly higher than for tidal swamp land despite a notable difference in yields.

The greater number of significant explanatory variables in the land price equations compared to the land rent equations confirms expectations—not only productivity of land per season but also productivity per year, market and social infrastructure, expected rate of economic growth, and other factors affect land prices. Thus, land prices are significantly higher in Java compared to Lampung and in Lampung compared to Kalimantan. The higher value of the coefficient of IRGR in the land price compared to the land rent equation seems to reflect the impact of irrigation on cropping intensity. As in the case of the land rent function, the coefficient of the modern variety adoption variable is positive but not significant. This result would be due, in part, to the close association between modern variety adoption and irrigation. The negative and significant coefficient of fertilizer-paddy price ratio is indicative of the factor-price effects as well as effects of location, including factor-price effects on the overall cost of living. However, DISTM, which measures distance from the market center, is not relevant.

SUMMARY OF FINDINGS

Our study confirms widespread evidence that modern variety adoption in Indonesia has been concentrated in irrigated and favorable rainfed production environments and has widened productivity differentials across environments. The analysis shows, however, that the potentially inequitable effects on regional income distribution have been mitigated by labor market adjustments in response to the increases in labor demand in the favorable areas. Instead of widespread mechanization, interregional migration, both permanent and seasonal, is the principal instrument for equalizing wages across regions. As a result, neither production environment nor modern variety adoption can account for cross-sectional differences in wages. The higher wage observed in the outer islands can be largely explained by the higher cost of living and lower supply of labor in those areas. It can therefore be inferred that rural labor markets in Indonesia are generally well integrated.

This study also provides evidence that modern varieties and irrigation contribute to disparities in returns to land. The much higher farm size in the unfavorable areas compared to irrigated and rainfed areas, however, suggests that land market adjustments may be occurring to reduce income disparities across regions. Moreover, rapid growth in the overall Indonesian economy, which raises real wages, means that employment opportunities have become increasingly available to poor farmers in the unfavorable areas.

Nonetheless, it is important to examine statistically whether and to what extent adjustments in land use and time allocation would have minimized potentially inequitable effects of differential technology adoption on household income distribution. The next chapter represents such an attempt.

Figure 5.1   Location of study areas, extensive survey, Indonesia, 1987

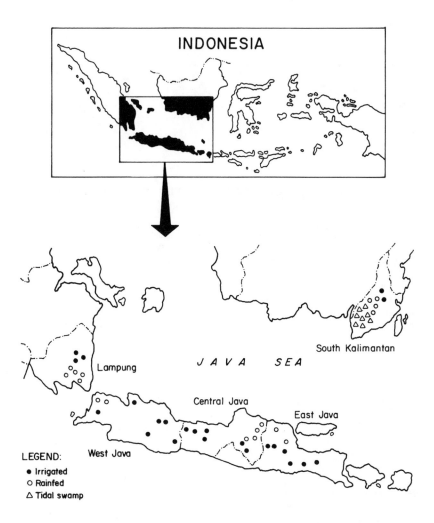

Table 5.1   Distribution of rice-production environments and total rice production, Indonesia, 1987.[a]

Production environment	% of area	% of total production
Irrigated	58	71
Good water control	11	17
Moderate water control	21	27
Poor water control	26	27
Rainfed lowland	20	18
Upland (or dryland)	11	6
Tidal swamp	11	5

a. Adapted from Heytens (1991b).

Table 5.2   Distribution of sample villages by production environment, extensive survey, Indonesia, 1987.

Province	Irrigated	Rainfed	Tidal swamp	Total
West Java	6	2	—	8
Central Java	6	4	—	10
East Java	6	2	—	8
Lampung	4	3	—	7
South Kalimantan	2	4	8	14
Total	24	15	8	47

Table 5.3   Selected socioeconomic characteristics of sample villages, extensive survey, Indonesia, 1987.

	Irrigated	Rainfed	Tidal swamp
Farm size (ha)	0.5	0.5	2.4
Man-land ratio (person/ha)	14.6	5.8	1.6
Ratio of landless households (%)	26	11	8
Area under owner cultivation (%)	77	86	74
Rice cropping intensity (%)	181	117	106

Table 5.4   Technology adoption, paddy yields, and rice cropping intensity by production environment, extensive survey, Indonesia,
1970–1987.

	Irrigated	Rainfed	Tidal swamp
Ratio of irrigated area (%)			
1970	76	0	0
1980	86	0	0
1987	93	4	0
Modern variety adoption (%)[a]			
1970	53	8	0
1980	91	42	0
1987	98	81	0
Fertilizer use (kg NPK/ha)			
1987	144	107	56
Yield (t/ha)			
Traditional varieties			
1970	1.9	1.8	2.3
1980	2.0	1.9	2.4
1987	2.9	2.6	1.7
Modern varieties			
1970	3.8	3.3	—
1980	4.3	3.0	—
1987	5.8	4.4	—
Rice cropping intensity (%)			
1970	136	105	100
1980	169	100	100
1987	181	117	106

a. Percentage of total wetland area in the village.

Table 5.5   Regression results of modern variety adoption and fertilizer use functions, extensive survey, Indonesia, 1987.[a]

	MVR	Ln Fertilizer	
	(1)	(2)	(3)
Intercept	0.77**	5.50**	3.79**
	(4.31)	(19.08)	(8.94)
IRGR	0.10*	0.11**	0.17
	(1.98)	(2.39)	(0.73)
SWAMPY	−0.56**	0.05	0.32
	(−2.43)	(0.12)	(0.63)
MVR	—	—	1.40**
			(2.85)
Ln FSIZE	−0.05	−0.15	0.06
	(−0.38)	(−0.71)	(0.26)
TENANCY	−0.06	−0.60	−0.15
	(−0.36)	(−1.28)	(−0.31)
Ln FPPRICE	−0.12	0.24	0.07
	(−0.55)	(0.55)	(0.16)
JAVA	0.20*	0.32	−0.14
	(2.23)	(1.24)	(−0.43)
LAMPUNG	0.31*	0.48	0.01
	(2.24)	(1.27)	(0.03)
R^2	0.82	0.38	0.38
F-value	29.79	5.01	4.38

a. Numbers in parentheses are t-statistics.
** Indicates significance at 1% level; * at 5% level.

Table 5.6   Regression results of yield and rice cropping intensity functions, extensive survey, Indonesia, 1987.[a]

	Ln Yield			Rice cropping intensity	
	(1)	(2)	(3)	(4)	(5)
Intercept	8.47** (6.58)	8.27** (6.24)	6.67** (6.31)	0.94** (4.12)	0.77** (2.38)
IRGR	0.30** (2.54)	0.27* (2.17)	0.26* (2.01)	0.60** (3.62)	0.56** (3.18)
SWAMPY	-0.88** (-3.84)	-0.76** (-2.74)	—	0.38 (1.19)	0.54 (1.40)
MVR	—	0.20 (0.74)	0.71** (3.29)	—	0.28 (0.75)
Ln FSIZE	0.12 (1.01)	0.13 (1.07)	-0.04 (-0.44)	-0.35* (-2.16)	-0.34* (-2.07)
TENANCY	-0.11 (-0.40)	-0.09 (-0.35)	-0.29 (-1.03)	-0.01 (-0.04)	0.006 (0.02)
Ln FPPRICE	-0.32 (-0.23)	-0.23 (-0.17)	0.98 (0.87)	0.06 (0.18)	0.08 (0.24)
JAVA	0.34* (2.26)	0.30* (1.87)	0.16 (1.33)	-0.04 (-0.22)	-0.10 (-0.45)
LAMPUNG	0.32 (1.47)	0.26 (1.11)	—	0.10 (0.32)	0.01 (0.04)
R^2	0.77	0.78	0.72	0.52	0.53
F-value	18.37	15.96	16.9	5.92	5.19

a. Numbers in parentheses are t-statistics.
** Indicates significance at 1% level; * at 5% level.

Table 5.7   Demographic characteristics of sample villages by production environment, extensive survey, Indonesia, 1987.

	Irrigated	Rainfed	Tidal swamp
Annual population growth rate 1980–1987 (%)	1.7	1.4	0.8
Man-land ratio (persons/ha)			
Wetland	18.1	15.0	2.0
All agricultural land	14.6	5.8	1.6
Farm size (ha)	0.5	0.5	2.4
Ratio of agricultural landless households (%)	26	11	8

Table 5.8   Regression results of population growth rate functions, extensive survey, Indonesia, 1980–1987.[a]

	(1)	(2)	(3)
Intercept	0.73** (2.32)	0.79** (2.44)	0.72* (2.30)
ΔIRGR	0.77* (1.87)	—	0.74* (1.80)
ΔMVR	−0.25 (−0.80)	−0.19 (−0.60)	—
Ln MLR80	−0.28 (−0.84)	−0.28** (−2.79)	−0.27** (−2.80)
Ln DISTM	0.21* (1.84)	0.18 (1.54)	0.19* (1.72)
JAVA	1.21* (4.10)	1.28** (4.23)	1.22** (4.14)
LAMPUNG	0.73* (2.07)	0.86** (2.40)	0.66* (1.94)
R^2	0.47	0.43	0.47
F-value	6.76	6.87	7.84

a. Numbers in parentheses are t-statistics.
** Indicates significance at 1% level; * at 5% level.

Table 5.9   Prices and wage rates[a] by production environment, extensive survey, Indonesia, wet season, 1987.

	Irrigated	Rainfed	Tidal swamp
Paddy price (Rp/kg)			
Traditional varieties	—	161	208
Modern varieties	181	161	—
Land price (thou Rp/ha)	8,373	3,147	786
Land rent (thou Rp/ha/season)[b]	265	163	90
Wage rates (Rp/day)			
Land preparation			
Daily wage (hoeing)	2,174	1,916	2,500
Imputed wage (hoeing)	—	3,344	3,995
Daily wage (plowing)	5,816	4,208	—
Imputed wage (plowing)	6,338	5,256	—
Transplanting			
Daily wage	1,824	1,196	—
Imputed wage	2,885	2,669	2,500
Weeding	1,780	1,816	1,941
Harvesting and threshing			
Imputed wage	2,852	2,991	3,754

a. Rp 1,652 = US$1.
b. Refers to wetland.

Table 5.10   Regression results of wage functions, extensive survey, Indonesia, wet season, 1987.[a]

	Ln Hoeing	Ln Transplanting	Ln Weeding	Ln Harvesting and threshing
Intercept	5.61** (16.04)	5.09** (18.54)	5.62** (19.39)	5.90** (15.28)
IRGR	0.004 (0.03)	0.03 (0.29)	0.08 (0.58)	0.08 (0.69)
SWAMPY	−0.05 (−0.19)	−0.16 (−0.72)	−0.46* (−1.71)	0.04 (0.10)
MVR	0.03 (0.11)	0.005 (0.02)	−0.16 (−0.80)	0.30 (1.05)
Ln FPPRICE	−0.05 (−0.17)	−0.33 (−1.46)	−0.22 (−0.80)	−0.28 (−1.05)
Ln MLR87	−0.05 (−0.62)	0.02 (0.33)	0.03 (0.33)	−0.007 (−0.08)
Ln DISTM	0.06 (0.09)	0.17** (2.75)	0.007 (0.98)	−0.009 (−0.12)
CONT2	0.35* (1.84)	0.42** (3.74)	—	—
JAVA	−0.28 (−1.29)	−0.46** (−2.40)	−0.37** (−3.07)	−0.44* (−1.72)
LAMPUNG	−0.08 (−0.33)	−0.46* (−1.98)	−0.07 (−0.25)	−0.16 (−0.52)
R^2	0.41	0.57	0.34	0.08
F-value	4.58	7.66	3.88	1.41

a. Numbers in parentheses are t-statistics.
** Indicates significance at 1% level; * at 5% level.

Table 5.11   Regression results of land rent and land price functions, extensive survey, Indonesia, wet season, 1987.[a]

	Ln Land rent	Ln Land price
Intercept	4.74** (19.37)	6.86** (19.37)
IRGR	0.46** (3.97)	0.69** (4.34)
SWAMPY	−0.32 (−1.46)	−0.45 (−1.41)
MVR	0.30 (1.22)	0.34 (0.34)
Ln FPPRICE	0.14 (0.61)	−0.03** (−2.89)
Ln MLR87	−0.02 (−0.27)	−0.03 (−0.34)
Ln DISTM	0.04 (0.67)	−0.09 (−1.04)
JAVA	0.09 (0.51)	1.30** (4.89)
LAMPUNG	−0.18 (−0.81)	0.87** (2.71)
R^2	0.70	0.88
F-value	14.29	42.63

a. Numbers in parentheses are t-statistics.
** Indicates significance at 1% level; * at 5% level.

6

Varietal Improvements, Productivity Change, and Income Distribution: The Case of Lampung, Indonesia

■

TUMARI JATILEKSONO

Analysis of data from an intensive village-level survey in Lampung Province essentially completes the study of modern rice technology adoption in Indonesia, and its productivity and equity impact on the nation as a whole. The previous chapter focused on the determinants of technology adoption based on an extensive survey, concentrating mainly on rice production in irrigated, favorable rainfed, and tidal swamp environments. The intensive survey in Lampung included the upland environment as a major rice producer.

Lampung, at the south end of Sumatra Island (Figure 6.1), has been a major destination of government transmigration programs and spontaneous migration. Population density has increased fourfold over the past three decades, yet it is still only 26% of Java's density (Table 6.1).

The proportion of rice in Lampung grown in relatively less favorable production environments is greater than that of Indonesia as a whole and of Java in particular. Facilities built during the 1970s provide irrigation to 43% of cultivated area planted to rice. Two-thirds of that land can grow two rice crops, but a single rice crop is grown in the remaining third. Expansion of irrigation, plus the newer modern varieties' greater pest resistance, better grain quality, shorter growth duration, and higher tolerance for adverse physical conditions, increased the diffusion of modern varieties.

As irrigated area expanded, rainfed lowland areas' share of total cultivated rice area diminished to less than 20%. Upland areas, however, continue to be a major production environment for rice, accounting for more than a third of total cultivated rice area. The upland areas are still totally planted with traditional rice varieties, but crop area planted with modern varieties in the lowlands increased from 6% in 1970 to 90% in 1988.

Although no successful modern varieties were developed for the upland areas, upland paddy yields increased from 1 t/ha in the early 1970s to about 1.7 t/ha in recent years, mainly because of greater fertilizer use. Observed yield increases in other areas were due not only to adoption of modern varieties and expansion of irrigation, but also to factors such as the decline in

129

fertilizer-paddy price ratios as substantial price subsidies were provided over time (Jatileksono 1987; Timmer 1989; Heytens 1991a).

Simple productivity analysis of modern varieties versus traditional varieties is inadequate for the analysis of the impact of Green Revolution in Indonesia because improvements in the characteristics of modern varieties contributed to their wider dissemination and continued growth in yields. My intensive study for Lampung quantifies the impact of differential adoption of various generations of modern varieties on productivity and income distribution. Previous analyses of technology impact have not distinguished variety-specific effects but have implicitly assumed that different generations of modern rice varieties have had uniform characteristics and, hence, unchanging productivity effects.

I used cross-section and time-series data, generated by farmers' recall, to identify the impacts of a series of modern varieties. The analysis of income distributional effects of differential technology adoption across production environments focuses on the effects on returns to land, an issue largely ignored in the Green Revolution literature. Lampung is a suitable choice of study site for such an analysis for several reasons:

- The relatively similar production environments among lowland areas in the late 1960s and subsequent changes in irrigation and adoption of modern varieties provide a rare opportunity to identify the impacts of irrigation and modern varieties on productivity and returns to land in isolation from other factors.
- Dramatic changes in demographic patterns, land development, and technology adoption generated substantial land market transactions.
- The presence of relatively large tracts of upland areas that have been bypassed by modern varieties but where alternative crops can be grown facilitates the investigation of the indirect effect of differential technology adoption on product market adjustments through changes in cropping patterns.

VILLAGE SURVEYS AND CHARACTERISTICS

Four villages for each Lampung production environment—irrigated, rainfed, and upland—were selected, and forty farm households were randomly selected from the population of rice farmers in each village. The villages were in six subdistricts, as shown in Figure 6.1. The number of sample villages and sample farm households was predetermined to be equal among the three production environments. The irrigated villages were served by a unit operated by the national irrigation system. The distance from villages to the nearest subdistrict market ranged from 1 to 9 km.

Farm households were surveyed twice—in the wet season (November

1987 to April 1988) and the dry season (May to October 1988). The questionnaire covered detailed information on household characteristics, technology adoption, input use, yields, prices, wages and labor contracts, tenure pattern, and income from all sources. A special questionnaire was used for historical data (by recall) on technology adoption, fertilizer use, productivity, and land prices.

Village Characteristics

Table 6.2 presents selected socioeconomic characteristics of the villages by production environment. The man-land ratio, defined as the ratio of village population to the total cultivated area, is significantly higher in the irrigated and rainfed villages than in the upland villages despite an equal distribution of land to original migrant households. This disparity is explained partly by the fact that native inhabitants, who cultivate much larger areas than migrants, are included in the upland village sample and partly by the fact that spontaneous immigration took place in the lowland villages following the initial transmigration program.

Size of landownership and operational farm size is higher in the less favorable areas than in irrigated areas. Note also that farmers in irrigated and rainfed villages typically own some upland tracts. Owner cultivation dominates the tenure patterns, and the proportion of leasehold and share tenancy is highest in the more favorable rice-growing villages. Household size, number of working family members, and age of household head is highest in the rainfed villages; those in the irrigated and upland villages are fairly similar. Average education of household heads in all production environments is less than six years—i.e., less than a full primary school education.

Table 6.3 gives cropping patterns in the study area. Rice is grown twice a year in irrigated areas. The introduction of modern varieties in the mid-1970s made double cropping of rice also possible in certain favorable rainfed areas, where residual soil moisture remains after the wet season. Multiple cropping, including rice, is commonly practiced in the upland area.

MODERN VARIETIES, INPUT USE, AND PRODUCTIVITY

A key feature of this study is examination of the impact of changes in characteristics of modern varieties. Varieties bred at the International Rice Research Institute (IRRI) and in the Indonesian rice research system are currently grown. However, the first-generation varieties (IR5, IR8, and C4-63) have been completely replaced by the second-generation (IR36) and third-generation (IR64) modern varieties from IRRI, as well as by domestically bred varieties.

The Indonesian improved varieties are divided into IMV1 and IMV2 groups. IMV1 includes crosses of IR5 and Syntha (an Indonesian improved variety)—e.g., Pelita I-1 and Pelita I-2. IMV2 includes crosses between Pelita I-1 and other improved varieties and traditional varieties—e.g., Cisadane, Cimandiri, Cipunegara, Citarum, Citandui, Krueng Aceh, Semeru, and Sadang.

Current Patterns of Technology Adoption

Table 6.4 presents adoption rates and technology use for traditional varieties and different types of modern varieties by production environment.

The latest Indonesian-bred varieties (IMV2), particularly Cisadane and Krueng Aceh, dominate rice cultivation in the irrigated lowland villages for both growing seasons. In the rainfed lowland, IMV2 is also popular, but only in the wet season. IR36 covers almost half of the rainfed rice area, and IMV1 and IR64 each account for 22% in the dry season. The shorter growth duration of IR36 and the higher drought tolerance of IMV1 and IR64 make these varieties more suitable in rainfed areas. IR64, which was released only in the dry season of 1987, is expected to spread more widely.

Fertilizer use per hectare is significantly different among production environments, ranging from 82 kg/ha in the upland villages to 202 kg/ha in the irrigated lowland areas. Fertilizer use varies among breeds in the irrigated lowland but not in the rainfed lowland.

Application of pesticides, mainly insecticides and herbicides, is two to four times greater in the irrigated than in the rainfed areas; pesticide use in upland rice is minimal. Among varieties, the widest disparities in pesticide use is in irrigated areas. Average yield is higher in the more favorable production environments, and it generally increases with later generation modern varieties. Yields of all modern varieties are about the same in the rainfed lowland during the dry season and generally much lower than wet-season yields.

Modern variety adoption has often been reported to increase labor use per hectare by increasing labor requirements for crop care and harvesting (Barker and Cordova 1978; Otsuka, Gascon, and Asano 1994b). The pattern of labor use by task, production environment, season, and source is reported in Table 6.5. Labor use per hectare is not greatly different among different types of modern varieties within a production environment, but because no traditional varieties are grown in the lowlands, it is not possible to compare labor use per hectare between traditional and modern varieties.

Significant differences in labor use are observed between seasons and between lowland and upland areas. It should be noted that the variation in labor use is not due to differences in the degree of mechanization, because tractor adoption rate is low.

Almost all sample farms have adopted a simple thresher and use a sickle for harvesting. Lower labor use per hectare in upland areas is due mainly to differences in level of crop care, method of crop establishment, and lower yields—and, therefore, lower demand for harvesting and transplanting labor. Rice is transplanted in the irrigated and rainfed areas, whereas direct seeding is common in the upland area.

The higher proportion of hired labor in more favorable environments suggests that employment opportunities for the landless and near-landless farm households increase with adoption of modern varieties in these areas.

Fertilizer, Pesticide, and Labor Use Functions

Fertilizer, pesticide, and labor use functions in log-linear form were estimated to identify the effects of differences in varieties on input use. The input use function could be specified as a reduced-form equation using exogenous variables, including output and factor prices, as explanatory variables. Because paddy prices, fertilizer and pesticide prices, and wages are similar across villages in Lampung, the input use function per hectare was specified as a function of variables representing production environments, modern variety adoption, and socioeconomic characteristics. Note that choice of rice varieties may not be legitimately considered exogenous. The lack of exogenous variables, however, precluded the application of an instrumental variable method in this study.

Because the effects of rice varieties on factor use depend on the production environment, the production environment and varieties were specified as interaction terms. Thus, each of the three production environments—irrigated (IRG), rainfed (RF), and upland (UPLAND)—was expressed as a dummy variable and multiplied with dummy variables indicating variety or group of varieties (e.g., IRG*IR36). In upland areas, a distinction was made between traditional varieties planted as a single crop (UPLAND*TV) and those cultivated as part of a multiple cropping system (UPLAND*TV-MCT). The interaction term between rainfed lowland and the first generation of Indonesian modern varieties (RF*IMV1) served as the control in this set of environmental and technology variables.

Among the socioeconomic characteristics, the following variables were included: rice farm size in hectares (RFSIZE), tenure pattern as represented by the ratio of area under leasehold (LEASER) and share tenancy (SHARER), age of household head (AGE), years of schooling of household head (SCHOOL), and the number of workers in the family (WORKER). Except for the variables expressed as dummies and ratios, all continuous independent and dependent variables were specified in the natural logarithms in this and in all other functions estimated in later sections. However, linear specification of the dependent variable was also applied in estimating the Tobit model.

Table 6.6 presents the OLS estimates of fertilizer use functions of 1) lowland farmers by season and 2) the combined lowland and upland farmers during the wet season. Because some upland farmers do not use fertilizer at all, they were excluded in the estimation. However, the Tobit procedure was also applied to include all of the sample farms from both the lowland and upland villages. The results clearly indicate that newer modern varieties induced greater fertilizer use in the irrigated lowland areas during the wet season. Qualitatively, the same patterns are revealed in both the OLS and Tobit estimations based on the combined lowland and upland samples. Differences in fertilizer use between traditional upland varieties grown as monoculture or in multiple cropping systems (TV-MCT) also appear to exist. In contrast, there seems to be no significant difference in fertilizer use across varieties in the irrigated areas during the dry season or in the rainfed areas in almost all equations. The fact that more favorable production environments significantly affect fertilizer application implies that modern rice varieties have a greater response to fertilizer in favorable environments, especially in the irrigated environment.

The positive and significant effect of the leasehold tenure in three out of the four equations is somewhat surprising. Conversely, there is no significant effect for share tenancy. There is some indication that, at least in the lowland wet-season sample, smaller rice farms and younger farmers tend to apply higher rates of fertilizer.

Adoption of modern rice varieties is also associated with greater use of pesticides. Table 6.7 shows the regression results of pesticide use functions, which were estimated by the Tobit procedure because many sample farmers did not apply pesticides. Pesticide use appears to have increased with more recent varieties in the irrigated areas for both growing seasons. The coefficients of interaction terms between varieties and rainfed-lowland or upland production environments are not significant.

Continuous irrigated rice cropping creates environments hospitable to insects and diseases. Therefore, it is likely that continuous rice cropping, rather than the adoption of modern varieties, causes higher pesticide use in irrigated areas. Larger farms tend to apply higher rates of pesticides, particularly herbicides to save labor. Moreover, there is an indication that farms with a greater number of working family members tend to substitute labor for herbicides in weeding during the wet season. Age, schooling, and tenure are not significant explanatory variables.

Table 6.8 presents the estimation results of the labor use functions for preharvest and harvest labor. Production environment and varieties have a major effect on harvest labor during the wet season. That effect is consistent with the pattern of difference in yields observed earlier. Coefficients of the interaction terms between varieties and upland areas are significantly lower than those involving rainfed and irrigated areas for both preharvest and harvest labor. Some varieties, particularly IR64, IMV2, and IR36, appear to require greater preharvest labor. Among socioeconomic variables, larger farm size is clearly associated with lower labor use per hectare for preharvest and harvesting activities during both growing seasons. Age and years of schooling do not significantly affect labor use, but number of family workers slightly increases man-days of preharvest labor during the dry season. It is interesting to note that share tenants use more preharvest labor than owner-cultivators. Unexpectedly, the coefficients of the tractor-user dummy (TRUSER) are not significant in the preharvest labor regressions.

More interesting findings are shown by the regression results of labor-use functions disaggregated by family and hired labor (Table 6.9). Use of hired labor per hectare is significantly higher in the irrigated villages than in other environments. It is clear that the increase in labor demand resulting from modern variety adoption is met by hired labor, as none of the coefficients of the interaction terms between irrigation and varieties are significant in the family labor function for both seasons. There is also some indication that, at least for the irrigated areas, IR64 tends to require more hired labor than other modern varieties. For rainfed farms, family labor and hired labor both increase when modern varieties IMV2 and IR64 are grown during the wet season. In the dry season, however, there is no significant difference in labor use per hectare across varieties.

As expected, use of family labor decreases and use of hired labor increases as farm size increases, and family labor use declines as farmer age increases. Increase in the number of working members significantly raises family labor input and reduces hired labor. Leaseholding increases family labor use during the dry season, whereas share tenancy increases family labor use during both seasons.

Determinants of Land Productivity

Modern varieties increase land productivity by raising yield per hectare per season as well as by increasing cropping intensity. An attempt was made to identify the impact of varietal improvement on yield by estimating yield functions. The same set of exogenous variables as in the input use functions were specified.

The estimated yield functions (Table 6.10) clearly indicate that production environments and varieties are the important factors determining yields. Moreover, the pattern of the estimated coefficients of the interaction terms between production environment and varieties is consistent with a priori expectations—the adoption of more recent modern varieties has increased yields more significantly in the irrigated than in the rainfed lowlands. Because of the limited water supply, during the dry season in rainfed areas, varieties with shorter growth duration, such as IR36 and IR64, have higher yields than longer-growth-duration varieties, such as IMV1 and IMV2.

It should be noted that estimation results do not significantly change when the lowland and upland data are combined. In this equation, yields of upland rice under monoculture are found to be about 56% of IMV1 grown in the rainfed lowlands, slightly lower when grown in multiple cropping.

The coefficients of farm size and schooling are significant and of the expected signs in the wet season, but the magnitudes are comparatively small. Farmer's age, the number of working members, tenure, and tractor adoption, however, do not have a significant impact. Recent studies on the economics of tenancy strongly suggest that input use, technology choice, and productivity are not significantly affected by tenure status (Otsuka and Hayami 1988; Otsuka, Chuma, and Hayami 1992).

Historical Adoption of Modern
Varieties, Fertilizer Use, and Yields

Although the choice of rice varieties is determined by farmers, the availability of different generations of modern varieties is determined outside the village. Thus, the overall performance of the series of improved modern varieties can be evaluated more accurately by historical comparison based on time-series data than by cross-sectional comparison because of the exogenous nature of the availability of modern varieties.

The historical pattern of diffusion of different modern varieties in Lampung is depicted in Figure 6.2. The first-generation modern varieties from IRRI were adopted in a relatively small area in the mid-1970s and disappeared by 1980. The first Indonesian varieties, IMV1, spread over a larger area, but after 1977 their use declined. Although the adoption of IR36 leveled off in the 1980s, it continues to be planted over wide areas. The second-generation Indonesian varieties, IMV2, initially spread slowly, but by the mid-1980s their adoption surpassed that of IR36 by a wide margin.

To further examine the impact of varietal improvement on productivity, time-series data based on recall of sample farm households were used. Nearly all farmers had grown the various modern varieties on the same farm area. Therefore, it was possible to obtain information on average paddy yield, fertilizer use, and crop area associated with all rice varieties the farmers had grown.

According to farmers' recall, the modern varieties progressively produce higher yields (Table 6.11). The third-generation varieties produce yields more than double traditional varieties (TV) in irrigated areas in both seasons. Consistent with the findings from cross-sectional data, the increases in yields are lower in rainfed areas than in irrigated areas. Likewise, adoption of multiple cropping technology for upland rice also lowers yields over time despite higher application of fertilizer.

As expected, the changes in fertilizer use per hectare over time and differences in fertilizer use across production environments closely follow the pattern of modern variety adoption. It should be noted, however, that growth in fertilizer use is due not only to increased yield response to fertilizer but also to a favorable fertilizer-paddy price ratio resulting from substantial fertilizer price subsidies in the 1980s (Jatileksono 1987; Timmer 1989; Heytens 1991a).

To quantify the effects of changes in varieties on fertilizer use and paddy yields, equations similar to those used in earlier sections were estimated. Aside from the interaction terms between production environment and varieties, only farm size and schooling were retained as independent variables. In addition, however, the ratio of fertilizer price to paddy price was included. The sample observations were limited to owner-cultivators because tenants and leaseholders typically had only recently acquired tenancy rights. The upland sample was excluded because upland farmers grew no modern varieties. Because many sample farmers did not apply fertilizer, particularly in the earlier years, log-linear OLS regressions based only on fertilizer users were estimated along with a linear Tobit model fitted to all sample farmers.

The estimation results of the fertilizer use functions presented in Table 6.12 clearly show that changes in modern varieties over time have caused upward shifts in fertilizer use. As indicated by the coefficients of the interaction terms, these shifts have been more substantial in the irrigated than in the rainfed lowlands for both growing seasons. The second- and third-generation modern varieties apparently have induced greater increases in fertilizer use in the irrigated areas as compared with the rainfed low-lands.

The shifts in rice yield resulting from adoption of newer modern varieties can be observed from the regression coefficients in Table 6.13. The coefficient of RF*IR5 is not significant, indicating that IR5 yields the same amount as IMV1 in the rainfed lowland. Both of these varieties, however, have significantly higher yields than traditional varieties for both seasons. Adoption of IR36, IMV2, and IR64 progressively raised the yield functions in the rainfed lowland, but not as much as in irrigated areas. Not surprisingly, the estimated coefficients for the upland environment suggest that average yield of traditional varieties is significantly lower in that environment than in the rainfed lowland environment.

As noted earlier, the increase in fertilizer subsidies in the 1980s coincided with the introduction of IMV2 and IR64. The significant and negative coefficient of the fertilizer-paddy price ratio (FERTPP) indicates the significantly positive effects of fertilizer price subsidies on fertilizer use and yield. Even with subsidies taken into account, however, results similar to those for the analysis based on cross-section data were obtained, which strengthens the conclusion that newer modern varieties have increased fertilizer use and yields, particularly in the irrigated areas. Introduction of modern varieties and subsidies for fertilizer and irrigation have correspondingly raised productivity in the favorable rice-growing regions, thereby widening regional yield differentials.

VARIETAL IMPROVEMENT AND LAND PRICES

Land is the major production factor in rice cultivation. The effect of differential technology adoption on income distribution across production environments depends critically on how returns to land among adopters and nonadopters are affected (Chapter 3; Binswanger 1980; Evenson 1975). In this section I estimate the effects of modern varieties and production environments on returns to land over time. The relatively similar production environments among the study villages in the late 1960s and subsequent changes in irrigation and adoption of modern varieties in the study area provide a rare opportunity to identify the impacts of irrigation and modern varieties on the return to land.

Unfortunately, historical data on land rent were not available, and farmer recall of rents paid was poor. However, farmers who purchased land accurately recalled land price as well as the year of transaction. Instead of land rent, therefore, my focus is on the impact of varietal improvement on land prices based on the recall data for land prices. The main questions asked of farmers were: When did they buy the land, what was the parcel size, and how much did it cost? Was it an irrigated, rainfed-lowland or upland rice field; a dryland nonrice field; or a residential lot? What was the soil class? Had they adopted modern rice varieties before they bought the land? Among the 480 farm households, 160 land transactions (142 lowland parcels and 18 upland parcels) from 1969 to 1987 were reported.

Land price is not necessarily a good proxy for the current return to land, because price also reflects an expected increase in the future return to land (Alston 1986; Melichar 1979; Burt 1986; Castle and Hock 1982; Robison, Lins, and Venkataraman 1985; Reinsel and Reinsel 1979). If land rent grows at a constant rate of g% per year and the discount rate (r) is constant, the relation between land price (V_t) and land rent at year t (R_t) can be simply expressed (e.g., Alston 1986; Burt 1986; Melichar 1979; Shalit and Schmitz 1982) as

$$V_t = R_t/(r-g).$$

Accurate data on r and g are not readily available nor estimable; thus, they are assumed to be fixed over time. Land price then can be assumed to change proportionally with the current return to land, which implies that land price depends on the same exogenous variables determining land rentals identified in Chapter 3. Although restrictive, such assumptions may not be wholly untenable, for the following reasons. First, the construction of

---

Jatileksono and Otsuka (1993) is an expanded version of the section of this chapter headed "Varietal Improvement and Land Prices."

irrigation facilities and the adoption of modern varieties have essentially permanent effects on productivity and the return to land. Thus, farmers may not continuously change their expectation of future growth in returns to land because of changes in technology and production environment. Second, the real price of rice has been stable because of government market intervention, and the real price of fertilizer has been declining steadily as a result of a subsidy program. Price changes, therefore, might not cause substantial changes in farmers' expectation of future growth in the returns to land. Third, the government has provided subsidized credit for the purchase of production inputs such as fertilizer and pesticides at the fixed rate of 12% per year under the BIMAS (mass guidance) program since the late 1960s. Thus, r may be largely regarded as fixed.

Changes in Land Prices

Table 6.14 presents the number of land transactions, modern variety adoption rate, and land prices by production environment over time. The number of land transactions in irrigated and rainfed villages was about the same except during the recent period, when it accelerated more in the irrigated than in the rainfed villages. The average size of land transaction, conversely, tended to decline over time, mainly because of population pressure on a limited land supply. Population pressure seems to have been more pronounced in the irrigated and rainfed lowlands than in the uplands, where some mountainous areas remain unsettled.

Some farmers in the rainfed lowland had adopted modern varieties by 1970, and almost all farmers in the lowland area grew modern varieties by the mid-1970s. It is interesting to note from Table 6.14 and Figure 6.3 that land prices of irrigated and lowland areas in the early 1970s were about equal. This is as expected, because at that time most of the currently irrigated villages were still rainfed or inadequately irrigated. The price of irrigated lowlands increased sharply after the mid-1970s as a consequence of irrigation expansion and modern variety adoption. Further increases occurred in the 1980s as rice productivity continued to grow, in part because of adoption of improved modern varieties. The particularly rapid growth in real land prices in the irrigated villages since the early 1970s widened the gap in land prices across production environments. In fact, increases in real land prices in the rainfed areas were much smaller than in irrigated areas.

Such growth in land prices, particularly in the irrigated villages, cannot be explained solely by more favorable price incentives for rice, because the fertilizer-paddy price ratios changed significantly only in the early 1980s. It seems more reasonable to attribute the land price growth to the construction of irrigation facilities and the adoption of modern varieties in these areas. As a matter of fact, real land prices in upland areas, where no technological change took place, essentially remained constant.

Determinants of Land Price

According to Chapter 3, the reduced-form equation for the determination of land rental will depend on several factors. On the demand side, the relevant explanatory variables are those affecting the profitability of farming, such as input and paddy prices, technology, and production environments. On the supply side, man-land ratio, computed as the ratio of village population to cultivated area, can be a proxy for shifts in the land supply function. Another relevant variable affecting land price is distance from market center, which can be a proxy for access to urban markets. Although a farmer's decision to sell land may also depend on financial pressures arising from family or personal circumstance or from occupational and locational mobility (Herdt and Cochrane 1966), such situations must be assumed to be randomly occurring. Assuming changes in land rental to be proportional to land prices, a land price determination function in log-linear form was estimated.

The regression results are in Table 6.15. In the first equation, no distinction as to types of varieties was made. Production environment and varieties were specified simply as dummy variables for irrigation and modern variety adoption and as an interaction term between the two factors. These variables were indeed statistically significant, with the expected positive coefficients. Adoption of modern varieties and irrigation appear to contribute equally well to growth in rice productivity, as evidenced by the nearly equal estimated coefficients of these variables. The coefficient of the interaction term is considerably higher, suggesting a higher rate of increase in the land prices in irrigated, as opposed to rainfed lowland, areas as modern varieties were adopted.

Because profitability of rice farming will critically depend also on relative prices of paddy and inputs, fertilizer-paddy price ratio (FPPRICE) was inserted. The coefficient is highly significant and negative, as expected. Population pressure, as measured by man-land ratio (MLR), also drives up land prices. Only the coefficient of the distance variable (DISTC) is not significant, mainly because distance between village and town centers does not vary much across the sample villages.

As discussed in the previous section, newer modern varieties that are more fertilizer-responsive and have higher yields have been adopted in recent years. In equation (2) (Table 6.15), specific modern varieties or variety groups were paired in interaction terms with production environment. With this specification, the coefficients of the man-land ratio and fertilizer-paddy price ratio are not significant, nor is the distance variable. Most remarkable are the significance and magnitudes of the estimated coefficients of environment-variety interaction terms. The coefficients of RF*IR5, RF*IMV1, RF*IR36, and RF*IMV2 are highly significant and increase from

0.28 to 0.74, 1.00, and further to 1.43. These estimated coefficients imply that the adoption of improved modern varieties over time continuously increased land price and in recent years the land price in rainfed lowlands favorable to modern variety adoption increased to 4.1 times relative to land prices in rainfed areas planted to traditional varieties. These results indicate that the availability of improved modern varieties significantly and continuously contributed to the acceleration of productivity growth, even in rainfed areas.

The coefficient of IRG*TV is 0.45 and significant, implying that the land productivity improves with irrigation even in the absence of modern varieties. The value of land, however, dramatically increases with the adoption of modern varieties. In fact, the coefficient of IRG*IR5 is significantly larger than the coefficient of IRG*TV.

Improvement in the characteristics of modern varieties has further contributed to productivity growth in irrigated regions. The coefficient of IRG*IMV1 is 1.69, whereas the coefficient of IRG*IR36 is 1.99 and that for IRG*IMV2 is 2.19. The difference between the coefficient of IRG*IR5 and each of the latter three is significant. Thus, changing characteristics of modern varieties over time contributed to the increases in land values in irrigated areas. However, the rate of increase seems to be declining, which may indicate a declining contribution of modern varieties to productivity growth in the irrigated areas.

The estimated coefficients of the interaction terms between the modern variety variables and IRG are significantly larger than the corresponding coefficients of those modern variety variables interacted with RF. It seems clear that by increasing both rice cropping intensity and rice yields, the adoption over time of a series of improved modern varieties brought about larger increases in land prices in irrigated areas than in rainfed areas.

Even when the regression is based on the combined lowland and upland price data, as shown in equation (3) (Table 6.15), the results are essentially unchanged. Distance, man-land ratio, and fertilizer-paddy price ratio remain not significant, and the coefficients of the interaction terms are only slightly lower than those in equation (2). The coefficient of the upland dummy is 0.48, implying that the land price in upland areas is 61% higher than the price in rainfed lowlands planted to traditional varieties. This conclusion is not unreasonable, because the price of upland areas generally reflects the value of other crops grown in those areas.

The results of this statistical analysis strongly indicate that adoption of a series of improved modern varieties in favorable production environments significantly increases the productivity of land. However, the additional contribution of the most recent modern varieties over earlier ones seems rather limited, particularly in the irrigated area, which suggests that there will be growing difficulty in making further improvements to the modern varieties.

MODERN VARIETY IMPROVEMENT AND INCOME DISTRIBUTION

Agricultural technology affects farmers' income by influencing factor demand and factor prices, which, in turn, induce changes in allocation of farmers' own resources to different uses. In addition, the supply shift of agricultural product resulting from technical change will affect output price and thus crop choice.

In this section I attempt to identify the impact of varietal improvement on factor earnings and household income among producer groups across regions based on the cross-section data for 1987–1988.

Factor Income in Rice Farming

Table 6.16 presents product and factor prices in rice farming. There is no important price discrepancy among modern varieties in irrigated and rainfed lowland areas. Traditional varieties planted in upland areas command a higher price than modern rice varieties from the lowland areas because of their better quality. Paddy prices in the dry season are generally higher than in the wet season, but the differences are less than 10% and primarily reflect the effects of inflation. Differences in paddy prices reported by farmers may also be due to other factors (e.g., differences in moisture content and cleanliness) that cannot be easily measured.

The Indonesian government sets equal fertilizer prices across village unit cooperatives throughout the country. Thus, the small price variation of urea observed across production environments simply reflects differences in transportation cost. The wage rate for hoeing is higher in the more favorable areas, but the difference is only 12% or less. The wage rate for transplanting and weeding is generally higher for male than for female workers, although no specific pattern can be found across production environments. The rental of bullocks is higher in the dry season than in the wet season.

To quantify the differences in factor earnings among production environments, the conventional accounting technique was followed (see, e.g., Ranade 1977; Barker and Herdt 1985). The gross returns of rice per hectare were distributed among groups of factors of production. Returns to current inputs equaled the sum of expenses on seeds, fertilizer, and pesticides. Returns to hired capital included payment for use of draft animals and machines for land preparation, plus water fees for irrigation. Returns to hired labor were calculated as the sum of the hired labor man-days for all operations multiplied by the corresponding wage rates, including the value of food provided in the case of daily contracts; in the case of output-sharing contracts, this factor was simply measured as the value of output paid to hired laborers. Returns to owned capital and family labor were imputed using rental rate for hired capital and wage rate for hired labor, respectively. Finally, return to land was estimated as residual by subtracting total costs of current inputs, capital, and labor from the gross value of output.

The computed factor earnings and factor shares are presented in Table 6.17. The gross returns in rice farming in irrigated villages are more than double that in upland villages. Gross returns in the rainfed villages are about 82% of those in irrigated villages during the wet season and 67% during the dry season. These figures indicate that modern varieties are less productive during the dry season than during the wet season in the rainfed area. The absolute returns to current inputs, rented capital, hired labor, and the residual are substantially higher in the more favorable areas. In terms of factor shares, however, there are less pronounced patterns. Broadly observed, owners of each factor input receive a proportionally larger income from a given land in more favorable areas. The much higher value of the residual in the more favorable environments corresponds to the fact that both the differences in production environments and the differential adoption of modern varieties create significant gaps in the returns to land across the survey villages. The residual is much smaller in the upland area because of a low return to land as well as single rice cropping. The surplus, defined as the difference between the residual and cash land rent, was higher in the more favorable areas during the wet season, but it was higher in the rainfed than in the irrigated area during the dry season.

Sources and Determinants of Household Income

The analysis presented in the previous subsection highlighted the effects of technology on functional distribution of rice income. Household income, however, is determined not only by the distribution of rice income but also by the possession of productive resources such as land, human capital, and capital assets, as well as by market and institutional factors such as opportunities for nonrice production, access to nonfarm employment opportunity, and land tenure. In this section, factors affecting differential level of household income are examined. Household income was decomposed by source—i.e., rice production by factor ownership, other farm income, and nonfarm income.

Table 6.18 shows the average annual income of farm households by source and by production environment. Rice production accounts for slightly more than half of total household income in the irrigated villages, with returns to land having by far the highest contribution. In less favorable areas, income from rice cultivation as a whole, as well as returns to land, is relatively small. However, nonrice income in the less favorable areas is higher absolutely than in the irrigated villages, which suggests that the lower income from rice production in less favorable environments is substantially compensated for by allocation of more family resources to production of other crops and livestock and to nonfarm activities. Total household incomes in the rainfed and upland villages are, respectively, about 88% and 75% of that in the irrigated villages. It should be noted that farm income in the upland villages does not substantially differ from that in other villages, mainly because of larger farm size in the upland compared to the rainfed and irrigated villages.

Income determination functions for rice are estimated separately for the wet and dry seasons and for component incomes decomposed into imputed returns to family labor, owned capital, and income from land (net of rent payment for tenant farmers). The land income reflects not only the returns to land but also returns to management and errors in imputing income of family labor and owned capital. In estimating the determinants of rice income, each component was regressed on the interaction terms between production environments and various modern varieties and socioeconomic characteristics— i.e., rice farm size, tenure pattern, ownership of draft animals, age, schooling of household head, and number of working members.

The estimation results of rice income determination functions shown in Table 6.19 are remarkably consistent with a priori expectations. Production environments as well as types of varieties clearly affect returns to land, labor, and, to some extent, capital income. Upland rice clearly provides lower returns. Whereas farms in irrigated areas obtain higher returns from access to land, rainfed farms receive relatively more labor income than irrigated farms in the wet season, although the opposite is true in the dry season. This result is consistent with the earlier observation that irrigated farms using modern varieties employ relatively more hired labor than rainfed farms. Irrigated farms earn greater labor income in the dry season simply because the majority of rainfed farmers do not plant a second crop of rice. There seems to be no difference in capital income between irrigated and rainfed farms, as only two out of the twelve coefficients are significant.

Within the irrigated environment during the dry season, IMV2 and IR64 bring a higher return to land than older modern varieties, such as IR36. In the rainfed environment during the dry season, IR64 seems to raise the land income as well as the labor income most significantly. IMV2 and IR64 have the largest effects on the return to land in both irrigated and rainfed areas during the wet season.

Farm size is one of the most important variables affecting all of the different components of rice farm income for both growing seasons. The coefficient of farm size in the land income equation is close to unity, suggesting constant returns to scale in rice farming. Larger farms provide more income opportunities to landless and near-landless farm households, as evidenced by the coefficients of farm size in the labor and capital income equations, which are significantly less than unity. Schooling of household head has no significant effect on any of the income components from rice farming. The coefficients of the tenure variables in both seasons confirm expectations that leaseholders, and especially share tenants, would obtain much less income from land than owner-operators. However, share tenants in particular, and leaseholders during the dry season, allocate more family labor and thus obtain more labor income from rice farming than owner-operators. It is obvious that ownership of bullocks (ANOWNER) significantly affects the capital income from rice farming.

The econometric analysis of determinants of total annual household income and its different components (i.e., rice, nonrice, and nonfarm incomes) is reported in Table 6.20. The same explanatory variables were specified except for the interaction terms, which this time were between production environments and two rice varieties grown in the wet and dry season. The control variable pertained to rainfed farms growing any modern varieties during the wet season and growing nonrice crops or lying fallow during the dry season.

The rice income equation shows the best statistical fit, with an R^2 of 0.86. Except for age, schooling, and number of working members, all the coefficients are highly significant and have the expected signs. The size of land, including its tenure pattern and quality, and ownership of bullocks also significantly explain differences in rice income across farm households. The coefficients of leasehold and share tenancy are equal despite leaseholders' lower rent payments because share tenants devote relatively more family labor to rice farming. The ability to plant a second crop and control water matter, as evidenced by significant differences in the coefficients across upland, rainfed lowland, and irrigated farms. The effect of difference in varieties planted seems most pronounced in the irrigated areas. Moreover, it is quite clear that in both the irrigated and the rainfed areas, IMV2 and IR64 provide the highest income.

Although the size of rice land (RFSIZE), nonrice land (NRFSIZE), and ownership of bullocks (ANOWNER) explain nonrice farm income, it is interesting to note that the characteristics of the family labor force— specifically, age of the household head and number of working members— significantly determine the size of nonfarm income. The negative coefficients of age, rice farm size, and bullocks in the nonfarm income equation simply imply that farm households who have younger heads, less rice area, and other assets devote more family labor time for nonfarm employment. This suggests that the smaller income in rice farming in less favorable production environments is compensated for by income from other sources of employment.

Household Income Distribution

The effects of varietal improvement on household income distribution were examined by a decomposition analysis of the Gini measure of income inequality as developed by Fei, Ranis, and Kuo (1978) and Pyatt, Chen, and Fei (1980) (see Chapter 3 for details).

Table 6.21 shows the estimated overall Gini ratios and the absolute contributions of factor components measured by the product of income share, rank correlation ratio, and component Gini ratio. The overall Gini ratios based on total household income are not significantly different across production environments. In fact, the ratio is slightly lower in more favorable villages, as shown by the Lorenz curves (Figure 6.4a). The Gini ratios of income components suggest that income generated from nonfarm activities and returns to owned capital in rice farming are most unevenly distributed among farm households in any production environment. Moreover, the distribution of income from nonrice farming is more skewed than that of land income or family labor earnings from rice farming.

In the irrigated villages, the most important source contributing to the overall income inequality is nonfarm activities (38%), followed by nonrice farming (29%) and returns to land in rice farming (27%). In the rainfed villages, it is nonrice farming (55%), followed by nonfarm activities (35%), whereas in the upland villages it was almost solely nonrice farming (91%).

The pooled data of all households show that the most important source contributing to the overall income inequality is nonrice farming (55%), followed by nonfarm activity (25%) and land income from rice farming (16%). Family labor income is more equally distributed, whereas the distribution of capital income is clearly more skewed than the overall income (Figure 6.4b). However, the inequality of capital income does not significantly contribute to the overall income inequality because its share in total income is quite small.

Gini ratios based on per capita income were also estimated to take account of differences in family size. The distribution of overall income is generally more unequal for per capita income than for household income, as are individual income components, indicating that lower-income households tend to have larger family size. It is also clearly shown that income distribution is more uneven in the upland area, in which modern varieties were not grown. Income distribution in the rainfed area is only slightly less equitable than in the irrigated areas. In terms of contributions of the various income sources to income inequality, the patterns are similar to those of household income.

The fact that adoption of newer modern varieties increases land income from rice farming in the irrigated area more than in the rainfed lowland and upland areas suggests that overall income inequality will increase in Indonesia. The contribution of newer modern varieties to overall income inequality, however, is largely offset by substantially greater contributions from nonrice farming and nonfarm employment. Thus, modern variety improvement does not seriously contribute to overall income inequality among farm households across rice production environments in Lampung.

RESEARCH SHOULD CONTINUE

Examination of the variations in performance of different generations of modern varieties across production environments in Lampung clearly indicates that improvements in the characteristics of modern varieties—specifically, greater pest resistance, higher tolerance for adverse production environments, better grain quality, and shorter growth duration—have led to their wide adoption. The only exception is in the upland areas, where traditional varieties continue to be grown.

Analysis of the Lampung data also clearly shows that the more recently released modern varieties are more fertilizer-responsive and thus produce progressively higher yields. Yet improvements in the modern varieties have had a greater impact in the irrigated areas than in the rainfed lowlands.

Analysis of the distributional consequences of differential technology adoption in this study focuses on its impact on returns to land. It was clearly demonstrated that productivity growth resulting from modern variety adoption in the favorable rice-growing areas increases land prices. Consistent with patterns of yield growth, increases in land price for irrigated areas have been higher than for rainfed areas. During the same time, land values in upland areas bypassed by the new technology have tended to stagnate.

Despite the greater disparity in returns to land between favorable and unfavorable rice-production environments, distribution of household income has not significantly worsened. Moreover, profitable nonrice income opportunities exist in less favorable areas so that family labor and land are reallocated to production and employment in nonrice farming and the nonfarm sector. In consequence, upland farmers are generally not much poorer than other farmers.

In other words, the trade-off between efficiency and equity associated with the diffusion of modern varieties is not as severe as commonly thought. Therefore, rice research for the favorable rice-growing areas should continue. In addition, research investment is also warranted where there is potential to develop modern technologies for the nonrice food and commercial crops grown in the less favorable environments.

Figure 6.1   Location of study areas, intensive survey, Lampung, Indonesia, 1987–1988

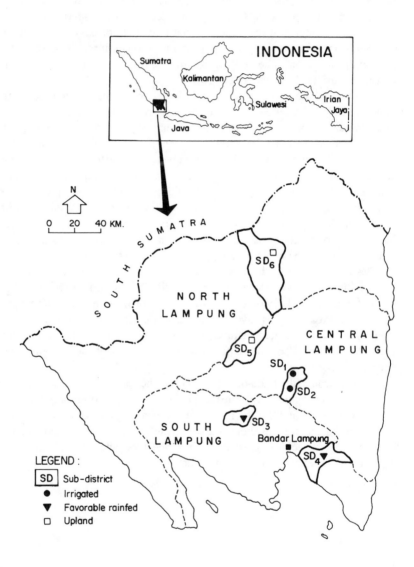

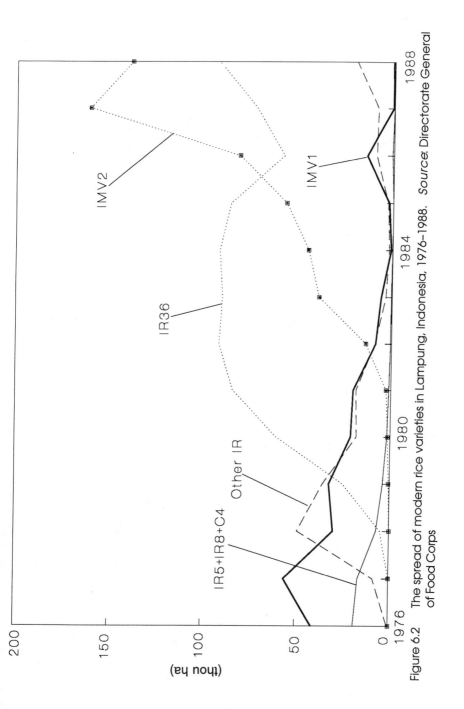

Figure 6.2   The spread of modern rice varieties in Lampung, Indonesia, 1976–1988.   *Source:* Directorate General of Food Corps

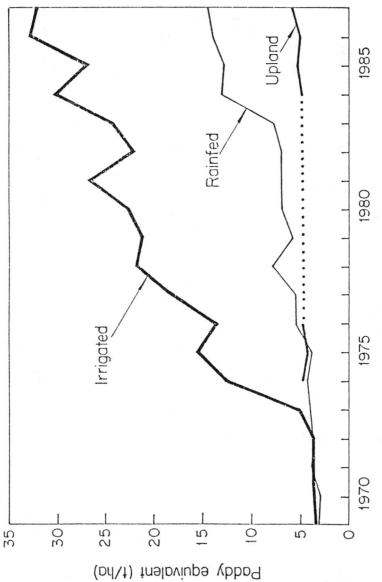

Figure 6.3   Trends in land prices, Lampung, Indonesia, 1969–1987

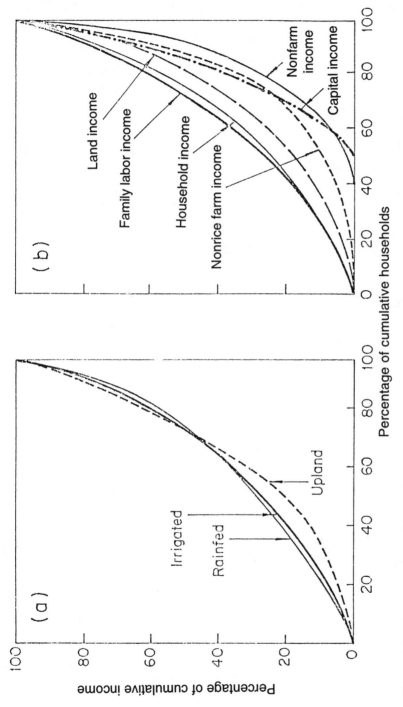

Figure 6.4   Lorenz curves of household incomes, intensive survey, Lampung, Indonesia, 1987–1988

Table 6.1   Selected indicators of Lampung compared to Java and Indonesia, 1961–1988. Sources: Statistical Yearbook of Indonesia 1975, 1983, and 1989.

Selected indicators	Years	Lampung	Java	Indonesia
Physical area (thou km^2)		33	132	1,919
Irrigated lowland (thou ha)		128	2,523	4,315
Rainfed lowland (thou ha)		53	894	2,215
Upland (thou ha)		119	347	1,213
Population (millions)	1961	1.7	63	97
	1988	6.9	105	176
Population growth (%)	1961–1971	5.3	1.9	2.1
	1971–1980	5.8	2.0	2.3
	1980–1985	5.0	1.8	2.2
Population density (person/km^2)	1961	50	476	15
	1988	207	800	91
Paddy yield (t/ha)	1971	1.6	2.8	2.4
	1980	2.5	3.9	3.3
	1988	3.4	4.8	4.1
Rice production per capita (kg)	1971	93	111	115
	1980	101	137	137
	1988	123	161	159

Table 6.2   Socioeconomic characteristics of villages and farm house-holds by production environment, intensive survey, Lampung, Indonesia, 1987–1988.

	Irrigated	Rainfed	Upland
Sample villages (no)	4	4	4
Man-land ratio (person/ha)[a]	6	7	2
Ratio of landless households (%)	5	4	2
Sample farm households (no)	160	160	160
Land ownership (ha)	1.3	1.7	2.2
Lowland	0.9	1.0	-
Upland	0.4	0.7	2.2
Operational farm size (ha)	1.3	1.6	1.9
Rice farm	0.9	0.9	1.5
Other crops	0.4	0.7	0.4
Tenure of rice farm (%)			
Owner	85	89	98
Leasehold	5	4	0
Share tenancy	10	7	2
Farm household characteristics			
Household size	5.7	6.3	5.6
Family workers (no)[b]	3.6	4.0	3.6
Age of household head	47.0	51.0	45.0
Years of schooling of head	5.4	3.8	4.5

a. Ratio of village population to cultivated area.
b. Family members between fifteen and sixty-five years old.

Table 6.3   Cropping patterns by production environment (% of area), intensive survey, Lampung, Indonesia, 1987–1988.

Cropping pattern	Irrigated	Rainfed	Upland
Rice-rice	100	27	0
Rice–nonrice food crop[a]	0	61	0
Rice-fallow	0	12	18
Multiple cropping including rice	0	0	82
Rice cropping intensity (%)	200	127	100
Total cropping intensity (%)	200	188	182

a. Includes maize, peanut, mungbean, soybean, cassava.

Table 6.4   Technology adoption, input use, and paddy yield by varieties, season, and production environment, intensive survey,
Lampung, Indonesia, 1987–1988.

	Wet season			Dry season	
	Irrigated	Rainfed	Upland	Irrigated	Rainfed
Variety adoption (% of area)[a]					
TV[b]	0	0	100	0	0
IMV1	0	16	0	0	22
IR36	6	5	0	27	48
IMV2	92	69	0	70	8
IR64	2	10	0	3	22
Fertilizer use (kg NPK/ha)					
TV	—	—	82	—	—
IMV1	—	105	—	—	113
IR36	179	118	—	190	108
IMV2	183	117	—	177	117
IR64	202	118	—	183	116
Pesticide use (thou Rp/ha)					
TV	—	—	1.7	—	—
IMV1	—	6.4	—	—	8.5
IR36	26.6	16.5	—	21.3	7.8
IMV2	36.5	18.2	—	38.4	8.8
IR64	46.4	9.6	—	24.2	6.4
Yield (t/ha)					
TV	—	—	1.76	—	—
IMV1	—	2.80	—	—	2.52
IR36	4.22	3.37	—	3.64	2.67
IMV2	4.46	3.57	—	4.04	2.64
IR64	4.49	3.46	—	4.19	2.77
Labor use (man-days/ha)					
TV	—	—	85	—	—
IMV1	—	162	—	—	131
IR36	175	170	—	146	133
IMV2	177	188	—	142	140
IR64	182	176	—	154	141
Tractor adoption (% of farms)	5	0	0	5	0

a. IMV1 includes crosses between IR5 and the national improved variety, Syntha:
Pelita I-1 and Pelita I-2. IMV2 includes crosses between Pelita I-1 (IMV1) and other
improved varieties: Cisadane, Krueng Aceh, etc.
b. TV = traditional variety.

Table 6.5   Labor use (man-days/ha) in rice farming by season, source, production environment, and task, intensive survey, Lampung, Indonesia, wet and dry season, 1987–1988.

Activities	Wet season			Dry season		
	Family	Hired	Total	Family	Hired	Total
Irrigated villages						
Land preparation	13	8	21	12	7	19
Seedlings and						
transplanting	8	25	33	7	28	35
Crop care	32	12	44	31	12	42
Harvesting	11	48	59	9	38	47
Total	63[a]	93	156	59	84	143
Rainfed villages						
Land preparation	21	7	28	19	5	24
Seedlings and						
transplanting	9	31	40	5	16	21
Crop care	43	6	49	43	4	48
Harvesting	11	47	58	11	32	43
Total	83	91	174	78	57	135
Upland villages						
Land preparation	9	3	12			
Planting	6	12	17			
Crop care	18	5	23			
Harvesting	4	14	19			
Total	36	34	70			

a. Total may not equal sum of activities because of rounding.

Table 6.6   Regression results of fertilizer use (per ha) functions, intensive survey, Lampung, Indonesia, wet and dry season, 1987–1988.[a]

	OLS			Tobit
	Lowland		Lowland + upland	Lowland + upland
	Wet season (1)	Dry season (2)	Wet season (3)	Wet season (4)
Intercept	5.14	4.90	4.65	127.36
RF*IR36	0.13 (1.20)	−0.07 (−0.87)	0.13 (0.85)	13.93 (0.55)
RF*IMV2	0.10 (1.59)	0.07 (0.71)	0.08 (0.93)	13.03 (0.98)
RF*IR64	0.16* (1.85)	0.11 (1.13)	0.17 (1.40)	18.58 (0.92)
IRG*IR36	0.51** (4.77)	0.58** (7.33)	0.50** (3.55)	69.05** (3.88)
IRG*IMV2	0.60** (9.48)	0.51** (6.73)	0.59** (7.07)	82.88** (6.37)
IRG*IR64	0.71** (4.21)	0.48** (2.46)	0.69** (3.04)	99.26* (1.92)
UPLAND*TV	—	—	−0.62** (−5.30)	−54.16** (−3.79)
UPLAND*TV–MCT	—	—	−0.23** (−2.50)	−20.11 (−1.48)
Ln RFSIZE	−0.04* (−1.72)	−0.02 (−0.83)	0.002 (0.07)	0.50 (0.10)
LEASER	0.19* (1.65)	0.27* (2.23)	0.19 (1.25)	33.09** (2.33)
SHARER	0.13 (1.57)	0.09 (1.00)	0.14 (1.28)	14.65 (1.16)
Ln AGE	−0.14* (−1.79)	−0.08 (−0.83)	−0.003 (−0.03)	−5.39 (−0.52)
Ln SCHOOL	−0.001 (−0.07)	0.003 (0.34)	−0.001 (−0.18)	0.21 (0.23)
Ln WORKER	−0.007 (−0.17)	0.02 (0.40)	−0.03 (−0.54)	−3.33 (−0.60)
R^2	0.49	0.51	0.52	—
F-value	24.83	19.82	34.64	—
Samples (no)	320	240	469	480
Log likelihood	—	—	—	−2,394

a. Numbers in parentheses are t-statistics.
** Indicates significance at 1% level; * at 5% level.

Table 6.7   Regression results of pesticide use (per ha) functions, intensive survey, Lampung, Indonesia, wet and dry season, 1987–1988.[a]

	Lowland		Lowland + upland
	Wet season (1)	Dry season (2)	Wet season (3)
Intercept	13.08	0.14	13.92
RF*IR36	2.84	0.49	2.92
	(0.33)	(0.07)	(0.37)
RF*IMV2	5.99	1.92	5.48
	(0.88)	(0.22)	(0.89)
RF*IR64	1.76	–0.61	1.51
	(0.18)	(–0.01)	(0.17)
IRG*IR36	13.68*	13.21**	14.21*
	(1.82)	(2.72)	(2.09)
IRG*IMV2	24.70**	26.59**	24.31**
	(3.73)	(5.65)	(4.07)
IRG*IR64	34.45**	27.64*	34.78**
	(2.98)	(2.16)	(3.25)
UPLAND*TV	—	—	–7.99
			(–1.24)
UPLAND*TV-MCT	—	—	–5.28
			(–0.84)
Ln RFSIZE	3.74**	2.55*	4.32**
	(2.34)	(1.95)	(3.55)
LEASER	3.39	3.28	2.82
	(0.53)	(0.52)	(0.48)
SHARER	4.18	0.28	0.96
	(0.84)	(0.07)	(0.23)
Ln AGE	1.02	3.03	0.77
	(0.23)	(0.57)	(0.20)
Ln SCHOOL	0.10	0.18	0.14
	(0.30)	(0.44)	(0.52)
Ln WORKER	–5.46**	–1.18	–4.74**
	(–2.56)	(–0.70)	(–2.65)
Samples (no)	320	240	480
Log-likelihood	–1,252	–917	–1,749

a. Numbers in parentheses are t-statistics.
** Indicates significance at 1% level; * at 5% level.

Table 6.8   Regression results of labor use (per ha) functions disaggregated into preharvest and harvest labor, intensive survey, Lampung, Indonesia, wet and dry season, 1987–1988.[a]

	Wet season		Dry season	
	Preharvest labor (1)	Harvest labor (2)	Preharvest labor (3)	Harvest labor (4)
Intercept	4.58	3.40	4.45	3.72
RF*IR36	0.16	0.30**	–0.03	–0.17*
	(1.46)	(2.40)	(–0.59)	(–2.20)
RF*IMV2	0.31**	0.35**	0.007	–0.06
	(4.96)	(4.86)	(0.10)	(–0.60)
RF*IR64	0.17*	0.33**	0.16*	–0.14
	(1.97)	(3.30)	(2.13)	(–1.48)
IRG*IR36	0.14	0.43**	0.20**	0.05
	(1.39)	(3.65)	(3.50)	(0.59)
IRG*IMV2	0.06	0.36**	0.16**	0.11
	(1.05)	(5.20)	(2.90)	(1.51)
IRG*IR64	0.14	0.52**	0.20	0.24*
	(0.84)	(2.73)	(1.38)	(1.88)
UPLAND*TV	–0.30**	–0.48**	—	—
	(–3.81)	(–5.12)		
UPLAND*TV-MCT	–0.19**	–0.43**	—	—
	(–3.50)	(–6.61)		
TRUSER	0.05	—	0.02	—
	(0.56)	—	(0.32)	—
Ln RFSIZE	–0.18**	–0.13**	–0.12**	–0.14**
	(–9.13)	(–5.62)	(–5.30)	(–4.85)
LEASER	0.02	0.10	0.10	0.10
	(0.16)	(0.80)	(1.15)	(0.83)
SHARER	0.22**	0.10	0.11*	0.12
	(2.80)	(1.06)	(1.78)	(1.43)
Ln AGE	–0.04	0.08	–0.04	0.002
	(–0.57)	(0.96)	(–0.57)	(0.02)
Ln SCHOOL	0.004	–0.005	–0.005	0.005
	(0.82)	(–0.94)	(–0.03)	(0.65)
Ln WORKER	0.02	–0.004	0.05*	–0.01
	(0.48)	(–0.11)	(1.69)	(–0.28)
R^2	0.68	0.80	0.18	0.18
F-value	64.34	131.58	3.91	4.36
Samples (no)	480	480	240	240

a. Numbers in parentheses are t-statistics.
** Indicates significance at 1% level; * at 5% level.

Table 6.9   Regression results of labor use (per ha) functions disaggregated into family and hired labor, intensive survey, Lampung, Indonesia, wet and dry season, 1987–1988.[a]

	Wet season		Dry season	
	Family labor (1)	Hired labor (2)	Family labor (1)	Hired labor (2)
Intercept	4.67	4.08	4.70	3.73
RF*IR36	0.36**	0.007	–0.08	–0.11
	(2.35)	(0.05)	(–0.84)	(–1.62)
RF*IMV2	0.31**	0.26**	–0.06	0.01
	(3.51)	(3.02)	(–0.48)	(0.13)
RF*IR64	0.24*	0.20*	0.14	–0.07
	(2.00)	(1.72)	(1.26)	(–0.74)
IRG*IR36	0.06	0.40**	–0.12	0.38**
	(0.40)	(2.84)	(–1.36)	(5.43)
IRG*IMV2	–0.05	0.34**	–0.04	0.30**
	(–0.64)	(4.13)	(–0.43)	(4.62)
IRG*IR64	–0.02	0.51*	–0.04	0.50**
	(–0.10)	(2.23)	(–0.17)	(2.87)
UPLAND*TV	–0.18	–0.75**	—	—
	(–1.61)	(–6.77)		
UPLAND*TV-MCT	–0.33**	–0.06	—	—
	(–4.29)	(–0.84)		
TRUSER	–0.03	0.04	–0.05	0.06
	(–0.19)	(0.29)	(–0.42)	(0.72)
Ln RFSIZE	–0.39**	0.09**	–0.29**	0.06*
	(–13.68)	(3.12)	(–8.49)	(2.21)
LEASER	0.04	0.05	0.27*	–0.006
	(0.25)	(0.35)	(2.00)	(–0.05)
SHARER	0.36**	0.009	0.34**	–0.05
	(3.01)	(0.08)	(3.51)	(–0.70)
Ln AGE	–0.20*	0.08	–0.21*	0.11
	(–2.07)	(0.87)	(–1.99)	(1.38)
Ln SCHOOL	–0.00	0.00	–0.00	0.00
	(–0.03)	(0.13)	(–0.42)	(0.24)
Ln WORKER	0.16**	–0.18**	0.12**	–0.06
	(3.34)	(–3.72)	(2.51)	(–1.46)
R^2	0.63	0.66	0.36	0.45
F-value	52.18	60.11	9.81	14.00
Samples (no)	480	480	240	240

a. Numbers in parentheses are t-statistics.
** Indicates significance at 1% level; * at 5% level.

Table 6.10   Regression results of paddy yield functions, intensive survey, Lampung, Indonesia, wet and dry season, 1987–1988.[a]

	Lowland		Lowland + upland
	Wet season (1)	Dry season (2)	Wet season (3)
Intercept	8.02	7.40	7.77
RF*IR36	0.17* (3.61)	0.11* (1.85)	0.17* (2.36)
RF*IMV2	0.24** (8.47)	0.07 (0.85)	0.25** (5.82)
RF*IR64	0.20** (5.39)	0.17* (2.22)	0.21** (3.60)
IRG*IR36	0.38** (8.31)	0.50** (8.28)	0.39** (5.55)
IRG*IMV2	0.46** (16.91)	0.58** (10.11)	0.47** (11.40)
IRG*IR64	0.47** (6.49)	0.63** (4.21)	0.47** (4.20)
UPLAND*TV	—	—	-0.58** (-10.58)
UPLAND*TV-MCT	—	—	-0.66** (-14.56)
TRUSER	0.02 (0.36)	-0.09 (-1.20)	0.02 (0.31)
Ln RFSIZE	-0.03** (-2.44)	-0.03 (-1.32)	-0.02* (-1.72)
LEASER	-0.05 (-0.94)	-0.001 (-0.01)	-0.04 (-0.48)
SHARER	0.03 (0.83)	0.03 (0.45)	0.05 (1.01)
Ln AGE	-0.02 (-0.61)	0.09 (1.23)	0.04 (0.88)
Ln SCHOOL	0.004* (1.77)	0.002 (0.28)	0.007* (2.03)
Ln WORKER	-0.005 (-0.29)	-0.008 (-0.23)	-0.008 (-0.33)
R^2	0.62	0.55	0.88
F-value	38.31	21.23	228.57
Samples (no)	320	240	480

a. Numbers in parentheses are t-statistics.
** Indicates significance at 1% level; * at 5% level.

Table 6.11   Paddy yield and fertilizer use based on historical data by production environment, season, and varieties, intensive survey, Lampung, Indonesia, 1987–1988.

Environment, season, variety	Yield (t/ha)	Fertilizer (kg/ha)[a]			
		Urea	TSP	KCl	ZA
Irrigated					
Wet season					
TV	1.93	40	25	0	0
IR5	3.47	192	128	0	0
IMV1	3.62	206	138	0	0
IR36	3.44	201	142	5	3
IMV2	4.37	246	204	41	9
IR64	4.49	269	154	77	77
Dry season					
TV	1.74	55	34	0	0
IR5	2.92	183	125	0	0
IMV1	3.03	219	139	0	0
IR36	3.14	202	131	14	4
IMV2	3.89	250	212	28	16
IR64	4.19	243	208	35	35
Rainfed					
Wet season					
TV	1.90	0	0	0	0
IR5	2.76	85	58	0	0
IMV1	2.81	105	69	0	0
IR36	2.82	146	111	0	0
IMV2	3.14	176	141	2	0
IR64	3.46	172	136	11	0
Dry season					
TV	1.75	0	0	0	0
IR5	2.60	114	85	0	0
IMV1	2.67	142	98	0	0
IR36	2.84	154	126	0	0
IMV2	2.70	174	110	0	0
IR64	2.77	192	137	5	0
Upland					
Wet season					
TV	1.18	59	28	0	0
TV-MCT	0.90	136	72	18	0

a. TSP is triple superphosphate, KCl is potassium chloride, and ZA is ammonium sulfate.

Table 6.12   Regression results of fertilizer use (per ha) functions based on historical data in the lowland area, intensive survey, Lampung, Indonesia, wet and dry season, 1987–1988.[a]

	OLS		Tobit	
	Wet season (1)	Dry season (2)	Wet season (3)	Dry season (4)
Intercept	4.41	4.44	40.71	24.41
RF*TV	—	—	-225.79 (-0.04)	-78.90 (-0.76)
RF*IR5	0.008 (0.14)	0.11 (1.42)	2.39 (0.43)	26.16** (3.82)
RF*IR36	-0.01 (-0.12)	-0.02 (-0.27)	30.11 (0.84)	29.64** (3.35)
RF*IMV2	0.17** (3.39)	0.02 (0.17)	38.47** (6.49)	23.15* (2.10)
RF*IR64	0.11 (1.10)	0.27** (2.39)	43.35** (2.38)	75.45** (2.36)
IRG*TV	-1.02** (-15.75)	-1.11** (-13.94)	-31.24** (-3.44)	3.14 (0.15)
IRG*IR5	0.15* (1.96)	0.01 (0.11)	78.46** (5.69)	76.22** (2.80)
IRG*IMV1	0.21** (2.77)	0.16* (1.83)	73.21** (4.63)	78.45** (4.71)
IRG*IR36	0.29** (5.95)	0.28** (4.28)	65.08** (8.95)	87.39** (10.31)
IRG*IMV2	0.63** (13.27)	0.61** (8.53)	112.86** (16.46)	130.14** (11.61)
IRG*IR64	0.74** (3.66)	0.64** (2.56)	129.92 (0.64)	123.30* (1.95)
Ln FPPRICE	-0.04 (-0.44)	0.10 (0.89)	-65.12** (-6.06)	-38.34** (-2.83)
Ln RFSIZE	-0.17** (-7.70)	-0.18** (-6.34)	-15.64** (-5.28)	-20.12** (-4.43)
Ln SCHOOL	0.007 (1.60)	0.01 (1.69)	0.56 (0.86)	0.94 (0.87)
R^2	0.63	0.69	—	—
F-value	97.54	90.85	—	—
Samples (no)	750	502	1,048	565
Log-likelihood	—	—	-4,188	-2,812

a. Numbers in parentheses are t-statistics.
** Indicates significance at 1% level; * at 5% level.

Table 6.13   Regression results of paddy yield functions based on historical data, intensive survey, Lampung, Indonesia, wet and dry season, 1987–1988.[a]

	Lowland		Lowland + upland
	Wet season (1)	Dry season (2)	Wet season (3)
Intercept	7.85	7.77	7.88
RF*TV	–0.30** (–7.95)	–0.35* (–1.86)	–0.30** (–9.04)
RF*IR5	0.04 (1.20)	0.01 (0.26)	0.03 (0.78)
RF*IR36	0.05 (0.79)	0.10* (1.77)	0.05 (0.57)
RF*IMV2	0.11** (3.88)	0.06 (0.91)	0.11** (2.73)
RF*IR64	0.18** (2.77)	0.20** (2.57)	0.19* (2.28)
IRG*TV	–0.29** (–8.00)	–0.30** (–6.02)	–0.29** (–5.96)
IRG*IR5	0.28** (5.89)	0.23** (3.01)	0.29** (4.58)
IRG*IMV1	0.29** (5.79)	0.25** (4.36)	0.31** (4.59)
IRG*IR36	0.25** (8.42)	0.28** (6.94)	0.26** (6.47)
IRG*IMV2	0.47** (16.04)	0.48** (10.59)	0.48** (12.19)
IRG*IR64	0.48** (3.49)	0.55** (2.99)	0.50** (2.71)
UPLAND*TV	—	—	–0.99** (–25.17)
UPLAND*TV-MCT	—	—	–1.27** (–32.14)
Ln FPPRICE	–0.10* (–1.89)	–0.04 (–0.62)	–0.10 (–1.31)
Ln RFSIZE	–0.05** (–4.30)	0.003 (0.15)	–0.004 (–0.28)
Ln SCHOOL	0.004* (1.79)	0.006 (1.38)	0.002 (0.51)
R^2	0.59	0.47	0.76
F-value	104.40	34.87	264.20
Samples (no)	1,048	565	1,347

a. Numbers in parentheses are t-statistics.
** Indicates significance at 1% level; * at 5% level.

Table 6.14   Number and size of land transactions, modern variety adoption, and land price by period and production environment, intensive survey, Lampung, Indonesia, 1969–1987.

	Irrigated	Rainfed	Upland
Transactions (no)			
1969–1973	14	15	0
1974–1978	15	14	3
1979–1983	16	15	0
1984–1987	35	18	15
Size of transaction (ha)			
1969–1973	0.41	0.75	—
1974–1978	0.53	0.64	2.00
1979–1983	0.42	0.67	—
1984–1987	0.26	0.45	1.83
Modern variety adoption (% of area)			
1969–1973	0	7	0
1974–1978	84	91	0
1979–1983	100	100	0
1984–1987	100	100	0
Land price (t/ha paddy equivalent)			
1969–1973	3.9	3.5	—
1974–1978	16.3	5.4	4.6
1979–1983	23.3	6.9	—
1984–1987	30.5	13.5	5.3

Table 6.15   Regression results of land price determination functions, intensive survey, Lampung, Indonesia, 1987–1988.[a]

	Lowland		Lowland + upland
	(1)	(2)	(3)
Intercept	8.18	8.00	7.99
IRG	0.39** (2.13)	—	—
MV	0.42** (3.77)	—	—
IRG*MV	0.67** (3.40)	—	—
RF*IR5	—	0.28** (2.81)	0.27** (2.86)
RF*IMV1	—	0.74** (5.09)	0.71** (5.57)
RF*IR36	—	1.00** (5.14)	0.97** (5.61)
RF*IMV2	—	1.43** (9.95)	1.40** (11.31)
IRG*TV	—	0.45** (3.15)	0.44** (3.22)
IRG*IR5	—	1.22** (8.82)	1.21** (9.10)
IRG*IMV1	—	1.69** (15.50)	1.69** (16.08)
IRG*IR36	—	1.99** (12.31)	1.97** (13.66)
IRG*IMV2	—	2.19** (15.62)	2.16** (18.13)
UPLAND	—	—	0.48** (3.98)
Ln DISTC	0.03 (0.70)	–0.01 (–0.23)	–0.00 (–0.05)
Ln MLR	0.14* (1.76)	0.07 (1.07)	0.08 (1.40)
Ln FERTPP	–1.00** (–6.86)	0.04 (0.21)	0.01 (0.04)
R^2	0.84	0.91	0.91
F-value	117.53	108.84	118.54
Samples (no)	142	142	160

a. Numbers in parentheses are t-statistics.
** Indicates significance at 1% level; * at 5% level.

Table 6.16   Paddy and urea prices, wage rates, and rental of capital by season and production environment, intensive survey, Lampung, Indonesia, 1987–1988.

	Wet season			Dry season	
	Irrigated	Rainfed	Upland	Irrigated	Rainfed
Paddy price (Rp/kg)					
TV	—	—	215	—	—
IMV1	—	189	—	—	195
IR36	180	180	—	196	195
IMV2	187	197	—	195	197
IR64	190	190	—	200	198
Urea price (Rp/kg)	129	128	135	130	130
Wage (Rp/day)					
Hoeing	1,978	1,848	1,789	1,993	1,784
Transplanting					
Male	1,838	1,763	—	1,881	—
Female	1,439	1,378	—	1,452	1,521
Weeding					
Male	1,696	1,763	1,519	1,729	1,777
Female	1,503	1,457	1,565	1,510	1,456
Bullock rental (Rp/day)	3,604	3,278	3,474	3,781	3,854
Tractor rental (Rp/hour)	3,109	—	—	3,340	—

Table 6.17   Factor payments (thou Rp/ha) and factor shares (%) of rice farm by production environment, intensive survey, Lampung, Indonesia, wet and dry season, 1987–1988.[a]

	Wet season			Dry season	
	Irrigated	Rainfed	Upland	Irrigated	Rainfed
Gross value of output	830 (100)	681 (100)	323 (100)	768 (100)	515 (100)
Current inputs	120 (14)	80 (12)	65 (20)	115 (15)	65 (13)
Capital	90 (11)	71 (10)	46 (14)	84 (11)	65 (13)
Owned	22 (3)	32 (5)	19 (6)	22 (3)	22 (4)
Hired	68 (8)	39 (6)	27 (8)	62 (8)	43 (8)
Labor	300 (36)	303 (44)	121 (38)	319 (42)	188 (37)
Family	99 (12)	119 (18)	43 (13)	94 (12)	91 (18)
Hired	202 (24)	183 (27)	79 (24)	225 (29)	97 (19)
Residual	320 (39)	228 (34)	90 (28)	250 (33)	197 (38)
Cash land rent	174 (21)	101 (15)	67 (21)	174 (23)	101 (20)
Surplus	146 (18)	127 (19)	23 (7)	76 (10)	96 (19)
Farm income[b]	441 (53)	379 (57)	152 (47)	366 (48)	310 (60)

a. Numbers in parentheses are percentages of total gross value of output.
b. The sum of returns to owned capital and family labor plus residual.

Table 6.18   Average annual income (thou Rp) of farm households by production environment, intensive survey, Lampung, Indonesia, 1987–1988.

Source of income	Irrigated	Rainfed	Upland
Rice production	724	447	251
Labor[a]	171	126	65
Capital[b]	40	33	29
Land[c]	513	288	157
Nonrice farm income	368	514	708
Land rental earnings	100	79	26
Off-farm wage earnings	53	37	18
Nonrice food crops		22	278
Perennial crops; vegetables	124	196	290
Livestock, poultry, fishery	91	180	96
Nonfarm income[d]	317	276	103
Total income	1,409	1,237	1,062
Household size	5.7	6.3	5.6
(no of working members)[e]	(3.6)	(4.0)	(3.6)
Income per person	247	196	190
(per working member)	(391)	(309)	(295)

a. Imputed family labor income in owned farms.
b. Imputed return to owned machineries and carabao.
c. Residual for owner-cultivators and residual minus actual rent payments for tenants.
d. Includes labor earnings from nonfarm employment, other assets, pensions, and remittances.
e. Above fifteen and below sixty years old.

Table 6.19   Regression results of rice income functions disaggregated by factor income, intensive survey, Lampung, Indonesia, wet and dry season, 1987–1988.[a]

	Wet season			Dry season		
	Land (1)	Labor (2)	Capital (3)	Land (4)	Labor (5)	Capital (6)
Intercept	11.25	11.73	−0.003	11.00	11.60	−1.73
RF*IR36	0.12 (0.60)	0.31* (2.02)	−0.27 (−0.68)	0.22 (1.18)	−0.12 (−1.30)	0.76* (1.70)
RF*IMV2	0.42** (3.51)	0.48** (5.28)	−0.23 (−1.02)	0.11 (0.44)	−0.12 (−0.98)	0.20 (0.35)
RF*IR64	0.43** (2.61)	0.29** (2.37)	−0.40 (−1.27)	0.39* (1.61)	0.22* (1.85)	−0.06 (−0.11)
IRG*IR36	0.64** (3.24)	0.12 (0.81)	−0.54 (−1.45)	0.37* (1.93)	0.25** (2.73)	0.06 (0.13)
IRG*IMV2	0.71** (6.12)	0.22** (2.59)	−0.51* (−2.31)	0.70** (3.87)	0.31** (3.54)	0.21 (0.48)
IRG*IR64	0.69* (2.18)	0.13 (0.54)	−0.52 (−0.87)	0.90* (1.91)	0.40* (1.77)	−0.44 (−0.39)
UPLAND*TV	−0.62** (−4.08)	−0.32** (−2.76)	−0.52* (−1.79)	—	—	—
UPLAND*TV-MCT	−0.80** (−6.24)	−0.45** (−4.66)	−0.48* (−1.99)	—	—	—
Ln RFSIZE	0.97** (24.68)	0.66** (22.25)	0.30** (4.05)	0.92** (12.50)	0.65** (18.25)	0.44** (2.52)
LEASER	−1.13** (−5.34)	0.02 (0.15)	−0.27 (−0.66)	−2.15** (−7.48)	0.24* (1.73)	−0.53 (−0.78)
SHARER	−1.87** (−12.63)	0.30** (2.65)	−0.25 (−0.89)	−2.17** (−10.60)	0.34** (3.48)	−0.33 (−0.68)
ANOWNER	0.01 (0.17)	−0.03 (−0.69)	10.42** (107.71)	−0.14 (−1.56)	0.07 (1.68)	9.94** (47.71)
Ln AGE	0.18 (1.37)	−0.18* (−1.76)	0.14 (0.54)	0.27 (1.26)	−0.20* (−1.89)	0.47 (0.91)
Ln SCHOOL	0.02 (1.63)	−0.01 (−0.82)	−0.00 (−0.11)	0.01 (0.65)	−0.004 (−0.36)	0.03 (0.72)
Ln WORKER	−0.01 (−0.28)	0.12** (2.42)	0.06 (0.50)	−0.19 (−1.19)	0.17** (3.36)	0.14 (0.57)
R^2	0.75	0.64	0.97	0.66	0.79	0.92
F-value	74.57	55.38	953.98	33.68	65.01	205.62
Samples (no)	480	480	480	240	240	240

a. Numbers in parentheses are t-statistics.
** Indicates significance at 1% level; * at 5% level.

Table 6.20   Regression results of annual household income functions by source, intensive survey, Lampung, Indonesia, 1987–1988.[a]

	Rice income	Nonrice income	Nonfarm income
	(1)	(2)	(3)
Intercept	12.53	13.90	20.57
RF*IMV1–IR36	0.35**	–0.16	–0.19
	(5.12)	(–0.30)	(–0.13)
RF*IMV2–IR36	0.48**	–0.27	–1.84
	(5.88)	(–0.42)	(–1.10)
RF*IMV2–IMV2	0.45**	–0.85	–2.44
	(4.09)	(–0.97)	(–1.08)
RF*IMV2–IR64	0.52**	–0.48	–0.66
	(6.28)	(–0.73)	(–0.39)
IRG*IR36–IR36	0.52**	0.12	–0.17
	(4.58)	(0.14)	(–0.07)
IRG*IMV2–IR36	0.66**	0.32	–1.11
	(11.57)	(0.71)	(–0.94)
IRG*IMV2–IMV2	0.76**	0.43	0.91
	(17.29)	(1.25)	(1.01)
IRG*IMV2–IR64	0.83**	0.11	1.75
	(6.17)	(0.10)	(0.63)
UPLAND*TV	–0.77**	–0.82	–0.68
	(–12.01)	(–1.61)	(–0.51)
UPLAND*TV–MCT	–0.96**	0.52	–1.006
	(–23.06)	(1.57)	(–1.17)
Ln RFSIZE	0.83**	–0.40*	–1.45**
	(34.25)	(–2.09)	(–2.90)
Ln NRFSIZE	0.03*	0.89**	–0.27
	(1.98)	(8.55)	(–0.98)
LEASER	–0.78**	–0.06	4.05
	(–6.57)	(–0.07)	(1.56)
SHARER	–0.78**	0.49	0.47
	(–9.55)	(0.75)	(0.28)
ANOWNER	0.16**	0.80**	–1.55**
	(5.62)	(3.48)	(–2.61)
Ln AGE	0.06	–0.46	–4.02**
	(0.81)	(–0.77)	(–2.57)
Ln SCHOOL	0.00	–0.05	0.08
	(0.75)	(–1.19)	(0.78)
Ln WORKER	0.03	–0.42	2.06**
	(0.79)	(–1.39)	(2.64)
R^2	0.86	0.23	0.12
F-value	162.02	7.86	3.35
Samples (no)	480	480	480

a. Numbers in parentheses are t-statistics.
** Indicates significance at 1% level; *at 5% level.

Table 6.21   Income shares, Gini ratios, and contribution of income components by production environment, intensive survey, Lampung, Indonesia, 1987–1988.

Environments	Total income	Rice income			Nonrice income	
		Land	Family labor	Owned capital	Farm	Nonfarm
Income shares						
Irrigated	1.000	0.333	0.127	0.030	0.274	0.236
Rainfed	1.000	0.191	0.107	0.028	0.439	0.235
Upland	1.000	0.130	0.062	0.028	0.681	0.099
Pooled	1.000	0.227	0.102	0.029	0.447	0.196
Gini ratios based on household income						
Irrigated	0.347	0.394	0.288	0.725	0.531	0.725
Rainfed	0.363	0.363	0.286	0.664	0.552	0.744
Upland	0.385	0.470	0.306	0.594	0.535	0.681
Pooled	0.369	0.476	0.354	0.675	0.568	0.743
Percentage contribution of household income components						
Irrigated	100	27	4	2	29	38
Rainfed	100	7	2	1	55	35
Upland	100	8	–1	2	91	0
Pooled	100	16	2	2	55	25
Gini ratios based on per capita income						
Irrigated	0.370	0.435	0.333	0.740	0.539	0.732
Rainfed	0.371	0.394	0.338	0.681	0.567	0.734
Upland	0.425	0.488	0.298	0.622	0.561	0.687
Pooled	0.396	0.507	0.390	0.689	0.592	0.743
Gini ratios based on individual income						
Irrigated	0.350	0.419	0.309	0.714	0.533	0.713
Rainfed	0.371	0.399	0.328	0.690	0.559	0.720
Upland	0.440	0.497	0.287	0.643	0.590	0.660
Pooled	0.394	0.498	0.367	0.692	0.595	0.726

7

Modern Variety Adoption, Factor-Price Differential, and Income Distribution in Thailand

∎

SOMPORN ISVILANONDA AND SARUN WATTANUTCHARIYA

Improvements in infrastructure, extension work, and public research have supported sustained agricultural growth and increasing crop diversification in Thailand over the past four decades. Between 1970 and 1988 rice production almost doubled, largely because of crop area expansion and to a lesser extent because of increases in yields per hectare. Rice declined in importance in Thai agriculture, but it remains a dominant crop and a major export.

The modern rice varieties developed at IRRI and elsewhere in Asia are suited to favorable production environments, notably irrigated areas (Barker and Herdt 1985). In Thailand, however, only 24% of the rice-growing area is irrigated. Furthermore, modern varieties generally have low-quality grain by Thailand's standards, which require high quality for the export market.

Research to adapt modern rice varieties to Thai conditions has been under way since the late 1960s (Jackson, Panichapat, and Awakul 1969). By 1985, however, modern varieties were grown in only 13% of the nation's total rice area and were concentrated largely in irrigated areas of the Central Plain. That adoption pattern has important implications for the regional productivity differential and income distribution.

The yield gap between favorable and unfavorable rice-production environments has widened. Fears are widely expressed in Thailand that the productivity differential has created a regional income disparity (World Bank 1986). Moreover, a strategy to increase rice production through wider dissemination of modern varieties in favorable areas may further worsen regional income distribution (Lipton and Longhurst 1989; Falcon 1970).

The distributional effects of modern rice technology on rice farmers and farm laborers depend on the characteristics of the new technology—its factor-use bias, scale neutrality, and environmental or locational specificity.

This chapter is based on Isvilanonda, Wattanutchariya, and Otsuka (1992).

Previous studies show that the adoption of modern varieties directly increases the demand for labor by raising labor requirements for crop care, harvesting, and threshing (Barker and Cordova 1978; Otsuka, Gascon, and Asano 1994b) and by increasing cropping intensity (Bartsch 1977; Barker and Herdt 1985).

Changes in factor use in favorable rice-production environments cause changes in factor demands and factor prices in those areas, calling for adjustments in interregional factor markets. The greater the mobility of labor, the greater the adjustment of labor markets to the differential adoption of modern varieties. The adjustment of the labor markets through migration affects the land market: An increased man-land ratio in favorable production environments will increase demand for cultivated land and thus increase rental values. The rental value of land will also increase in favorable areas because of technological change. Thus, income disparity between favorable and unfavorable areas is expected to arise largely from the land income differential but not necessarily from the labor income differential.

In this chapter we examine the differential impact of modern rice technology on income distribution among rural households across different production environments in Thailand. An extensive survey collected village-level information on production environments, adoption of new technology, yield, and factor and output prices across wide areas. An intensive survey obtained detailed information on rice production and on incomes of farmer and landless-laborer households by source.

VILLAGE SURVEYS

Two sets of data were collected. The first was from an extensive survey of seventy-one villages in six provinces representing irrigated and nonirrigated areas in the North, Northeast, and Central Plain regions (Figure 7.1). Villages where deepwater rice are grown in the Central Plain were included. The second set of data was taken from an intensive survey of six villages in the provinces of Suphan Buri in the Central Plain and Khon Kaen in the Northeast (Figure 7.2). Ban Koak (KK1) is an irrigated village; Ban Kaina (KK2) and Ban Meng (KK3) are rainfed villages in Khon Kaen. In Suphan Buri, Wang Yang (SP1), Sa Ka Chome (SP2), and Jora Khae Yai (SP3) represent irrigated, rainfed, and deepwater environments, respectively.

Extensive Survey

Villages for the extensive survey were selected from six major rice-growing provinces in proportion to the relative importance of rice production in the provinces—sixteen villages from the North, twenty-two from the Northeast, and thirty-three from the Central Plain. Because irrigation is the most important determinant of production environments, villages were first stratified by the presence of irrigation, and then sample villages were randomly selected. Villages with gravity irrigation systems constructed and maintained by the Royal Irrigation Department were considered favorable production environments. Villages dependent on rainfall were further classified into rainfed and deepwater categories. A group interview with the village headman and knowledgeable farmers collected information on technology adoption, factor prices, and the socioeconomic characteristics of village households, such as farm size and tenure, in the 1986 wet season.

The distribution of sample villages and their socioeconomic characteristics by region and by production environment are seen in Table 7.1. Irrigated farms are smaller than rainfed farms in each region, and irrigated farms in the North are smallest (0.9 ha). Note that although the farm size data in Table 7.1 are for cultivated area during the wet season, some farmers in deepwater areas grow rice in some parts of their lands only during the dry season. Thus, the average total cultivated area will substantially exceed 5.3 hectares in this environment.

Consistent with the patterns of farm size by production environment, the man-land ratio, defined as the ratio of population to cultivated area, is highest in irrigated areas. At the same time, there are relatively more landless households in the irrigated areas of all regions. The percentage of owner-cultivators is only slightly different among irrigated and rainfed villages within regions, but wide variations exist across regions. Villages in the North and Northeast are located relatively close to large regional centers (Chiang Mai and Khon Kaen, respectively), whereas villages in the Central Plain are far from Bangkok.

Double cropping of rice is not common in the North and Northeast (Table 7.2). By contrast, most of the irrigated area in the Central Plain is double cropped in rice. Dry-season irrigation water is usually insufficient in the Northeast, and 40% of the irrigated area grows a single rice crop. Rice-fallow is the most common cropping pattern in nonirrigated areas, but some farms grow a crop after rice because of a relatively even rainfall pattern.

Intensive Survey

The intensive-survey villages were selected to represent the different production environments. An October 1987 census provided information on general characteristics of households, demographic data, history of migration and changes in technology, and landownership patterns. Sample farms for the intensive survey were randomly selected in accordance with proportions of the tenure groups. Because of the limited number of landless households, almost all were interviewed. The survey was conducted during the wet and dry seasons to obtain accurate information on farm and nonfarm activities for the 1988 crop year. Table 7.3 shows the farm size and other characteristics of the sample villages.

Despite the higher man-land ratio in the favorable areas, the ratio of landless households is relatively small, even smaller than in the less favorable areas. Permanent migration of landless agricultural laborers from less favorable to favorable areas is not common in Thailand because of the availability of unexploited land and employment opportunities in big cities. Seasonal migration is common, however. Landless family members migrate seasonally to find construction work in cities. They also have access to fisheries for more than six months each year.

Tenure patterns in the Northeast differ somewhat from those of the Central Plain. There are relatively more owner-operators in Khon Kaen than in Suphan Buri. In contrast to the Khon Kaen area, which was opened for cultivation relatively recently, Suphan Buri is an old settled area, and absentee landlordism prevails. Share tenancy is most prevalent in KK3—22% of the total cultivated area—and may be preferred because of irregular rainfall and unstable yields. Leasehold tenancy is more common in the more favorable areas except for SP3.

Cropping patterns in the intensive-survey villages in Khon Kaen and Suphan Buri are quite similar (Table 7.4). Most of the rainfed areas (SP2, KK2, and KK3) grow rice in the wet season only. Only a small portion of land can be planted to other crops. During the dry season, rice land is pasture for draft animals. The deepwater area has special characteristics: Because the land is flooded for six months or more each year, only traditional floating rice varieties are grown. However, deepwater areas adjacent to canals, which provide water for irrigation, are usually left idle during the wet season, plowed as soon as the water has drained away during the early dry season, and planted to rice. Thus, the deepwater area grows either a single wet-season or a single dry-season rice crop.

MODERN VARIETY ADOPTION
AND PRODUCTIVITY DIFFERENTIAL

Relatively low population pressure on land resources, the high quality requirement of the export market, and the small proportion of irrigated rice area were all important reasons for the slow adoption of IRRI modern rice varieties in Thailand (Sriswasdilek 1973). National research worked to develop varieties suited specifically to the Thai domestic and international markets.

In 1969, a series of Thai varieties, RD1, RD2, and RD3, were released by domestic rice breeders in collaboration with IRRI. By 1988, nineteen RD-type rice varieties had been released. Most of those were not photoperiod-sensitive (Setboonsarng, Wattanutchariya, and Puthigorn 1988). Seven (RD5, RD6, RD8, RD13, RD15, RD17, and RD19) were photoperiod-sensitive; RD varieties with even numbers are nonglutinous rice.

The modern RD varieties have gained acceptance among Thai farmers in irrigated areas, especially in the Central Plain. An important acceptance factor is that they are not photoperiod-sensitive, which enables farmers to increase cropping intensity as well as yield.

Production Environments,
Modern Variety Adoption, and Productivity

The modern variety adoption rate increased in all regions from 1980 to 1986, suggesting that the rice economy in Thailand is changing from total dependence on traditional varieties to more widespread adoption of modern varieties.

The adoption of modern varieties is lower in the North and Northeast than in the Central Plain (Table 7.5). The low adoption rates are explained mainly by the fact that farmers in the two regions grow glutinous rice for their own consumption; only a few glutinous rices can be classified as modern varieties.

Because of the fertilizer responsiveness of the RD varieties, fertilizer application has increased in the irrigated areas of the Central Plain. No fertilizer is applied in deepwater areas, where low-yielding, traditional floating rice is generally grown. Other than in those two areas, fertilizer use is similar, which suggests that choice of varieties is most closely related to fertilizer responsiveness.

Yields of modern varieties are generally higher than those of traditional varieties, particularly in the irrigated areas of the Central Plain. This characteristic partly explains why modern varieties have been most widely adopted in that area. However, it is also important to observe that the yields of traditional varieties in irrigated areas of the North are almost as high as the yields of modern varieties in the Central Plain, reflecting the relatively higher soil fertility and milder climate in the North, as well as improvements in traditional glutinous varieties. Low average yields in the Northeast reflect its unfavorable, drought-prone environment.

Determinants of Modern Variety Adoption

The probability of adoption of a new technology critically depends on the difference in profitability between the old and the new. Also important is the farmer's ability, often measured by education, farming experience, and exposure to extension services, to perceive an advantage and efficiently use the new technology.

For our study, farmer-specific variables were not available, and only village-specific variables were used. Modern variety adoption was hypothesized to be determined by environmental factors in the form of irrigation ratio (IRGR) and socioeconomic factors as indicated by paddy price (PADDYP), distance to regional center (DISTC), farm size (FSIZE), and owner-cultivator ratio (OWNERR). Distance was supposed to capture the influence of urban centers on wages, other input prices, and access to new information. The owner-cultivator ratio was used to capture the possible impact of differences in land tenure on technology adoption. The linear relation was specified, and the two-limit probit regression method developed by Rosett and Nelson (1975) was used to explain rate of modern variety adoption (MVR), defined as the ratio of area planted to modern varieties. Three regional dummies (NORTH, NORTHEAST, and DPWATER) were inserted to capture the effect of region-specific environments, particularly rainfall patterns and flooding.

Regression results of the modern variety adoption function are shown in Table 7.6. The estimated coefficient of irrigation ratio is positive and highly significant, confirming the critical importance of irrigation in the adoption of modern varieties. The coefficient of the NORTHEAST dummy is negative and significant, which seems to reflect the adverse impact of an unfavorable production environment on modern variety adoption. Despite the better natural environment for rice production in the North, the coefficient of the NORTH dummy is negative and significant. This result is primarily due to quality preference for improved glutinous rice varieties over modern varieties.

The coefficient of farm size (FSIZE) is unexpectedly negative but significant at the 5% level according to the two-tailed t-test, implying that small farm size is not a constraint on the adoption of modern varieties in Thailand. Tenure does not significantly affect the adoption rate of modern varieties, either, as has been found in other countries (see Chapters 4, 5, and 8–10). Because access to credit is positively associated with farm size and landownership (Feder et al. 1988), our findings suggest that credit is not a major constraint on modern variety adoption.

Determinants of Fertilizer Use and Land Productivity

Because modern varieties are not photoperiod-sensitive and are responsive to fertilizer, their adoption is expected to increase the use of fertilizer, yield per hectare, and cropping intensity—and have a profound impact on land productivity. In estimating the determinants of fertilizer use, yield, and cropping intensity functions, the recursive equation system was assumed. Thus, the ratio of modern variety area was included as an explanatory variable in these functions, along with the same set of the exogenous variables used in estimating the modern variety adoption function. The ordinary least squares technique was used for the estimation.

The regression results shown in Table 7.6 indicate that irrigation plays a significant role in increasing use of fertilizer, yield, and cropping intensity. The estimated coefficients imply that the presence of irrigation increases fertilizer application by 53 kg/ha, the wet-season yield by 1 t/ha, and cropping intensity by 85%. As expected, modern variety adoption has significant effects on fertilizer use and yield but not on cropping intensity.

Thus, modern varieties are high-yielding but do not necessarily promote higher cropping intensity. This conclusion is consistent with the fact that traditional glutinous rice varieties dominate in the North and Northeast, as well as the fact that cash crops are widely grown after rice in these regions. Note, however, that the adoption of modern varieties may have increased rice cropping intensity in the Central Plain.

It is remarkable that the NORTH dummy has a significant coefficient in yield and cropping intensity functions. This result implies that the North has a climate favorable to the production of rice and other crops. In contrast, the effect of nearly six months of flooding in the deepwater rice areas, as captured by the coefficient of the DPWATER dummy, seems particularly negative on fertilizer use.

The positive and significant coefficient of DISTC in the fertilizer use equation is unexpected. Fertilizer is used most intensively in irrigated areas of the Central Plain, and many of these areas are far from Bangkok. Fertilizer transportation costs are frequently subsidized through institutions such as farm cooperatives.

In summary, unequal access to irrigation, coupled with differential modern variety adoption across production environments and regions, results in significant productivity differential in rice farming in Thailand.

MODERN VARIETY ADOPTION AND LABOR DEMAND

Increased land productivity achieved by the adoption of modern varieties requires higher labor use, especially for crop care, harvesting, and threshing. Intensive use of farm land resulting from increased cropping intensity also raises the labor requirement. The upward shift in labor demand would affect wage rates positively in favorable areas and may act as an inducement to adopt labor-saving technology, particularly tractors, threshers, and direct seeding (pregerminated direct seeding and broadcasting methods).

We first examined the determinants of labor-saving technology adoption using village-level data from the extensive survey. The set of farm-level data from the intensive survey was then used to estimate the determinants of labor use.

Modern Varieties and Labor-Saving Technology

If high demand for labor makes wage rates relatively high in the favorable rice-growing areas, labor-saving technology may be introduced, as predicted by the theory of induced innovation (Hayami and Ruttan 1985; Binswanger and Ruttan 1978). In Thailand, labor-saving technologies, particularly tractors, were introduced long before the advent of modern varieties. However, the imported tractors were used for the cultivation of upland crops, especially in opening new land. The importation of large tractors increased sharply after the construction of highways to the North and Northeast during the early 1950s. Contract tractor service spread rapidly and was used in broadcast rice areas in the Central Plain (Wattanutchariya 1983).

Small tractors, or power tillers, were imported from Japan during the early 1960s. Those were simplified by local manufacturers, and locally produced two- and four-wheel tillers and tractors were rapidly adopted in irrigated areas, particularly in the Central Plain. Increased cropping intensity in irrigated areas, improvement of farm income, and the low interest rate of agricultural credit were major factors in stimulating farmers in irrigated areas to adopt the power tillers (Onchan 1983).

Table 7.7 shows the adoption rates of tractors, threshers, and direct seeding, which are known to be labor-saving (Binswanger 1978; Jayasuriya and Shand 1985; Otsuka, Gascon, and Asano 1994b). Mechanization tended to be more widespread in more favorable areas. The major exception was deepwater areas, where the adoption of both tractors and threshers was already complete by 1986. Large farm areas without bunds, as well as quick flooding when the rainy season started, increased the comparative advantage of using large tractors in the deepwater areas.

Mechanical threshers were introduced in the Central Plain during the 1970s. No adoption was reported in 1980, but by 1986 they had been fully adopted in the Central Plain. In irrigated areas of the North and Northeast, the thresher adoption rate was higher in irrigated than in rainfed areas, partly because they save turnaround time required to plant a second crop.

Transplanting has been a traditional method of rice crop establishment in Thailand, except in rainfed and deepwater areas of the Central Plain, where the instability of rainfall or uncontrollable flooding necessitates direct seeding as soon as the first rain comes. In the irrigated area of the Central Plain, pregerminated direct seeding was introduced to replace transplanting and has been increasingly adopted in recent years. This conversion may suggest that modern variety technology raised labor demand and wage rates, which in turn induced the adoption of a labor-saving crop-establishment method.

The mechanization and diffusion of new methods of crop establishment continue to spread in Thailand. As Schultz (1975) argued, an economy characterized by rapid changes in technology is likely to be in a state of dynamic disequilibrium and moving toward a new, long-run equilibrium. In such an adjustment process, substantial wage differentials across environments may be observed. These differentials, however, may be reduced as labor-saving technology, which reduces labor demand and wage rates, is adopted in favorable rice-growing areas.

Determinants of Adoption of Labor-Saving Technology

In addition to the ratio of irrigated area and modern variety adoption rate, farm size (FSIZE), paddy price (PADDYP), distance from regional center

(DISTC), and ratio of owner-cultivated area (OWNERR) were included as explanatory variables in the labor-saving technology adoption functions. The estimation results of the two-limit probit regression for tractor, thresher, and direct-seeding adoption functions are shown in Table 7.8. We dropped the DPWATER dummy from tractor and direct-seeding adoption equations and the NORTH dummy from the latter equation because of a problem of singularity in estimation.

Irrigation ratio has positive and highly significant coefficients in the tractor and thresher regressions, implying that an irrigated environment is conducive to the adoption of labor-saving technologies. The adoption of modern varieties, however, does not increase adoption of tractors and threshers, as evidenced by the insignificant coefficients of MVR. These observations suggest that the adoption of those labor-saving technologies coincided with but were not caused by the spread of modern varieties. Neither distance from regional markets nor paddy prices significantly affect the adoption of labor-saving technology. Furthermore, the insignificance of the coefficient of the tenure variable would imply that wealthier farm owners' better access to credit does not affect the adoption of labor-saving technology positively.

Only farm size was a significant factor in the adoption of direct-seeding methods. Because larger farms need larger labor inputs for crop establishment, the difficulty of supervising a number of laborers, as well as a shortage of labor during the peak season, may induce farmers to substitute direct seeding for transplanting, particularly in the Central Plain, where relatively lucrative nonfarm jobs attract laborers.

Technology and Labor Use

Technology directly affects productivity and factor use. An increase in productivity in an irrigated area as a result of modern variety adoption is likely to be associated with increases in employment, because intensive cultivation requires greater use of labor, particularly for crop care, harvesting, and threshing. Cropping intensity, because it affects labor use throughout the year, also affects labor demand. Thus, it is reasonable to hypothesize that labor demand per unit of land is highest in irrigated areas because of their higher rice yields and cropping intensities. Because of the difficulty of obtaining data on labor use at the village level, analysis of the labor use function here employs farm-level data from the intensive survey.

Another important issue is the impact of modern variety adoption on the use of family and hired labor. Because most hired workers are landless laborers or marginal farmers, modern variety technology has equitable effects to the extent that its adoption increases the demand for hired labor.

There are at least two possible reasons to expect greater use of hired labor with the modern variety technology. First, because of the shorter growth duration of modern varieties, the peak season for hired labor tends to be longer. Second, the adoption of modern varieties increases farmers' incomes, which facilitates the substitution of hired for family labor through the income effect. Family and hired labor functions are estimated separately in this study.

Table 7.9 shows adoption patterns of modern varieties and other technologies across the intensive-survey villages. The rate of modern variety adoption is highest in wet and dry seasons in irrigated areas of Suphan Buri (SP1). Floating rice varieties are planted during the wet season in the deepwater area (SP3), and modern varieties are grown only in areas where water can be pumped from the canal during the dry season. Negligible amounts of modern varieties are planted in the rainfed area of the Central Plain (SP2). In Khon Kaen, the wet-season rice crop is grown mostly for home consumption, and improved native glutinous varieties are preferred. However, modern variety adoption in the irrigated village (KK1) is 100% in the dry season.

Modern variety adoption has resulted in increased use of chemical fertilizer in irrigated areas. Only one rice crop is grown in rainfed villages, but rice cropping intensity is as high as 181% in the irrigated village in the Central Plain. For deepwater areas, chemical fertilizer is heavily applied only during the dry season.

Marked differences in paddy yield per hectare across villages reflect the productivity impact of modern rice technology. Yield and adoption rate of modern varieties tend to be higher in the dry season. In the Central Plain, paddy yields in the irrigated areas planted to modern varieties are at least three times as high as those in rainfed and flood-prone areas planted to traditional varieties during the wet season. In the Khon Kaen irrigated village, however, the yield of modern varieties is not significantly higher than that of traditional varieties during the wet season, which may explain why the adoption of modern varieties is low in KK1 during the wet season.

The labor requirement for crop care and harvesting in irrigated areas increases with modern variety adoption. Table 7.10 shows labor use per hectare by activity and the adoption rate of labor-saving technology. It is clear that the use of tractors for land preparation substantially reduces the amount of labor per hectare in most areas. The higher labor use in land preparation in KK2 and KK3 can be attributed to the use of draft animals for plowing.

In areas with good water control (SP1), the pregerminated direct seeding method is now common (Isvilanonda 1990). In SP2 and SP3, plowing is done before the rainy season starts, and direct seeding has long been practiced. Direct seeding uses less labor for planting but requires more herbicides because weeding is difficult in direct-seeded fields. Thus, labor use in crop establishment in Suphan Buri is distinctly smaller than in Khon Kaen, where transplanting is common. More labor is used in crop care in irrigated areas

(SP1 and KK1) than in rainfed and deepwater areas, despite greater use of herbicides in irrigated areas. Harvesting in all areas is done manually, whereas threshing is done manually or with threshers.

In Suphan Buri, the use of labor-saving technology is relatively uniform, and total labor use is highest in the most favorable environment. This suggests that the adoption of modern varieties in the irrigated environment increases labor use per hectare. Also, it is important to note that the use of hired labor is larger in more-favorable environments, although use of hired labor is common in the deepwater area (SP3) because of large farm size.

In sum, it seems reasonable to hypothesize that both the adoption of modern varieties and the presence of irrigation increase labor use, particularly hired labor.

Determinants of Labor Use

The effect of modern variety technology adoption on labor use or employment has an important bearing on rural poverty, because labor constitutes the main source of earning for the rural poor.

In this subsection, we estimate the labor-use function to quantify the effect of modern rice technology on the use of family and hired labor. The adoption of modern varieties is confined only to irrigated environments, including parts of some deepwater areas that are irrigated during the dry season. Thus, it is difficult to separate the effects of modern varieties on labor use from those of production environment with cross-section data. We specified the technology factors in terms of the production environments interacted with modern variety and traditional variety adoption. Four technology variables were specified: modern varieties adopted in irrigated areas (MVR*IRG); modern varieties adopted in deepwater areas (MVR*DPWATER); traditional varieties adopted in irrigated areas (TV*IRG); and traditional varieties adopted in deepwater areas (TV*DPWATER). The variable left out to serve as a control in the regression was traditional varieties adopted in rainfed areas. Other socioeconomic variables included in the regression equations were farm size (FSIZE); the number of working members in the household between age thirteen and sixty (WORKER); age of household head (AGE); education, as represented by the dummy for schooling of household head beyond grade four (SCHOOL); tenure variables, defined as leasehold (LEASER) and share-tenant area ratios (SHARER); adoption dummies of tractors and threshers (HTUSER and THUSER); a dummy variable for direct seeding (DSEED); and a regional dummy (NORTHEAST).

Table 7.11 shows the estimation results of family and hired labor use functions. It is remarkable to find the positive and significant coefficient of modern varieties planted in irrigated areas (MVR*IRG) in the hired labor regression. This result implies that modern variety adoption associated with irrigation increases hired labor use by almost eighteen days per hectare compared to that of rainfed farms planted to traditional varieties, supporting the hypothesis that modern rice technology is biased toward hired labor. However, the coefficient of MVR*DPWATER in the hired labor regression is not significant, probably because the relatively small area planted to modern varieties during the dry season allows family labor to perform most activities.

The coefficient of TV*IRG in the hired labor regression is positive and significant, which would imply that irrigation also increases the demand for hired labor. However, the coefficient of (MVR*IRG) is significantly larger than that of (TV*IRG), suggesting that the *pure* effect of modern variety adoption on hired labor use is positive. The coefficients of both TV*IRG and TV*DPWATER are negative and significant in the family labor regression but positive and significant in the hired labor regression. Thus, in the irrigated areas and the deepwater areas planted to traditional varieties, hired labor is substituted for family labor.

The coefficients of farm size (FSIZE) and tractor use (HTUSER) are negative and significant in the family labor regressions. These results indicate that larger-scale farmers prefer to enjoy more leisure and that tractor use facilitates the reduction of family labor. As expected, the number of household workers has a positive effect on family labor use. Tenure factors affect neither family nor hired labor use.

Direct seeding (DSEED) has a negative and significant coefficient in the hired labor regression, suggesting that direct seeding lessens the requirement for hired labor. The Northeast regional dummy has a negative and significant coefficient in the hired labor function and a significantly positive coefficient in the family labor function, which indicates a structural difference in the labor market between the Central Plain and the Northeast.

The estimation results of labor use functions strongly indicate that the adoption of modern varieties and the presence of irrigation increase hired labor use, which would raise the market wage of hired labor in favorable areas. As we noted earlier, however, tractors and threshers were introduced in irrigated areas at least partly in response to higher wages. Thus, the increased labor demand in favorable areas would have been offset partially by the use of labor-saving methods.

LABOR MARKET ADJUSTMENT AND REGIONAL FACTOR-PRICE DIFFERENTIALS

If modern variety adoption increased wage rates in favorable areas in the short run, adjustments would have occurred in the labor market to equalize wage rates across production environments. We first examined the impact of technological change on labor supply adjustments. Then we examined factor-price differential across environments and regions.

Labor Supply Adjustment

In a rapidly growing economy such as Thailand's, the dominant labor migration flow, permanent as well as seasonal, is from rural to urban areas (Watanabe 1987). The possible impact of higher labor demand in favorable crop-growing areas could be to deter the rate of out-migration from favorable areas to cities rather than to attract labor from less favorable areas. However, seasonal migration from unfavorable to favorable crop-growing areas or from rice-growing areas in the Northeast to cassava- or sugarcane-growing areas also occurs during the peak season (Panpiemras and Krusuansombat 1985).

Ideally we would have used data on out-migration, or population growth, at the village level to examine interregional labor market adjustments in response to any wage differential created by the differential adoption of modern variety technology. However, such data for Thailand were not available. Therefore, we used man-land ratio (i.e., the ratio of village population to cultivated area) and landless household ratio (i.e., ratio of village landless laborer to farmer households) as proxies for the cumulative shift of labor supply in the past.

As seen in Table 7.1, there is quite a consistent difference in man-land ratio and landless laborer–farmer household ratio among the three regions and between the irrigated and nonirrigated areas within each region. Man-land ratio is highest in the North, second highest in the Northeast, and lowest in the Central Plain.

The fact that man-land ratio is highest in the North may be explained by high yield, high cropping intensity, and good access to nonfarm jobs. The fact that the Central Plain's man-land ratio is lower than that of the Northeast, however, is difficult to account for. One explanation is that job opportunities in Bangkok particularly attracted migrants from the Central Plain because of geographical proximity. This explanation would not imply, however, that labor supply is insensitive to differences in the labor demand. In fact, the man-land ratio is substantially higher in the irrigated than in the nonirrigated areas in each region.

Landless laborers are geographically more mobile than farmers. Thus, the ratio of landless households is a good indicator of migration patterns in the past. The ratio of landless households, however, is generally low in Thailand, which would reflect the availability, until recently, of unexploited land, particularly in the Northeast.

The high landless ratio in the North may be explained partly by the greater availability of nonfarm jobs and partly by more intensive farming, which requires more hired laborers. The consistently higher landless household ratio in the irrigated (as against nonirrigated) areas in each region is consistent with the hypothesis that favorable production environments coupled with modern variety technology increase demand for hired labor.

To identify the factors affecting regional differences in man-land ratio and landless household ratio, regression analysis was conducted wherein irrigation ratio (IRGR) and modern variety adoption rate (MVR) were specified as explanatory variables. Other socioeconomic variables, such as paddy price (PADDYP), distance to regional center (DISTC), and ratio of owner-cultivators (OWNERR), were also included. Regional dummies (NORTH and NORTHEAST) and a deepwater dummy (DPWATER) were inserted to control the effects of differences in other environmental factors. Table 7.12 shows the estimation results of the man-land ratio and landless household ratio functions. The estimated coefficient of irrigation (0.46) in the man-land ratio function suggests that the man-land ratio is about 50% higher in the irrigated area than in the nonirrigated areas. This finding supports the hypothesis that interregional labor market adjustments took place to increase the supply of labor in areas where the labor demand increased.

The coefficient of MVR is positive but not significant. The greater impact of irrigation on man-land ratio is expected because irrigation increases not only the use of hired labor per season, as do modern varieties, but also cropping intensity, thereby increasing labor demand throughout the year. The estimated coefficients of the North and Northeast regional dummies are also significant and even larger in magnitude than the coefficients of irrigation ratio, implying that a large, unexplained difference in man-land ratio exists.

In the landless ratio function, the estimated coefficient of IRGR is significant only at the 10% level. This result may be due to the relatively small variation in the landless ratio across villages. High geographical mobility of the landless, however, was observed in India (Oberai and Singh 1980; Ahluwalia 1978; Lal 1976; Johl 1975) and in the Philippines (Otsuka, Cordova, and David 1990). Although the evidence of interregional labor market adjustments is not as conclusive as we would wish to have, there are indications that the higher labor demand is associated with a larger labor supply.

Wages, Land Rent, and Machinery Rentals

Factor prices classified by rice-production environment and region are shown in Table 7.13. Only the peak season activities of transplanting and harvesting are considered under wage rates because hired labor is not used for other activities in many of the unfavorable-area villages. Wage data for transplanting are not available in some Central Plain villages because of the complete adoption of pregerminated direct seeding, which has eliminated the use of hired labor for crop establishment. Transplanting is done by daily wage or piece-rate contracts, based on area transplanted; harvesting is done by daily wage or output-sharing contracts. In the case of piece-rate and output-sharing contracts, the imputed daily wages are derived on the basis of the average daily earnings of typical hired labor. In villages where two types of contracts are used, the wage of the more dominant form is considered.

The data in Table 7.13 suggest three broad patterns concerning the regional wage differentials:

- Daily wages are substantially lower than imputed wages. Such differences between daily wages and piece-rate or output-sharing contracts may arise because of the weaker work incentives in wage contracts. Or they may arise because the more able workers select piece-rate or output-sharing contracts to receive higher remuneration for higher levels of performance (Otsuka et al. 1992; Roumasset and Uy 1980; Stiglitz 1975).
- Wages tend to be slightly but consistently higher in irrigated than in the nonirrigated villages in each region.
- Wages are generally highest in the Central Plain and lowest in the Northeast. These interregional wage differences could reflect either the high cost of interregional migration or a short-run disequilibrium in the labor market.

All contracts for tractor rentals are on an area basis, but there are rates for one and two passes. Tractor rental rates in the North are substantially higher than in other regions because charges for two passes of plowing and for puddling are included. For thresher rentals, all contracts are piece-rate, based on the amount of threshed paddy.

Relevant comparisons of tractor and thresher rentals across regions and production environments are difficult to make because of the difference in contracts and the lack of observations in areas where tractors and threshers are not used. However, there seems to be rough equality of these machine rentals across areas.

Remarkably larger regional differences are observed in land rent per hectare during the wet season. Land rent seems to be significantly affected by technological and environmental factors. In contrast, paddy prices are largely equalized across areas, which suggests the integration of local paddy markets throughout the country. It is also noteworthy that only small differences are observed between prices of traditional and modern varieties, which suggests that the quality of Thai modern varieties is largely comparable to that of traditional varieties.

Determinants of Factor-Price Differentials

We estimated the factor-price determination functions to examine the impacts of adoption of modern rice technology and irrigation on the regional wage, land rent, and machinery rental differentials. In addition to technology and environmental factors, represented by ratios of modern variety adoption (MVR) and irrigation (IRGR), we included socioeconomic variables: owner-cultivator ratio (OWNERR); distance to regional center (DISTC); paddy price

(PADDYP); farm size (FSIZE); and regional dummies (NORTH, NORTHEAST, and DPWATER). A piece-rate contract dummy (CONT2) for transplanting wage and an output-sharing contract dummy (CONT3) for harvesting wage were included. For the tractor rental regression, the dummies for hand tractor (HTUSER), as distinct from the four-wheel tractor, and for two passes (TWOPASS), as distinct from one, were inserted.

Table 7.14 shows the estimation results of the wage and land rent determination functions. Because of the endogeneity of MVR, the functions are estimated with and without this variable. Although MVR is not significant for transplanting and the harvesting wage, the estimated coefficients of irrigation are positive and highly significant, implying a net positive effect of an irrigated environment on wage rates. This conclusion is consistent with the regression results of a number of cross-sectional studies of rural labor markets in India, which found significantly positive effects of modern variety technology (irrigation or modern variety adoption) on wage rates (Johl 1975; Lal 1976; Rosenzweig 1984). Our estimated coefficients, however, are in the vicinity of 0.10 or less—i.e., wage rates are higher in the irrigated areas by only about 10%.

The coefficients of the contract dummies are positive and highly significant, whereas the coefficients of the distance variable are negative and significant. These findings indicate that the returns to labor under piece-rate and output-sharing contracts are substantially higher than under daily wage contracts and that wages tend to be higher in locations closer to urban labor markets.

The significance of the estimated coefficients of regional dummies in the wage regression varies, but the magnitudes of the estimated coefficients suggest that wage rates are from 6 to 27% lower in the North and Northeast than in the Central Plain. Such differences are not unexpected and may reflect migration cost. Historically, the Northeast has been the poorest part of the country, and there has been migration to Bangkok and other areas. Out-migration from the North has also been substantial in recent years (Tirasawat 1985).

The estimation result of the land rent regression shows much larger differentials in returns to land between irrigated and nonirrigated areas and among regions. The estimated coefficient of irrigation is around 0.6, which implies nearly an 80% difference in land rents between irrigated and nonirrigated areas. The coefficient of modern variety adoption ratio is also significantly positive in equation (5), and its estimated coefficient, 0.32, is far from negligible. Thus, it is clear that the regional land rent differentials are substantially larger than the wage differentials between favorable and unfavorable areas.

These findings are consistent with the large positive coefficient of the regional dummy in the land rent regression for the North, where the production environment is favorable. Conversely, the estimated coefficient of the Northeast regional dummy is negative and relatively small. This result may be partly due to the modest differences in climate between the Northeast and the Central Plain and/or to inadequate interregional adjustments in labor supply, which result in a relatively high man-land ratio in the Northeast.

Because machinery is more mobile than labor, similar machine rental rates across areas would be expected. According to the estimation results of the tractor and thresher rental regression shown in Table 7.15, neither irrigation nor modern variety adoption has a significant effect. The dummy for the North region has significantly positive coefficients in the tractor rental regression, largely because the puddling operation is included. The estimated coefficient of the dummy variables for two passes of tractor operation is about 0.8, implying that this rental is about twice as high as for a single operation. The hand tractor dummy is significant, but the coefficients are relatively small. In the thresher rental regression, none of the variables are significant. In general, therefore, differences in machinery rentals are largely insignificant across production environments and regions.

Thus, the regression analysis of the regional factor-price differentials suggests that differences in production environment and the differential adoption of modern variety technology in Thailand have resulted in large regional variations in land rent, modest differences in wages, and no difference in machine rentals. Differences in mobility or migration costs would explain some, if not most, of the differences in factor-price differentials. We do not assert that the interregional labor market adjustment alone mitigates the regional wage disparity; another possible mechanism is the adoption of labor-saving technology in high-wage regions.

MODERN RICE TECHNOLOGY AND HOUSEHOLD INCOME DISTRIBUTION

Household income depends on payments to factors of production owned and supplied by the household. Such payments critically depend on technology and factor prices. Table 7.16 compares output and factor prices in the wet season in the intensive-survey villages. Farm gate prices of paddy within each region differ slightly across villages in accordance with the location. Fertilizer prices, in terms of nitrogen, are almost the same across villages, except in SP2, where few farmers report the use of fertilizer.

Because farm tasks differ in effort, intensity, and skill requirement, wage rates differ from task to task. Consistent with the findings on regional wage differentials based on the extensive survey, wage rates are higher in the more favorable area. In fact, the village in the most unfavorable area in the less favorable region KK3 has the lowest wage rate. We note that piece-rate contracts are common for most activities in irrigated and deepwater villages in Suphan Buri. Wage rates in the irrigated village (SP1) and deepwater village (SP3), which are very close to each other, are very similar despite significant differences in technology and production environments.

Seasonal (rather than permanent) rural-to-rural migration from unfavorable to favorable areas is common in Thailand. Therefore, the regional difference in wage rates is closely related to the distance and the transportation costs between regions. Because less favorable villages (i.e., KK3 and SP2) are located in more remote areas than favorable villages (i.e., SP1 and KK1), a part of the wage difference between KK1 and KK3 and between SP1 and SP2 can be explained by the cost of short-distance seasonal migration. There are, however, more substantial differences in wage rates between the Northeast and Central Plain. We cannot address the extent to which those differences can be explained by migration cost.

Because machinery is more mobile than labor, we expect to observe small regional differences in machinery rentals. In fact, custom rates of tractors for the service of two passes are not different across locations. However, custom rates of threshers are lower in Suphan Buri, perhaps because of its proximity to the industrial center, Bangkok.

Although we found certain differences in factor prices, we observed more marked differences in rice technology, or productivity, among intensive-survey villages. We now examine how those differences are reflected in the difference in factor payments. Table 7.17 shows the average factor payments and relative factor shares per hectare per season, estimated as a weighted average of wet and dry seasons based on the ratios of cultivated areas of the two seasons. As expected, the gross value of output per hectare is highest in the most favorable village (SP1) and lowest in the most unfavorable (KK3). We note that gross value of output for the deepwater area (SP3) is relatively high because of the high yield of modern varieties during the dry season.

Actual costs paid to hired and purchased inputs and imputed costs accruing to the family-owned input were used in estimating factor payments. The absolute factor payment to each factor is higher in the more favorable villages, which implies that the adoption of modern rice technology in favorable areas increases the return to all inputs. To account for actual and imputed payments to owners of productive inputs, the factor payments to labor and capital were divided into those accruing, respectively, to hired and family labor and to rented and farmer-owned capital. Residual income was derived by deducting the costs of current inputs, labor, and capital from the gross value of output. It was assumed to include returns to land and management. By subtracting average leasehold rent in the village from the residual, the surplus was computed.

There are several important findings:

- The factor share of labor is higher in less favorable environments. Thus, it appears that modern rice technology as a whole, including modern varieties, tractors, and threshers, is labor-saving. In fact, in

KK2 and KK3, where no major technological change occurred, labor share is close to 50%.

• Absolute factor payments to labor, particularly to hired labor, tend to be higher in the more favorable environments. Thus, hired labor income seems to increase with technological change, even though the rate of its increase is smaller relative to that of other factors.

• Both the relative share and the absolute amount of residual income are larger in more favorable areas. In SP1, the residual accounts for more than 50% of the gross revenue. Because most farmers in our survey villages are owner-operators—except in SP3 (Table 7.3)—farmers gain from increased returns to land.

These observations suggest that landless and small farmers, who depend on labor income, lose relative to large farmers unless lucrative employment opportunities are available outside the rice sector.

Household Income by Source

Even though the intensive-survey villages are rice-dependent, income from other agricultural activities, as well as from nonfarm employment, contributes significantly to the total household income. In this study, we classified household rice income into imputed returns to family labor, owned capital, and land. The land income for the owner-cultivator is the residual, whereas it is the residual minus actual rent for tenants. Other farm income consists of earnings obtained from working as hired labor on other farms, renting out capital equipment and land, and growing other crops and raising livestock. Nonfarm income includes nonfarm labor earnings, remittances, and pensions.

Table 7.18 presents the average annual income of farm households by village and by source. Rice income accounts for more than half of total farm household income in all the Suphan Buri villages. In Khon Kaen, nonrice income, including nonfarm income, is more important than rice income. Irrigation, modern varieties, and rice cropping intensity appear to be important factors contributing to higher rice income, as evidenced by the fact that SP1 has the smallest farm size but the highest cropping intensity, the highest yields, and the largest rice income. Even though the deepwater village, SP3, has the lowest wet-season yield, the cultivation of modern variety rice in some dry-season fields, coupled with large farm size, results in high rice income.

We note that average rice income is significantly different among the six villages primarily because of the difference in land income. Thus, the difference in land income is a major source of income inequality among farm households.

Although the most favorable village (SP1) is basically rice-dependent, farm income from other crops is also high, indicating that the production environment in the village is favorable not only for rice but also for other crops, such as water chestnuts.

Nonfarm income is largest in the deepwater village because the cropping intensity (Table 7.9) and labor requirement of growing deepwater rice are low (Table 7.10) whereas access to nonfarm job opportunities in the Bangkok area is relatively good. Nonfarm income is also important in villages in Khon Kaen, because rice-fallow is the dominant cropping pattern in the rainfed villages (Table 7.4) and farm size is particularly small in the irrigated villages (Table 7.3). Many working family members seasonally migrate to sugarcane areas in the Central Plain and to industrial and commercial areas in Bangkok to supplement their farm income.

The total income of farm households, both on a per household and per person basis, is by far the highest in irrigated village SP1, followed by that of deepwater village SP3. Aside from these two villages, the average farm household incomes are relatively similar, primarily because of the absence of particular technological and locational advantages.

Table 7.19 shows the average annual income of agricultural landless households by source and village. Landless households derive income from farm and nonfarm activities. Income from farm activity comes from employment not only in the production of rice and other crops but also in poultry raising and fishing.

The income of landless households from farm work is highest in the most favorable village, SP1, which has year-round work opportunities in water chestnut production. The landless in the rainfed village of KK3 receive the highest income from nonfarm sources, including cane cutting, remittances, and pensions. As a result, the total income of landless households is higher in KK3 than in SP2 and SP3.

Determinants of Household Income

Household income is determined partly by the ownership of productive resources such as land, human capital, and capital assets and partly by technology and factor prices, which affect the demand for productive resources. To identify the effects of production environments and other factors on household income, we estimated the income determination functions separately by income source and by farm and landless households.

Each income was regressed as a function of technology factors: farm size (FSIZE) and leasehold and share tenancy area ratios (LEASER, SHARER); dummies for the ownership of power tillers (HTOWNER) and threshers (THOWNER); the number of working members aged between thirteen and sixty (WORKER); age of household head, as a proxy for labor quality (AGE); schooling, represented by the dummy for the completion of compulsory education (SCHOOL); and other factors, represented by a regional dummy (NORTHEAST). The technology variables were specified by interaction terms between the dummy variable of production environments, the ratio of area planted to the specific type of rice varieties (i.e., modern or traditional), and farm size. The farming conditions in the favorable villages of SP1 and KK1, where modern and traditional varieties coexist, were represented by irrigated area planted to modern varieties (MVR*IRG*FSIZE) and irrigated area planted to traditional varieties (TVR*IRG*FSIZE). Flood-prone areas planted to modern varieties (MVR*DPWATER*FSIZE) and to traditional varieties (TVR*DPWATER*FSIZE) served as technology factors representing SP3. Rainfed areas planted to traditional varieties were left out to serve as a control variable. The estimated equation was specified in linear form, in which the dependent variable, household income by source, was expressed by 1,000 baht. The coefficient of technology demonstrates the joint effects of technology, environment, and cropping intensity. (See Chapter 3 for the justification of linear specification with interaction terms).

The regression results of the farm household income determination functions are shown in Table 7.20. Most of the coefficients have the expected signs. In particular, the estimated result of the land income equation clearly shows that technology, farm size, tenure, and schooling are important factors explaining variations in residual income from rice production. Examination of the coefficients of the four technology-related variables suggests that returns to land increase with availability of irrigation and modern variety adoption and that deepwater areas, particularly when planted to modern varieties during the dry season, are significantly more favorable than rainfed areas. Note that although the pure effect of irrigation may be seen from the coefficient of (TVR*IRG*FSIZE), the pure effect of modern variety adoption may be judged from the difference in the estimated coefficients between (MVR*IRG*FSIZE) and (TVR*IRG*FSIZE).

As expected, the coefficients of farm size are significantly different from zero. The coefficients of leasehold and share tenancy are negative and significant, essentially reflecting the payment of land rents. The positive and significant coefficient of the schooling variable suggests the importance of management skills in rice production in Thailand.

Technology-environment interaction terms affect labor and capital income from rice production but generally do not affect nonrice and nonfarm income. Labor and capital income from rice, as well as other farm income, tend to be higher in irrigated areas planted to modern varieties, reflecting the higher rice cropping intensity as well as diversification of cropping patterns in irrigated areas of the Central Plain.

In the deepwater environment, the adoption of modern varieties is associated with increased labor and capital income from rice production. Thus, the shift from floating rice to dry-season modern varieties in the deepwater area significantly increases income-earning opportunities.

The farm size variable has significantly positive effects on labor, capital, and residual income but has no influence on other farm and nonfarm income. As expected, the coefficients of the number of working family members are positive and significant in the labor income and nonrice farm income regressions but not in the nonfarm income regression. Socioeconomic variables (age and schooling of household head and tenure status) are generally insignificant, except in the land income regression, but the ownership dummies of hand tractors and threshers are significant not only in capital income but also in labor income. This result may be explained by the fact that machinery owners use family labor to operate their machines. The hand tractor dummy also has a positive and significant coefficient in the nonrice farm income regression, which partly reflects the rental revenue of tractors.

The negative and significant coefficients of the Northeast dummy in land income and nonrice farm income seem to reflect the lower productivity of land, not only in rice farming but also in production of other crops, in the Northeast compared to the Central Plain.

In the estimation of income determination functions of landless households, income is classified into farm and nonfarm sources. Characteristics of family labor, such as age, schooling, and number of working family members, are employed as independent variables, along with village-specific variables of farm size (MVR*IRGV*FSIZE and MVR*DPWATER*FSIZE). The omitted variable, which serves as a control, is traditional varieties cultivated in rainfed areas.

The regression results of landless household income by source are shown in Table 7.21. The number of working family members and the adoption of modern varieties in irrigated areas seem to have significant effects on farm income, a result consistent with increased use of hired labor in irrigated areas. The positive and significant effect of modern varieties in the deepwater area in the nonfarm income equation seems to suggest that because of this area's proximity to Bangkok and low rice cropping intensity, landless households actively seek seasonal employment in nonfarm activities. This hypothesis does not imply, however, that landless workers in the Northeast earn less than workers in other areas. According to the last equation, which includes the Northeast village dummy to represent the regional difference in the structure of labor earnings, the landless in the Northeast earn significantly more income from nonfarm sources than do the landless in the Central Plain.

Income Inequality of Households

We used the Gini ratio decomposition formula developed by Fei, Ranis, and Kuo (1978) to assess income inequality in the intensive-survey villages. Table 7.22 shows the estimation results of overall Gini ratios and the absolute contributions of each factor component measured as the product of income share, rank correlation ratio, and component Gini ratio (see Chapter 3 for methodology).

Among five income components considered, the most important source of inequality in the Northeast is nonfarm income. Moreover, the lowest Gini ratio is found in the irrigated village of KK1. These findings seem to imply that the presence of irrigation does not create particularly inequitable income distribution in KK1. The inequality seems to arise from unequal access to nonfarm employment opportunities.

In Suphan Buri, where farms are relatively larger, modern variety adoption seems to have increased the contribution of land income distribution to overall income inequality (compare the contribution of land in SP1 and SP3 with that of SP2). Significant inequality, however, also arises from nonrice farm income in SP1 and nonfarm income in SP3. As a result, the overall Gini ratio is highest in the deepwater village and lowest in the rainfed village.

The most relevant measures of income inequality in relation to the impact of differential adoption of modern rice technology are the overall Gini ratio and the contributions by component incomes using the pooled sample of six villages, which is shown in the last line of Table 7.22. The contribution of land income to overall Gini ratio is relatively large, and that of labor income is quite small. Although somewhat less important than that of land income, the contributions of nonrice farm income and nonfarm income are also significant.

These results suggest that not only the differential adoption of modern rice technology but also the differential access to various sources of income critically affect the income distribution among rural households.

SOME POLICY IMPLICATIONS

We have analyzed the direct and indirect effects of production environments and the adoption of modern rice varieties on income distribution in rural households in Thailand. We found that difference in production environments, as determined by the availability of irrigation, is the major factor affecting the adoption of modern varieties. We also found that widespread adoption of modern varieties in favorable areas results in increased fertilizer use, land productivity, and cropping intensity.

The adoption of tractors and threshers is influenced by the presence of irrigation, but they continue to spread to unfavorable areas. In the commercial rice-growing areas of the Central Plain, the adoption of tractors, threshers, and direct seeding methods is almost complete in all production environments.

Of more importance is our finding that the adoption of modern varieties in the Central Plain significantly increases the demand for hired labor. Crop care and harvesting have particularly large effects, which implies that modern varieties are characteristically biased toward hired labor use. The increase in hired labor demand generates rural employment, to the advantage of the rural poor.

Among the factors of production, labor is relatively mobile. The shift in hired labor demand associated with modern variety adoption would have raised wage rates in favorable areas in the short run. In the long run, however, market adjustments induced by the wage differentials between favorable and unfavorable areas have tended to equalize the wage rate across production environments.

The analysis of regional factor-price differentials shows that although rentals of tractors and threshers, the most mobile factors, equalize across production areas, wage rates are slightly different between favorable and unfavorable production areas. This difference may result from a lag in the adjustment process of the labor market, as the Green Revolution in Thailand started recently, and from the high cost of migration and relocation.

Increased land productivity in favorable production areas generates higher land rent, resulting in large regional land rent differentials.

The ultimate negative impact of modern variety adoption on the income distribution of rural households does not appear to be as serious as generally thought. The adoption of modern varieties has increased returns to land in irrigated and deepwater environments, thereby making owner-cultivators better off. Our income determination analysis shows, however, that modern variety technology significantly increases rice income but not nonrice income. The decomposition analysis of income distribution demonstrates that the more uneven income distribution among rural households results more from nonrice income than from rice income. For rice income, land returns are most unequally distributed, and the contribution of modern variety adoption to such distribution is significant. Yet modern variety adoption has increased labor income, which must have contributed to the equalization of overall income distribution, even though we cannot quantify such effects from our cross-section data.

Considering all these effects, it seems fair to conclude that the introduction of modern varieties in Thailand increases income inequality only to a limited extent.

Our analysis provides several important policy implications:

- Considering the fact that the productivity impact of modern varieties is substantial only in irrigated areas, further irrigation investment is necessary to reap the gain from modern rice technology.
- Given the slow adoption of modern varieties, even in irrigated areas of the North and Northeast, serious attention should be paid to the profitability of developing modern varieties particularly suitable for those regions.

- To increase the income of rural households in the rainfed environments prone to drought, research should be directed toward crops other than rice.
- In deepwater areas, however, the effective way to raise productivity and farmers' income seems to be to facilitate the shift of wet-season, floating rice cultivation to dry-season cultivation with modern varieties. The profitability of promoting such a shift should be further investigated.

Because of the interregional labor market linkages, the benefits of increases in labor demand in specific locations due to technological change have been widely shared by the landless and near-landless. In this respect, there is no strong trade-off between efficiency and equity. The inequity arises, however, from the fact that technological change brings about increases in returns to land only in favorable areas. Thus, a policy to redistribute income gains of landowners should be considered to achieve efficiency and equity associated with the Green Revolution in Thailand.

Figure 7.1 Location of study areas, extensive survey, Thailand, 1987

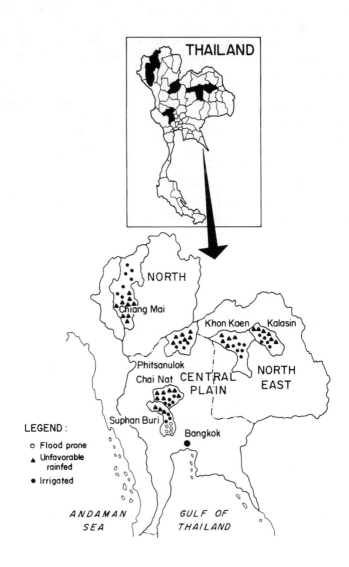

Figure 7.2 Location of study areas, intensive survey, Thailand, 1987

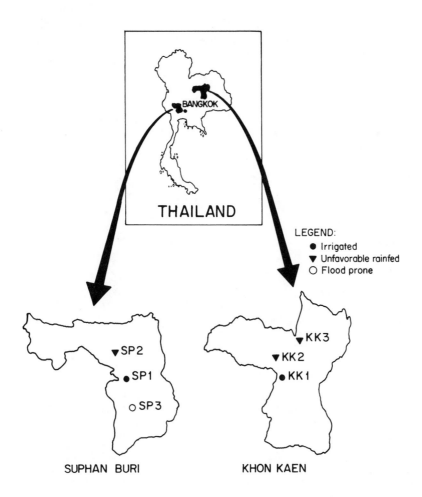

Table 7.1   Selected socioeconomic characteristics of sample households by production environment and region, extensive survey, Thailand, wet season, 1986.

	North		Northeast		Central Plain		
	Irri-gated	Rain-fed	Irri-gated	Rain-fed	Irri-gated	Rain-fed	Deep-water
Sample villages (no)	7	9	11	11	12	16	5
Farm size (ha)[a]	0.9	2.3	1.9	2.4	3.9	5.4	5.3
Man-land ratio[b] (person/ha)	7.9	3.2	3.5	3.2	1.9	1.3	1.7
Ratio of landless households (%)[c]	14	11	5	3	12	7	9
Ratio of owner-cultivators (% of area)	62	66	91	87	53	58	49
Distance to regional center (km)	31	48	48	56	260	286	131

a. Cultivated area during the wet season.
b. Ratio of village population to cultivated area.
c. Ratio of landless laborer to farmer households.

Table 7.2   Cropping patterns (% of area) by production environment
and region, extensive survey, Thailand, wet season, 1986.

	North		Northeast		Central Plain		
Cropping pattern	Irri-gated	Rain-fed	Irri-gated	Rain-fed	Irri-gated	Rain-fed	Deep-water
Rice-rice	1	0	15	0	93	2	20
Rice-fallow	9	54	40	75	0	87	78
Rice–other crops	78	13	26	1	7	6	2
Other crops	12	33	19	24	0	5	0

Table 7.3   Selected socioeconomic characteristics of sample households by production environment and region, intensive survey, Thailand, 1987.

	Khon Kaen			Suphan Buri		
	Irrigated	Rainfed		Irrigated	Rainfed	Deepwater
	KK1	KK2	KK3	SP1	SP2	SP3
Sample farm households (no)	49	54	50	45	56	41
Sample landless households (no)	1	3	9	9	7	14
Ratio of landless households[a]	5	5	10	6	6	15
Farm size (ha)	1.4	1.7	2.7	2.8	6.5	8.4
Man-land ratio (person/ha)[b]	4.1	4.0	2.4	1.9	0.9	0.8
Tenure (% of area)						
Owner	92	100	75	72	82	52
Leasehold	8	0	3	28	4	48
Share tenancy	0	0	22	0	14	0

a. Ratio of total landless laborer households to total farm households in the village.
b. Ratio of village population to cultivated area.

Table 7.4   Cropping patterns (% of area) by production environment and region, intensive survey, Thailand, 1987.

	Khon Kaen			Suphan Buri		
	Irrigated	Rainfed		Irrigated	Rainfed	Deepwater
	KK1	KK2	KK3	SP1	SP2	SP3
Rice-rice	89	0	0	77	0	0
Rice-fallow	0	96	95	0	90	99[c]
Rice–nonrice crops[a]	4	0	1	18	1	0
Other crops[b]	7	4	4	5	9	1

a. Nonrice crops include vegetables, soybean, and water chestnut.
b. Other crops include cassava, mulberry, banana, tobacco, and jute.
c. 67% of area was planted to wet-season rice and 32% to dry-season rice.

Table 7.5   Technology adoption, paddy yields, and cropping intensity by production environment and region, extensive survey, Thailand, wet season, 1986.[a]

	North		Northeast		Central Plain		
	Irri-gated	Rain-fed	Irri-gated	Rain-fed	Irri-gated	Rain-fed	Deep-water
Ratio of irrigated area (%)	83	0	77	0	97	0	0
Modern variety adoption (%) (1)[b]	15 (1)	4 (2)	4 (0)	2 (26)	71 (2)	11 (0)	0.6
Fertilizer use (kg NPK/ha)[c]	100	104	110	74	262	103	0
Yield (t/ha)							
Traditional varieties	4.1	2.8	2.6	1.9	1.9	2.1	1.9
Modern varieties	4.7	4.1	3.2	1.8	4.4	3.3	1.8
Total cropping intensity (%)	228	122	143	100	180	107	132

a. Except total cropping intensity, which refers to 1986 calendar year.
b. Numbers in parentheses are adoption rates of modern varieties in wet season, 1980.
c. The amount of fertilizer is the sum of weights of different kinds of fertilizers (mostly 16-20-0 and 21-0-0) in the wet season.

Table 7.6   Regression results of modern variety adoption, fertilizer use, paddy yield, and cropping intensity functions, extensive survey, Thailand, wet season, 1986.[a]

	MVR	Fertilizer	Yield	Cropping intensity
Intercept	0.86 (1.24)	−13.97 (−0.12)	1.78* (1.66)	0.31 (0.76)
IRGR	0.50** (5.30)	52.88** (2.32)	0.98** (4.63)	0.85** (10.40)
DPWATER	−0.15 (−0.57)	−64.58* (−1.74)	0.10 (−0.30)	0.08 (0.58)
MVR	—	135.18** (3.15)	1.08** (2.72)	0.22 (1.46)
FSIZE	−0.06* (−1.83)	5.72 (1.40)	−0.02 (−0.62)	−0.004 (−0.25)
OWNERR	−0.06 (−0.25)	−36.34 (−1.02)	0.04 (0.13)	0.16 (1.22)
PADDYP	−0.25 (−1.01)	10.68 (0.26)	−0.02 (−0.06)	0.21 (1.41)
DISTC	0.38 (0.63)	300.93** (2.47)	1.72 (1.52)	0.63 (1.45)
NORTH	−0.41* (−2.15)	62.74 (1.54)	1.15** (3.02)	0.47** (3.22)
NORTHEAST	−0.63** (−3.19)	58.86 (1.47)	0.09 (0.23)	−0.08 (−0.59)
R^2	—	0.59	0.69	0.83
F-value	—	9.90	15.38	33.65
Log-likelihood	−22.78	—	—	—
(Chi-square)	71.93	—	—	—

a. Numbers in parentheses are t-statistics.
** Indicates significance at 1% level; *at 5% level.

Table 7.7   Adoption of labor-saving technologies (%) by production environment and region, extensive survey, Thailand, wet season, 1980 and 1986.

| | North | | Northeast | | Central Plain | | |
	Irri-gated	Rain-fed	Irri-gated	Rain-fed	Irri-gated	Rain-fed	Deep-water
Tractor[a]							
1980	39	8	2	0	49	34	60
1986	89	93	82	11	100	82	100
Thresher							
1980	16	0	0	0	0	0	0
1986	46	1	50[b]	3	100	100	100
Direct seeding							
Broadcast	0	0	0	0	0	65	100
Pregerminated	0	0	5	0	70	0	0

a. Includes power tillers and riding tractors.
b. Includes beating device (machine) as well as portable threshers.

Table 7.8   Regression results of tractor, thresher, and direct-seeding adoption functions, extensive survey, Thailand, wet season, 1986.[a]

	Tractor	Thresher	Direct seeding[b]
Intercept	0.57 (0.56)	10.35 (0.001)	-2.70 (-1.23)
IRGR	0.87** (3.36)	2.04** (2.60)	0.51 (0.80)
DPWATER	—	-2.48 (-0.00)	—
MVR	0.59 (0.70)	0.72 (0.30)	0.58 (0.66)
FSIZE	0.08 (1.18)	0.23 (0.95)	0.28** (2.55)
OWNERR	-0.52 (-0.19)	-1.60 (-1.10)	-0.69 (-1.04)
PADDYP	-0.09 (-0.26)	-1.08 (-1.00)	0.76 (0.88)
DISTC	1.29 (0.96)	-7.56 (-0.61)	2.10 (1.26)
NORTH	0.24 (0.70)	-8.09 (-0.001)	—
NORTHEAST	-0.43 (-1.25)	-7.58 (-0.00)	-0.22 (-0.39)
Log-likelihood	-27.98	-24.47	-45.68
(Chi-square)	58.82	91.87	71.24

a. Numbers in parentheses are t-statistics.
b. Refers to both pregerminated direct seeding and broadcasting for crop establishment.
** Indicates significance at 1% level; * at 5% level.

Table 7.9   Ratio of irrigated areas, adoption of modern varieties, fertilizer use, cropping intensity, and paddy yields, intensive survey, Thailand, wet and dry season, 1987.

| | Khon Kaen | | | Suphan Buri | | |
| | Irrigated | Rainfed | | Irrigated | Rainfed | Deepwater |
	KK1	KK2	KK3	SP1	SP2	SP3
Ratio of irrigated area (%)						
Wet season	100	0	0	100	0	0
Dry season	100	0	0	100	0	32
Adoption of modern varieties (%)						
Wet season	0.2	0	0	61	0.2	0
Dry season	100	—	—	100	—	100[a]
Fertilizer use (kg N/ha)[b]						
Wet season	46	36	15	77	4	0
Dry season	65	—	—	112	—	91
Yield (t/ha)[c]						
MV wet season	2.8	—	—	4.1	—	—
MV dry season	3.0	—	—	4.7	—	4.1
TV wet season	2.7	1.6	1.4	3.3	1.3	1.1
Rice cropping intensity (%)	147	100	100	181	100	100

a. Adoption rate in irrigated rice dry-season crop.
b. Refers to ammophos (16-20-0), ammonium sulfate (21-0-0), and urea (45-0-0).
c. MV = modern varieties, TV = traditional varieties.

Table 7.10   Labor use (man-days/ha) and adoption of labor-saving technologies (%) in rice farming by production environment and region, intensive survey, Thailand, 1987.[a]

	Khon Kaen			Suphan Buri		
	Irrigated	Rainfed		Irrigated	Rainfed	Deepwater
	KK1	KK2	KK3	SP1	SP2	SP3
Land preparation	5	14	14	7	6	5
(% area tractor)[b]	(94)	(29)	(2)	(100)	(98)	(100)
Crop establishment	24	26	27	7	3	2
(% area PDS)	(32)	(0)	(0)	(89)	(0)	(20)[c]
(% area BC)[d]	(0)	(0)	(0)	(0)	(100)	(80)
Care of crop	11	4	4	15	3	8
(% area herbicide)	(15)	(4)	(0)	(92)	(82)	(80)
Harvesting and threshing	30	31	26	29	28	22
(% area threshers)	(91)	(13)	(0)	(100)	(100)	(100)
Total labor	70	75	71	58	40	37
(% hired labor)	(32)	(5)	(12)	(49)	(28)	(50)

a. Weighted average of wet and dry seasons, weights being ratios of planted areas.
b. Using four-wheel tractors in SP2 and SP3 and two-wheel tractors in other villages.
c. PDS (pregerminated direct seeding) is adopted only in the dry season.
d. BC is broadcasting.

Table 7.11   Regression results of labor use functions in rice production, intensive survey, Thailand, average of wet and dry season, 1987.[a]

	Family labor	Hired labor
Intercept	42.87**	14.81**
	(5.01)	(2.66)
MVR*IRG	−2.26	17.73**
	(−0.59)	(7.15)
MVR*DPWATER	14.81*	3.97
	(1.65)	(0.68)
TV*IRG	−11.81*	12.10**
	(−2.23)	(3.51)
TV*DPWATER	−18.77**	6.54**
	(−4.64)	(2.49)
FSIZE	−1.39**	0.31
	(−4.41)	(1.51)
LEASER	−1.41	1.77
	(−0.48)	(0.93)
SHARER	−3.14	2.48
	(−0.94)	(1.14)
TRUSER	−12.23**	2.64
	(−3.12)	(1.04)
THUSER	−1.80	1.49
	(−0.41)	(0.52)
DSEED	4.41	−8.24**
	(0.84)	(−2.40)
AGE	0.01	−0.02
	(0.07)	(−0.38)
SCHOOL	1.13	1.02
	(0.42)	(0.58)
WORKER	1.45**	−0.38
	(2.94)	(−1.19)
NORTHEAST	26.00**	−9.50**
	(4.38)	(−2.41)
R^2	0.83	0.68
F-value	43.69	16.99

a. Numbers in parentheses are t-statistics.
** Indicates significance at 1% level; * at 5% level.

Table 7.12   Regression results of man-land ratio and landless ratio functions, extensive survey, Thailand, wet season, 1986.[a]

	Ln Man-land ratio	Ln Landless ratio
Intercept	−0.45	−2.26*
	(−0.62)	(−2.21)
IRGR	0.46*	0.44
	(2.26)	(1.55)
DPWATER	0.39	0.10
	(1.29)	(0.23)
MVR	0.21	−0.14
	(0.60)	(−0.28)
OWNERR	−0.20	−0.72
	(−0.62)	(−0.63)
Ln PADDYP	0.77	0.72
	(0.95)	(0.63)
Ln DISTC	0.03	−0.09
	(0.25)	(−0.50)
NORTH	1.32**	0.51
	(4.01)	(1.11)
NORTHEAST	1.02**	−0.60
	(3.27)	(−1.37)
R^2	0.53	0.32
F-value	8.64	3.66

a. Numbers in parentheses are t-statistics.
** Indicates significance at 1% level; * at 5% level.

Table 7.13   Paddy price, wage rates, tractor and thresher rentals, and land rent by production environment and region, extensive survey, Thailand, 1986.[a]

	North		Northeast		Central Plain		
	Irri-gated	Rain-fed	Irri-gated	Rain-fed	Irri-gated	Rain-fed	Deep-water
Paddy price (B/kg)							
Traditional variety	2.3	2.2	2.2	2.3	2.4	2.2	2.5
Modern variety	2.4	2.2	2.2	2.0	2.2	2.2	2.3
Wage rates (B/day)							
Transplanting							
Daily wage	38	33	35	33	42	35	—
	(5)	(8)	(11)	(11)	(3)	(2)	
Imputed wage	48	44	—	—	52	50	—
	(2)	(1)			(3)	(4)	
Harvesting							
Daily wage	38	35	36	34	—	35	—
	(6)	(8)	(11)	(11)		(8)	
Imputed wage	54	44	—	—	56	53	55
	(1)	(1)			(12)	(8)	(5)
Tractor rental (B/ha)							
One pass	—	—	—	630	440	440	440
				(2)	(1)	(3)	(5)
Two pass[b]	1,640	1,610	1,050	1,130	1,020	1,000	—
	(7)	(9)	(11)	(5)	(11)	(13)	
Thresher rental (B/ton)	100	—	93	112	91	95	88
	(2)		(7)	(2)	(12)	(15)	(5)
Land rent (B/ha)	4,100	2,900	1,600	1,100	2,800	1,300	1,300
	(7)	(8)	(11)	(11)	(12)	(16)	(5)

a. Figures in parentheses are the number of sample villages.
b. In the North, puddling is also included.

Table 7.14   Regression results of wage and land rent functions, extensive survey, Thailand, 1986.[a]

	Ln Transplanting		Ln Harvesting		Ln Land rent	
	(1)	(2)	(3)	(4)	(5)	(6)
Intercept	3.67**	3.68**	3.89**	3.42**	5.24**	5.42**
	(29.72)	(31.38)	(26.22)	(27.86)	(15.57)	(16.02)
IRGR	0.07**	0.08**	0.07**	0.10**	0.51**	0.62**
	(2.45)	(3.13)	(2.36)	(3.68)	(6.48)	(9.30)
DPWATER	—	—	0.06	0.04	−0.14	−0.20*
			(1.30)	(0.96)	(−1.18)	(−1.69)
MVR	0.02	—	0.08	—	0.32*	—
	(0.40)		(1.64)		(2.29)	
Ln FSIZE	−0.09	−0.09	0.12	0.09	0.18	0.07
	(−0.72)	(−0.73)	(1.04)	(0.80)	(0.60)	(0.22)
OWNERR	0.01	0.01	0.02	0.02	−0.06	−0.07
	(0.27)	(0.24)	(0.50)	(0.48)	(−0.49)	(−0.56)
Ln DISTC	−0.06**	−0.06**	−0.04*	−0.04*	−0.08*	−0.08
	(−3.13)	(−3.21)	(−1.91)	(−1.84)	(−1.65)	(−1.52)
Ln PADDYP	−0.08	−0.09	0.05	0.04	−0.13	−0.17
	(−0.71)	(−0.78)	(0.40)	(0.32)	(−0.41)	(−0.53)
CONT2	0.26**	0.26**	—	—	—	—
	(8.67)	(8.76)				
CONT3	—	—	0.36**	0.37**	—	—
			(11.33)	(11.50)		
NORTH	−0.26**	−0.27**	−0.06	−0.08	0.61**	0.51**
	(−3.85)	(−4.39)	(−0.91)	(−1.33)	(4.13)	(3.52)
NORTHEAST	−0.25**	−0.26**	−0.10*	−0.12**	−0.29*	−0.39**
	(−3.85)	(−4.53)	(−1.85)	(−2.35)	(−2.20)	(−3.10)
R^2	0.86	0.86	0.89	0.90	0.85	0.84
F-value	28.79	33.03	53.64	58.34	38.15	39.56

a. Numbers in parentheses are t-statistics.
** Indicates significance at 1% level; * at 5% level.

Table 7.15   Regression results of tractor and thresher rental functions, extensive survey, Thailand, 1986.[a]

	Ln Tractor rental		Ln Thresher rental	
	(1)	(2)	(3)	(4)
Intercept	4.26**	4.25**	4.42**	4.37**
	(25.15)	(25.92)	(12.15)	(12.90)
IRGR	0.003	−0.004	0.02	−0.01
	(0.08)	(−0.12)	(0.19)	(−0.22)
DPWATER	−0.02	−0.02	−0.02	−0.02
	(−0.27)	(−0.26)	(−0.26)	(−0.21)
MVR	−0.02	—	−0.06	—
	(−0.32)		(−0.46)	
Ln FSIZE	−0.05	−0.04	0.33	0.39
	(−0.31)	(−0.25)	(0.98)	(1.21)
OWNERR	−0.13*	−0.13*	−0.001	0.01
	(−2.28)	(−2.29)	(−0.001)	(0.06)
HTUSER	0.07*	0.07*	—	—
	(1.67)	(1.69)		
Ln PADDYP	0.11	0.11	0.00	0.01
	(0.71)	(0.76)	(0.01)	(0.05)
Ln DISTC	−0.00	0.00	0.03	0.03
	(−0.01)	(0.00)	(0.65)	(0.59)
TWOPASS	0.78**	0.79**	—	—
	(11.80)	(12.06)		
NORTH	0.47**	0.48**	0.23	0.26
	(5.68)	(6.18)	(1.20)	(1.41)
NORTHEAST	0.07	0.08	0.05	0.07
	(0.96)	(1.21)	(0.38)	(0.58)
R^2	0.95	0.95	0.10	0.09
F-value	97.00	108.53[a]	0.39	0.42

a. Numbers in parentheses are t-statistics.
** Indicates significance at 1% level; * at 5% level.

Table 7.16 Comparison of output and factor prices by production environment and region, intensive survey, Thailand, wet season, 1987.

	Khon Kaen			Suphan Buri		
	Irrigated	Rainfed		Irrigated	Rainfed	Deepwater
	KK1	KK2	KK3	SP1	SP2	SP3
Paddy price (B/kg)	3.3	3.4	3.2	3.8	3.6	3.8
Nitrogen price (B/kg)[a]	13	12	12	12	15	—
Wages (B/day)						
Land clearing	40	35	30	54	35	50
Chemical application	40	35	30	60	50	50
Hand weeding	40	35	30	50	35	50
Crop establishment	40	35	30	56[b]	35	56[b]
Harvesting	40	35	30	57[b]	50[b]	55[b]
Threshing	40	35	30	50	35	50
Custom rental						
Tractor (B/ha)						
One pass	—	—	—	—	450	375
Two passes	—	1,225	1,250	1,250	1,250	—
Buffalo (B/ha)						
One pass	438	—	—	—	438	—
Two passes	—	876	876	—	—	—
Thresher (B/ton)	100	100	100	80	80	80

a. Refers to price of nitrogen from ammophos (16-20-0).
b. Imputed daily earnings under piece-rate contract.

Table 7.17   Factor payments (thou B/ha) and factor shares (%) in rice farming by production environment and region, intensive survey, Thailand, 1987.[a]

	Khon Kaen			Suphan Buri		
	Irrigated	Rainfed		Irrigated	Rainfed	Deepwater
	KK1	KK2	KK3	SP1	SP2	SP3
Gross value of output	8.9	5.6	4.4	15.3	4.6	7.4
	(100)	(100)	(100)	(100)	(100)	(100)
Current inputs	1.2	0.7	0.4	2.3	0.5	1.5
	(14)	(12)	(9)	(15)	(11)	(20)
Fixed capital	1.1	0.7	0.5	1.4	0.6	0.7
	(12)	(12)	(11)	(9)	(13)	(10)
Owned[b]	0.7	0.6	0.4	1.1	0.3	0.5
Hired	0.4	0.1	0.1	0.3	0.3	0.2
Labor 3.0	2.6	2.1	3.5	1.6	2.0	
	(34)	(47)	(48)	(23)	(35)	(27)
Family[c]	2.1	2.5	1.9	1.8	1.2	1.1
Hired	0.9	0.1	0.2	1.7	0.4	0.9
Land[d]	3.6	1.6	1.4	8.1	1.9	3.2
	(40)	(29)	(32)	(53)	(41)	(43)
Leasehold rent[e]	2.2	—	1.4	3.4	1.6	1.9
Surplus[f]	1.4	—	0	4.7	0.3	1.3

a. Weighted average of wet and dry seasons, weights being the ratios of planted areas. Figures in parentheses are factor shares.
b. Imputed cost using average machinery rental in each village.
c. Imputed labor cost using average daily earnings under piece-rate contracts in various tasks.
d. Estimated as residual.
e. Average leasehold rent in each village.
f. Residual minus average leasehold rent.

Table 7.18   Average annual income (thou B) of farm households by source and production environment, intensive survey, Thailand, 1987.

	Khon Kaen			Suphan Buri		
	Irrigated	Rainfed		Irrigated	Rainfed	Deepwater
	KK1	KK2	KK3	SP1	SP2	SP3
Rice production	17.3	8.1	9.3	51.5	19.8	32.6
Labor[a]	5.8	4.3	5.2	9.1	7.9	9.1
Capital[b]	1.9	1.1	1.2	5.4	1.9	3.8
Land[c]	9.6	2.7	2.9	37.0	10.0	19.7
Nonrice production	20.1	20.9	21.4	40.9	17.6	29.4
Farm[d]	3.7	4.1	6.0	33.4	10.0	4.8
Nonfarm[e]	16.4	16.8	15.4	7.5	7.6	24.6
Total income	37.4	29.0	30.7	92.4	37.4	62.0
Household size	6.9	6.7	6.5	5.4	6.0	6.5
(no of working members)[f]	(4.0)	(4.8)	(5.1)	(4.1)	(4.4)	(5.0)
Income per person	5.4	4.3	4.8	17.1	6.2	9.6
(per working member)	(9.3)	(6.0)	(6.0)	(22.6)	(8.5)	(12.5)

a. Imputed family labor income in owned farms.
b. Imputed return to owned machinery and draft animals.
c. Residual for owner-cultivators and residual minus actual rent payments for tenants.
d. Includes nonrice crops, livestock, poultry raising, fishing, actual labor earnings, and actual rental earnings outside owned farms.
e. Includes labor earnings from nonfarm employment, other assets, pensions, and remittances.
f. Between ages thirteen and sixty.

Table 7.19   Average annual income (thou B) of landless households by source and production environment, intensive survey, Thailand, 1987.

| | Khon Kaen | Suphan Buri | | |
| | Rainfed | Irrigated | Rainfed | Deepwater |
	KK3	SP1	SP2	SP3
Households (no)	9	9	7	14
Farm income[a]	8.5	22.2	8.2	6.5
Nonfarm income	11.0	7.0	1.9	7.3
Labor earnings	7.5	6.7	0.8	5.1
Remittance and pensions	3.5	0.3	1.1	2.2
Total income	19.5	29.2	10.1	13.8
Household size	4.8	4.7	4.7	4.5
(no of working members)[b]	(3.9)	(2.4)	(2.1)	(2.5)
Income per person	4.1	6.2	2.1	3.1
(per working member)	(5.0)	(12.2)	(4.8)	(5.5)

a. Includes labor earnings from rice and nonrice crop production, livestock and poultry raising, and fishing.
b. Number of household members between ages thirteen and sixty.

Table 7.20   Regression results of farm household income functions, intensive survey, Thailand, 1987.[a]

	Rice income (owned farms)			Nonrice farm income	Nonfarm income
	Land	Labor	Capital		
Intercept	8.95*	−0.73	−0.04	11.77*	8.51
	(2.09)	(−0.67)	(−0.09)	(1.85)	(0.71)
MVR*IRG*FSIZE	11.01**	1.37**	1.07**	4.50**	−2.99
	(12.04)	(5.90)	(11.65)	(3.30)	(−1.17)
MVR*DPWATER* FSIZE	2.57**	0.88**	0.80**	−1.29	0.18
	(4.56)	(6.19)	(14.07)	(−1.54)	(0.11)
TVR*IRG*FSIZE	7.48**	0.97**	0.74**	1.16	−0.42
	(9.60)	(4.91)	(9.50)	(0.99)	(−0.19)
TVR*DPWATER* FSIZE	1.29**	−0.66**	−0.24**	−0.26	1.39
	(3.18)	(−6.47)	(−5.86)	(−0.43)	(1.22)
FSIZE	0.85**	1.12**	0.33**	−0.20	−0.63
	(3.05)	(15.89)	(11.80)	(−0.49)	(−0.80)
LEASER	−12.16**	−0.80	−0.44*	−2.30	4.52
	(−5.47)	(−1.43)	(−1.99)	(−0.69)	(0.72)
SHARER	−4.45*	−0.31	−0.02	3.35	−7.65
	(−1.75)	(−0.48)	(−0.09)	(0.88)	(−1.07)
HTOWNER	1.15	1.58**	1.84**	7.79**	−1.88
	(0.56)	(3.03)	(8.95)	(2.54)	(−0.33)
THOWNER	5.48	1.80*	2.27**	2.38	1.37
	(1.38)	(1.79)	(5.69)	(0.40)	(0.12)
AGE	−0.06	0.002	−0.003	−0.04	−0.01
	(−1.03)	(0.13)	(−0.53)	(−0.39)	(−0.07)
SCHOOL	4.15*	0.64	0.10	−1.87	1.37
	(2.08)	(1.27)	(0.52)	(−0.63)	(0.24)
WORKER	−0.16	0.29**	0.03	1.11*	1.18
	(−0.44)	(3.10)	(0.82)	(2.02)	(1.13)
NORTHEAST	−9.05**	0.63	−0.18	−11.05**	2.76
	(−5.18)	(1.43)	(−1.04)	(−4.24)	(0.56)
R^2	0.68	0.77	0.88	0.24	0.04
F-value	45.94	71.95	154.21	6.72	0.90

a. Numbers in parentheses are t-statistics.
** Indicates significance at 1% level; * at 5% level.

Table 7.21   Regression results of landless household income functions, intensive survey, Thailand, 1987.[a]

	Farm income		Nonfarm income	
	(1)	(2)	(1)	(2)
Intercept	3.70	9.87	30.27*	7.05
	(0.30)	(0.76)	(2.13)	(0.60)
AGE	-0.21	-0.12	0.01	0.04
	(-1.32)	(-0.62)	(0.03)	(0.20)
SCHOOL	-0.30	1.63	2.02	3.96
	(-0.06)	(0.26)	(0.33)	(0.68)
WORKER	3.17*	2.75	-2.81	-2.62
	(1.88)	(1.34)	(-1.42)	(-1.35)
Village-specific variables:				
FSIZE	1.22	—	-3.69*	—
	(0.86)		(-2.22)	
MVR*IRGV*FSIZE	1.34**	—	-0.59	—
	(3.56)		(-1.34)	
MVR*DPWATER*FSIZE	-0.30	—	0.71*	—
	(-0.80)		(1.76)	
NORTHEAST	—	-6.63	—	9.65*
		(-1.23)		(1.89)
R^2	0.64	0.27	0.40	0.34
F-value	3.73	0.67	0.99	1.14

a. Numbers in parentheses are t-statistics.
** Indicates significance at 1% level; * at 5% level.

Table 7.22   Overall Gini ratio for all households and contributions by income component, intensive survey, Thailand, 1987.

| Villages | Overall Gini ratio | Contribution by | | | Nonrice farm income | Nonfarm income |
| | | Rice income (owned farms) | | | | |
		Land	Labor	Capital		
Khon Kaen						
KK1	0.26	0.05	0.02	0.00	0.02	0.17
KK2	0.39	0.02	0.01	0.01	0.03	0.32
KK3	0.38	0.03	0.01	0.01	0.03	0.30
Suphan Buri						
SP1	0.30	0.13	0.01	0.01	0.13	0.02
SP2	0.26	0.06	0.04	0.01	0.09	0.06
SP3	0.41	0.16	0.05	0.03	0.01	0.16
All	0.40	0.14	0.03	0.02	0.09	0.12

8
Production Environments, Modern Variety Adoption, and Income Distribution in Bangladesh
■

MAHABUB HOSSAIN, M. ABUL QUASEM, M. A. JABBAR, AND M. MOKADDEM AKASH

Bangladesh's population of 110 million (770 persons/km^2 density) grows annually at 2%, a rate that adds nearly 2 million people every year. Two-thirds of per capita income is spent on food—nearly 40% on rice alone. The demand for food grains is still growing at around 3% per year. Maintaining the food-population balance, which is already precarious, depends mainly on technological progress.

The area of cultivated land has remained stagnant at around 8.5 million hectares since the early 1960s. Cropping intensity has reached nearly 179% (Bangladesh Bureau of Statistics 1986). Nearly 75% of the cropped land is devoted to rice, and there is little scope for the diversion of land from nonfood to food crops. Bangladesh's labor intensity in rice cultivation is among the highest in the world. The scope of increasing rice production through additional use of labor is severely limited. Therefore, growth in rice production must come from an increase in land productivity.

Rice in Bangladesh is grown in three distinct seasons: *boro* (January to June), *aus* (April to August), and *amon* (August to December). Modern rice varieties were introduced for the *boro* and *aus* seasons in 1967 and for the *amon* seasons in 1970. After an initial surge in adoption, the rate decreased during 1973–1976. Since 1976 there has been uninterrupted expansion of modern varieties (Figure 8.2). Gains in the food-grain sector that Bangladesh has achieved since 1970 are mostly due to technological progress in rice cultivation. During the 1980s the area under rice did not increase, but production increased at 2.8% per year because of adoption of modern varieties (Table 8.1).

When modern varieties were introduced, yield was about 5 t/ha, but it declined to about 3.5 t/ha by the mid-1970s and has remained stagnant at that level since then (Figure 8.3). The overall paddy yield, however, has continued to increase as a result of the diffusion process—i.e., reallocation of land from the low-yielding traditional to high-yielding modern varieties. There is still great potential for diffusion, as only 50% of the paddy area is now covered by modern varieties.

Technological progress in rice production has been uneven across regions. Rapid progress has occurred in the districts of Chittagong, Comilla, Bogra, Jessore, and Dhaka, where there is development of irrigation facilities. Progress has remained slow, however, in the districts of Barisal, Patuakhali, and Khulna, where rice lands suffer from the intrustion of saline water from the sea. Progress also has been slow in the districts of Faridpur and Sylhet, which are subject to deep flooding caused by excessive rainfall and the overflowing of rivers from July to October.

The objective of this study is to analyze factors behind the differential adoption of the new rice technology in Bangladesh and its impact on the well-being of people in rural areas. The main focus is on the role of environmental factors in influencing the effects of the technology on income distribution. We also analyze the impact of technology diffusion on input use and productivity and the operation of factor markets such as land and labor.

VILLAGE AND HOUSEHOLD SURVEYS

Data for the study were drawn from a sample survey of sixty-two randomly selected villages conducted jointly by the Bangladesh Institute of Development Studies (BIDS) and the Bangladesh Rice Research Institute (BRRI) during 1987–1988. The survey covered crops grown during 1987 calendar year.

Survey Methodology

A list of all local self-government unions of the country (excluding those in the Chittagong Hill Tracts region) was prepared from reports of the 1981 population census, and sixty-four unions were randomly selected from the list. Two unions were later dropped because of difficulty in administering of the survey.

Information on the number of households, land area, total population, and literacy rates was obtained for all villages of each selected union. Two villages having 100 to 250 households and a land-person ratio and literacy rate similar to those for the union as a whole were then selected. Thus, 124 villages were selected, with the first choice among each pair being the village most representative of the union. A community-level survey (extensive survey) collected data for all villages through group interviews of local leaders and schoolteachers. An in-depth household survey (intensive survey) was done in each first-choice village. Seven second-choice villages were surveyed because of lack of cooperation from respondents in the first-choice village.

The in-depth household survey collected information on size of household, ownership and utilization of land, major sources of income, type of housing, and age and educational status of the head of the household. The households were then classified into four landownership groups: functionally landless (less than 0.2 ha), small owner (0.2 to 1 ha), medium owner (1 to 2 ha), and large owner (2 ha or more). Each of the landownership groups was further classified into two groups according to whether the household was engaged in tenancy cultivation or not. Then twenty households were selected from each village by proportionate random sampling. In a few villages, the sample size was twenty-one because of rounding error. The total sample was 1,245 households. A few sample households were dropped from the analysis because the data were suspected to be unreliable.

The extensive survey collected aggregate village-level data through group interviews. Information was collected on land elevation, soil type, salinity problems, trends in the coverage of irrigation facilities, the history of the adoption of new agricultural technology, the potential of the village regarding technology diffusion and irrigation development, normal yield for various crops, prices of major agricultural inputs and outputs (including prices of land and labor), and the access of the village to various infrastructure facilities.

The intensive survey collected information on the demographic characteristics of household members, characteristics of different plots of land owned by the household, allocation of the plots to various crops and their production, the pattern of employment for working members, terms and conditions of the labor and tenancy markets, the marketing of agricultural produce, and access to the agricultural extension system.

In addition, a detailed survey on inputs and outputs was undertaken for a small sample of selected plots for the study of the costs and returns of modern varieties compared to those of traditional varieties. The field investigators collected information from five cultivators in each of the sixty-two sample villages for the major crop varieties grown in the village. The sample respondent was requested to provide information for one plot that was not severely affected by floods or droughts and for which the respondent could accurately recall input-output information. One respondent was selected from each of five land tenure groups: small owner-cultivator, small tenant-cultivator, medium owner-cultivator, medium tenant-cultivator, and large owner-cultivator. Thus, 60% of the sample plots were covered from the owner-cultivator group, which roughly corresponds to the proportion of owner-farmers for the country.

Representativeness of the Sample

The unions selected for the study constitute 1.4% of the 4,401 unions in the country. The census of the selected villages enumerated 9,874 households, or 159 households per village. The enumerated households make up about

0.07% of the households in the country. The Bangladesh Bureau of Statistics (BBS) uses a sample size of about 6,400 households for its periodic household-level surveys. Thus, the estimates obtained from the survey for this study will compare favorably with those obtained by the BBS.

The representativeness of the study sample is indicated by the similarity of the pattern of the distribution of landownership obtained from the survey to that obtained from the 1983–1984 agricultural census.

CHARACTERIZATION OF THE PRODUCTION ENVIRONMENT

The agricultural production environment is basically determined by physical and climatic factors. The farmer chooses crop varieties that suit the particular environment of a plot of land. Thus, favorableness of the environment depends on the requirement of a particular variety and the characteristics of the plot.

It is necessary at the outset to define the production environments and characterize the study areas to determine whether environments are favorable or unfavorable for the adoption of modern varieties. Also, because the villages were selected randomly and the sample size is quite large, the study gives an opportunity to assess the importance of various environmental factors in Bangladesh.

Initially, a large number of variables were chosen to examine the differential in adoption of modern varieties and rice yields across the villages. These included socioeconomic factors such as average farm size of the village, ratio of land owned by large landowners (those with more than 2 ha), and the importance of nonfarm activities. These variables were dropped, however, because no systematic variation in the adoption of modern varieties and rice yield was found with respect to them. Three variables were found to have a substantial effect on modern variety adoption and crop yield; elevation of land (topography), rainfall, and salinity (Table 8.2).

Topography

One distinctive feature of modern varieties is that they are short-statured and less tolerant of flooding—and drought—than traditional varieties. Average rainfall in Bangladesh is more than 2,000 mm per year, with more than 75% of that occurring from June to September. As a result, excessive waterlogging during the rainy season and inadequate moisture in the soil during the dry season (January to April) adversely affect rice production.

The topography variable was defined in terms of the depth of flooding during the peak of the monsoon season. Land that is not flooded at all was defined as high land, land flooded up to 30 cm depth as medium land, from 30 to 90 cm depth as low land, and more than 90 cm depth as very low land. This information was collected from farmers for each of the plots owned by them and was used to get a distribution of land at the village level by depth of flooding. In a large number of villages, substantial variation in topography of the plot exists, and quite a few villages have both high and very low land. The implication of this finding is that even if topography adversely affects adoption of modern varieties, at least some land is favorable for adoption of modern varieties. Also, where the farmer operates a number of plots at different elevations within a village, there is a good chance that at least one of his plots will be planted to modern varieties. Thus, for analyzing the impact of the new technology, it would be improper to classify a village or farmer as either an adopter or nonadopter of modern varieties.

Because it is difficult to classify villages neatly according to topography, we have classified them according to the type of elevation that occupies the major portion of the land in the village. An unfavorable production environment is defined as one with either high land (inadequate soil moisture) or very low land (excessive waterlogging). About 45% of the land area in the study villages is unfavorable by this criterion.

For all seasons taken together, the rate of modern variety adoption is highest on medium high land, followed by high land and very low land. During the dry season, modern variety adoption is highest on very low and medium high land and lowest on high land. This pattern results from the easy availability of surface water in extreme low-lying villages and the higher incidence of groundwater irrigation in the medium high land villages. Adoption of modern varieties during the wet season, however, varies directly with the elevation of land.

The unfavorableness of the lowland areas with respect to the adoption of modern varieties is compensated for by relatively higher yields. Average yield for modern varieties is about 4.5 t/ha in very low land, which is about 40% higher than the yield in high land and 15% higher than in medium high land. Regular flooding due to the prolonged overflow of rivers enriches the soil in the low-lying villages. For traditional varieties, the yield is low on high land because of moisture stress during the early and late monsoon seasons; for the other three categories of land, no systematic relationship emerges.

The combined effect of soil fertility and modern variety adoption is reflected in the overall yield of rice. Average yield is highest for the very low-lying villages and lowest for villages with high land. Thus, one may conclude that for Bangladesh, the most unfavorable environment for growing rice is in the extreme high land villages—i.e., the drought-prone areas.

Rainfall

Information on normal rainfall for the sample villages is based on the available data for the district. The villages were classified into three groups—those with less than 1,800 mm/yr (low), those with 1,800 to 2,400 mm/yr (moderate), and those with more than 2,400 mm/yr (high).

The rate of adoption of modern varieties is positively related to the incidence of rainfall during the dry season. For the whole year, modern variety adoption is substantially lower in low-rainfall villages than in high- or medium-rainfall villages, even though adoption of modern varieties during the wet season is high in the low-rainfall villages. Average yield for traditional varieties and modern varieties is relatively low in both high- and low-rainfall villages compared to the medium-rainfall villages. These observations indicate that the production environment for rice is unfavorable in both low- and high-rainfall villages.

Soil Salinity

Bangladesh has a long coastal area that suffers from saltwater intrusion, particularly during the dry season, when salt is deposited in the soil in some areas. Modern varieties available in Bangladesh are not sufficiently tolerant of salinity to grow in such areas.

Fourteen of the sixty-two study villages are in the coastal regions of Chittagong, Noakhali, Barisal, Patuakhali, and Khulna. No village reports extreme soil salinity, and moderate salinity affects seven villages, representing 13% of land area in the survey. In a few of the salinity-affected villages, farmers recently started growing modern varieties by extracting groundwater through shallow tubewells. Farmers report that the salt content of that groundwater is not high enough to severely affect rice yield.

In the villages with salinity problems, the proportion of area under irrigation is substantially lower than in other villages, but yields of traditional varieties are higher (Table 8.2). This pattern is due to the allocation of land exclusively to transplanted *amon* (favorable rainfed varieties) in these villages. It has a higher yield than local *aus* (upland variety) or broadcast *amon* (deepwater variety) grown extensively in other parts of the country.

Classification of Production Environments

In view of the diverse factors mentioned above, it is difficult to neatly classify the villages according to production environments. Some kind of classification is necessary, however, in order to assess the impact of modern variety adoption in various environments. However imperfect it might be, the following system was used to classify the sample villages according to environmental status:

Irrigated. The irrigated group includes villages where more than 50% of the land area has modern irrigation facilities. Access to irrigation allows farmers to overcome constraints imposed by other environmental factors, such as high elevation of land or inadequate rainfall.

Villages with less than 50% of the land under irrigation were classified into four environmental groups as follows:

Drought-prone. The drought-prone group includes upland villages where average annual rainfall is less than 1,800 mm and more than 50% of the land is not flooded at all. The soil in these villages suffers from drought from November to May. During years of low rainfall, droughts may affect both the *aus* (in June) and transplanted *amon* (in October) varieties.

Flood-prone. The flood-prone group includes villages where more than 50% of the land is flooded at a depth of more than 30 cm. The major portion of the land in these villages is not suitable for growing short-statured modern varieties during the monsoon season. Even traditional varieties may suffer from temporary submergence at times of excessive rains.

Saline-affected. The saline-affected group includes villages that report problems of soil salinity, mainly in tidal wetlands in coastal areas. During the monsoon season, the salt content of the tidal water is relatively low. In the dry season, however, the salt content is high, and the land becomes unsuitable for growing rice.

Favorable rainfed. The favorable rainfed group includes villages not covered under the above groups. These are basically shallow rainfed lowlands with uniform land elevation and a medium or high intensity of rainfall.

The location and environmental conditions of villages are shown in Figure 8.1. The status of adoption of modern varieties in villages of different environmental status appears in Table 8.3. Saline-affected villages have the lowest ratio of irrigated area, modern variety adoption, and fertilizer use. The flood-prone villages have a higher ratio of irrigation because of their better access to surface and groundwater. However, the modern varieties are grown in those villages mostly during the dry season, because deep wet-season flooding does not allow cultivation of modern varieties. Use of modern varieties during the wet season has spread most widely in the drought-prone areas, where the ratio of irrigated area is about equal to that of the sample as a whole.

ADOPTION OF MODERN VARIETIES

The literature on adoption of modern varieties argues that large farmers and owner-cultivators are in a more favorable position to adopt them than small farmers and tenant farmers. For an excellent survey of that literature and a review of empirical studies, see Griffin (1974), Pears (1980), Feder, Just, and Zilberman (1985), and Lipton and Longhurst (1989).

Nearly 70% of farmers in Bangladesh have holdings of less than 1 ha; more than 40% are tenants or partial tenants, and about 23% of the area is farmed under tenancy (Bangladesh Bureau of Statistics 1986). Thus, a priori one would expect the agrarian structure of Bangladesh to constrain the diffusion of modern varieties. Technical factors such as topography, soil salinity, and access to irrigation facilities may also affect adoption of modern varieties.

Physical Environment and Modern Variety Adoption

Irrigation is particularly important for cultivation of modern varieties in Bangladesh during the dry season. Information on irrigation was collected for each plot owned and operated by the sample household. We estimated from the survey that 27% of the total land is irrigated during one season or another. If noncultivated land (homestead, orchard, water bodies, etc.) is excluded, the irrigation ratio is about 31%.

Of the total irrigated land, about 25% is irrigated by traditional methods (such as swing baskets), which are labor intensive and are basically used to provide supplementary water. Nearly 60% of the land is irrigated by exploitation of groundwater using mostly privately owned tubewells, which is a high-cost source; only 15% of land is irrigated by low-lift pumps or gravity canals under the public sector–operated surface water irrigation system.

The pattern of land use in plots irrigated by traditional methods differs from that of plots irrigated by modern methods (Table 8.4). Most of the plots using traditional methods are near water bodies and are extremely low-lying. Their intensity of cropping is somewhat lower, and the proportion of area planted to modern varieties is substantially lower than in plots irrigated by modern methods.

Adoption of modern varieties is highly facilitated by modern irrigation. Only 5% of the nonirrigated land grows modern varieties (mostly modern *aus* varieties) during the dry season; for irrigated land, the proportion is 66%. Irrigation also increases modern variety adoption during the *amon* season, although to a much smaller extent.

Because of crop substitution, the impact of irrigation on cropping intensity is insignificant. Rice cropping intensity increases but the expense of other crops (e.g., land) is shifted from other crops to rice when irrigation facilities are developed. Total cropped area does not change.

Land elevation is an important factor affecting adoption of modern varieties, particularly during the *amon* season. Modern varieties do not tolerate deep flooding and are unsuitable for land that is flooded above a certain depth for a considerable period of time. The cropping pattern and intensity on lands of different topography and irrigation are shown in Table 8.5.

On nonirrigated land, the intensity of cropping is substantially higher for plots on medium and low land than for plots on high and very low land. When irrigation is available, cropping intensity increases on high and medium land but declines on low and very low land. The major cropping patterns on nonirrigated low land are single-cropped deepwater *amon*, a mixed *aus* crop with broadcast *aus* and *amon* varieties, and deepwater *amon* followed by pulses and oilseeds. When irrigation is available, the farmer keeps the land fallow during the monsoon season and grows modern rice varieties during the dry season. This change in cropping pattern is more profitable for the farmer, although it reduces cropping intensity. On high and medium land, the availability of irrigation allows farmers to shift from other crops to modern variety rice during the dry season or to use land that is seasonally fallow (because of inadequate moisture) to grow modern varieties. These types of land are also suitable for a shift from traditional to modern varieties of rice during the monsoon season.

Investment in irrigation thus facilitates the adoption of modern varieties, but the extent to which irrigation facilities are used by farmers depends on the elevation of the land. With irrigation, the cropping intensity with modern varieties of rice increases to more than 100% on high and medium high land, compared to 6 to 23% under nonirrigated conditions, depending on the elevation of land (Table 8.5).

Socioeconomic Characteristics and Modern Variety Adoption

The requirement for working capital in cultivating a given amount of land is higher for modern varieties than for traditional varieties. Farmers who grow modern varieties need to invest in irrigation equipment, such as tubewells and pumps, or pay water charges to owners of the equipment for purchase of the services. Unless the government bears the cost of irrigation development, access to capital in the form of accumulated savings or low-cost credit from financial institutions may become an important factor determining the extent of modern variety adoption. Because small landowners and tenants have little capital and limited access to institutional credit, a priori it would be expected that they would adopt modern varieties less heavily than large owner-cultivators.

Table 8.6 reports the findings of our survey regarding the use of irrigation and the extent of adoption of modern varieties by various socioeconomic groups. Contrary to the a priori hypothesis, the proportion of area irrigated is invariant with the size of landholdings. Availability of irrigation in Bangladesh seems to be exogenously determined. In the early years, irrigation facilities were developed by the government, largely through externally funded projects that benefited cultivators irrespective of the size of landownership. Even with private ownership of irrigation equipment, which has increased considerably since the late 1970s, the small- and medium-sized farms have an equal chance of having some of their plots located within the command area of the equipment because of the random location of scattered holdings. This may explain why access to irrigation is invariant across farm sizes.

Nearly 70% of the cultivator households grow modern varieties, according to the survey. The intensity of adoption is inversely related to the size of landownership, which is contrary to the findings reported in the early Green Revolution literature. Similar findings have been noted in earlier studies (Asaduzzaman 1979; Hossain 1988). Large holdings allocate 35% of cultivated land to modern varieties, compared to 44% for small holders and 54% for the marginal ones, who are basically tenant farmers. The inverse relationship of modern variety adoption with the size of landownership is observed for both growing seasons, although the difference is more pronounced for the wet season. Because access to irrigation facilities is invariant across the landownership scale, it is evident from these findings that smaller farms use irrigation facilities more intensively than large farms for growing modern varieties.

The impact of tenancy on the extent of adoption of modern agricultural technology has been a subject of considerable controversy in the literature. Bhaduri (1973) cites an East Indian experience to argue that the landlord who derives income from rent as well as from usury would not allow a tenant to adopt a new technology because it would increase the tenant's income and thereby free him from the landlord's clutches. Newbery (1975), however, argues that under uncertain labor and product markets, share tenancy may be a preferred arrangement for the adoption of the new technology because the risk can be shared by the tenant and the landlord. Also, because the tenant is usually a small-scale farmer with surplus labor and high subsistence pressure, adoption of the relatively more labor-intensive modern varieties may be easier for the tenant than for the owner-cultivator. Recent reviews of the literature by Otsuka and Hayami (1988) and Otsuka, Chuma, and Hayami (1992) suggest that tenurial status of the farm would not affect modern variety adoption.

It is estimated from our survey that 43% of the cultivators rent some land and that about 23% of the cultivated land is under tenancy. Nearly 71% of the rented land is occupied under a sharecropping arrangement in which the tenant pays 50% of the gross produce to the landowner as rent. Most of the tenants own some land and rent some more for higher utilization of the capacity of the fixed endowment of family workers and farm establishment. Only 14% of farmers are pure tenants—i.e., farmers who own no cultivated land themselves.

Data on access to irrigation and adoption of modern varieties across land tenure groups are reported in Table 8.6. The use of irrigation as well as adoption of modern varieties is highest for owner cum tenant cultivators, who own the major portion of their holdings. However, the intensity of adoption of modern varieties is not much different between owner and tenant farms or between owned and rented land. But for each tenure class, the rate of adoption is lower for rented land compared to owned land.

Determinants of Modern Variety
Adoption: A Multivariate Analysis

To identify the factors affecting modern variety adoption, the following linear regression model was estimated using the Tobit procedure:

MVP   =   f (FSIZE, TENANCY, IRGP, PHIGH, PLOW,
             FPPRICE, SCHOOL, LAND, SUBP, RFALL,
             SALINE, ELECT, INFR)

where

MVP	=	ratio of harvested rice area under modern varieties (percent)
FSIZE	=	amount of land cultivated by the sample household (ha)
IRGP	=	ratio of cultivated area under irrigation (percent)
PHIGH	=	land at high elevation as a percentage of total cultivated land
PLOW	=	land at low and very low elevation as a percentage of cultivated land
SUBP	=	subsistence pressure, measured by the number of family members per earner
FPPRICE	=	price of fertilizer in the village relative to price of paddy
SCHOOL	=	completed years of formal schooling for the head of the household
LAND	=	pressure of the population on land at the village level, measured by the average size of land owned per household in the village (ha)
TENANCY	=	percentage of cultivated land rented
RFALL	=	village-level dummy with value 1 for villages with annual rainfall over 2,500 mm, 0 otherwise
SALINE	=	village-level dummy with value 1 for villages reporting soil salinity, 0 otherwise
ELECT	=	village-level dummy with value 1 for villages with electricity, 0 otherwise
INFR	=	village-level dummy with value 1 for villages with easy access to bus or rickshaw transport, 0 otherwise.

Because modern varieties are more fertilizer-responsive than traditional varieties, relative profitability may depend on the price of fertilizer relative to that of paddy. An earlier specification of the model included wage rates relative to paddy prices as an independent variable, but the results showed wage rate to be positively and significantly associated with modern variety adoption. This result was contrary to a priori expectations that as wage rate increases, profitability—and hence the adoption rate of modern varieties—decreases. It appears that wage rate is an endogenous variable—the higher the rate of modern variety adoption, the larger the demand for labor and hence the higher the wage rate. Therefore, wage rate was dropped from the list of explanatory variables in the final estimation of the equation.

Access to information about sources of new inputs, knowledge about how they can be optimally used, and methods of marketing additional output could also be important factors in determining the differential rate of adoption. The level of education of the farmer, SCHOOL, was used as a proxy for this variable.

The effect of infrastructure was be captured by village-level dummy variables ELECT and INFR. The environmental factors, such as elevation of the parcel of land, susceptibility to droughts, submergence, and soil salinity, were captured by the variables PHIGH, PLOW, RFALL, and SALINE.

The model was estimated separately for two seasons. For the overlapping *boro* and *aus* seasons, irrigation is a prerequisite for the adoption of modern varieties; rainfall is scanty, and puddling of soil for transplanting of seedlings cannot be done without irrigation. Because this is also a relatively slack season for agricultural activity—as a significant proportion of land remains fallow—factors such as labor shortage may not constrain the spread of modern varieties. During the *amon* season, however, rainfall is plentiful enough in large parts of the country that modern varieties can be grown as a rainfed crop. Because most of the land is cropped during this season, occasional labor shortages may appear. Because of these differences, analysis at the seasonal level could provide useful information.

The estimated values of the parameters of the model are reported in Table 8.7. It is found that technical and environmental factors are more important in determining the adoption of modern varieties than socioeconomic factors. The most important factors, as indicated by the very high t-values, are provision of irrigation, susceptibility to soil salinity, and access to electricity. The estimated value of the regression coefficient suggests that a 10% increase in irrigated area would increase modern variety adoption by 7.4%. This factor is the major determinant of adoption for the dry season; for the wet season, the coefficient is positive but not statistically significant. The coefficients of other environmental factors suggest that during the wet season modern varieties are adopted less on the lowlands and in villages with excessive rainfall, indicating the need to develop taller varieties or varieties tolerant to submergence. For the dry season, however, the land elevation factors do not affect the rate of adoption. Soil salinity affects adoption for the dry as well as the wet season; the rate of adoption is about 48% lower in villages reporting soil salinity.

Access to electricity and better transport facilities contribute to higher rates of adoption, particularly for the dry season. The rate of adoption is 29% higher in villages with access to electricity compared to those lacking this infrastructural facility.

The coefficient of fertilizer-paddy price ratio is negative and statistically significant, which suggests that the adoption rate is lower in villages with higher input-output prices. Thus, farmers respond to economic incentives in deciding whether to allocate land to modern varieties. Other socioeconomic factors affecting the rate of adoption are the pressure of population on land and the subsistence pressure in the family. The statistically significant negative coefficient of LAND suggests that the rate of adoption is higher in villages with lower per capita land endowment. This finding is contrary to a popular view that the economically favorable areas with better land endowments have benefited more from the availability of modern rice varieties than areas with lesser endowments (Lipton and Longhurst 1989). The positive coefficient of SUBP supports the Chayanovian hypothesis that the larger the subsistence pressure in the family, the greater the need to increase income and hence to adopt modern varieties.

It is important to note that when the effects of all other variables are controlled, the tenurial status of the farm does not affect the adoption rate. But the coefficient of farm size is positive and statistically significant for the dry season, suggesting higher rates of adoption on larger farms, contrary to the observations noted from the bivariate analysis presented in Table 8.6. The higher rates of adoption on smaller farms shown in the table may be due to higher subsistence pressure in the household, the availability of more labor in relation to land on small farms, and the low land endowment in the high-adopter villages.

MODERN RICE TECHNOLOGY, INPUT USE, AND LAND PRODUCTIVITY

This section assesses the impact of the adoption of modern varieties on the use of labor and fertilizer, cropping intensity, and returns to land. The direct effect of the technology on farm income will depend not only on changes in crop yields but also on input requirements. The impact of modern variety adoption on the demand for labor is particularly important in assessing the equity implications of the new technology.

Specification of Estimated Equations

It is postulated that demand for inputs at the farm level depends on the size of cultivated holding (FSIZE), the size of nonland fixed assets (CAPITALQ), and the number of workers in the household (WORKER). The variable CAPITALQ has been measured as the replacement cost of the value of farm animals, agricultural tools and implements, and transport equipment.

The ownership of irrigation equipment poses a measurement problem for this variable. Irrigation equipment is owned by a few households; others pay water charges when irrigating land. The water charge includes the depreciation of machinery as well as the operating expenses of fuel and labor, which account for about half of the water charges. We assumed the working life of irrigation equipment as six years in order to impute the value of irrigation equipment for individual farmers.

The proportion of area under tenancy may also affect the demand for inputs because of the disincentive effect of sharecropping, which is the predominant form of tenancy arrangement in Bangladesh. Access to knowledge and the quality of farm management may also affect input demand. This factor was incorporated by taking the years of schooling of the head of the household (SCHOOL) as an explanatory variable. Because demand for an input is a derived demand, it depends on its own price, as well as the price of output and the prices of other inputs. Therefore, we included the price of fertilizer (FPRICE), the wage rate (WAGE), and the price of paddy (PADDYP) as explanatory variables in the equation. The information on prices was collected at the farm level from households who participated in the market. The farm-level prices may to some extent be influenced by the level of demand for the input and the level of supply of the output and hence may be endogenously determined. In order to avoid this problem, following Bardhan (1979) we used village-level prices, including wage rates, collected through the extensive survey.

The technology variables were represented by the proportion of cultivated area under modern varieties (MVR) and the proportion of area under irrigation (IRGR). Because the adoption of modern varieties is highly related to the proportion of area under irrigation (see Table 8.7), two interaction variables (MVR*IRGR and MVR*RFR) were included to avoid the problem of multicollinearity. The regression coefficient of the MVR*IRGR variable measured the effect of modern varieties when they are adopted under irrigation, whereas the coefficient of MVR*RFR measured the effect when they are adopted as a rainfed crop.

The effect of environmental factors on input demand should be indirectly captured through the MVR variable, because they were found to be a significant determinant of adoption of modern varieties. But these factors might have independent effects on input use alongside their indirect effects through technology adoption. Therefore, we estimated regression equations incorporating village-level dummy variables to represent the environmental factors. The flood-prone villages were represented by the dummy variable DPWATER, drought-prone villages by DPRONE, and saline-affected villages by SALINE. The villages with favorable rainfed conditions were used as the control group. The independent effects of infrastructural variables were captured by dummy variables ELECT and INFR.

We estimated the demand functions in log-linear forms for ease of interpretation of the coefficients. Because a small number of farm households did not use fertilizer or hired labor, they were excluded from the regression analysis, which may create a bias in the estimated value of the regression coefficients. To check whether this exclusion substantially affected findings, we also estimated the functions in linear form. The results were not qualitatively different.

Fertilizer Demand

The average fertilizer use is 77 kg/ha of cultivated land (Table 8.8). This figure gives an estimate of fertilizer consumption of 0.70 million tons for Bangladesh, which is close to the officially recorded sale of 0.71 million tons in the 1987–1988 financial year. The level of consumption is highest in irrigated villages and lowest in saline-affected areas.

Demand for fertilizer is highly price-elastic (Table 8.9). Price elasticity of demand is estimated at -2.1, which suggests that a 10% increase in fertilizer prices would reduce fertilizer demand by 21%. The price of paddy does not seem to exert significant influence on fertilizer demand. The demand for fertilizer is positively related to the size of farm capital and to the level of education of the head of the household. The coefficient of farm size is substantially lower than unity, which suggests an inverse relationship between farm size and fertilizer use. The coefficient of the tenancy variable is negative but not statistically significant.

Modern variety adoption significantly increases fertilizer demand. The values of the coefficients suggest that a 10 percentage point increase in the area growing modern varieties would increase fertilizer use by 6.8% for irrigated varieties and 3.5% for rainfed ones. Thus, irrigation has a significant additional effect on fertilizer demand.

When the effects of other variables are controlled, fertilizer use is not significantly different in flood-prone and drought-prone areas than in areas with favorable rainfed conditions. However, for saline-affected areas, fertilizer use is found to be about 42% lower.

Labor Demand

Average total labor use is 222 days per hectare of cultivated land (Table 8.8). This figure yields an estimate of 3.5 billion person-days of labor use in crop cultivation activity in Bangladesh, which is equivalent to about 197 days per worker in the agricultural labor force and 148 days per worker in the rural labor force. The labor use per unit of land is highest in irrigated villages and lowest in saline-affected areas. Hired labor constitutes about 35% of total labor.

As expected, the demand for hired labor is significantly and positively associated with farm size and ownership of nonland assets. The elasticity of the demand for hired labor with respect to farm size is slightly less than unity, which suggests that the use of hired labor does not increase proportionately with farm size. But the coefficient of family labor is significantly lower than unity, indicating that larger farms prefer leisure, a characteristic of the farm economy that has a positive income distribution effect. This result suggests that total labor use per unit of land declines with farm size, which is consistent with the inverse size-productivity relationship in Asian agriculture (Berry and Cline 1979). The coefficient of the tenancy variable is negative and highly significant in the equations for both family and hired labor, meaning that tenant farmers use proportionately less labor than do owner-farmers.

The coefficient of the schooling variable has a negative sign in the equation for family labor but a positive sign in the equation for hired labor, and the coefficient is statistically highly significant. These results imply that with higher levels of education, the household supplies less labor for farming activities and substitutes by hiring labor. An educated laborer presumably has better earning opportunities outside farming; hence, the opportunity cost of allocating labor on owned farms increases with higher levels of education.

The new rice technology increases the demand for hired labor, but the increase is significant only when modern varieties are adopted under irrigated conditions. The values of the coefficient of MVR*RFR are positive but not statistically significant. The coefficient of MVR*IRGR is not only statistically significant but also substantially higher (0.40) in the equation for hired labor than for family labor (0.16). Because hired labor is supplied mainly by poorer families, this finding suggests that the positive employment effect of the technological change favors the poor.

Cropping Intensities

Rice cropping intensity is highest in villages with favorable environments (Table 8.8). The average rice cropping intensity for sample villages is 134, and average total cropping intensity is 175. The drought-prone areas have the lowest total cropping intensity, whereas cropping intensity for the flood-prone and favorable rainfed areas is similar.

The regression model does not explain much of the variation in cropping intensity, as evidenced by the low R^2 (Table 8.10). The technology variables, however, are statistically significant in the equation for rice cropping intensity. The estimated coefficient suggests that rice cropping intensity increases by about 31% when irrigated land is shifted from traditional to modern varieties. Modern variety adoption under irrigation, however, increases rice cropping intensity at the expense of other crops, so that it does not have any significant effect on total cropping intensity.

The tenancy variable has a negative and significant effect on total cropping intensity, which implies that the tenant allocates more land to rice than nonrice crops compared to owner-cultivators.

When the effects of other variables are controlled, the drought-prone and saline-affected areas have significantly lower rice cropping intensities than favorable rainfed areas. For all crops, however, only the drought-prone areas have a significantly lower intensity of land use.

Land Productivity

Table 8.8 shows average paddy yield for all varieties and the value of production per hectare for the whole year for all crops (measured in takas), classified by production environment. Average yield is highest in the irrigated villages because of higher rates of modern variety adoption. Among the nonirrigated villages, productivity of land in value terms is highest in favorable rainfed villages because of higher intensity of land use and production of relatively more profitable nonrice crops such as sugarcane, vegetables, and fruits.

To assess the effect of modern varieties on paddy yield and value of production, we estimated a multivariate regression model on the determinants of land productivity. The same explanatory variables specified in the input demand regression were used, except for the price variables. Because the dependent variable was output per unit of land, WORKER and CAPITALQ variables were measured per unit of land rather than in absolute values per household. The estimated values of the parameters are presented in Table 8.10.

The regression coefficient of the farm size variable in the paddy yield regression is negative and significant. This figure suggests that paddy yield is higher on smaller farms, a finding reported extensively in numerous studies of Asian agriculture (Hossain 1977; Mandal 1980; and Verma and Bromley 1987).

The regression coefficient of the tenancy variable is negative and significant, contrary to generalizations made in recent studies by Otsuka and Hayami (1988) that tenancy does not have any disincentive effect on production. More recently, Otsuka, Chuma, and Hayami (1992) raised the possibility that yield is generally lower under share tenancy than under owner cultivation because of legal restrictions on tenure choice in Bangladesh. Because Bangladesh's agriculture is characterized by surplus labor, the marginal contribution of family workers to productivity is not significantly different from zero, as indicated by the insignificant value of the WORKER variable. The elasticity of output with respect to ownership of farm capital is estimated at 0.09, and the coefficient is highly significant.

Adoption of modern varieties contributes significantly to raising the yield of both paddy and all crops. The value of the coefficient of MVR*RFR in the equation for paddy yield is 0.25, which suggests that when modern varieties are grown in rainfed fields, paddy output increases by about 25%. When modern varieties are grown in irrigated fields, the increase in paddy output is about 46%. Thus, irrigation has a significant beneficial effect on paddy output.

The estimated coefficients in the equation for all crops suggest that modern varieties increase output for the whole year by 39% when grown as rainfed crops and by 49% when grown as irrigated crops. The differential effect on output between rainfed and irrigated land is smaller for all crops than for paddy alone, which may be explained by two factors. First, when modern varieties are irrigated they may replace other crops; hence, an increase in paddy output is achieved to some extent at the expense of other crops. Second, and perhaps more important, the availability of irrigation under flood-free conditions allows two modern variety crops to be grown during the same year. Thus, although total output for the year as a whole is high, the paddy yield for each season is lower because of the more intensive use of land.

The estimated coefficients of the village-level dummy variables show that land productivity is not lower in flood-prone villages. But drought-prone areas have about a 14% lower paddy yield and 21% lower land productivity than favorable rainfed areas.

A result that may surprise many is that the saline-affected coastal areas have a significantly higher paddy yield and land productivity for all crops. These areas are regularly flooded by high tides, so the land is enriched by deposits of silt. Also, most of the land in coastal areas is located at medium elevations, which are suitable for growing local, transplanted *amon*, the highest-yielding traditional variety. In noncoastal areas, a substantial portion of the land is allocated to traditional broadcast *aus* and deepwater *amon*, which are low-yielding.

MODERN RICE TECHNOLOGY AND FACTOR-MARKET ADJUSTMENTS

The literature on the impact of modern varieties has emphasized their direct effects on income distribution across socioeconomic groups and geographical regions (Lipton and Longhurst 1969). It is argued that the diffusion of modern varieties is likely to benefit already well-off farmers and regions in a country.

The spread of the new technology may, however, have a significant indirect effect through the operation of the factor markets; it may change the terms and conditions of transactions of land and labor markets, thereby indirectly affecting income distribution through an adjustment process. We have already noted that labor demand increases with the spread of modern varieties. In the short run, labor supply may be inelastic, resulting in an upward pressure on the wage rate. This increase in employment and wage rate may affect migrant agricultural laborers from less favorable areas. If so, labor supply will meet demand, and an increase in wage rate in the adopter villages will be prevented. At the same time, a reduction in surplus labor in nonadopter villages will push the wage rate upward in those locales. This process should eventually narrow the employment and income differentials of the agricultural wage laborers between adopter and nonadopter villages (Binswanger 1980).

Similar adjustments may take place through the operation of the land market. An increase in land productivity would initially raise land prices and rents, increasing the factor share of land at the expense of labor. This trend would provide incentives to people to permanently migrate to areas with higher land productivity, reducing average farm size in adopter villages and increasing the same in nonadopter villages. This process should reduce the gap in farm incomes between adopter and nonadopter villages.

Diffusion of modern varieties may lead to changes in tenurial arrangements and terms and conditions in the tenancy market. Because modern varieties require more labor per unit of land, the large landowner, faced with the problem of supervision of additional labor, may want to have the modern varieties grown by labor-abundant tenant households.

The terms of sharecropping may discourage modern variety adoption by the sharecropper, as he will have to share with the landowner the returns from the additional investment in fertilizer and water. This consideration may lead to changes in tenancy arrangements from sharecropping to fixed-rent contracts. With changes in the incidence and terms of tenancy contracts, some income adjustments may take place across socioeconomic groups.

In this section, we study the operation of the land and labor markets across production environments to assess whether income adjustments take place across regions and socioeconomic groups through the operation of the market forces mentioned above. For the purpose of the descriptive analysis, the villages are classified into three groups: 1) low-adopter villages, with less than 10% of the land growing modern varieties; 2) medium-adopter villages, with a 10 to 50% adoption rate; and 3) high-adopter villages, with adoption rates of over 50%.

Land Market Adjustments

The pattern of landownership in the low- and high-adopter sample villages is shown in Table 8.11. Although there are few large landowners, land distribution is fairly unequal. In low-adopter villages, 69% of the households in the landownership scale own land in sizes of less than 0.6 ha, which accounts for 17% of the land owned. At the other end, 10% of the households owning more than 2 ha control 51% of the land. The Gini concentration ratio is 0.65. Thus, if ownership of land were the main source of income growth, the incremental income from land would be highly unequally distributed.

In the high-adopter villages, average size of landholding is only 0.53 ha, about 24% lower than in the low-adopter villages. The concentration in landownership is marginally lower, as evidenced by the Gini concentration ratio of 0.63. The proportion of households owning land in sizes of 2 ha or more is lower (7%), and they control only 39% of the total land owned, compared to 51% for the low-adopter villages. These figures support the findings reported earlier that modern varieties have spread relatively more quickly in villages with a low average size of holding. Also, with the increase in land productivity, population pressure on land may have increased through in-migration of people from low-adopter villages or through reduction of rural-to-urban migration. Small and marginal landowners may increase their size of holding by purchasing land from households who use it less intensively. Ex post, therefore, the incremental gains in land productivity from modern variety adoption would be relatively more equally distributed.

Table 8.12 provides information on land transactions. Only 6% of households purchased land during 1987; 5% sold land. Slightly more than 1% of the total land was sold or purchased during the year. In the low-adopter villages, 2.3% of land was sold and 1.2% was purchased. The incidence of land transactions, however, did not increase with technology diffusion. The hypothesis that the diffusion of new technology leads to accumulation of land by allowing larger farmers to buy off marginal holdings is not valid for Bangladesh.

Land transactions also occur among households through the operations of the tenancy market. The most important tenancy arrangement in Bangladesh is the sharecropping system. Under share tenancy, actual outputs, and in some cases certain inputs, are shared by the landowner and the tenant according to a fixed proportion. The common practice is to share at a 50:50 ratio.

Under the fixed-rent tenancy, the tenant pays the landowner a predetermined amount, either in cash or in kind, irrespective of output. Cash is usually paid at the time of rental and is often contracted on a yearly basis. In-kind payments are made after the harvest, and contracts are on a seasonal basis.

An arrangement under which land is transferred from small to large landowners is known as *dai-shudi*. It is basically a credit arrangement (referred to as a mortgaging contract in this study). The tenant gives a loan to the landowner against a collateral of land, which the tenant cultivates until the loan is repaid. If the landowner cannot repay after the specified number of years, the tenant has the right to purchase the land. *Dai-shudi* is sometimes the first step in the process of land transfer through purchase and sale. It is relatively more common in low- and high-adopter villages.

The incidence of tenancy appears to increase with modern variety adoption (Table 8.13). The proportion of tenant cultivators and the percentage of cultivated area under tenancy are slightly higher in the high-adopter villages compared to the low-adopter villages. This finding is contrary to observations for other South Asian countries that, by increasing profitability of land, the spread of modern varieties leads to tenancy eviction and thereby accentuates income inequality (Ladejinsky 1977; Pears 1980).

With modern variety adoption, the sharecropping system gives way to fixed-rent tenancy (Table 8.13). In high-adopter villages, 42% of the land transacted in the tenancy market is under fixed-rent contract, compared to only 6% for the low-adopter villages.

The estimated values of land rent under different tenancy arrangements are reported in Table 8.14. The rent is substantially higher for modern varieties than for traditional varieties, which is a reflection of the higher absolute share of land in the output of modern varieties. But the rental value under the fixed-rent contract is about 45% lower than that under the sharecropping contract. Thus, the change in the form of tenancy from sharecropping to fixed rent helps redistribute some of the gains in factor shares of land from the landowner to the tenant.

Labor Market Adjustments

Labor is supplied by four categories of farm workers: family workers, attached farm workers, casual workers, and contract workers.

Attached farm workers are hired for at least a year, after which the employment is reconsidered; employment for a crop season also exists. In both cases, the attached worker usually lives with the farm family and is paid fixed wages and provided free meals and clothing.

Casual workers are employed on a daily basis at the prevailing market wage at the time of employment. Even marginal cultivators sometimes employ casual laborers because of the highly seasonal demand for labor in rice cultivation.

Contract workers are hired to complete a specific operation against a piece-rate wage. This type of labor contract is gaining importance relative to casual labor because of the problem of supervision; the casual worker receives the stipulated wage after the day irrespective of the amount of work done and hence has an incentive to shirk. Piece-rate workers can increase earnings by working more intensively and can take up another job or look after their own business if they can finish the work early.

Adoption of the new technology seems to affect the composition of hired labor (Table 8.15). The importance of attached workers declines with modern variety adoption. Only 8% of the total labor is supplied by attached workers in high-adopter villages, compared to about 36% in low-adopter villages.

Additional probing during the village surveys determined that the employment of attached workers is poverty-driven. Working conditions for attached workers are precarious, as the employer can ask them to do any job at any time. A worker will prefer this type of employment when there is large labor surplus in the village and hence the uncertainty of finding a job in the market is high.

Some poor households hire out their children as apprentice-attached workers in large landowning households, where they receive free meals and lodging. It saves poor families the cost of rearing children. With reduction in surplus labor and alleviation of poverty, the supply of attached labor goes

down. In India, however, the incidence of attached labor contracts increased
with modern variety adoption (Bhalla 1976).

The adoption of new technology also seems to have some positive
impact on the use of contract labor. In the high-adopter group, 53% of the
sample villages report at least some use of contract labor for transplanting,
weeding, and harvesting (Table 8.15).

A major change in the labor market following adoption of modern
varieties involves employment of migrant workers. About 24% of sample
cultivators in the high-adopter villages report use of migrant labor, compared
to only 8% in the low-adopter villages. Seasonal migration of labor may
occur as a response to labor shortages caused by modern variety cultivation
during a particular time of the year. Labor shortages take place in 76% of the
villages in the high-adopter group, compared to 44% in the medium-adopter
and 55% in the low-adopter group.

When the labor market becomes tight, the increase in labor demand
following modern variety adoption should also increase the wage rate, unless
the increased demand is met either by migrant workers or machines. In
Bangladesh, mechanization is rarely practiced except in irrigation. Among the
sixty-two villages studied, power tillers and mechanical threshers are used in
only two. There are reports, however, that over the last three years, large
farmers from areas in which the labor market has become tight and wages
have increased have started acquiring power tillers.

The estimates of wage rates for different operations are presented in
Table 8.16. It appears that the rate of adoption of modern varieties has a
slightly positive effect on the wage rate. The data suggest that migration
of labor tends to equalize regional wages, though not fully. Thus, some
income transfers seem to have taken place between high- and low-adopter
villages.

Determinants of Land Prices and Wage Rates

To assess the impact of modern varieties on factor prices, reduced-form
equations of land prices and wage rates incorporating supply and demand
variables were estimated using the village-level extensive-survey data. For the
price of land, the following equation was estimated:

$$\text{LANDP} = f\,(\text{LMR, PLARGE, MVR, IRGR, RFR, PADDYP,} \\ \text{PFLW, PNF, PHIGH, PLOW, SALINE, ELECT, INFR}),$$

where LANDP equals price of land in the village (Tk/ha), LMR equals
amount of land per person (ha), PLARGE equals percentage of land controlled
by large farmers (households with more than 3.0 ha of land), PFLW equals
percentage of functionally landless households (those with less than 0.2 ha of
land), and PNF equals percentage of households reporting nonfarm activities
as major sources of income. The other variables are defined as before.

Both supply and demand of land will depend on the amount of land available in relation to population (LMR). If there is a higher concentration of land among large landowners (PLARGE), more land will be supplied in the tenancy and land markets, reducing land rental and land prices. The demand for land will depend on the proportion of landless households to total population (PFLW). The demand would be lower if there were alternative job opportunities in the nonfarm sector, the effect of which is supposed to be captured by PNF. The development of infrastructure facilities such as paved roads (INFR) and access to electricity (ELECT) may increase productivity and profitability of land and hence raise land prices. These factors may be also related to employment opportunities in the nonfarm sector and hence reduce the demand for land, thereby putting downward pressure on land prices. The net effect depends on the relative strength of these opposing forces. By increasing the productivity and profitability of land, the adoption of modern varieties (MVR) and the expansion of area under irrigation (IRGR) increase demand and hence put upward pressure on prices.

The reduced form equation with land prices as a dependent variable was estimated in log-linear form using the OLS method. The estimates of the regression equation are presented in Table 8.17. Among infrastructural variables, electricity has a significantly positive coefficient: Land prices in villages with access to electricity are 33% higher than in other villages. Structural variables—i.e., incidence of landlessness, concentration of land in the hands of large farmers, or the importance of nonfarm occupations—do not seem to significantly influence land prices.

The coefficient of the interaction variable between modern variety adoption and favorable rainfed environments (MVR*RFR) is not significant. But the coefficient of MVR*IRGR is positive and significantly different from zero. The value of the coefficients suggests that when modern varieties are grown as irrigated crops, land prices increase by about 48%. These findings are consistent with the fact that the productivity gains from modern variety adoption in irrigated areas are substantial for the dry season. Wet-season gains are marginal.

The same set of independent variables was estimated to analyze wage differentials across villages. However, because the demand for hired agricultural labor would depend on the endowment of cultivated land relative to family workers, the amount of cultivated land per unit of agricultural worker in farm households (CLAWF) was added as an explanatory variable in this equation. The supply of agricultural labor in the market depends on the wage rate, population per unit of land in the village (LMR), the proportion of functionally landless households (PFLW), and the opportunity for employment in the nonfarm sector (PNF). The demand for agricultural labor depends not only on the wage rate but also on the availability of land in relation to agricultural workers (LANDWKR), the proportion of land held by large farmers (PLARGE), the proportion of area irrigated (IRGR), and the proportion of area cultivated with modern varieties (MVR). The estimates of the coefficients of the reduced-form equation with wage rate as the dependent variable are presented in Table 8.17. Separate estimates were made for harvesting wage and transplanting wage.

The coefficient of the land-man ratio is negative and highly significant. This suggests that as the potential supply of labor declines relative to land, the wage rate falls. This result is counterintuitive but can be explained. As reported earlier, the farm size in the high-adopter villages is smaller than in the low-adopter villages. Thus, it may well be that in those villages where land is abundant relative to labor, primarily traditional varieties are grown and less labor-intensive methods of cultivation are practiced.

Landlessness does not have a significant influence on the transplanting and harvesting wage rates. The coefficient of the nonfarm job variable is not significantly different from zero. The amount of land available per worker in the village is expected to put an upward pressure on the wage rate by increasing the demand for hired labor, but the coefficient is statistically significant only in the equation for transplanting wage rate.

The new rice technology has a positive effect on the wage rate only when adopted in rainfed villages, i.e., during the monsoon season. The coefficients of MVR*IRGR are negative and significant in the harvesting wage equation.

Because the dry winter season is relatively slack for agricultural activities, the increase in the demand for labor from modern variety adoption may not significantly increase the wage rate. At that time, migration from low-adopter to high-adopter villages can meet the temporary labor shortage in the latter group. Moreover, because the crop is irrigated, the seasonality in the demand for labor is probably less pronounced.

Because most of the land is cropped during the monsoon season, the increase in the labor demand from modern variety adoption puts upward pressure on the wage rate. The effect of modern variety adoption on harvesting wage, however, is insignificant. Furthermore, none of the estimated coefficients of village-level environmental variables are significant. Taken together, the estimation results of wage functions indicate that wage rates are largely equalized across production environments in Bangladesh through interregional labor market adjustments.

MODERN RICE TECHNOLOGY, INCOME DISTRIBUTION, AND POVERTY

Some qualifications on the quality of information on income are in order. Because rural households do not keep records of their income-earning activities, it is difficult to estimate income accurately, particularly for activities conducted on a self-employed basis. Most rural households are also involved in many expenditure-saving activities, such as producing fruits and vegetables in kitchen gardens, rearing poultry, fishing from nearby creeks and canals, processing food, and manufacturing personal household effects for family consumption.

There is a tendency for respondents to overreport the cost of production and underreport earnings from self-employed activities, which many of them do not consider sources of income. Thus, income estimates from the survey may be biased downward. Also, the year of the survey was affected by a disastrous flood, which extensively damaged the *amon* crop in a few sample villages. The intensive survey collected information on the extent of damage to rice crops by the 1987 floods. Damage was estimated at 2,087 takas (Tk) per household—16% of the income from crop cultivation and 8% of total household incomes.

Factor Shares

Before we present the findings of the survey on the composition and distribution of household income, it is useful to look at the factor shares of land, labor, and capital in rice cultivation with traditional and modern varieties. The composition of gross value of output in the cultivation of modern varieties as compared to traditional varieties is presented in Table 8.18. The estimates are derived from variety-level input-output structure obtained from the small sample of plots. The following points may be noted from the table:

- The share of current inputs (a measure of working capital requirement) increases substantially with the cultivation of modern varieties. This increase is due to a nearly eightfold jump in the cost of purchased inputs (i.e., fertilizers, pesticides, and irrigation).
- The share of draft power (a measure of fixed capital) decreases from 17% for traditional varieties to 8% for modern varieties. The cost of animal power per hectare remains almost the same, but because gross value of output is about 93% higher for modern varieties, the animal cost per unit of output for traditional varieties is about half of that for modern varieties. If current inputs and draft power are taken as a measure of user cost of total capital (working plus fixed), then the share of capital in the gross value of production increases from 26% for traditional varieties to 28% for modern varieties. In absolute terms, users' cost of capital is about 115% higher for modern varieties than for traditional varieties.
- The share of labor declines substantially from 31% for traditional varieties to 23% for modern varieties, but the absolute return to labor per unit of land increases by about 37%. The increase is more pronounced for hired labor, which goes to the landless and marginal landowners. The income of hired labor is estimated at Tk 3,008 per

hectare for modern varieties, compared to Tk 1,839 for traditional varieties, an increase of nearly 64%.

- The share of land decreases marginally from 47% for traditional varieties to 43% for modern varieties. Note that the contribution of land has been measured by the amount of rent paid by the sharecropper to the landowner minus the amount of inputs paid by the landowner to the tenant. The cost-sharing practice is more prevalent in the cultivation of modern varieties. For modern variety *boro*, the landowners contribute nearly 16% of the cost of material inputs, compared to 8% for traditional transplanted *amon* and only 6% of traditional *aus*. The absolute return for land is 79% higher for modern varieties compared to traditional varieties.

- The farm operator surplus, which is defined as the gross value of production minus total input costs, is negative in the cultivation of traditional varieties. This result suggests that in the crop year under study, the tenant received a lower rate of return for labor than its opportunity cost (i.e., the wage it would fetch in the market) and the owner-cultivator received a lower return for land than the landowner who had land cultivated by a tenant. For modern varieties, however, the farm operator surplus is positive. The surplus is estimated at about 6% of the gross value of production.

As the return to land and capital increases, the owner-cultivator seems to contribute less labor to production and depends relatively more on hired labor, which benefits those who hire out labor services in the market. Thus, although return to total labor is 37% higher for modern varieties than for traditional varieties, the return to hired labor is about 64% higher. Because of the income adjustments taking place between larger landowners (who are dependent more on their land and capital for income) and the landless and marginal landowners (who are dependent more on labor), the inequality in the distribution of incremental incomes between cultivators and wage laborers is substantially less than that indicated by the difference in factor shares of land, capital, and labor.

The return to the tenant's family resources (farm income on rented land) is substantially lower than the return to those of owner-cultivators (farm income on owned land). But both incomes are about 60% higher from cultivation of modern varieties than from traditional varieties. Thus, the tenant also gains substantially in absolute terms.

The Structure of Household Income

Rice cultivation is one of the many economic activities undertaken by rural households. To assess the impact of the new technology on income distribution, the structure and determinants of household income must be examined. The following major points may be noted from the patterns of rural household incomes by source shown in Table 8.19.

- Agriculture accounts for about 60% of total household income, crop cultivation only 46%. Noncrop agriculture and nonfarm activities are important sources of rural household income.
- About 60% of the income from the crop sector originates from rice, but income from rice accounts for only 28% of total household income. If wages paid to hired workers are included, the share of rice cultivation in total household income increases to about 40%. Although modern rice technology favors larger landowners, its impact on the inequality in the distribution of total household income would be moderated because of the importance of nonrice sources of income.
- Nonfarm households (landless and functionally landless households) do not gain directly from the cultivation of rice but profit substantially as hired workers. Whereas the average annual income in crop cultivation for all households is estimated at Tk 3,210 per household, nonfarm households earn 2.7 times more than farm households from hiring out labor services in crop cultivation.
- Agricultural wages account for only one-fourth of the income of nonfarm households. Nonfarm households earn about one-third more from nonagricultural sources than farm households.
- Noncrop agricultural activities (livestock, fisheries, and forestry) are more important sources of income for farm households than for nonfarm households. Farm households earn about twice as much as nonfarm households from such activities. The disparity is almost the same as that found with income from the crop sector.

The structure of household income classified by production environment is seen in Table 8.20. Income from rice cultivation has been decomposed into shares of land, labor, and capital. Labor income consists of the income earned from wages in rice cultivation plus the imputed value of family labor employed in rice cultivation on owned farms. Income from capital is imputed at 16% of the replacement value of nonland fixed assets plus water charges for the use of irrigation equipment. The opportunity cost of services of family-owned capital is evaluated at 16% in interest rate, because the farmers could obtain credit from the financial institutions at that rate. Income from land is obtained as the residual, after deducting the labor and capital incomes from the income from rice cultivation.

In spite of their smaller land endowment, irrigated villages have the highest agricultural income (Table 8.20). The main contributing factor is the higher income from rice cultivation. Income from this source is about 82% higher in irrigated villages than in drought-prone areas and 47% higher than in favorable rainfed villages. Income shares of land, labor, and capital are also higher for the irrigated villages than for villages with unfavorable environments. Nonrice income, however, tends to be both relatively and absolutely larger in nonirrigated villages. As a result, the difference in per capita income across environments is relatively small.

Determinants of Household Income

Multivariate regressions on determinants of income were estimated to identify the effect of technology and environmental factors on household income. The same variables were used as in the case of land productivity reported earlier. The proportion of nonagricultural workers in the household (NAGRW) was added as a separate variable to identify the marginal contribution of nonagricultural workers to household income.

The regression equations were estimated separately for different components of income. Because of the ease of interpretation of the regression coefficients, the equations were estimated in log-linear form using the OLS method.

The effect of the new technology on incomes should be captured by the variables MVR and IRGR. Because the two variables are highly interdependent, two interaction terms (MVR*IRGR and MVR*RFR) were used to measure the separate effect of modern variety adoption in rainfed and irrigated areas. The estimated parameters of the income equation for farm households are reported in Table 8.21.

Income from rice cultivation is not found to be significantly associated with the number of agricultural workers in the farm family because of its offsetting effects on labor and capital incomes. However, rice income is significantly determined by the use of technology. The coefficient of MVR*RFR is positive and highly significant in the land and capital income equations. The adoption of modern varieties in rainfed areas increases rice income by 55%. If modern varieties are grown in irrigated areas, the income increase is stronger—66%.

Modern variety adoption significantly increases income from both land and capital in rice cultivation under irrigated as well as rainfed conditions, but it contributes to higher labor income only as an irrigated crop. The coefficient of MVR*RFR in the income equation for labor is insignificant.

The estimated coefficient of MVR*IRGR in the equation for labor income suggests that adoption of modern varieties in irrigated areas increases income from labor in rice cultivation by 42% but land income by about 70%. Thus, landowners gain proportionately more from the adoption of modern varieties than do workers.

Technology adoption, however, does not increase income from nonrice sources in either agriculture or nonagricultural activities. Income from nonrice sources is determined significantly by the amount of land and capital assets owned by the family and by the number of nonfarm income earners in the household. A 10 percentage point increase in the proportion of nonagricultural workers in the household would increase nonagricultural incomes by 12%.

Occupational mobility from farm to nonfarm occupations depends largely on the level of education of the worker. The independent effect of education is found to be positive in the case of nonagricultural income. The increase in nonagricultural income because of education, however, is achieved partly at the expense of income from rice cultivation. The regression coefficients of the education variable, however, are not statistically significant. Similar results are reported from a sixteen-village survey conducted in Bangladesh in 1982 (Hossain 1990).

We noted earlier that environmental factors are significant determinants of modern variety adoption; hence, those variables indirectly affect household income. Apart from the indirect effect, some of the environmental factors directly affect household income. For example, the income from rice cultivation is significantly higher in saline-affected villages than in favorable rainfed villages, but lower in drought-prone villages. The unfavorable effect on rice income in the drought-prone villages is mostly due to substantially lower income shares from land. Return to capital is significantly lower in flood-prone villages, but income from nonrice crops and nonagricultural sources is significantly higher compared to that of favorable rainfed villages. In contrast, the saline-affected areas earn significantly lower income from nonagricultural sources than favorable rainfed villages do.

The coefficient of the dummy variable representing access to electricity is significantly positive in the equation for nonagricultural income. It has a negative effect on rice income, but this is offset by the higher income from nonagricultural activities.

Separate income functions were estimated for nonfarm households, which account for nearly one-third of all households in the sample. Some of these households earn income from rice cultivation as wage laborers, and a few of them receive rent from a small amount of land given out to others under sharecropping arrangements. Most of them also operate a part of the homestead land and earn income from vegetables and fruits grown in kitchen gardens. We included the size of land owned (LANDOWN) as an explanatory variable instead of land cultivated, which has zero value for these households. Also included were the number of agricultural workers (AGRIC) and the number of nonagricultural family workers (NAGRIC). The equation was estimated in linear form because of the large number of zero values for dependent variables. The findings are reported in Table 8.22.

An agricultural worker in a nonfarm household earns Tk 3,795 from rice cultivation as a wage laborer, which is only 35% of the income earned by a nonagricultural worker in the nonfarm sector. Indeed, the major portion of income for nonfarm households is derived from nonrice and nonagricultural sources. The primary contributors of income from nonagricultural sources are the number of nonagricultural workers and the size of nonland assets. One taka of investment in nonland assets increases nonagricultural income at the margin by Tk 0.54, which seems higher than the increase estimated for farm households. Rice income for nonfarm households is significantly lower in drought-prone villages than in flood-prone villages and in villages with a favorable environment. The income from nonagricultural sources is also significantly higher in the flood-prone villages.

Education, as measured by the schooling of the household head, has a positive effect on nonagricultural income, as in the case of farm households. The coefficient of education, however, is negative and significant in the rice-income equation. These results indicate that education enhances one's earning ability only in the nonagricultural sector.

Household Income Distribution

The sample households were ranked on the basis of per capita income, and the income shares of the successive decile groups were estimated to see the pattern of income distribution in the sample. The impact of modern variety adoption was examined by comparing the income shares of various groups in the low-adopter and high-adopter villages.

The income distribution is fairly unequal (Table 8.23). The inequality in income distribution is highest in saline-affected coastal areas, and the most equitable income distribution is found in the drought-prone areas.

The degree of inequality in income distribution is often summarized by the Gini concentration ratio. The estimated values of the Gini coefficient for the distribution of per capita income for groups of villages classified by environment and modern variety adoption status are shown in Table 8.23. The Gini ratio is 0.36 for the entire sample, which is almost the same as for the favorable rainfed villages. But for saline-affected areas, the Gini coefficient is estimated at 0.39, indicating high inequality, and 0.30 for drought-prone areas, indicating low inequality.

The diffusion of modern varieties does not seem to increase the concentration of income. The income shares of different groups and the Gini ratio are almost the same in the high- and low-adopter villages. For the medium-adopter villages, income inequality is slightly higher.

A change in the distribution of total income is a function of the changes in the distribution of different components of income. The distribution of total income may change because of changes in the distribution of an individual component of income, as well as changes in the income share for the component. If additional income is derived from a relatively equally distributed source, income distribution will improve (see Chapter 3 for analytical methodology). The pattern of income distribution is expected to change with the adoption of the new technology, so a Gini decomposition was conducted to identify factors behind the change.

Because the economic position of a household depends on per capita income of the household rather than the total household income, we measured income inequality for all components in the scale of per capita income. The findings of the decomposition of the income for the entire sample are presented in Table 8.24. It will be seen that the share of agricultural income is substantially higher than the relative contribution of this income to overall income inequality. This implies that agricultural income is less unequally distributed than nonagricultural incomes. Nearly half of the inequality in the distribution of total household income is due to nonagricultural income, despite the fact that its income share is only 40%. Rice cultivation contributes only 36% of the overall income inequality.

The decomposition of income inequality for areas classified by frequency of modern variety adoption is shown in Table 8.25. The Gini ratio of per capita household income is almost identical for the low- and medium-adopter villages and slightly lower for the high-adopter villages, suggesting that income distribution does not deteriorate with the diffusion of the new technology. But the distribution of income from rice cultivation alone is skewed by diffusion of modern varieties. In low-adopter villages, about 29% of the inequality in household income is due to rice cultivation, whereas the share for high-adopter villages is 56%. The main reason for this disparity is the increase in the share of rice income in total household income—from 21% in the low-adopter villages to 36% in the high-adopter villages. The larger contribution of rice income to overall inequality in the high-adopter villages, however, is compensated for by an improvement in the distribution of nonagricultural income.

The findings on decomposition of income inequality in villages classified by environment are presented in Table 8.26. Gini ratio is lower for irrigated villages than for favorable rainfed villages, indicating an equalization in the distribution of income with the expansion of irrigation facilities. The share of household income from rice cultivation increases with irrigation expansion, and because rice income is more equally distributed, the overall distribution of income improves.

Rice cultivation accounts for 62% of the household income inequality for irrigated villages, compared to 34% in rainfed villages. The main reason for the high concentration of household income in saline-affected areas, especially as compared to flood-prone and drought-prone areas, is that the distribution of nonagricultural income is highly skewed in favor of the rich in the former group. Income from rice cultivation contributes most significantly to the overall income inequality in the drought-prone villages.

The comparison of overall Gini ratios across five environments does not indicate any clear-cut association between income inequality and production environments.

Alleviation of Poverty

From the welfare point of view, the most appropriate indicator of the effectiveness of a development strategy or policy is its effect on the poor. There has been a recent surge of interest in measuring changes in the incidence of poverty.

A conventional way to measure poverty is to establish a poverty line, defined as the threshold level of income needed to satisfy basic subsistence requirements, and count the number of people below that line—the "head-count" method of measuring poverty.

A number of studies in Bangladesh have used the head-count method to measure changes in poverty over time. (See, among others, Hossain et al. [1993], Rahman and Haque [1988], Muqtada [1986], and Ahmed and Hossain [1984].) These studies show that the level of poverty deteriorated alarmingly in the 1970s compared to the 1960s, although some improvement took place in the early 1980s.

The usual approach has been to take the normative requirement of different kinds of food as a minimum consumption bundle, which gives a per capita intake of 2,112 kilocalories per day, and estimate its cost by applying retail prices for these items. Some adjustment is then made for the requirement of nonfood necessities. Using this method and assuming that 30% of the poverty-level income is spent on nonfood basic needs, the per capita poverty-level income is estimated at Tk 4,300 (US $135) per year.

The estimates of poverty using the above methodology are reported in Table 8.27. For all villages in the study, 59% of the households have incomes below the poverty line. Among groups of villages under different production environments, the poverty ratio is the highest in the drought-prone villages (72%) and lowest in the saline-affected coastal areas (46%). The poverty ratio is 56% for irrigated villages.

The adoption of new technology seems to have a positive effect on the alleviation of poverty. The head-count poverty ratio is 56% for the high-adopter villages, as against 64% for medium-adopter villages. The improvement in the poverty level is appreciable in view of the fact that the average size of landholding is 0.53 ha for the former compared to 0.64 for the latter (Table 8.11). The poverty ratio is 58% for the low-adopter villages, but improved economic conditions of households for these villages are partly due to relatively greater access to nonagricultural sources of income (Table 8.25).

SUMMARY AND CONCLUSIONS

In this chapter we analyzed the factors affecting the differential adoption of modern rice varieties in Bangladesh and their impact on the well-being of the people. The main focus was on the role of environmental factors in influencing the income distribution effects of the new technology.

Major Findings

The adoption of modern varieties in Bangladesh is determined more by technical and environmental factors (access to irrigation facilities, topography, soil salinity, and amount of rainfall) than by socioeconomic factors (farm size, tenurial status of the farmer). Infrastructure variables, measured by access to electricity and transport facilities, and subsistence pressure at the household and village levels are also important factors behind the technology diffusion.

The adoption rate of modern varieties is high in villages with unfavorable land endowments, low nonfarm employment opportunities, or both. Because such villages have a large proportion of small farms, there is an inverse relationship between the farm size and the adoption rate, a result contrary to the findings of early studies on the Green Revolution in India.

The diffusion of the new technology has some impact on the operation of land and labor markets. The land market is relatively thin, as 5 to 6% of the households participate in land transactions in a given year. The market is more active in high-adopter villages than in low-adopter villages. Average farm size is 20% lower in the high-adopter villages than in the low-adopter villages. Thus, it is the land-poor regions that have adopted the modern rice technology, more because of the subsistence pressure of augmenting household incomes.

The incidence of tenancy increases with the adoption of modern varieties, as land is transferred from large to small landowners through tenancy transactions. With modern variety adoption, tenancy arrangements shift away from sharecropping in favor of fixed rent. Thus, through the operation of the tenancy market, a part of the incremental income from land is transferred from landowners to relatively low-income tenant farmers in the high-adopter villages.

The size of the labor market increases with modern variety adoption. The demand for hired labor increases at a higher rate than the use of family labor. The type of labor shifts away from the relatively low-wage attached labor toward high-wage casual labor. The technology has a positive effect on the use of migrant labor. The wage rate for casual labor tends to be slightly higher in the high-adopter villages, which suggests that the incremental demand for labor is largely, but not fully, met by migrant labor. Thus, although part of the incremental labor income in the high-adopter villages is transferred to low-adopter villages through seasonal migration of labor, the agricultural workers in favorable areas benefit to some extent from additional employment, higher wage rates, and changes in labor contracts.

The diffusion of the new technology increases land prices. This suggests that, because of the inequality of land income across different production environments, considerable inequality remains in the distribution of the incremental income from modern variety adoption across socioeconomic groups and regions.

The income gains from the cultivation of modern varieties are shared by all factors of production, but they are distributed relatively more in favor of capital and land at the expense of labor. The increase in income for labor, however, is distributed in favor of the landless and marginal landowners, who supply agricultural labor in the market. Therefore, the inequality in the distribution of gains from modern variety adoption between the land-rich and the land-poor is less pronounced than that suggested by changes in income shares of different factors.

Rice cultivation accounts for only 40% of rural household incomes. Households engage simultaneously in other farm and nonfarm activities. Although income gains from modern variety adoption are higher for larger landowners, the inequality in the distribution of household income is mitigated because of the importance of nonrice agriculture and nonagricultural activities, from which landless and near-landless households earn a large proportion of their income. The Gini ratios estimated for the high-adopter, low-adopter, and medium-adopter villages are almost the same, suggesting that the diffusion of technology has a neutral effect on the distribution of household income.

Inequality in household income from rice cultivation increases with the adoption of the new technology. For low-adopter villages, only 29% of the inequality in household income is due to inequality in income from rice cultivation; the corresponding figure for the high-adopter villages is 56%. However, the increase in inequality from the cultivation of rice is compensated for by lower inequality in income from nonagricultural sources.

The diffusion of modern rice technology has had a positive effect on the alleviation of poverty. The proportion of poor households is substantially smaller in villages with a higher rate of adoption of modern varieties. This statistic is remarkable because the high-adopter villages have substantially lower land endowments. The poor in the villages with lower land endowments manage to earn higher incomes than their counterparts in villages with higher land endowments.

The flood-prone areas enjoy the highest net gains from the adoption of the new technology. The traditional cropping pattern for these areas is deepwater *amon* rice followed by low-yielding pulses or oilseeds. With relatively greater availability of surface water during the dry season, farmers are increasingly shifting land to single cropping with modern variety *boro* or double cropping with oilseeds followed by modern variety *boro*.

The drought-prone highland areas have benefited the least from modern rice technology because irrigation expansion for these areas has been difficult and costly.

There is still good potential for further diffusion of the new rice technology in Bangladesh. As demonstrated by this study, concerns about the negative effect of the technology on alleviation of poverty are unfounded. Although income inequality from rice cultivation increases with the diffusion of the new technology, poor families gain in absolute terms through the adjustments of labor and tenancy markets. The negative effect of the technology on the distribution of household incomes is not pronounced, partly because rice accounts for only two-fifths of household income and partly because the low-income group benefits from the linkage effects of the growth of farm incomes on nonfarm rural activities.

It is also noteworthy that the new technology has been adopted more heavily in areas with lower endowments of land and hence has helped reduce the income disparity across regions. Thus, the government should actively support further diffusion of the technology.

Conditions for Further Diffusion of Modern Varieties

A necessary condition for the increase in area under modern varieties during the dry season is the expansion of irrigation facilities. If rice prices remain favorable, the private sector may come forward to invest in small-scale irrigation equipment in areas with favorable sources of surface and groundwater. But large-scale water resource development will not be possible without public sector involvement.

For areas not subject to deep flooding, investment for drainage and supplementary irrigation is needed for greater diffusion of modern varieties during the wet season. The productivity and profitability gaps between modern varieties and traditional varieties are relatively low for this season, which may constrain adoption. Rice breeders should give attention to development of modern varieties that are more tolerant of temporary submersion and drought.

Although the deeply flooded areas cannot grow the short-statured modern varieties during the wet season, they have taken advantage of the new technology by changing the cropping pattern during the dry season. However, when farmers opt for modern variety *boro*, they forgo planting deepwater *amon*, because it is too late to broadcast *amon* seeds after the modern variety *boro* is harvested. If development of modern varieties for deepwater *amon* is difficult, research should focus on development of tall, fast-growing varieties that can be transplanted during the early months of flooding.

Finally, we emphasize that in extremely land-scarce and labor-abundant countries such as Bangladesh, farmers will welcome any labor-using technology that provides scope for increasing production from a given amount of land. Resources must therefore continue to be allocated for research in development of higher-yielding varieties. This need should not be overlooked because of concern over the prevailing environmental issues, which dictate development of varieties that would reduce the dependence on the use of agrochemicals.

Figure 8.1 Location of study areas, extensive and intensive survey, Bangladesh, 1987

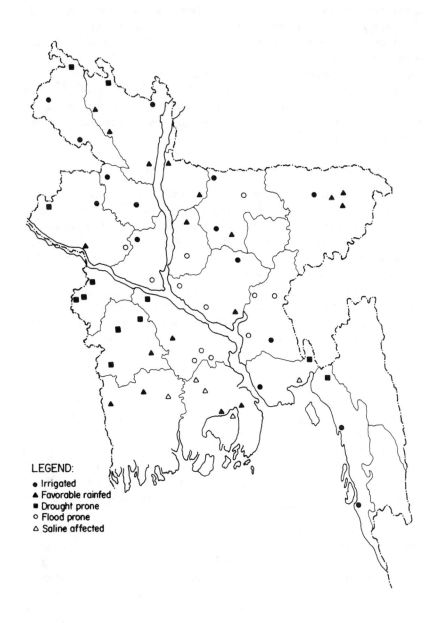

LEGEND:
- • Irrigated
- ▲ Favorable rainfed
- ■ Drought prone
- ○ Flood prone
- △ Saline affected

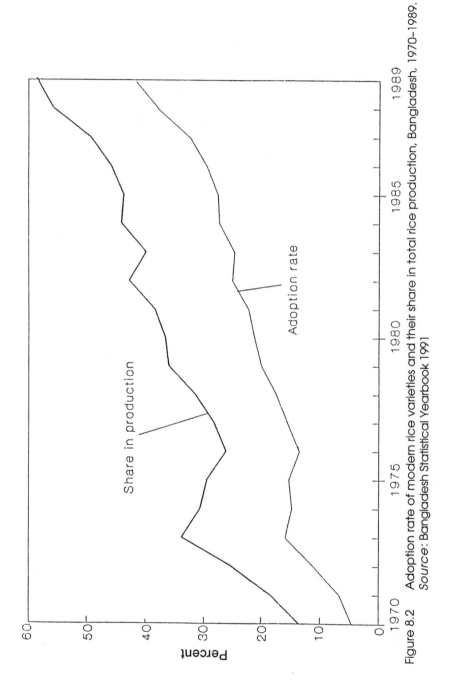

Figure 8.2   Adoption rate of modern rice varieties and their share in total rice production, Bangladesh, 1970–1989.
Source: Bangladesh Statistical Yearbook 1991

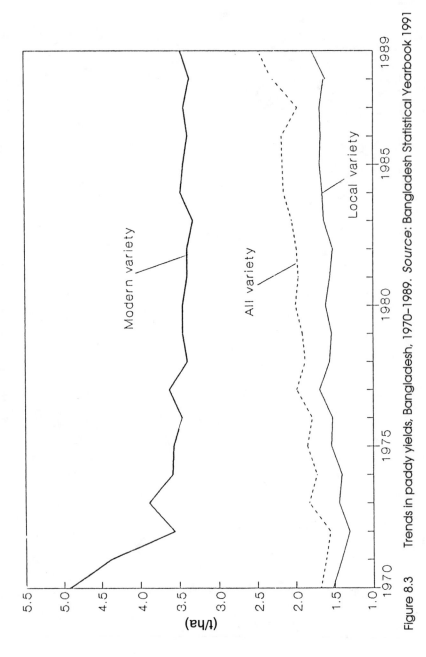

Figure 8.3   Trends in paddy yields, Bangladesh, 1970–1989. *Source: Bangladesh Statistical Yearbook* 1991

Table 8.1   Growth (%) in paddy production, area, and yield in Bangladesh, 1971–1989. Source: Estimated from Bangladesh Bureau of Statistics, *Monthly Statistical Bulletin* (various issues).

Period	Production	Area	Yield
1971–1980	3.1	1.0	2.1
1980–1989	2.8	0.1	2.7
1971–1989	3.0	0.6	2.4

Table 8.2   Characteristics of the survey sample by environmental classification, intensive survey, Bangladesh, 1987.

Village groups by characteristics	Percent of land under this group	Irrigated area (%)	Area under modern varieties (%)	Average yield of rice (t/ha) Traditional varieties	Modern varieties	All varieties
Land elevation[a]						
High	28	26	40	1.8	3.2	2.4
Medium	38	31	49	2.0	3.9	2.9
Low	18	32	25	1.9	4.2	2.8
Very low	16	37	40	2.0	4.5	3.2
Rainfall[b]						
Low	32	18	29	1.8	3.9	2.7
Medium	53	34	43	2.1	4.2	2.9
High	15	41	44	2.0	3.4	2.7
Salinity						
Low	87	34	43	1.9	3.9	2.8
Moderate	13	10	12	2.2	4.0	2.4

a. Classification by land elevation: High = not flooded; Medium = flooded up to 30 cm depth; Low = flooded 30 to 90 cm depth; Very low = flooded more than 90 cm depth.
b. Classification by rainfall: Low = less than 1,800 mm/yr; Medium = 1,800 to 2,400 mm/yr; High = more than 2,400 mm/yr.

Table 8.3   Adoption of modern rice varieties and irrigation in villages classified by environmental status, plot-level survey, Bangladesh, 1987.

| | | % of area under modern varieties | | |
Village groups	Irrigated area (%)	Dry season	Wet season	Total
Irrigated	70	6	29	35
Favorable rainfed	35	28	17	45
Drought-prone	31	18	34	52
Flood-prone	39	30	2	32
Saline-affected	10	7	4	11
Average	30	22	18	40

Table 8.4   Adoption of modern varieties and cropping intensity by irrigation status, plot-level survey, Bangladesh, 1987.

| Irrigation status of the plot | % of the cultivated area under | | | | | Total cropping intensity (%) |
	Traditional rice	Modern rice Boro/aus	Modern rice Amon	Total rice	Nonrice crops	
No irrigation	99	5	13	117	58	175
Irrigation by traditional methods	72	35	11	118	52	170
Irrigation by mechanical methods	54	66	34	154	22	176
Total	85	22	18	125	49	174

Table 8.5   Cropping pattern and cropping intensity (% of land area) by topography and irrigation facilities, plot-level survey, Bangladesh, 1987.[a]

Major cropping pattern	High I	High NI	Medium I	Medium NI	Low I	Low NI	Very low I	Very low NI
Single cropped	25	45	12	38	37	36	79	51
MV[b]	17	5	7	5	27	4	50	3
TV[c]	3	13	4	28	9	28	29	40
Other crops	5	27	1	5	1	4	—	8
Double cropped	68	37	82	43	59	35	21	37
TV + TV rice	2	16	6	18	8	20	4	19
MV + MV rice	31	3	28	1	6	1	—	—
TV + MV rice	24	7	39	5	37	2	12	2
MV + others	9	3	3	4	1	1	1	1
TV + others	2	8	6	15	7	11	4	15
Triple cropped	7	3	4	16	3	26	1	7
MV + MV + others	5	1	1	1	—	1	—	—
MV + TV + others	1	1	1	3	1	1	—	1
TV + TV + others	1	1	2	12	2	24	1	6
Total cropping intensity	181	160	196	179	166	192	121	161
Cropping with modern rice varieties	120	23	108	21	78	8	63	6

a. I = irrigated; NI = nonirrigated.
b. Modern variety.
c. Traditional variety.

Table 8.6   Intensity of adoption of modern rice varieties for farms classified by size and tenure, intensive survey, Bangladesh, 1987.

Groups of cultivators	Irrigated area as % of cultivated area	Modern variety area (% of cultivated land)				
		Owned land	Rented land	Wet season	Dry season	Total[a]
Land ownership (ha)						
Up to 0.2	32	65	52	27	27	54
0.2 to 1.0	32	47	37	18	25	43
1.0 to 2.0	30	42	25	19	21	40
2.0 and more	30	35	30	15	20	35
Tenure						
Owner	31	40	—	18	21	40
Owner cum tenant	35	44	37	16	26	42
Tenant cum owner	28	43	42	19	22	42
Average	31	40	40	18	22	40

a. Total of wet and dry season.

Table 8.7   Regression results of modern variety adoption functions, intensive survey, Bangladesh, 1987.[a]

Variables	All seasons	Wet season	Dry season
Intercept	2.19 (0.17)	42.87 (1.66)	-29.28 (-1.37)
F SIZE	5.38** (2.42)	6.23 (1.46)	10.88** (3.41)
TENANCY	-0.10 (-1.40)	0.04 (0.31)	-0.02 (-0.22)
LAND	-32.17** (-3.26)	-28.27 (-1.52)	-68.11** (-4.42)
IRGP	0.74** (11.27)	0.17 (1.41)	1.16** (9.65)
SCHOOL	0.54 (1.04)	0.78 (0.86)	0.90 (1.23)
SUBP	3.07** (2.86)	5.13** (2.57)	2.40 (1.59)
FPRICE-18.69*	-80.92** (-1.81)	-30.23* (-3.37)	(-1.93)
PHIGH-0.03	0.16 (-0.57)	-0.09 (1.61)	(-0.96)
PLOW-0.10	-0.68** (-1.62)	-0.07 (-5.11)	(-0.87)
SALINE-48.28**	-89.36** (-5.92)	-50.62** (-4.87)	(-4.45)
RFALL0.02	-20.34** (0.00)	13.60* (-2.50)	(1.90)
INFR	7.89 (1.45)	15.08 (1.58)	30.93** (3.69)
ELECT	29.41** (5.03)	34.49** (3.42)	53.49** (5.75)
Chi-square	244.68	146.59	350.66
Log-likelihood	-2,298	-1,621	-1,948
F-value	22.03**	12.29**	34.19**

a. Numbers in parentheses are t-statistics.
** Indicates statistical significance at 1% level; * at 5% level.

Table 8.8   Input use and land productivity by production environment
of sample villages, intensive survey, Bangladesh, 1987.

	Fertilizer nutrient (NPK kg/ha/yr)	Labor use (days/ha/yr)		Cropping intensity		Yield	
		Family	Hired	Rice	Total	Rice (t/ha)	All crops (Tk/ha/yr)
Irrigated	109	158	85	149	170	3.6	14,635
Favorable rainfed	94	135	74	145	180	2.7	12,078
Drought-prone	75	162	77	122	163	2.2	8,532
Flood-prone	67	143	83	131	182	3.2	10,990
Saline-affected	36	133	76	141	175	2.4	9,761
Average	77	144	78	134	175	2.6	10,500

Table 8.9   Regression results of fertilizer and labor use functions, intensive survey, Bangladesh, 1987.[a]

Variables	Ln Fertilizer	Ln Family labor	Ln Hired labor
DPRONE	-0.03 (-0.34)	0.46** (3.45)	-0.09 (-0.86)
DPWATER	-0.03 (-0.03)	0.26 (1.83)	0.16 (-1.38)
SALINE	-0.47** (-3.31)	0.51* (2.62)	-0.05 (-0.31)
MVR*IRGR	0.54** (7.22)	0.16 (1.35)	0.36** (3.73)
MVR*RFR	0.31** (2.82)	0.03 (0.13)	0.16 (1.16)
Ln FPPRICE	-2.07** (-3.93)	1.15 (1.42)	-8.01* (-2.55)
Ln PADDYP	-0.26 (-1.25)	0.19 (0.59)	0.28 (1.05)
Ln WAGE	-0.31** (-2.82)	-0.71** (-3.62)	-0.59** (-3.92)
TENANCY	-0.10 (-1.06)	-0.34* (-2.32)	-0.33** (-2.79)
Ln FSIZE	0.59** (7.31)	0.60** (8.93)	0.85** (15.02)
Ln WORKER	0.03 (0.39)	0.30** (2.76)	0.03 (0.36)
Ln SCHOOL	0.02** (2.99)	-0.02* (-1.97)	0.08** (1.79)
Ln CAPITALQ	0.19** (5.11)	0.11* (1.94)	0.12** (2.84)
INFR	-1.00 (-1.15)	-0.01 (-0.07)	-0.01 (-0.05)
ELECT0.11	0.28* (1.15)	0.17 (1.92)	(1.46)
R^2	0.50	0.31	0.53
F-statistics	38.84**	15.79**	44.15**

a. Numbers in parentheses are t-statistics.
** Indicates significance at 1% level; * at 5% level.

Table 8.10 Regression results of yield and cropping intensity functions, intensive survey, Bangladesh, 1987.[a]

Variables	Ln Rice cropping intensity	Ln Total cropping intensity	Ln Paddy yield	Ln All crops yield
DPRONE	-21.15** (-5.12)	-15.25** (-3.13)	-0.14** (-2.79)	-0.21** (-4.48)
DPWATER	2.26 (-0.51)	8.24 (1.58)	0.06 (1.05)	0.04 (0.79)
SALINE-12.48*	-9.96 (-2.04)	0.14* (-1.38)	0.16* (1.94)	(2.19)
MVR*IRGR	30.89** (8.48)	3.82 (0.87)	0.46** (10.07)	0.49** (11.20)
MVR*RFR	33.25** (6.31)	29.83** (4.82)	0.25** (3.99)	0.39** (5.23)
Ln PADDYP	18.47* (1.80)	5.95 (0.50)	—	—
Ln FPPRICE	33.28 (1.19)	22.65 (0.70)	—	—
Ln WAGE	0.86 (0.15)	-25.38** (-3.70)	—	—
TENANCY	-0.64 (-0.14)	-16.02** (-3.05)	-0.20** (-3.71)	-0.31** (-5.95)
Ln FSIZE	-4.63 (-1.42)	2.23 (-0.58)	-0.07* (-1.78)	-0.06 (-1.64)
Ln WORKER	3.63 (1.06)	-2.86 (-0.70)	0.02 (0.55)	-0.02 (-0.38)
Ln SCHOOL	0.49 (1.20)	0.32 (0.66)	0.01 (1.28)	0.01 (1.03)
Ln CAPITALQ	0.87 (0.57)	3.08 (1.52)	0.09** (4.16)	0.09** (4.51)
INFR	7.97* (1.96)	1.80 (0.37)	-0.01 (-0.14)	0.07* (1.66)
ELECT6.38	2.96 (1.45)	-0.07 (0.57)	0.02 (-1.27)	(0.40)
R^2	0.19	0.08	0.23	0.32
F-statistics	15.37**	4.53**	15.38**	25.55**

a. Numbers in parentheses are t-statistics.
** Indicates significance at 1% level; * at 5% level.

Table 8.11 Pattern of distribution of landownership by status of technology adoption, intensive survey, Bangladesh, 1987.

Size of land ownership (ha)	Low-adopter villages[a]		Medium-adopter villages[b]		High-adopter villages[c]	
	% of house-holds	% of land owned	% of house-holds	% of land owned	% of house-holds	% of land owned
0.0-0.2	45	3	44	4	50	4
0.2-0.6	24	14	22	13	22	15
0.6-1.0	9	10	12	16	12	17
1.0-2.0	12	22	14	31	9	25
2.0-3.0	5	17	5	19	5	23
3.0 and more	5	34	3	17	2	16
Total	100	100	100	100	100	100
Average size of land ownership (ha)		0.65		0.64		0.53
Gini ratio		0.65		0.61		0.63

a. Villages with less than 10% of the cultivated area under modern varieties.
b. Villages with 10 to 50% of the cultivated area under modern varieties.
c. Villages with more than 50% of the cultivated area under modern varieties.

Table 8.12   Incidence of land transactions by modern variety adoption scale, intensive survey, Bangladesh, 1987.

	Low-adopter villages	Medium-adopter villages	High-adopter villages	Total sample
Households purchasing land (%)	5	6	6	6
Households selling land (%)	4	4	6	5
Households mortgaging-In land (%)	4	2	4	3
Households mortgaging-out land (%)	6	4	6	5
Percentage of land:				
Purchased	1.2	1.2	1.0	1.1
Sold	2.3	0.6	0.9	1.3
Mortgaged-in	1.8	0.5	1.3	1.2
Mortgaged-out	1.7	1.0	2.6	1.8

Table 8.13   Incidence of tenancy by status of modern variety adoption, intensive survey, Bangladesh, 1987.

Indicators	Low-adopter villages	Medium-adopter villages	High-adopter villages
Tenant farmers (% of cultivators)	39	42	43
Rented-out land (% of owned land)	20	10	14
Rented-in land (% of cultivated land)	21	23	26
Percent of rented land under:			
Sharecropping	94.0	77.3	56.9
Fixed rent	6.0	22.4	42.0
Mortgage arrangement	—	0.3	1.1

Table 8.14   Difference in land rent (Tk/ha) under sharecropping and fixed-rent contract, costs-and-returns survey, Bangladesh, 1987.

Tenancy type	Traditional varieties	Modern varieties
Fixed-cash rent		
Low-adopter	2,552	3,705
Medium-adopter	2,305	3,705
High-adopter	4,150	6,373
Fixed-kind rent	—	6,225
Share rent	6,286	11,240

Table 8.15   Importance of different labor hiring arrangements classified by modern variety adoption status, Bangladesh, 1987.

Labor market characteristics	Low-adopter villages	Medium-adopter villages	High-adopter villages
Cultivators employing permanent workers (%)	23	13	12
Permanent workers (per 100 households)	33	20	15
Cultivators hiring casual labor in a week (%)	28	37	42
Villages reporting use of contract labor (%)[a]	38	54	53
Cultivators reporting use of migrant labor (%)	8	8	24
Share (%) of hired labor			
Attached worker	36	18	8
Casual worker	50	69	67
Migrant worker	12	7	20
Contract worker	2	6	5

a. From extensive-survey and intensive-survey data.

Table 8.16   Wage rates by type of labor and modern variety adoption and costs-and-returns survey, Bangladesh, 1987.

Production activity	Low-adopter villages (Tk/day)	Medium-adopter villages (Tk/day)	High-adopter villages (Tk/day)
Land preparation	32	31	35
Transplanting	33	30	37
Weeding	32	28	34
Harvesting	33	29	36
Threshing	31	28	33

Table 8.17   Regression results of land prices and wage rate functions, extensive survey, Bangladesh, 1987.[a]

Variables	Ln Land prices	Ln Transplanting wage	Ln Harvesting wage
DPWATER	-0.11 (-0.55)	-0.08 (-0.88)	-0.11 (-1.24)
DPRONE	-0.26 (-1.24)	-0.10 (-1.00)	-0.06 (-0.66)
SALINE	0.10 (0.36)	0.09 (0.73)	0.08 (0.67)
MVR*IRGR	0.48* (1.72)	-0.19 (-1.51)	-0.23* (-1.87)
MVR*RFR	0.44 (1.47)	0.38** (2.83)	0.17 (1.30)
Ln LMR	-0.82* (-1.89)	-0.53* (-2.17)	-0.68** (-2.88)
Ln LANDWKR	—	0.28* (1.87)	0.24* (1.67)
PLARGE	0.78 (0.91)	0.12 (0.32)	0.26 (0.69)
PFLW	-0.47 (-0.50)	-0.71 (-1.64)	-0.57 (-1.35)
PNF	0.09 (0.18)	0.11 (0.36)	0.005 (0.02)
ELECT	0.33* (1.93)	-0.02 (-0.20)	-0.03 (-0.37)
INFR	-0.09 (-0.51)	0.18* (2.09)	0.22** (2.62)
R^2 0.47		0.46	0.50

a. Numbers in parentheses are t-statistics.
** Indicates significance at 1% level; * at 5% level.

Table 8.18   Factor shares in cultivation of traditional and modern rice varieties, costs-and-returns survey, Bangladesh, 1987.

Inputs/output	Traditional variety[a]		Modern variety[b]	
	Tk/ha	% of gross value of product	Tk/ha	% of gross value of product
Gross value of production	13,533	100	26,176	100
Current input:	1,240	9	5,305	20
Self-supplied[c]	689	5	921	3
Purchased[d]	551	4	4,384	17
Draft power	2,253	17	2,196	8
Family	2,034	15	1,916	7
Hired	219	2	280	1
Labor	4,241	31	5,796	23
Family	2,402	18	2,788	12
Hired	1,839	13	3,008	12
Land	6,286	47	11,240	43
Farm operator surplus	-487	-4	1,639	6
Farm family income				
Owned land	10,235	76	17,583	67
Rented land	3,949	29	6,343	24

a. Averages for local *aus*, broadcast *amon*, and local transplanted *amon* weighted by the proportion of areas under these varieties.
b. Averages for modern *boro*, *aus*, and *amon* weighted by the proportion of area under these varieties.
c. Includes seeds and manure.
d. Includes fertilizer, pesticides, and water charges.

Table 8.19   Structure of rural household incomes by source, intensive survey, Bangladesh, 1987.

Sources of income	All households Tk/yr	% share	Nonfarm households Tk/yr	% share	Farm households Tk/yr	% share
Agriculture	16,582	60	9,238	41	20,382	67
Crop cultivation	12,825	46	7,040	31	15,818	52
Rice	7,820	28	1,267	6	11,211	37
Nonrice	1,795	6	258	1	2,590	8
Wages	3,210	12	5,515	24	2,017	7
Noncrop agriculture	3,757	14	2,198	10	4,564	15
Non-agriculture	11,123	40	13,342	59	9,975	33
Processing	2,124	8	2,518	11	1,920	6
Trade	3,162	11	4,856	22	2,285	8
Transport	663	2	1,220	6	375	1
Construction	335	1	523	2	238	1
Services	2,777	10	2,348	10	3,000	10
Remittances	816	3	494	2	982	3
Other	1,246	5	1,383	6	1,175	4
Total income	27,705	100	22,580	100	30,357	100
Family size (no)	6.13		5.22		6.60	
Per capita income	4,520		4,326		4,600	

Table 8.20   Components of household income by production environment, intensive survey, Bangladesh, 1987.

Sources of income	Irrigated		Favorable rainfed		Drought prone		Flood prone		Saline affected	
	Tk/yr	%	Tk/yr	%	Tk/yr	%	Tk/yr	%	Tk/yr	%
Agriculture	20,467	71	15,310	59	14,680	64	14,972	55	20,415	72
Rice cultivation	15,094	52	10,284	39	8,291	36	9,808	36	13,257	47
Land	8,434	29	6,408	24	3,787	17	5,376	20	7,152	25
Labor	5,541	19	3,151	12	3,776	16	3,846	14	5,086	18
Capital	1,119	4	725	3	728	3	586	2	1,019	4
Nonrice agriculture	5,373	19	5,026	20	6,389	28	5,164	19	7,158	25
Nonagriculture	8,425	29	10,876	41	8,331	36	12,388	45	7,813	28
Processing, trade, transport, construction	5,968	21	7,339	28	6,070	26	7,397	27	4,465	16
Salaries and remittances	2,457	8	3,537	13	2,261	10	4,991	18	3,348	12
Household income	28,892	100	26,186	100	23,011	100	27,360	100	28,228	100
Household members (no)	5.73		6.26		6.13		6.09		5.94	
Income per capita	5,042		4,183		3,754		4,493		4,752	

Table 8.21 Regression results of farm household income, intensive survey, Bangladesh, 1987.[a]

Variables	Ln Income from rice cultivation				Ln Nonrice agriculture	Ln Nonagriculture
	Land	Labor	Capital	Total		
DPRONE	-0.66**	0.10	-0.28**	-0.52**	0.17*	-0.01
	(-4.26)	(0.66)	(-7.11)	(-6.30)	(1.67)	(-0.04)
DPWATER	0.09	-0.05	-0.10**	-0.16*	0.21*	0.45**
	(0.06)	(-0.30)	(-2.50)	(-1.87)	(1.99)	(3.47)
SALINE	0.38*	0.43*	-0.01	0.26**	0.39**	-0.35*
	(1.89)	(2.08)	(-0.02)	(2.25)	(2.72)	(-2.21)
MVR*IRGR	0.70**	0.42**	0.19**	0.66**	-0.11	-0.05
	(5.32)	(3.27)	(5.74)	(9.25)	(-1.27)	(-0.49)
MVR*RFR	0.64**	0.10	0.12**	0.55**	-0.09	-0.13
	(3.82)	(0.53)	(2.56)	(5.80)	(-0.78)	(-0.97)
Ln FSIZE	0.70**	0.63**	0.04*	0.81**	0.28**	0.10*
	(9.47)	(8.76)	(1.89)	(20.33)	(5.94)	(1.82)
TENANCY	-0.42**	-0.17	0.14**	-0.25**	-0.17*	0.03
	(-2.84)	(-1.09)	(3.30)	(-3.03)	(-1.70)	(0.22)
Ln CAPITALQ	0.10*	0.14**	1.02**	0.08**	0.20**	0.21**
	(1.78)	(2.38)	(5.61)	(2.38)	(5.13)	(4.83)
Ln WORKER	-0.09	0.25*	-0.05*	-0.05	0.15*	0.33**
	(-0.80)	(2.20)	(-1.78)	(-0.76)	(1.96)	(3.63)
NAGRW	-0.05	-0.32*	-0.02	-0.08	0.06	1.23**
	(-0.35)	(-1.82)	(-0.46)	(-0.94)	(0.56)	(10.59)
SCHOOL	-0.03*	-0.02	0.01	-0.01	-0.01	0.02
	(-1.91)	(-1.02)	(1.38)	(-1.10)	(-0.36)	(1.40)
ELECT	-0.22	0.32*	0.03	-1.16*	-0.02	0.35**
	(1.42)	(2.20)	(0.67)	(-1.85)	(-0.20)	(2.91)
INFR	0.11	-0.18	-0.03	-0.08	0.00	0.15
	(0.90)	(-1.55)	(-0.95)	(-1.12)	(0.01)	(1.61)
R^2	0.34	0.29	0.90	0.58	0.23	0.35
F-value	20.10**	18.50**	472.35**	75.43**	17.03**	22.20**

a. Numbers in parentheses are t-statistics.
** Indicates significance at 1% level; * at 5% level.

Table 8.22   Determinants of income for nonfarm households, intensive survey, Bangladesh, 1987.[a]

Variables	Rice income	Nonrice agriculture	Nonagricultural
DPRONE	-1,974** (-2.33)	-885* (-1.86)	194 (0.13)
DPWATER	-398 (-0.47)	-373 (-0.79)	3,146* (2.14)
SALINE	1,174 (0.98)	286 (0.42)	-47 (-0.02)
LANDOWN	9,183** (11.37)	1,020* (2.25)	1,830 (1.31)
SCHOOL	-197* (-1.87)	25 (0.42)	334* (1.96)
AGRIC	3,795** (8.36)	53 (0.21)	-197 (-0.25)
NAGRIC	-1,923** (-4.09)	147 (0.56)	10,836** (13.27)
CAPITALQ	-0.13* (-2.18)	0.12** (3.56)	0.54** (5.26)
INFR	-2,263** (-3.34)	-1,184** (-3.12)	23 (0.02)
ELECT876	-92 (1.02)	984 (-0.19)	(0.66)
R²	0.45	0.11	0.50
F-value	33.82	5.15	39.43

a. Sample size is 409. Numbers in parentheses are t-statistics.
** Indicates significance at 1% level, * at 5% level.

Table 8.23   Pattern of income distribution and concentration of income (% of total income), intensive survey, Bangladesh, 1987.

	Bottom 40%	Middle 40%	Top 10%	Top 5%	Gini ratio
Environment group					
Irrigated	18	39	27	16	0.355
Favorable rainfed	18	40	25	15	0.359
Drought-prone	22	40	24	14	0.302
Flood-prone	18	40	27	16	0.355
Saline-affected	18	35	33	24	0.394
Modern variety adoption status					
Low	19	40	25	15	0.346
Medium	18	39	28	17	0.363
High	19	40	26	16	0.340
All households	18	39	27	17	0.358

Table 8.24   Concentration of income and its decomposition by source of income for all households, intensive survey, Bangladesh, 1987.

Sources of income	Income share (%)	Pseudo-Gini ratio[a]	Absolute contribution to income inequality	Relative contribution to income inequality (%)
Agriculture	59.9	0.30	0.178	51.7
Rice cultivation	28.2	0.44	0.123	35.8
Other crops	6.5	0.36	0.023	6.7
Noncrop agriculture	13.6	0.20	0.027	7.8
Agricultural wage	11.6	0.04	0.005	1.4
Nonagriculture	40.1	0.41	0.166	48.3
Salaries and wages	13.0	0.51	0.066	19.2
Others	27.1	0.37	0.100	29.1
Total income	100.0	0.34	0.344	100.0

a. See equations (35) to (36) in Chapter 3.

Table 8.25   Contribution to income inequality by income component and status of modern variety adoption, intensive survey, Bangladesh, 1987.

Sources of income	Low-adopter villages Income share	Low-adopter villages Absolute contribution to inequality	Medium-adopter villages Income share	Medium-adopter villages Absolute contribution to inequality	High-adopter villages Income share	High-adopter villages Absolute contribution to inequality
Agriculture	0.52	0.137	0.65	0.200	0.68	0.231
Rice	0.21	0.094	0.28	0.116	0.36	0.175
Other crops	0.08	0.026	0.08	0.032	0.05	0.018
Noncrop	0.11	0.022	0.16	0.034	0.14	0.030
Wages	0.13	-0.005	0.13	0.017	0.12	0.008
Nonagriculture	0.48	0.192	0.35	0.136	0.32	0.082
Wages and salaries	0.17	0.093	0.12	0.063	0.09	0.034
Others	0.31	0.099	0.23	0.073	0.22	0.048
Overall Gini ratio	1.00	0.329	1.00	0.336	1.00	0.313

Table 8.26   Absolute contribution to income inequality by income component and by environmental status, intensive survey, Bangladesh, 1987.

Sources of income	Irrigated	Favorable rainfed	Drought-prone	Flood-prone	Saline-affected
	Concentration ratio				
Agriculture	0.246	0.196	0.164	0.120	0.089
Rice	0.199	0.122	0.105	0.067	0.068
Other crops	0.016	0.030	0.041	0.019	0.013
Noncrop activity	0.026	0.037	0.031	0.017	0.016
Wages	0.005	0.007	-0.013	0.018	-0.008
Nonagriculture	0.073	0.168	0.125	0.176	0.342
Wages and salaries	0.032	0.082	0.051	0.079	0.083
Others	0.041	0.086	0.074	0.097	0.259
Overall Gini ratio	0.320	0.364	0.289	0.296	0.431

Table 8.27   Incidence of poverty for villages classified by technology adoption and environment status, intensive survey, Bangladesh, 1987.[a]

	Head-count ratio	
	Household	Population
Environment status		
Irrigated	0.555	0.561
Favorable rainfed	0.601	0.601
Drought-prone	0.724	0.724
Flood-prone	0.540	0.582
Saline-affected	0.462	0.488
Modern variety adoption status		
Low-adopter	0.576	0.589
Medium-adopter	0.639	0.643
High-adopter	0.555	0.575
All cases	0.588	0.605

a. Poverty line was estimated at US$135 per capita per year, on the assumption of an energy need of 2,110 kilocalories and 30% expenditure on nonflood basic needs.

9
Modern Variety Adoption, Wage Differentials, and Income Distribution in Nepal
■

HARI K. UPADHYAYA AND GANESH B. THAPA

Nepal is predominantly agriculture-dependent. About 90% of the population is engaged in agriculture, which contributed about 60% of gross domestic product in 1990. Rice is Nepal's most important crop. It occupies about half the total cultivated area, which is split among two ecologically distinct regions—the hills and the lowlands (*tarai*).

The Nepalese population was concentrated in the hills region, including the Kathmandu Valley, prior to the 1950s. Since then, growing population pressure in the hills, eradication of malaria in the *tarai*, and construction of highways linking the eastern and western *tarai* have induced migration of a large proportion of the population to the lowlands. The availability of arable land in a favorable production environment was a factor that attracted migrants from the hills (Khadka 1977; Dahal, Raj, and Manzando 1977; New Era 1981).

Modern rice varieties were introduced to Nepal in the mid-1960s and are now grown on almost 40% of the rice crop area. The increase in rice yields following adoption of modern varieties has not, however, been as dramatic as in other Asian countries.

It is well known that adoption of modern varieties is constrained by the availability of irrigation water (Barker and Herdt 1985). Nepal's irrigation systems cover only about 23% of the total rice area. Moreover, these systems are largely underutilized, and the supply of irrigation water is unstable in many areas (Upadhyaya and Bhatta 1989).

Because of environmental constraints, the popular modern varieties in Nepal are not the IRRI-bred varieties but rather the taller improved varieties, which are less responsive to fertilizer application and, hence, produce lower

This chapter is based on Upadhyaya (1988); Thapa (1989); Upadhyaya et al. (1990); Thapa et al. (1992); and Upadhyaya et al. (1993).

281

yields. The performance of these taller varieties is relatively uniform across large areas (Upadhyaya et al. 1993). As a result, they are widely grown in poorly irrigated and favorable shallow rainfed areas. In less favorable areas, low-yielding traditional varieties are widely planted.

The concentration of modern varieties in the more favorable areas has raised concern that Nepal's Green Revolution has accentuated existing regional income disparities. For Nepal, this means income disparities between irrigated and rainfed areas and between the *tarai* and hills regions; most large-scale irrigation projects are in the *tarai*, and modern varieties are more widely adopted there than in the hills region. Moreover, even before the introduction of modern varieties, the income of the *tarai* farm population was generally higher than that of hills farmers because of larger landholdings (Islam 1984).

The equity effects of the new rice technology depend not only on its direct influence on productivity and factor use but also on its indirect influence on output and factor prices. It is therefore necessary to consider both the direct and the indirect effects in analyzing the trade-off between growth and equity associated with differential adoption of the new technology.

Although differential adoption of the new technology may widen the gap in productivity across regions, it is possible that subsequent adjustments in land, labor, and output markets may mitigate this potentially adverse impact on regional income distribution. Because labor is a mobile factor and the main resource of the rural poor, the equity effect of differential technology adoption would critically depend on the extent to which favorable and unfavorable areas are linked by interregional migration. If people move from unfavorable to favorable areas in response to the wage differential initially created by the differential adoption of the new technology, wages in the two areas will tend to equalize. If the interregional labor market does not adjust efficiently to the wage differential, interregional income disparity will widen, or at least persist, as adoption of the new technology increases in the favorable areas (Chapter 3; Evenson 1975; Quizon and Binswanger 1983).

Conversely, land is an immobile factor of production, and its supply is inelastic, at least in the short run. Hence, an increase in the demand for land resulting from modern variety adoption in favorable areas will increase returns to land in those areas, thereby creating a gap in land income. Moreover, distribution of landownership is more skewed than the distribution of labor. Therefore, the differential productivity growth resulting from differential adoption of new technology is likely to worsen the distribution of land income across production environments.

The objective of this chapter is to analyze the impact of differential adoption of modern rice technology on income distribution in Nepal.

VILLAGE SURVEYS

Data was gathered by two sets of surveys. The first was an extensive survey of forty-four hill and *tarai* villages representing different production environments. The second was an intensive household survey of *tarai* villages included in the extensive survey (Figure 9.1).

First, we selected study areas in the Eastern, Central, and Western regions, which account for about 85% of Nepal's total paddy area and production. Rupandehi, the largest rice-growing *tarai* district of the Western Region, was selected; from the Eastern Region, the two largest rice-growing *tarai* districts, Morang and Sunsari, were selected. From the Central Region, four leading rice-growing districts (two hills and two *tarai*) were selected.

A stratified random sampling procedure based on the presence of irrigation and importance of rice crop was adopted to select sample villages. Information about representative villages was obtained from the Agricultural Development Office in each district.

The intensive-survey villages represent the irrigated and rainfed production environments. The irrigated villages have run-of-the-river gravity irrigation systems constructed and managed by farmers. A few farmers in the rainfed villages use shallow tubewells.

Extensive Survey

The distribution of sample villages between the two ecological regions (the hills and *tarai*) closely followed the distribution of total rice area in the country. The number of sample villages in irrigated and rainfed environments was initially intended to be equal, but two rainfed villages in the hills were dropped because they had only a small rice-growing area.

A broad knowledge of the irrigation systems and farming conditions was obtained from extension workers before a survey was conducted in a particular village. Data on production environments, technology adoption, cropping patterns and crop yields, prices, labor migration and wage rates, land tenure, and other physical, environmental, and socioeconomic characteristics of each village were obtained by interviewing a group of knowledgeable farmers. The extensive-survey data are for the 1987 wet season.

Table 9.1 presents the distribution of the sample villages and their selected socioeconomic characteristics by production environment and ecological region. Irrigated villages are those where most of the rice fields are served by run-of-the-river systems. There are two categories of rainfed villages. Favorable rainfed villages are primarily located in the *tarai* in areas not prone to severe drought. Unfavorable rainfed villages, usually situated on sloping land in the hills, suffer frequent droughts and significant yield losses. Average farm size is similar for the irrigated and rainfed villages within an ecological region. However, farm size in the *tarai* is nearly twice as large as in the hills, and a greater proportion of farms in the *tarai* are devoted to rice. However, the proportion of owner-cultivators is generally higher in the hills than in the *tarai* and lower in the irrigated than in the rainfed villages of the *tarai*.

Irrigated villages have a higher ratio of landless population than rainfed villages in both environments because landless households are generally more mobile than farm households and migrate to favorable areas seeking better employment opportunities. The ratio of agricultural landless households is substantially higher in the *tarai* than in the hills, which may be explained by the greater availability of seasonal in-migrants in the hills during peak seasons. Many different crops with different peak seasons are grown in hills villages. Therefore, short-distance seasonal migrants are readily available in the hills, even though the transportation network is poorly developed in this region. The availability of off-farm jobs may also be an important factor in the rural labor market. The rainfed villages are generally more remote than the irrigated villages.

Intensive Survey

The intensive survey was taken in two stages between August 1987 and January 1988. First, a complete enumeration of all households was done to obtain basic information on farm and household characteristics, family history and migration, technology adoption, cropping patterns, and land tenure. Sample households were then randomly selected to collect detailed information on technology adoption, input use, yields, labor contracts and wages by activity, family farm assets, and incomes from all sources. A sample of landless households were interviewed separately for information on employment, assets, and incomes from different sources.

The intensive survey in the Central Region, however, focused on rice production and income of farm households, and income data from landless households was not collected.

Table 9.2 shows some selected socioeconomic characteristics of the intensive-survey villages. Average farm size is similar between the irrigated and rainfed villages in the Western Region (WR1 and WR2), but in the Central Region (CR2) it is higher in the rainfed village (CR2) than in the irrigated village (CR1). Almost all of the land area in both production environments is planted to rice in the Western Region. In the Central Region, however, the average size of the rice farm is higher in the irrigated village than in the rainfed village, and the number of working family members between fifteen and sixty years of age is also generally larger. Irrigated villages have a larger proportion of leaseholders than rainfed villages. It is interesting—and consistent with extensive-survey findings—that the ratio of agricultural landless households is significantly higher in the irrigated than in the rainfed villages in both regions.

MODERN VARIETY ADOPTION AND
ITS IMPACT ON LAND PRODUCTIVITY

We analyzed the effect of modern variety adoption on fertilizer use, paddy yield, and total cropping intensity in the extensive-survey villages.

Production Environments, Modern
Variety Adoption, and Productivity

Table 9.3 presents the patterns of technology adoption, paddy yields, and cropping intensities in the extensive-survey villages by production environment and ecological region. Only 40% of the rice areas of irrigated villages in the hills and 70% of the rice areas of irrigated villages in the *tarai* regions are actually irrigated. A small proportion of rice area in the rainfed villages is irrigated by shallow tubewells and natural springs.

As expected, the proportion of rice area planted to modern varieties follows the same patten as irrigated rice area, suggesting that modern varieties have been adopted where there is irrigation. However, despite limited irrigation, modern varieties have been also adopted to a considerable extent in rainfed villages, especially in the *tarai*.

The most widely planted modern variety in Nepal is Mahsuri, which was developed in Malaysia in 1965 (Kawakami 1983) and introduced in Nepal in 1973 (Yadav 1987). Mahsuri is medium-statured and less responsive to fertilizer application than modern varieties originating from the International Rice Research Institute (IRRI), and its yield advantage over traditional varieties is smaller. However, Mahsuri performs relatively well and has more stable yields than IRRI modern varieties when grown in moderately adverse environments. Mahsuri is most widely adopted in rainfed areas.

It was not possible to collect reliable extensive-survey data on the proportion of area planted to IRRI versus non-IRRI (predominantly Mahsuri) modern varieties at the village level because proportions of area planted to these varieties change from year to year. It was possible to identify the villages that have adopted only non-IRRI varieties or both types of varieties.

The non-IRRI varieties are invariably planted in villages that have adopted IRRI varieties, which include about 20% of irrigated villages. The degree of IRRI variety adoption is low in the *tarai* rainfed villages and nil in the hills rainfed villages. In contrast, the non-IRRI varieties alone have been adopted in more than a third of the rainfed villages in the hills and 90% of the rainfed villages in the *tarai*. It should be noted that in terms of rice-production environment, rainfed villages in the *tarai* are more favorable than rainfed villages in the hills. Degree of water control apparently affects adoption of IRRI varieties more than adoption of non-IRRI varieties.

Mechanization, which often follows modern variety adoption (Jayasuriya and Shand 1985), is low—even in the irrigated villages. The adoption of tractors seems to be constrained more by other factors than by production environment.

Modern varieties, particularly the IRRI type, are more fertilizer-responsive than traditional varieties, and this feature, together with lower production risks in more favorable areas, affects farmers' incentive to invest in cash inputs. Fertilizer use is highest in irrigated areas in the hills, where adoption of modern varieties is high and yields are stable. Fertilizer use is about the same in irrigated and rainfed areas in the *tarai*, because most rainfed areas in the *tarai* are favorable rainfed. In contrast, rainfed areas in the hills are prone to drought, and, hence, fertilizer use is largely limited to the irrigated portion of the areas and to areas where the Mahsuri varieties are planted.

The differences in adoption rates of IRRI and non-IRRI varieties and in fertilizer use per hectare across production environments are related to the corresponding differences in productivity, as reflected in yield levels. Because we expected yields of IRRI and non-IRRI varieties to be similar in those villages where both types are grown, we recorded average village-level yield data classified by modern varieties and traditional varieties (Table 9.3). The yield difference between modern and traditional varieties in irrigated and rainfed villages adopting IRRI varieties is significant. In contrast, the yield difference between modern and traditional varieties among villages adopting only non-IRRI modern varieties is quite small across production environments. IRRI varieties generally have higher yield potential than non-IRRI modern varieties, but their performance significantly decreases as degree of water control declines.

Total and rice cropping intensities are higher in the irrigated villages than in the rainfed villages in both ecological regions. Rice cropping intensities are generally higher in the *tarai* villages than in the hills villages, which reflects the more favorable rice-production environment in the *tarai*.

Determinants of Modern Variety Adoption, Fertilizer Use, Paddy Yields, and Cropping Intensity Across Villages

Previous studies in Nepal identified several socioeconomic and institutional factors—education, exposure to extension activities, tenure, and formal sources of credit—affecting farmers' decisions to adopt modern varieties (Rawal 1981; Flinn et al. 1980). Our study included, as independent variables, ratio of irrigated rice area (IRGR), farm size (FSIZE), ratio of owner-cultivators (OWNERR), distance to nearest commercial center (DISTM), and a *tarai* dummy (TARAI) to explain intervillage variations in the level of modern variety adoption.

Farm size and owner-cultivator ratio variables were both included to account for the better accessibility of large owner-cultivators to institutional services, particularly credit. As in other developing countries, large owner-cultivators in Nepal are shown to have better access to cheap formal-sector loans (Yadav, Otsuka, and David 1992).

The *tarai* dummy was included to control other environmental factors, such as topography, that are not captured by the irrigation ratio. Because the ratio of rice area planted to modern varieties (denoted as MVR) is zero in some sample villages, we used the Tobit regression method. The regression results are presented in Table 9.4.

Only irrigation is significant in the modern variety adoption function. The results are consistent with accumulated evidence that irrigation is a major factor affecting modern variety adoption but that tenure and farm size are not (Barker and Herdt 1985; Ruttan 1977). The coefficient of the irrigation variable suggests that the rate of modern variety adoption in a completely irrigated village is about 79% higher than in a completely rainfed village.

Because of the strong causal relationship between irrigation and modern variety adoption, it was difficult to isolate the effects of these two variables on fertilizer use, paddy yield, and cropping intensities. Furthermore, modern variety adoption was endogenous in our framework and hence could not be used as an independent variable. Ideally, we should have applied a simultaneous regression technique. As in other village studies, however, such a procedure was inapplicable because of the lack of exogenous variables. We therefore specified the modern variety variable as two dummy variables—villages where both IRRI and non-IRRI varieties are grown (IRMV+NIRMV) and villages where only non-IRRI varieties are grown (NIRMV); villages growing only traditional varieties served as the control variable. Such specification assumed that these dummy variables capture not only the pure effects of improved varieties but also the effects of exogenous environmental factors on the choice of varieties unaccounted for by the irrigation ratio.

Because fertilizer and paddy prices do not vary significantly across our sample villages, prices do not appear as explanatory variables in the fertilizer use function. Given that a number of villages do not apply fertilizers, we used linear, rather than log-linear, specification to avoid the sample bias caused by omission of villages with zero fertilizer application. Also, we employed the Tobit regression method.

Only the modern variety variables are significant in the fertilizer use function. The yield response of modern varieties to fertilizer application is generally higher than that of traditional varieties, so it becomes more profitable to use higher doses of fertilizer on modern varieties than on traditional varieties. The coefficients of the two modern variety variables suggest, however, that villages growing both IRRI and non-IRRI varieties apply more fertilizers than those growing non-IRRI varieties only. This result is to be expected because non-IRRI varieties, predominantly Mahsuri, are less responsive to fertilizer application. It should be emphasized, however, that these dummy variables also reflect environmental and physical characteristics specific to the villages, characteristics that affect the choice of varieties. In fact, the coefficient of irrigation is not significant, presumably because the modern variety variable also captures the impact of irrigation on fertilizer use.

The two modern variety dummy variables are significant in the paddy yield function estimated by the ordinary least squares (OLS) method. Yields in villages growing both types of modern varieties are higher by about 1.5 t/ha than in those growing traditional varieties, as implied by the coefficient of the IRMV+NIRMV variable. The coefficient of non-IRRI varieties is only 0.64, significantly smaller than the coefficient of IRMV+NIRMV. These results clearly indicate that IRRI varieties have a higher yield potential than non-IRRI varieties and traditional varieties.

Irrigation contributes positively to yield. In a completely irrigated village, average paddy yields are about 1 t/ha higher than those in a completely rainfed village, regardless of the type of variety grown. Farm size, tenure, and distance variables have no significant effect on differences in yield levels.

Intervillage differences in total cropping intensities are explained only by irrigation. Irrigation allows farmers to grow crops other than rice during the dry season, when rainfall is inadequate to meet water requirements for rice production. In fact, rice is rarely grown during the dry season in Nepal. The coefficient of IRGR suggests that introduction of irrigation in a rainfed village can increase the total cropping intensity by 50%—i.e., about half of the cultivated area of the village can be planted to an additional crop.

We expected adoption of shorter-growth-duration IRRI varieties to increase cropping intensity. The coefficient of IRMV+NIRMV, however, is positive but not significant, partly because the ratio of rice area planted to IRRI varieties is too small to significantly increase the total cropping intensity and partly because there is insufficient irrigation water for additional crops even in the favorable areas that adopt the IRRI varieties. We note, however, that the ratio of total area planted to rice during the wet season is significantly higher in the irrigated villages that grow IRRI varieties.

A major finding of the extensive survey was that lack of irrigation constrains the adoption of modern varieties in general and of IRRI modern varieties in particular, because higher fertilizer use and the yield advantage of IRRI varieties over non-IRRI varieties and traditional varieties are associated with more favorable production environments. Because the extensive survey did not have accurate information on the proportion of paddy area planted to IRRI varieties within a village, intensive-survey data for farm households in the four *tarai* villages were used to supplement the above analysis.

Determinants of Modern Variety Adoption, Fertilizer Use, and Paddy Yields Across Households in Tarai Villages

Intensive-survey data on levels of modern variety adoption and paddy yields by production environment are summarized in Table 9.5. Both irrigated villages have gravity irrigation systems, but irrigation is more reliable and complete in the Western Region village (WR1), which has fully adopted modern varieties for the wet season. Traditional varieties are still prevalent in large parts of the rainfed Central Region village, CR2. Overall adoption of modern varieties is 80% in the favorable rainfed village (WR2), but IRRI modern varieties have been adopted only in the fully irrigated part of WR2.

As in the extensive survey, the average fertilizer use and paddy yields are higher in the irrigated than in the rainfed villages. Between the two irrigated villages, the average levels of fertilizer use and paddy yield are higher where there is higher adoption of IRRI modern varieties and assured irrigation. The yield difference between IRRI and non-IRRI modern varieties becomes smaller as the degree of water control declines. Rice is grown only in the wet season, but total cropping intensity in the Western Region ranges from 170 in the rainfed village to 203 in the irrigated village, with its cultivation of nonrice crops in the dry season.

We used household-level intensive-survey data to analyze the factors affecting the adoption ratio of IRRI- and non-IRRI modern varieties. The results of the adoption functions by type of variety were estimated using the Tobit procedure and are presented in Table 9.6. Because the quality of irrigation is different between the Western and Central regions, two irrigation variables were specified—i.e., interaction terms between the ratio of irrigated area and the Western and Central Region dummies (IRGR*WEST and IRGR*CENT). We also included the Western Region dummy (WEST) to capture the effects of climatic and other regional differences. The rainfed area in the Central Region served as control. Education, represented by the proportion of farm workers between fifteen and sixty years old having more than three years of schooling (EDRATIO), was included to account for differences in decisionmaking ability. Tenancy was represented by two dummy variables to distinguish the effects of share (SHARE) and leasehold (LEASE) tenancy on technology adoption and productivity.

As seen in Table 9.6, these tenancy variables are not significant in regression analysis, which is consistent with the absence of significant effects of owner-cultivator ratio in the previous regression analysis. Consistent with the extensive-survey findings, environmental factors are the most important constraints on adoption of modern varieties. The adoption of IRRI varieties is particularly constrained by the quality of irrigation, as suggested by the significant coefficient of the IRGR*WEST dummy. The results indicate that Western Region villages are more favorable than others for modern variety adoption and that the presence of irrigation is critically important for the adoption of non-IRRI varieties in the Central Region. Farm size and education variables do not significantly affect the level of modern variety adoption.

To identify the pure effects of varieties on fertilizer use, paddy yield, and cropping intensities, simultaneous equation systems treating the IRRI and non-IRRI variety adoption rates as endogenous variables should have been specified. It was extremely difficult, however, to estimate such equation systems because of the absence of exogenous variables that significantly affect the choice of varieties but not fertilizer use, yield, and cropping intensity. Theoretically, we expected that all the variables affecting the former would affect the latter.

An alternative was the estimation of reduced-form equations using the same set of independent variables as those used in the estimation of the modern variety adoption functions. Although this approach was econometrically appropriate, it would not enable us to distinguish the differential effects of IRRI and non-IRRI varieties. Therefore, we applied the two-stage regression procedure, in which the predicted values of the adoption rates of the two types of varieties, based on the regression results of the modern variety adoption functions, were used as independent variables in the second-stage regressions. Because of the identification problem, however, the two environmental variables (IRGR*WEST and IRGR*CENT) could not be included in the second-stage regressions. The estimated coefficients of modern variety adoption in the second-stage regressions thus captured the effects not only of rice varieties but also of irrigation and other environmental factors. To at least partially control for such effects, a regional dummy variable, WEST, was included.

The differential effects of adoption of the two types of modern varieties on fertilizer use, paddy yield, and cropping intensities are shown in Table 9.7. The Tobit regression was applied for the fertilizer use function because some farmers did not apply fertilizers.

The results indicate that adoption of both types of modern varieties increases fertilizer use, but the IRRI varieties induce much higher levels of fertilizer use than the non-IRRI varieties. They do so because the IRRI varieties are more responsive to fertilizer than the non-IRRI varieties. Other things being equal, Western Region villages apply less fertilizer for rice than Central Region villages. Moreover, the results of yield regression indicate that the yield advantage of IRRI varieties over traditional varieties is much higher than that of non-IRRI varieties and that Western Region villages have lower yield levels than do villages of the Central Region.

The yield regression also indicates that leaseholders apply more fertilizer than owner-cultivators and obtain higher yields per hectare. Theoretically, there is no reason to expect leaseholders to apply more fertilizer and obtain higher yields than owner-farmers; both of them face undistorted incentives to apply inputs. Therefore, it is likely that leaseholders happen to apply more fertilizer for reasons other than difference in tenure. However, unless a severe penalty exists to deter opportunistic behavior, share tenants may apply fewer inputs because of the disincentive effect of output sharing. According to recent surveys of the empirical literature by Otsuka and Hayami (1988) and Hayami and Otsuka (1993), share tenants tend to apply as many inputs and obtain the same yields as do leaseholders and owner-farmers, unless the choice and terms of contracts are restricted by land reform laws.

The differential effect of IRRI and non-IRRI varieties on the total cropping intensity is evident. Total cropping intensity increases by about 38%

with the complete adoption of IRRI varieties. In contrast, the adoption of non-IRRI varieties does not have any significant effect on cropping intensity. Large farms cultivate their lands less intensively than small farms, as reflected in the significantly negative coefficients of FSIZE in the yield and total cropping intensity functions.

Statistical evidence based on the intensive survey of farm households largely supports the findings of the extensive survey—degree of water control is the critical factor affecting adoption of new rice varieties across villages and across farms within a village. This is particularly true for the IRRI varieties, which are more responsive to fertilizer and are higher-yielding than other varieties. The adoption rate of IRRI varieties in Nepal is generally low and concentrated in more favorable production environments, a situation that contributes to the widening of the productivity gap between favorable and unfavorable rice-growing areas. The relatively longer-growth-duration non-IRRI varieties are more popular in a wide range of production environments because their performance is more stable than the performance of shorter-duration IRRI varieties. We thus conclude that differential adoption of the new rice technology has widened the productivity gap between favorable and unfavorable rice-growing areas of the country.

IMPACTS ON LABOR DEMAND

Because labor is the main resource of the poorer segment of the society, particularly the landless, the distribution of benefits from productivity gains in the favorable rice-growing areas critically depends on the impact of the new technology on labor demand. We have shown that adoption of modern varieties in favorable areas does not induce mechanization, which saves labor and causes an adverse equity effect. An important question we address here regards the direct effect of technology on labor demand.

It has been established by a number of cross-sectional studies in other countries that adoption of the new rice technology increases labor demand (see Barker and Herdt 1985; Chapters 4, 6–8, and 10). Modern varieties considered in those studies were either the IRRI varieties or their crosses, which differ in nature from the dominant modern varieties in Nepal. To the extent that modern variety technology increases use of hired labor, the direct distributional impact of the technology may not be as inequitable as generally thought. Furthermore, the extent to which inhabitants of the unfavorable areas can, through interregional migration, share benefits from modern variety adoption in favorable areas is primarily determined by the extent to which the technology increases demand for hired labor in the favorable areas. Hence, to analyze the distributional consequences of modern variety adoption in depth, it is essential to separately examine the impacts of adoption on the demands for hired and family labor.

Labor Use in Rice Production

Table 9.8 shows labor use and adoption of labor-saving technology based on the intensive survey. Labor input increases with modern variety adoption, particularly in crop care activity. Studies elsewhere have shown that this increase results from greater application of fertilizer and the resulting need for weeding, as well as from the higher yield per hectare and the subsequent need to do more harvesting and threshing (Barker and Cordova 1978). However, because fertilizer application is quite low and the yield difference is relatively small, we found the aggregate labor demand effect of the modern variety technology to be relatively small.

Nonetheless, the composition of hired and family labor is significantly different between the irrigated and rainfed villages within each region. The share of hired to total labor input is 63% in WR1 compared to 46% in WR2, and a similar pattern can be observed in the Central Region villages. The relatively higher employment of hired labor in the irrigated villages suggests that adoption of modern variety technology creates greater employment opportunities for landless households.

Lower labor use in the Western Region is partly due to the use of tractors for land preparation. Labor input for crop care activities is also lower in the Western Region, possibly because of differences in the method of land preparation, which result in different weed intensities. Note, however, that the difference in labor use for crop care between the irrigated and rainfed villages is greater in the Western Region than in the Central Region. Note also that although the labor input for harvesting and threshing is the same in Central Region villages, the labor input for those activities differs among Western Region villages. These observations suggest that IRRI modern varieties have larger positive impacts on labor use.

Determinants of Labor Use

We estimated hired and family labor use functions by the Tobit regression method (Table 9.9). The dependent variables were expressed in terms of labor use per hectare. Again, the two modern variety variables are the predicted values of adoption rates of the two types of modern varieties based on the regression results of the modern variety adoption functions. Two additional variables were included: a mechanization, or tractorization, dummy (MECH), and number of family farm workers (WORKER). Wage rates and other factor and output prices were not included because they are largely uniform within and among villages.

Both technology variables are highly significant in the hired labor function. The coefficients suggest that, compared to traditional varieties, adoption of IRRI modern varieties increases the use of hired labor by almost seventy-three man-days/ha, whereas the corresponding increase resulting from adoption of non-IRRI modern varieties is about thirty-two man-days/ha.

The coefficients of these variables are not significant in the family labor function.

We expected that as income increases because of the adoption of modern variety technology, more hired labor would be substituted for family labor because leisure is a normal good (Roumasset and Smith 1981). We thus predicted that the modern variety technology would have a negative effect on family labor use. However, the coefficients, although negative, are not significant. These findings suggest that the increased use of hired labor in rice production is due more to increased peak-season demand for labor than to the income effect.

The coefficient of the education variable is positive and significant in the hired labor function but negative in the family labor function. This result suggests that better-educated family workers work off-farm, and hired laborers are substituted for them. As expected, the coefficient of farm size is positive and significant in the hired labor function but negative and significant in the family labor function.

Leasehold tenancy is not significant in the hired labor function, but the coefficient of share tenancy is negative and significant, indicating that share tenants use less hired labor than owner-operators.

As expected, the coefficient of the number of family farm workers is significantly negative in the hired labor function and significantly positive in the family labor function, because available family workers are substituted for hired laborers in various rice-production activities. More specifically, these figures suggest that an additional family worker will increase use of family labor by about seven man-days/ha and correspondingly decrease the use of hired labor by nearly five man-days/ha.

Mechanization does not seem to affect the demand for either hired or family labor. The coefficients of the Western Region dummy, which would reflect the effects of other socioeconomic, cultural, and environmental factors on labor use, suggest that less hired labor is used in the Western than in the Central Region.

To summarize, adoption of the modern rice technology significantly increases demand for hired labor in rice production. This increase is due largely to peak labor demand rather than to income effect. Because hired laborers are mostly landless or near-landless, the impact of new rice technology on labor use appears to have a desirable effect on household income distribution.

LABOR MARKET ADJUSTMENTS
AND REGIONAL WAGE DIFFERENTIALS

Because the modern variety technology promotes intensive use of labor, particularly hired labor, wage rates of hired labor should increase, at least in the short run, in areas that adopt the new technology. The wage differential is expected to induce migration from unfavorable to favorable areas and to equalize wages in the long run.

We examined the labor migration pattern and explored its causes and effects on the regional wage differential.

Technology Adoption and Interregional Migration

Permanent migration from the hills, the generally unfavorable rice areas, to the lowland *tarai* is a well-known demographic phenomenon. Official district-level data from the area of the extensive survey indicate a positive relation among land endowment, irrigation, and population growth (Nepal, Central Bureau of Statistics 1985). In general, man-land ratio was higher in the hills in 1971 but had largely equalized in the two regions by 1981 (Nepal, Central Bureau of Statistics 1987). An exception is the Sarlahi district (Figure 9.1), where the man-land ratio was higher than in the hills districts in both years. Sarlahi, however, has the highest proportion of irrigated area; much of the irrigation infrastructure was constructed there prior to 1970. The increase in the man-land ratio in the *tarai* was highest in Morang district, which initially had the lowest ratio.

The rapid growth in man-land ratio in the *tarai* was due mainly to the much higher growth in population, although the area cultivated also increased more there than in the hills districts. The average annual population growth rate from 1971 to 1981 in the hills districts covered by the extensive survey was 2.1%, whereas the corresponding figure in the *tarai* districts was 4.4%.

The large difference in the population growth rates indicates substantial migration from the hills to the *tarai* during the 1970s. Because labor was scarce relative to land in the *tarai* and the ratio of irrigated area was relatively high, the availability of land and modern rice technology in the *tarai* were important pull factors in this migration.

Note that average farm size and paddy area per farm were larger in the *tarai* than in the hills (see Table 9.1). Corresponding to the larger farm size, the ratio of landless households was much higher in the *tarai* than in the hills, and the ratio of landless households was higher in the favorable villages than in the unfavorable villages in both regions. These data are consistent with our hypothesis that modern rice technology induced migration among landless households. Yet the ratio of landless households in the hills was low even in the favorable villages, largely because of the greater availability of seasonal migrants in the hills during peak periods, such as the transplanting and harvesting seasons (Upadhyaya 1988).

It seems reasonable to hypothesize that an increase in the demand for hired labor arising from the adoption of modern rice technology was followed by a similar shift in the hired labor supply resulting from permanent in-migration of landless people and seasonal in-migration of other workers.

Determinants of Landlessness and Seasonal In-migration

We estimated the landless ratio function and seasonal in-migration function using the extensive-survey data, expressing the dependent variables as ratios and employing essentially the same set of independent variables in the two functions.

We did not analyze permanent migration because information on the rate of permanent migration obtained from the extensive survey was of dubious quality. Results of the intensive survey, however, indicate that the ratio of landless households is positively related to adoption of modern rice technology (Thapa 1989; Upadhyaya 1988). Hence, the ratio of landless households was used as a proxy variable for permanent in-migration. The regression results are shown in Table 9.10.

The first equation shows that irrigation positively affects the ratio of landless households, which supports our hypothesis that the adoption of modern rice technology represented by irrigation cum modern varieties shifts the labor supply by attracting the landless population from less favorable areas. The *tarai* dummy and average farm size both have positive and significant coefficients.

Our findings suggest that the landless migrated to the *tarai* not only because of the higher demand for hired labor associated with larger farm size but also because of other possible advantages, such as the lower man-land ratio and the greater opportunity to become tenants. Upadhyaya (1988) observed that some of the landless and near-landless people who migrated from other areas became tenants in the intensively surveyed *tarai* villages.

We considered farm size to be exogenous because its variation is not well explained by other exogenous variables, including irrigation. The lack of farm size adjustment to the difference in technology is likely to reflect imperfections in the land market, as emphasized by Binswanger and Rosenzweig (1984, 1986).

The distance to the market center (DISTM), whose coefficient is also significant, probably captures certain advantageous effects of remote areas on hired labor employment, such as the larger inequality in farm size distribution, which would increase aggregate hired labor demand.

The goodness of fit of the seasonal in-migration function is low, essentially because of the difficulty in obtaining accurate village-level information on the extent of seasonal in-migration during peak seasons. This information was particularly elusive in the hills, where production environments are quite diverse even within one village. It is remarkable, therefore, to find a positive and significant effect for irrigation and a negative and significant effect for the *tarai* dummy on seasonal in-migration during peak seasons. The positive effect of irrigation renders clear support for our major hypothesis that modern rice technology increases seasonal in-migration by increasing hired labor demand. The negative locational effect of *tarai* is consistent with our earlier observation that seasonal migration is less common in the *tarai* because of the dominance of synchronized growing seasons in rice production. We omitted the variable for ratio of owner-cultivators and included a contract dummy (CONT3) for the practice of output sharing in the seasonal in-migration function. There is no clear reason to assume that the ratio of owner-cultivators affects seasonal in-migration, whereas an output-sharing contract, as distinct from the daily-wage contract, is thought to attract seasonal in-migrants (because everybody can participate in harvesting and the effective daily wage is higher). This belief is confirmed by the positive and significant coefficient of the output-sharing harvesting contract dummy.

In summary, the differences in landless ratio and seasonal in-migration across different environments are consistent with the hypothesis of interregional labor market adjustments to differential adoption of modern rice technology and differential endowment of land relative to labor.

Technology and Regional Wage Differential

Paddy and fertilizer prices, as well as average wage rates across the hills and *tarai* villages, are given in Table 9.11. The prevailing prices of paddy are largely similar across production environments within regions, whereas fertilizer prices are similar within and across regions. Fertilizer prices are controlled by the government, and a subsidy for fertilizer transportation is provided for farmers in the hills. Paddy prices are higher in the hills than in the *tarai* because the latter is a rice-surplus zone and ships rice to the hills.

Wages were standardized to eight hours of work per day. The value of food provided by employers was estimated and included in wage payment. Gender-specific wage rates were included in Table 9.11 because female workers usually perform jobs that require relatively less physical strength, such as transplanting, weeding, manuring, and harvesting, whereas male workers are mostly engaged in plowing and threshing, which require more physical effort. In certain *tarai* villages, an output-sharing contract is practiced for harvesting. In such cases, we imputed labor earnings per day.

The difference in wage rates between the hills and *tarai* is generally small with one exception: The wage rate for land preparation is higher in the hills, partly because of the larger physical effort required to plow fields in mountainous terrain. The difference in wage rates between the favorable and unfavorable villages is small within both regions.

Imputed wage rates under output-sharing contracts are much higher than the daily wage for harvesting. According to the theory of contracts, a daily casual wage is likely to be lower than a contract wage. That is so partly because daily-wage workers are less motivated to work, as their income is fixed regardless of their efforts, and partly because the more able workers prefer the output-sharing contract, as it offers higher remuneration at higher levels of work effort (Stiglitz 1975; Roumasset and Uy 1980; Otsuka, Chuma, and Hayami 1992; Hayami and Otsuka 1993).

In general, wage rates are different for different activities. Therefore, we estimated the wage-rate functions separately for land preparation, transplanting, weeding and manuring, harvesting, and threshing. For the harvesting-wage function, we used the imputed wage rates where daily-wage and output-sharing contracts coexisted, as the latter contract was more prevalent in every case.

We did not have explicit data on labor quality, but the activities considered here are unskilled, standardized jobs; hence, it is unlikely that the differences in quality among workers can explain a major part of the regional wage differentials.

Determinants of Wage Rates

Ideally we should separately identify 1) the direct effect of modern rice technology on wage rate through its influence on the demand for hired labor and 2) its indirect, offsetting effects through its influence on the ratio of landless population and seasonal in-migration. We could not estimate such simultaneous equation systems, however, because of the paucity of exogenous variables. Therefore, we estimated the reduced-form wage functions employing the same set of independent variables used in the estimation of landless ratio and seasonal in-migration functions. The results are in Table 9.12.

None of the estimated coefficients of irrigation ratio is significant, even though all are consistently positive. Given that irrigation is a major determinant of modern variety adoption and that adoption of modern varieties significantly raises demand for hired labor, the nonsignificant wage effect of irrigation is of particular interest. One explanation is that the labor supply adjusts to the higher labor demand through increases in the landless population and seasonal in-migration.

Such an interpretation is reinforced by the finding that the *tarai* dummy has significant and negative coefficients for the nonpeak seasonal activities of land preparation and threshing but positive, although not always significant, coefficients for the peak-season activities of transplanting, weeding and manuring, and harvesting.

The schedule of nonpeak activities can be staggered, whereas peak-season activities cannot be delayed without significant production loss. Although labor demand for nonpeak-season activities is generally met by family labor and resident landless labor, seasonal migrants become an important source of labor supply during peak seasons. As shown in the previous section, the *tarai* has a larger supply of resident landless labor but fewer seasonal in-migrants than does the hills region. Lower wage rates during nonpeak seasons and somewhat higher wage rates during peak seasons in the *tarai* are clearly consistent with those differences. An important implication of this finding is that the average wage rates throughout the crop season are not substantially different between the hills and the *tarai.*

The coefficients of distance from village to the nearest market are consistently negative and significant, reflecting the difficulty of conveying labor market information and the large cost of traveling to distant areas.

Farm size has no significant effect on any wage rates, even though it is positively associated with hired labor demand. The ratio of owner-cultivators has a significant coefficient in transplanting, whereas the type of harvesting contract has a large and significantly positive coefficient in the harvesting wage regression.

The statistical evidence provided above strongly supports the hypothesis that regional labor markets in Nepal are sufficiently integrated so that the adjustment of supply and demand in local labor markets leaves no significant differences in wage rates over wide rural areas. This adjustment is remarkable in view of the fact that favorable and unfavorable areas are, in large measure, geographically separated and transportation and communication facilities are underdeveloped in Nepal.

MODERN RICE TECHNOLOGY AND HOUSEHOLD INCOME DISTRIBUTION

We have shown that modern rice technology is biased toward the use of hired labor and that subsequent labor supply adjustment, through seasonal and permanent migration of landless households to favorable areas, has largely equalized wages across favorable and unfavorable areas. We next analyze the effects of modern variety adoption on household income distribution within and across the intensive-survey villages.

Factor Shares in Rice Production

Changes in factor payments and factor shares in rice production have a significant impact on household income distribution because rice production constitutes a major source of household income in the study villages. A standard technique in functional income distribution analysis is to compare shares accruing to different factors and earners before and after technological change (Hayami and Kikuchi 1982; Ranade and Herdt 1978; Herdt 1987). If a higher share of increased output goes to the poorer segments of society, then technological change contributes to an equitable distribution of income. Conversely, if increased benefit is captured by landholders, then technological change may accentuate income disparity. Because of a lack of time-series data, it was not possible to compare factor shares before and after technological change. Instead, we compared factor shares between intensive survey villages characterized by different technologies but similar market conditions.

Average factor payments and relative factor shares per hectare of rice production in the study villages are shown in Table 9.13. The gross value of output is much higher in irrigated villages than in rainfed villages. Factor payments to different inputs are also higher, in absolute terms, in irrigated villages, indicating that adoption of modern rice varieties leads to higher returns to all factors of production. Relative share of labor in rainfed villages, where technology adoption has been limited by lack of irrigation, is generally higher than in irrigated villages.

Because household income distribution is closely related to actual payments to owners of factor inputs, factor payments to labor are divided into those accruing to hired and to family labor, whereas factor payments to land are divided into actual average rent and surplus to farm operators. The share accruing to land, as measured by the residual, constitutes between 50% and 60% of gross value of output in the study villages. In contrast, the share accruing to hired labor is roughly between 15% and 25% of gross revenue. The estimated surplus, defined as residual minus leasehold rent, is significantly higher in irrigated villages, partly because leasehold rents are set by the land reform law. This policy works to the great advantage of those who rent irrigated land.

The analysis of factor shares shows that employment opportunities for hired labor in rice production are relatively limited and that the important sources of farm operators' income from rice are the residual returns to land and the surplus. Consequently, a farm operator's total income share from capital, family labor, and land per hectare far exceeds that of hired labor, even though the share of family labor is lower than that of hired labor in rice production. These data clearly show that landless workers will be much worse off than farmers unless remunerative employment opportunities are available outside rice production.

Determinants of Household Income

Household income in the study villages consists of income from rice, nonrice crops, livestock, and nonfarm sources. Table 9.14 shows the average annual incomes of farm households in the survey villages. Nonrice farm income and nonfarm income account for significant shares of total income in all villages. Several studies in other countries have reported that nonfarm income constitutes a significant proportion of total income for agricultural households (Shand 1987; Anderson and Leiserson 1980; Chinn 1979).

In the Western Region, average income of farm households is significantly higher in the irrigated village than in the rainfed village. Much of this difference can be explained by the much higher level of farm income from nonrice crops grown during the dry season in the irrigated village—income due largely to the presence of irrigation. In the Central Region, however, the availability of more profitable nonrice crops in the rainfed village more than offsets the higher rice income in the irrigated village.

Rice income is divided into earnings of the household's own labor, capital, and land (or tenancy right) from rice production. Labor income refers to returns to family labor, imputed by applying appropriate market wage rates for different tasks. Similarly, capital income refers to returns to owned capital, imputed by prevailing custom rates. Land income for owner-operators is the residual, whereas for tenants it is the surplus (i.e., the residual net of rent payments). Note that the residual represents not only returns to land but also returns to management and errors in imputing income of family labor and family-owned capital.

Landless households, whose major source of income is labor earnings, have a considerably lower total income than farm households, mainly because of the difference in land income from rice and nonrice crop production. Landless households in the Western Region irrigated village receive more income from the rice sector than landless households in this region's rainfed village (Table 9.15; data were not collected from landless households in the Central Region). However, total household and per capita incomes are not greatly different between villages because landless households in the rainfed village have higher nonfarm income than those in the irrigated village. Because employment in the crop sector in the rainfed village is limited during the dry season, landless households find employment in the nonfarm sector.

Household income determination functions were estimated to identify the determinants of each component of household income. Theoretically, the estimated functions were reduced-form equations derived from utility maximization behavior of households with respect to allocations of labor, land, and other family-owned resources for different uses.

The technology variables were specified as interaction terms between farm size and adoption rates of IRRI and non-IRRI modern varieties. Other explanatory variables included farm size, interaction terms between farm size and tenancy, value of nonland fixed assets (ASSET), number of family workers between ages fifteen and sixty, and ratio of educated workers. An irrigated village dummy variable (IRGV) was also included. Linear functional form was again adopted in estimating income determination functions because several observations had zero labor earnings from rice production and zero nonfarm incomes.

The technology and tenure variables were specified as interaction terms with farm size because component incomes are expressed on a per farm basis (see Chapter 3 for further details). Because many households did not have labor and nonfarm incomes, we used the Tobit model to estimate the labor and nonfarm income determination functions.

Table 9.16 has the regression results of household income determination functions by income component based on the intensive survey. The estimation results conform with a priori expectations. The coefficient of

IRRI modern varieties interacted with farm size is positive and significant, whereas the coefficient of the non-IRRI modern varieties is close to zero in the land income regression. These coefficients suggest that, compared to traditional varieties, IRRI varieties will generate an additional surplus of nearly 4,300 rupees per hectare, whereas each hectare planted to non-IRRI varieties will not generate any additional surplus. The surplus net of rent payments will be lower than that of owner-operators by about Rs 2,500 for share tenants and Rs 2,000 for leasehold tenants, as suggested by the coefficients of the tenure variables interacted with farm size. These coefficients essentially reflect the amounts of land rent paid by the share and fixed-rent tenants to their landlords. As expected, share rents are slightly higher than leasehold rents, presumably because of the difference in risk premium (Otsuka and Hayami 1988).

The positive and significant coefficient of the irrigated village dummy variable may indicate the effect of irrigation as well as the locational advantages of irrigated villages, such as better soil and other environmental conditions.

The coefficient of the WEST dummy variable suggests that Western Region villages generally have lower land incomes than Central Region villages. The coefficient of farm size represents the per-hectare land income from owner-operated farms planted to traditional rice varieties, which is estimated to be about Rs 3,000. This number is close to the land income per hectare in the rainfed villages shown in Table 9.13.

Because labor income mainly consists of imputed earnings from family labor in rice production, the specification of the labor income regression was similar to that of the family labor use regression, except that the technology and tenure variables were expressed as interaction terms with farm size. On a per farm basis, adoption of modern varieties, particularly the non-IRRI type, seems to increase the labor income from rice production. The negative and significant coefficient of farm size implies that family labor input in rice production per hectare declines significantly as farm size increases, which is consistent with the results of the labor use functions.

Tenancy variables have positive and significant coefficients in the labor income function. Tenants are generally less well off than owner-farmers, so they allocate more labor time and earn higher labor income per farm from rice production than owner-farmers. The positive and significant coefficient of the variable for number of workers suggests that as the number of family workers increases, use of hired labor decreases, resulting in higher labor income.

The negative and significant coefficient of ASSET in the labor income function is partly due to the fact that farmers with more assets tend to be better off and, hence, work less, and partly due to the fact that such farmers own certain assets that provide opportunities for family workers to work outside rice farms. Overall, results of the labor income regression are largely consistent with the labor use functions.

As expected, farm size has a positive and significant coefficient in the nonrice farm income equation; each additional hectare of land increases nonrice farm income by about Rs 8,300 per farm per year. The negative and significant coefficient of non-IRRI modern varieties implies that these varieties are generally grown on relatively less favorable lands, where cultivation of nonrice crops is not so profitable. The positive and significant coefficient of ASSET may be partly explained by the fact that households with more fixed assets have greater access to credit, which positively affects income from nonrice sources.

Irrigated villages seem to have an advantage in producing nonrice crops because of better production environments unaccounted for by the modern variety variables, as reflected by the significantly positive coefficient of the irrigated village dummy variable. The negative and significant coefficient of the regional dummy variable suggests that Western Region villages have significantly lower nonrice farm incomes than Central Region villages.

Nonfarm income includes labor earnings from nonfarm employment, remittances, pensions, and income from self-employed petty trade. It is understandable, therefore, that farm households with more irrigated and favorable lands, where IRRI modern varieties are grown, earn significantly lower nonfarm income than other farm households, as implied by the coefficient of FSIZE*IRMV in the nonfarm income regression. The coefficients of ASSET and the irrigated village and regional dummy variables are all positive and significant, which means that asset-rich farmers in the irrigated villages, and in Western Region villages in general, have an advantage in terms of access to nonfarm employment opportunities.

Estimation results of household income determination functions for landless households in the Western Region are presented in Table 9.17. The coefficient for education is significant and positive in the nonfarm income regression but significant and negative in the rice income equation. Judging from the magnitudes of these coefficients, the net effect of schooling on total income is positive, which implies that human capital is an important determinant of landless household income, particularly because of the high payoffs to human capital for nonfarm jobs.

The coefficient of number of family workers is significantly positive in rice and nonrice farm income functions, which is plausible because income here refers to labor earnings from simple peak-season activities in crop production. As expected, the value of nonland fixed assets, which include buildings for petty trade, is an important explanatory variable in the nonfarm income regression.

We could not specify household-specific technology variables for the landless household income determination functions. Therefore, we considered the irrigated village dummy to capture, at least partly, the effects of environments and technology differences between the two villages. The estimated coefficients of the village dummy, however, are not significant.

The coefficient of this village dummy was also not significant when we estimated the total income function.

The above results are consistent with our earlier finding that agricultural wage rates are largely equalized between favorable and unfavorable areas in the *tarai*, primarily because of seasonal migration of the landless laborers from unfavorable to favorable areas. It seems that the benefits of increased demand for hired labor resulting from adoption of modern rice technology in favorable areas are shared with landless laborers at large.

Gini Decomposition Analysis

Several previous studies of the impact of technology on income distribution have used the Gini coefficient in comparing income inequality by use of cross-section data (Shand 1987; Raju 1976). Because the adoption of modern varieties affects various income components differently, it is essential to quantify the relative importance of each component in analyzing the issue of income inequality. The previous studies do not, however, consider the impact of technology on various income components.

We compare Gini coefficients for total and component incomes based on the procedure presented in Chapter 3 as derived by Fei, Ranis, and Kuo (1978) and later elaborated by Pyatt, Chen, and Fei (1980) (see Chapter 3 for further details on methodology).

The estimation results of Gini ratio for total income and absolute contributions of different income components (i.e., the product of income share, rank correlation ratio, and component Gini ratio) to total income inequality are shown in Table 9.18. Gini ratios are highest in the Central Region rainfed (CR2) and the Western Region irrigated (WR1) villages, where the most important income source contributing to total income inequality is nonrice farm income. In both of these villages, the share of this income source in total income is high (see Table 9.14). In addition, the component Gini ratio of nonrice farm income is higher in WR1 than in other villages, whereas the rank correlation ratio is higher in CR2 than in other survey villages. In WR2 and CR1, where the Gini ratios are equally low, rice income contributes most to the overall income inequality. These results indicate that the inequality in rice income is not a major contributor to overall income inequality, even though our survey villages are typical rice-dependent villages in Nepal.

The contribution of nonfarm income to total income inequality is significantly higher in Western Region villages than in Central Region villages, which may be due to the proximity of the former villages to an industrial city.

The contribution of rice income to overall income inequality is lowest in CR2 (28%), which would reflect product market adjustment away from rice resulting from the comparative advantage of alternative crops. In other villages, the distribution of rice income accounts for 41% to 54% of total income inequality. The most important contributor to rice income inequality is land income, whose component Gini ratio and rank correlation ratio are generally high in all survey villages. In contrast, the contribution of labor and capital income from rice farming to overall income inequality is relatively minor.

It is also important to note that the contribution of land income to overall income inequality is relatively low in the most favorable village for rice production, WR1. Moreover, the overall Gini ratio, based on pooled data of the four villages, is lower than Gini ratios in WR1 and CR2. These results suggest that the highly skewed distribution of ownership of or access to land, or both, is the most important factor accounting for household income inequality. We note that Thapa, Otsuka, and Barker (1992) did a counterfactual analysis indicating that the introduction of modern varieties did not significantly worsen household income distribution.

POLICY IMPLICATIONS

Our analysis indicates that the rate of development and quality of irrigation have constrained the adoption of high-yielding modern varieties. Because modern varieties have been adopted only in favorable production environments, significant regional productivity differential has emerged in Nepal. Our study also shows that the modern rice technology is biased toward the use of hired labor, and because hired laborers are mostly landless workers—usually the poorest in the village—the new rice technology has positively contributed to their welfare.

Despite the significantly positive effect of the new technology on hired labor demand, wage rates are largely equalized across different production environments because of permanent, as well as seasonal, migration from unfavorable to favorable areas. An important implication of this analysis is that adoption of new technology in favorable areas has not created significant regional income differentials among landless households whose livelihood depends on wage earnings.

Our household income distribution analysis demonstrates that modern variety adoption significantly increases returns to land but decreases earnings from nonrice production and nonfarm activities, as resources are shifted to rice production in the favorable rice-growing regions. Moreover, on a per hectare basis, family labor income from rice production decreases with modern variety adoption because hired labor is substituted for family labor. As a result, differential modern variety adoption has not significantly worsened household income distribution.

A major policy implication of our study is that more resources should be allocated to development and dissemination of improved rice technology suitable for the favorable areas. Such technology improves production efficiency without significantly worsening household income distribution. In fact, adoption of modern varieties has a positive effect on the income of landless laborers.

This study also underscores the importance of education in determining the income of landless households. This conclusion implies that, to alleviate the poverty of the landless, larger investments in their human capital are required. Such investments will improve both the efficiency and the equity of the Nepalese economy.

Figure 9.1 Location of study areas, extensive and intensive survey, Nepal, 1987

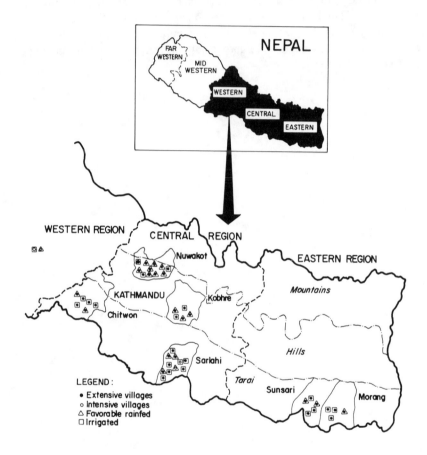

LEGEND:
- Extensive villages
- ○ Intensive villages
- △ Favorable rainfed
- □ Irrigated

Table 9.1   Selected socioeconomic characteristics of sample villages by production environment and ecological region, extensive survey, Nepal, wet season, 1987.

	Hills		Tarai	
	Irrigated	Rainfed	Irrigated	Rainfed
Sample villages (no)	5	11	18	10
Farm size (ha)	1.1	1.0	1.9	1.8
Rice farm size (ha)	0.6	0.4	1.5	1.3
Ratio of owner-cultivators (% of farm households)	89	90	50	71
Ratio of agricultural landless (% of total households)	5	2	30	19
Ratio of seasonal in-migrants (%)[a]	41	3	21	12
Distance to nearest market center (km)	2.6	5.3	2.8	4.8

a. Ratio to the total hired labor during peak seasons of transplanting and harvesting.

Table 9.2   Selected socioeconomic characteristics of *tarai* villages, intensive survey, Nepal, wet season, 1987.

	Irrigated		Rainfed	
	WR1	CR1	WR2	CR2
Farm size (ha)	2.0	1.6	2.1	2.1
Rice farm size (ha)	2.0	1.6	2.0	1.3
Family workers (no)[a]	2.4	4.0	2.8	3.6
Educated workers (%)[b]	76	65	63	61
Ratio of agricultural landless households (%)	19	31	11	21
Tenure (% of farmers)				
Owner-cultivators	67	80	88	75
Leasehold	15	11	5	10
Share tenancy	18	9	7	15

a. The number of family members between fifteen and sixty years old.
b. Education is defined as the completion of three years of primary school.

Table 9.3   Technology adoption, paddy yields, and cropping intensities by production environment and ecological region, extensive survey, Nepal, wet season, 1987.

	Hills		Tarai	
	Irrigated	Rainfed	Irrigated	Rainfed
Ratio of irrigated area (%)	40	6	71	10
Modern variety adoption (% of area)	76	24	73	46
Modern variety adoption (% of villages)	100	36	100	100
IRRI and non-IRRI	18	0	22	10
Non-IRRI only	82	36	78	90
Tractor use (% of area)	5	0	25	30
Fertilizer use (kg N/ha)[a]	39	15	26	27
Yield (t/ha)	2.9	1.8	3.0	2.5
Traditional varieties	1.7	1.4	2.2	2.0
IRRI & non-IRRI MVs[b]	3.7	—	3.4	2.7
Non-IRRI MVs only	2.2	2.1	2.8	2.5
Total cropping intensity (%)	221	192	214	192
Rice cropping intensity (%)	78	40	107	70

a. In many cases, farmers applied only nitrogen fertilizers, such as urea and ammonium sulfate. The amounts of nitrogen applied are calculated based on nitrogen content of a particular type of fertilizer—for example, urea (46%), ammonium sulfate (20%), and mixed fertilizer (20%).
b. MVs = modern varieties.

Table 9.4   Regression results of modern variety adoption, fertilizer use, paddy yield, and total cropping intensity functions, extensive survey, Nepal, wet season, 1987.[a]

	MVR	Fertilizer	Yield	Total cropping intensity
Intercept	-0.15 (-0.64)	-26.08 (-0.92)	1.42** (2.75)	1.68** (8.83)
IRGR	0.79** (4.01)	11.86 (0.63)	1.01* (2.15)	0.50** (2.91)
IRMV + NIRMV	—	52.80** (3.78)	1.52** (3.40)	0.06 (0.35)
NIRMV	—	41.17** (3.59)	0.64* (1.94)	0.04 (0.31)
FSIZE	0.01 (1.60)	0.82 (0.31)	-0.06 (-0.62)	-0.03 (-0.96)
OWNERR	0.38 (1.45)	12.28 (0.57)	0.17 (0.41)	0.25 (1.62)
DISTM	0.01 (0.48)	0.19 (0.13)	-0.01 (-0.57)	0.00 (0.40)
TARAI	0.13 (1.13)	-6.33 (-0.77)	0.06 (0.23)	0.00 (0.02)
R^2	—	—	0.60	0.31
F-value	—	—	7.74	2.30
Log-likelihood	-10.11	-116.93	—	—
(Chi-square)	24.86	17.14	—	—

a. Numbers in parentheses are t-statistics.
** Indicates significance at 1% level; * at 5% level.

Table 9.5   Technology adoption, paddy yields, and cropping intensities in selected *tarai* villages by production environment, intensive survey, Nepal, wet season, 1987.

	Irrigated		Rainfed	
	WR1	CR1	WR2	CR2
Sample households (no)	55	55	55	55
Irrigation (% of area)	100	89	11	9
Modern variety adoption (% of area)	100	85	80	5
IRRI varieties	41	5	6	0
Non-IRRI varieties	59	80	74	5
Fertilizer use (kg N/ha)	30	15	9	8
Yield (t/ha)	2.9	2.4	2.2	1.9
Traditional varieties	—	2.1	1.8	1.9
IRRI varieties	3.2	2.8	2.6	—
Non-IRRI varieties	2.6	2.4	2.3	—
Total cropping intensity (%)	203	193	170	196
Rice cropping intensity (%)	100	98	97	68

Table 9.6   Regression results of modern variety adoption functions by
type of variety, intensive survey, Nepal, wet season, 1987.[a]

	IRRI type	Non-IRRI type
Intercept	–2.20	–0.41**
	(–0.00)	(–3.94)
IRGR*WEST	0.88**	–0.02**
	(5.44)	(–2.59)
IRGR*CENT	–0.05	1.16**
	(–0.00)	(8.51)
FSIZE	0.02	–0.01
	(1.15)	(–0.44)
LEASE	–0.10	–0.04
	(–0.65)	(–0.63)
SHARE	–0.06	0.01
	(–0.37)	(0.13)
EDRATIO	0.11	–0.01
	(0.76)	(–0.27)
WEST	0.88**	1.27**
	(5.44)	(9.44)
Log-likelihood	–49.0	–65.11
(Chi-square)	125.8	162.83

a. Numbers in parentheses are t-statistics.
** Indicates significance at 1% level; * at 5% level.

Table 9.7　Regression results of fertilizer use, paddy yield, and total cropping intensity functions, intensive survey, Nepal, wet season, 1987.[a]

	Fertilizer	Yield	Total cropping intensity
Intercept	100.72** (8.23)	4.44** (16.09)	2.82** (19.30)
IRMV	45.60** (8.62)	0.97** (8.32)	0.38** (6.08)
NIRMV	10.63* (2.07)	0.44** (4.51)	−0.06 (−1.23)
FSIZE	0.31 (0.32)	−0.04* (−2.31)	−0.03** (−3.45)
LEASE	10.14* (1.75)	0.33** (2.81)	0.05 (0.78)
SHARE	−6.96 (−1.51)	−0.12 (−1.07)	−0.01 (−0.19)
EDRATIO	−3.59 (−0.95)	−0.05 (−0.59)	−0.01 (−0.43)
WEST	−88.67** (−6.93)	−0.20** (−7.73)	−0.79** (−5.80)
R^2	—	0.34	0.21
F-value	—	14.78	7.89
Log-likelihood	−642.49	—	—
(Chi-square)	84.66	—	—

a. Numbers in parentheses are t-statistics.
** Indicates significance at 1% level; * at 5% level.

Table 9.8   Labor use (man-days/ha) and adoption of labor-saving tech-
             nologies (%) in rice farming by production environment,
             intensive survey, Nepal, wet season, 1987.[a]

	Irrigated		Rainfed	
	WR1	CR1	WR2	CR2
Land preparation[b]	21	38	31	33
(% of area using tractors)	(69)	(0)	(13)	(0)
Crop establishment	27	36	23	36
Crop care[c]	33	44	22	39
Harvesting and threshing	47	41	38	41
Total labor	128	159	114	149
(% of hired labor)	(63)	(74)	(46)	(68)

a. One man-day refers to eight hours of work per day.
b. Includes plowing, harrowing, puddling, and seedbed preparation.
c. Includes fertilizer and pesticide application, manuring, and irrigation.

Table 9.9   Regression results of labor use functions in rice production, intensive survey, Nepal, wet season, 1987.[a]

	Hired labor	Family labor
Intercept	81.18**	63.20**
	(10.69)	(16.28)
IRMV	72.84**	−2.19
	(2.60)	(−0.05)
NIRMV	31.73**	−21.44
	(2.85)	(−1.61)
FSIZE	7.35**	−13.82**
	(7.97)	(−5.57)
LEASE	6.12	−2.50
	(0.72)	(−0.22)
SHARE	−13.16*	7.22
	(−1.76)	(0.68)
WORKER	−4.56**	6.72**
	(−3.60)	(3.43)
EDRATIO	17.67**	−8.79
	(3.05)	(−1.14)
MECH	−1.84	−4.88
	(−0.18)	(−0.36)
WEST	−62.06**	14.24
	(−7.10)	(1.21)
Log-likelihood	−1,016.40	−1,005.60
(Chi-square)	119.69	49.74

a. Numbers in parentheses are t-statistics.
** Indicates significance at 1% level; * at 5% level.

Table 9.10   Regression results of landless ratio and seasonal in-migration functions, extensive survey, Nepal, 1987.[a]

	Landless ratio	Seasonal in-migration ratio
Intercept	–0.12 (–1.00)	–0.08 (–0.26)
IRGR	0.19* (2.10)	0.28* (2.02)
Ln FSIZE	0.04* (2.20)	–0.01 (–0.10)
OWNERR	–0.06 (–0.69)	—
DISTM	0.02** (2.39)	–0.01 (–1.07)
CONT3	—	0.23** (2.39)
TARAI	0.17** (2.90)	–0.20* (–1.82)
R^2	0.54	0.24
F-value	8.47	1.80

a. Numbers in parentheses are t-statistics.
** Indicates significance at 1% level; * at 5% level.

Table 9.11   Paddy price and wage rates by activity and by production
environment, extensive survey, Nepal, wet season, 1987.

	Hills		Tarai	
	Irrigated	Rainfed	Irrigated	Rainfed
Prices (Rs/kg)				
Paddy[a]	5.1	5.7	4.3	4.5
Nitrogen[b]	9.5	9.6	9.5	9.5
Wage rates (Rs/day)				
Land preparation[c]	38	38	25	26
Transplanting[d]	24	23	20	23
Weeding and manuring[d]	22	22	19	22
Harvesting[d]	22	23	19	22
			(62)[e]	(42)[e]
Threshing[c]	35	36	30	29

a. Only prices of medium-grain (Mahsuri) paddy are quoted.
b. Nitrogen derived from urea (46%). Fertilizer prices are controlled by the government and subsidized for transportation costs in the hills.
c. Refers to male wage.
d. Refers to female wage.
e. Imputed wage rates per day under output-sharing arrangements.

Table 9.12   Regression results of wage rate functions, extensive survey, Nepal, wet season, 1987.[a]

	Ln Land preparation	Ln Transplanting	Ln Weeding and manuring	Ln Harvesting	Ln Threshing
Intercept	1.87** (8.42)	1.24** (5.42)	1.28** (5.79)	1.42** (6.95)	1.88** (7.34)
IRGR	0.14 (0.85)	0.05 (0.27)	0.07 (0.46)	0.23 (1.58)	0.21 (1.15)
Ln FSIZE	−0.02 (−0.32)	−0.05 (−0.61)	−0.01 (−0.20)	−0.04 (−0.58)	−0.01 (−0.16)
OWNERR	0.10 (0.59)	0.37* (2.18)	0.23 (1.37)	−0.03 (−0.17)	0.04 (0.21)
CONT3	—	—	—	1.12** (11.17)	—
DISTM	−0.03* (−1.92)	−0.04** (−2.79)	−0.03* (−2.20)	−0.02* (−1.87)	−0.04* (−2.27)
TARAI	−0.22* (−2.10)	0.20* (1.85)	0.12 (1.17)	0.05 (0.46)	−0.28* (−2.30)
R^2	0.24	0.33	0.22	0.88	0.26
F-value	2.31	3.55	1.98	41.25	2.54

a. Numbers in parentheses are t-statistics.
** Indicates significance at 1% level; * at 5% level.

Table 9.13   Factor payments (Rs/ha) and factor shares (%) in rice farming by production environment, intensive survey, Nepal, 1987.[a]

	Irrigated		Rainfed	
	WR1	CR1	WR2	CR2
Gross value of output	9,776	9,655	6,723	7,507
	(100)	(100)	(100)	(100)
Current inputs[b]	644	411	281	366
	(7)	(4)	(4)	(5)
Capital[c]	1,702	418	1,056	380
	(17)	(4)	(16)	(5)
Labor	2,349	3,042	2,020	2,836
	(24)	(32)	(30)	(38)
Family[d]	1,011	783	914	981
Hired	1,338	2,259	1,106	1,855
Residual	5,081	5,784	3,366	3,925
	(52)	(60)	(50)	(52)
Leasehold rent	3,525	3,553	3,248	2,922
Surplus[e]	1,556	2,231	118	1,003

a. Figures in parentheses are the factor shares.
b. Includes seed, fertilizer, and pesticides.
c. Includes animal and machine use.
d. Imputed labor cost using average daily wage rates.
e. Residual minus leasehold rent.

Table 9.14   Average annual income (thou Rs) of farm households by source and production environment, intensive survey, Nepal, 1987.

	Irrigated		Rainfed	
	WR1	CR1	WR2	CR2
Rice production	11.5	11.8	9.2	8.4
Labor[a]	1.6	1.1	1.3	0.8
Capital[b]	3.2	0.6	2.4	0.6
Land[c]	6.7	10.1	5.5	7.0
Nonrice production	17.4	10.7	7.4	20.6
Farm[d]	11.8	9.2	4.5	20.4
Nonfarm[e]	5.6	1.5	2.9	0.2
Total income	28.9	22.5	16.6	29.0
Household size	6.7	6.8	7.2	6.9
(no of working members)[f]	(2.4)	(4.0)	(2.8)	(3.6)
Income per person	4.3	3.3	2.3	4.2
(per working member)	(12.0)	(5.6)	(5.9)	(8.1)

a. Includes family labor income imputed by using appropriate market wage rates for different tasks.
b. Includes returns to owned machinery and bullocks imputed by using prevailing custom rates.
c. Residual for owner-cultivators and surplus (residual minus actual rent payments) for tenants.
d. Includes income from nonrice crops and livestock, off-farm labor earnings, and actual rental earnings.
e. Includes labor earnings from nonfarm employment, remittances, pensions, and income from self-employed petty trade.
f. Members between fifteen and sixty years old.

Table 9.15   Average annual income (thou Rs) of landless households in Western Region survey villages by source and production environment, intensive survey, Nepal, 1987.

	Irrigated	Rainfed
	WR1	WR2
Rice production	4.7	2.5
Nonrice production	5.0	6.0
Farm	3.9	1.6
Nonfarm	1.1	4.4
Total income	9.7	8.5
Household size	6.9	7.1
(no of working members)	(2.4)	(2.8)
Income per person	1.4	1.2
(per working member)	(4.0)	(3.0)

Table 9.16   Regression results of farm household income functions by income component, intensive survey, Nepal, 1987.[a]

	Rice income		Nonrice farm income	Nonfarm income
	Land income	Labor income		
Intercept	−1.30 (−0.68)	−0.52 (−1.32)	1.65 (0.78)	−12.53** (−4.29)
FSIZE*IRMV	4.29** (2.95)	0.43* (1.85)	1.47 (0.91)	−6.41** (−3.28)
FSIZE*NIRMV	0.01 (0.02)	0.51** (3.14)	−9.22** (−11.64)	−1.52 (−1.33)
FSIZE	3.03** (5.73)	−0.32** (−2.45)	8.29** (14.05)	1.16 (1.30)
FSIZE*SHARE	−2.46** (−2.92)	0.53** (3.99)	−0.02 (−0.03)	−0.21 (−0.17)
FSIZE*LEASE	−1.99** (−3.06)	0.55** (9.04)	−0.60 (−0.83)	−0.89 (−0.73)
ASSET	0.01 (1.17)	−0.01** (−2.86)	0.05** (6.70)	0.03** (4.72)
EDRATIO	2.09* (1.83)	0.19 (0.72)	0.90 (0.71)	2.11 (1.09)
WORKER	0.52 (1.61)	0.35** (7.48)	−0.29 (−0.79)	0.87* (1.99)
IRGV	2.50* (2.15)	−0.04 (−0.16)	2.95** (2.27)	5.77** (3.52)
WEST	−4.05** (−3.08)	0.43 (1.45)	−3.23* (−2.20)	6.17** (3.13)
R^2	0.64	—	0.75	—
F-value	34.88	—	58.93	—
Log-likelihood	—	−321.12	—	−434.25
(Chi-square)	—	121.35	—	52.84

a. Numbers in parentheses are t-statistics.
** Indicates significance at 1% level; * at 5% level.

Table 9.17 Regression results of landless household income functions in Western Region survey villages, intensive survey, Nepal, 1987.[a]

	Rice income	Nonrice farm income	Nonfarm income
Intercept	1.51	–1.77	–2.12
EDRATIO	–0.25** (–2.81)	–0.05 (–0.47)	1.62** (2.99)
WORKER	0.97** (4.08)	1.77** (6.42)	–2.29 (–1.47)
ASSET	–0.01 (–0.97)	–0.01 (–0.76)	0.08** (5.70)
IRGV	0.89 (1.53)	0.58 (0.86)	2.49 (0.94)
R^2	0.68	0.70	—
F-value	13.18	14.72	—
Log-likelihood	—	—	–33.40

a. Numbers in parentheses are t-statistics.
** Indicates significance at 1% level; * at 5% level.

Table 9.18 Overall Gini ratios for all households and contribution by income components, intensive survey, Nepal, 1987.

Village	Overall Gini ratio	Contribution by			Nonrice farm income	Nonfarm income
		Rice income (owned farms)				
		Land	Labor	Capital		
WR1	0.50	0.15	–0.00	0.06	0.21	0.08
WR2	0.43	0.16	–0.00	0.07	0.09	0.11
CR1	0.44	0.21	0.01	0.01	0.20	0.01
CR2	0.51	0.13	–0.00	0.01	0.37	-0.00
All	0.48	0.16	0.00	0.04	0.24	0.04

10

Irrigation Quality, Modern Variety Adoption, and Income Distribution: The Case of Tamil Nadu in India

■

C. RAMASAMY, P. PARAMASIVAM, AND A. KANDASWAMY

Rice is India's most important food crop, and its production has acquired a remarkable degree of stability since the introduction of modern rice varieties in the mid-1960s.

Rice in India grows on 42 million hectares. Production increased from 1.3 t/ha and a total of 46 million tons in 1965–1966 to 2.6 t/ha and a total of 109 million tons in 1988–1989. The key factors that contributed to the rapid growth in rice production were adoption of modern varieties, expansion and improvement of irrigation, and increased fertilizer use.

The area planted to modern varieties was 27 million hectares by the late 1980s, constituting 69% of total rice-growing area. The use of chemical fertilizers increased fourteenfold, from 0.8 million tons in 1965–1966 to 11 million tons in 1988–1989. Irrigated rice area increased from 13 million hectares in 1965–1966 to 18 million hectares in 1986.

Despite its strong performance through the 1980s, the rice sector faces difficult challenges in the coming decade. Enormous fluctuations in India's food grain production occur because of the variability in rice production in rainfed areas, which occupy 56% of total rice-growing area. Regional variation in rice productivity is also considerable.

Examination of the results of application of modern technologies to Indian rice production reveals that the Green Revolution took place in areas with assured sources of irrigation. In favorable regions, such as the Punjab, even marginal and small-scale farmers adopted modern varieties and took risks to gain long-term improvement in farm productivity.

It is argued that the farm policies pursued by India's government from the 1960s onward tended to increase the degree of income inequality between

This chapter is based on Ramasamy, Paramasivam, and Otsuka (1992); and Ramasamy and Otsuka (1992).

irrigated regions and those regions dependent on rainfall (Dhanagare 1987; C.H.H. Rao 1989). The use of higher rates of fertilizers was also observed mainly in irrigated areas, which already had higher yields (Bagchi 1982).

Table 10.1 shows the differential adoption of modern varieties and fertilizer use across the major regions in India. North India and South India, with high proportions of rice area irrigated, high levels of fertilizer use, and high rates of modern variety adoption, have the highest yields. In contrast, East India, with heavy rain during the main growing season and poorly developed water-control facilities, has the lowest rate of modern variety adoption and consequently the lowest fertilizer use and yields. The gap in yields across regions has also widened over time, as adoption of modern rice technology in East India has lagged behind that of North and South India.

In this study we examine the distributional consequences of adoption of modern rice technology in Tamil Nadu, a major rice-growing state in South India. Development of irrigation through construction of canals and tanks has basically supported rice production in Tamil Nadu since A.D. 200. The development of modern irrigation systems in successive five-year-plan periods and rapid expansion of groundwater utilization greatly facilitated recent expansion of rice production.

Tamil Nadu accounts for 11% of India's total rice production; about 95% of the state's rice area is planted with modern varieties. Rice is grown on 2 million hectares—about 30% of the total crop area in Tamil Nadu. Total production, in terms of rough rice, was 8.1 million tons in 1987. Production was 2.6 million tons in 1950, when massive investments in irrigation started, and 5.6 million tons in 1966, when adoption of modern varieties started.

Although there is consensus on the positive productivity impact of modern rice varieties (Ramasamy and Rajagopalan 1973; Farmer 1977; Hazell and Ramasamy 1991), the equity impact of modern varieties is questioned on the ground that they are best suited for favorable environments with good irrigation facilities. In Tamil Nadu, availability of irrigation water has emerged as one of the key factors leading to a high rate of modern variety adoption and higher yields among all groups of cultivators (Prahladachar 1983). Thus, it is argued that modern varieties bypassed the less favorable production environments—those where the people are generally poor. Another dimension of modern variety adoption is that it appears to be followed by adoption of labor-saving technologies, which displace human labor and thereby hurt agricultural laborers dependent on wages for income. A major question is: What is the degree of complementarity among various rice technologies introduced since the mid-1960s?

Differential adoption of modern varieties across production environments may cause disequilibrium in labor and land markets, at least in the short run, resulting in regional income differentials (Lipton and Longhurst 1989). The ultimate distributional impact, however, depends on how the factor markets adjust to those differentials. In the case of the labor market, wage equalization may take place through interregional migration, because labor is the mobile factor of production (Connel, Dasgupta, and Lipton 1976). The behavior of the land market will be different because land is an immobile factor. We expect to find that differential technology adoption created income differentials across the environments, primarily because of the difference in returns to land.

The direct effects of modern variety adoption on yield and income gains have been sufficiently studied, but there has been no systematic attempt to examine the indirect effects of modern variety adoption on factor-market adjustments and, ultimately, on income distribution. With this in view, we took the following steps for this study:

- First, we analyzed the adoption behavior of modern varieties of rice and labor-saving technologies and their direct impact on productivity and factor use.
- Second, we examined the direct impacts of modern varieties and other technologies on labor demand.
- Third, having established the direct effect of modern variety technology on labor demand, we analyzed the indirect effects of modern variety adoption on labor markets through its effects on interregional migration from unfavorable to favorable areas, as well as its effects on regional wage differentials.
- Finally, we analyzed the consequences of direct and indirect impacts of the differential technology adoption on overall household income distribution in Tamil Nadu.

CHARACTERIZATION OF ENVIRONMENTS AND VILLAGE SURVEYS

Rice is grown in almost all the districts of Tamil Nadu, and adoption of modern rice technology is to a great extent conditioned by the source of irrigation and its reliability. Differences in the quality of irrigation are largely determined by the sources of water. Rainwater stored in tanks, river-fed canal systems, and wells are the major sources; about 93% of the rice area is irrigated from one or more of these. The rest of the rice area is classified as a semi-dry environment, defined as a rainfed area with one or two sequences of supplemental irrigation from tanks at late stages of crop growth.

Rice Production Environments

We identified five rice-production environments for our study based on source of irrigation. Listed in order of reliability of water supply, the irrigation sources are: 1) rainfed-tank; 2) tank; 3) tank-well; 4) river delta–canal; and 5) reservoir-canal. These represent progressively favorable rice-production environments and are found in different administrative districts (Figure 10.1).

The rainfed-tank area is in a coastal district where broadcast seeding at the start of the wet season is the common practice. The broadcast-seeded field is subsequently irrigated by rainwater stored in tanks. Farmers do their transplanting, however, when early rainfall is plentiful. A single crop of rice is usually grown.

In the tank area, rainfall is more reliable, and storage of rainwater in tanks is well established. Transplanting is common, but broadcast seeding is also practiced in a few areas. The total area under rice is dependent on rainfall, and a single crop of rice is usually grown.

The soil quality is moderate in both areas described above, but there are small areas with salinity and alkalinity problems. Groundwater in the rainfed-tank area is saline and cannot be used for rice production, which has led to stagnation in rice cropping intensity. The distribution of monsoon rains and the amount of water stored in the tanks determine the size of rice production.

The tank-well area is a classic case of conjunctive use of tank and well irrigation for rice production. Availability of supplementary water from wells, especially during the dry season, provides reliability of the irrigation system throughout the year. This stability has resulted in diversified cropping, and rice is sometimes grown three times a year. The first-season crop (August–January) is wholly tank irrigated. The second-season crop (January–April) is either tank irrigated and supplemented by wells or irrigated wholly by wells. When a third crop is grown (May–August), it is irrigated with well water. Expanded use of groundwater has substantially contributed to increasing rice production in this environment.

The river delta–canal area is in the Cauvery River delta, popularly known as the rice bowl of Tamil Nadu. It has been irrigated by a canal system for centuries and constitutes the major rice-growing region of Tamil Nadu. One short-duration crop and one medium-duration crop of rice have traditionally been grown in this region. The cropping pattern has recently changed to a single medium-duration rice crop, however, because release of water has become inadequate as a result of water use upstream, outside the borders of Tamil Nadu. Drainage is a problem in coastal pockets of the region in high-rainfall years.

The reservoir-canal area is characterized by a reliable water supply from a modern reservoir, good soils, and adequate drainage. Two successive rice crops are grown. Modern rice varieties have had their greatest impact in this area.

Village Surveys

The five production environments are located in different districts and thus are geographically separated. Two sets of data were collected by surveys conducted during 1987–1988. In the first survey, designated as the extensive survey, fifty villages, equally distributed among the five rice environments, were selected. In the first stage, two adjoining *taluks* typical of the production environments were identified in each district. (A *taluk* is an administrative unit below district level.) In the next stage of sampling, a random sample of five villages in each *taluk* was chosen, providing a total of ten selected villages in each environment.

The extensive survey collected village-level data on technology adoption, fertilizer use, labor contracts, wage rates, paddy prices, migration pattern, infrastructure, and other socioeconomic characteristics through group interviews of village leaders, knowledgeable farmers, and development workers. This survey provided a broad picture of labor markets, changes in rice farming, and differences in production environments.

The second survey, designated as the intensive survey, collected detailed information at the household level. A village was randomly selected from the ten extensive-survey villages in each of the five production environments. A total of 416 households, distributed about equally among the five villages, were then randomly selected. Half of the sample households in each village were farm households, and the remaining half were equally distributed between agricultural labor households and nonagricultural households. The intensive-survey data sets were used to examine the impact of modern rice technology on productivity, labor use, and income distribution.

Village Characteristics

Table 10.2 reports selected socioeconomic characteristics of the extensive-survey villages. Although the village population is larger in the more favorable production environments, there is no clear association between production environment and farm size, defined here as operational holding of rice land. However, the man-land ratio, defined as the ratio of village population to cultivated area, tends to be higher in more favorable villages. The extent of favorableness seems to positively affect population growth through in-migration resulting from high income-earning opportunities. The ratio of landless households in the village does not show any clear association with production environments. A higher proportion of leaseholds is found in the river-canal area, where tenants primarily operate temple lands, which predominate the village. Rents for the temple lands were fixed several decades ago, and the tenants are practically owner-cultivators, receiving most of the returns to land. Average distance between villages and the nearest market centers does not show any consistent relationship with production environments.

The intensive-survey data shown in Table 10.3 indicate that the variations in total farm size, which includes rice and nonrice lands, do not seem to be related to production environments. Household size varies from 4.2 members in the river-canal area to 5.5 members in the tank-well area. Share tenancy is negligible in the rainfed-tank area but common in the tank area, where production is more risky.

Table 10.4 shows the cropping pattern in the extensive-study villages. Though commonly rice-based, cropping sequences vary across the production environments. The primary differences are found in the number of rice crops grown in a year and the possibilities for crop diversification. Rice cropping intensity is evidently higher in more favorable environments, as evidenced by the dominance of a single rice crop in the rainfed-tank area and the prevalence of double cropping of rice in the reservoir-canal area.

The analysis of cropping patterns based on the intensive-survey data shows similar results (Table 10.5). It is interesting to note that when nonrice land is included in the analysis, cropping patterns in rainfed-tank and tank-well areas are found to be more diversified.

The reliability of irrigation generally improves across the spectrum of production environments from rainfed-tank to reservoir-canal areas. Table 10.6 shows precise sources of irrigation water. Irrigation intensity, defined as the ratio of gross irrigated to net irrigated area, reflects differences in the reliability of water supply from different irrigation sources. Intensity varies from about 100% in the rainfed-tank area to about 170% in the reservoir-canal area. The rainfall-dependent tank irrigation does not allow the same piece of land to be irrigated for more than one season per year, whereas at least some lands can be irrigated in more than one season in the other production environments. The difference in the reliability of the irrigation sources across environments is well reflected in cropping intensity, which is closely correlated with irrigation intensity.

Rice is the single most important crop in the villages across the five environments. The ratio of rice crop area to total crop area is lowest in the reservoir-canal environment. This ratio is lower in this environment because the canal system does not cover wide areas.

PRODUCTION ENVIRONMENT, MODERN VARIETY ADOPTION, AND LAND PRODUCTIVITY

More than 90% of the rice area in Tamil Nadu was planted to modern varieties by the late 1980s. The fact that rice farmers rapidly shifted to the new technologies suggests the profit advantage of modern varieties over traditional varieties (Anden-Lacsina and Barker 1978). Concerted extension efforts, promotion of fertilizer use, and increased investment in irrigation were also responsible for the rapid adoption of modern varieties.

The early modern varieties, however, were highly environment-specific and performed best in well-irrigated fields. Those early varieties, such as IR8 and IR5, also turned out to be susceptible to insects and diseases and were not tolerant of water stress. Work by Indian research institutions to develop varieties suitable for the rice-production environments in Tamil Nadu has played a significant role in the continued adoption of modern varieties over the past two decades.

Yield-Increasing Technologies

Recall data from our extensive survey provide a rough indication that early adoption of modern varieties did not vary significantly across production environments in Tamil Nadu (Table 10.7). From 1970 onward, however, adoption of modern varieties was more rapid in the better environments. A recent study on the production impact of the Green Revolution in Tamil Nadu showed that adoption of modern varieties alone accounted for 28% of growth in rice production between 1973–1974 and 1982–1983 (Hazell and Ramasamy 1991).

Because modern varieties are fertilizer-responsive and sensitive to the availability of irrigation water, their adoption raises the profitability of investing in fertilizer and irrigation. The gains from modern variety adoption, however, are smaller in less favorable areas, such as rainfed-tank and tank areas. According to the extensive survey, modern varieties are planted on 66% of rice-growing areas in rainfed-tank environments, 72% in tank environments, and 95 to 100% in the three more favorable environments.

A close association between modern variety adoption and fertilizer use can be seen from Table 10.7, which shows close similarity between the rates of modern variety adoption and chemical fertilizer use. About one-third of the farmers in the survey still do not apply chemical fertilizers in the rainfed-tank and tank areas.

Insect and disease management is an integral part of the modern rice technology package. Pesticide use is widely adopted in favorable areas, but about one-third of farmers in the two least favorable areas do not use pesticides. Higher adoption of modern varieties and higher fertilizer use increase demand for pesticides in favorable areas. It was observed during the extensive survey that the farmers are particularly conscious of optimal use of insecticides in these villages.

Table 10.7 also shows rice yields across the production environments. Yields in favorable areas are consistently higher than in unfavorable areas, reflecting the differential impact of modern rice technology. Yields of modern varieties are higher than those of traditional varieties within the unfavorable areas, partly because modern varieties are grown in the more favorable parts of those areas.

Determinants of Modern Variety Adoption

Physical environmental factors—irrigation, weather, soil characteristics, topography, etc.—basically determine the productivity advantage of modern varieties. In addition to such potential productivity gain, socioeconomic factors such as output and input prices, experience in farming, education, credit availability, land tenure, farm size, and infrastructure development could affect adoption of modern varieties.

We estimated the adoption function of modern varieties using extensive-survey data to identify the major factors influencing adoption. We included the following socioeconomic variables in the model: farm size (FSIZE), literacy rate in 1980 (LIT80), ratio of rice area under share tenancy (SHARER), distance to the nearest market (DISTM), and price of rough rice (PADDYP). The physical environmental variables, included as explanatory variables, were irrigation intensity (IRGR), quality of irrigation (QIRGR), and regional dummies. QIRGR refers to the ratio of area where irrigation water is available at sowing time during the main rice season.

Among the regional dummies, RF-TANK represented the rainfed-tank environment, and TANK represented the tank environment. RIV-CAN represented river-canal, and RES-CAN represented the reservoir-canal area more favorable for rice production. The tank-well area served as control variable.

For estimating the adoption function, the Tobit estimation procedure was employed because there was a 100% adoption ceiling. The dependent variable was expressed as the percentage of area adopting the modern varieties of rice.

The regression results are shown in Table 10.8. The irrigation variables, IRGR and QIRGR, were used alternatively, and QIRGR emerged as a significant variable in explaining the rate of modern variety adoption. This outcome is plausible for Tamil Nadu, where rice production with modern varieties is highly dependent on the availability of irrigation water at the time of sowing. None of the socioeconomic variables influences adoption of modern varieties to a significant extent, which is consistent with earlier findings in East India that adoption of modern varieties is more or less equal among all sections of the farming community irrespective of tenurial status and size of holdings (Mandal and Ghosh 1976). A field study in Chengalpattu district, Tamil Nadu, covering 1962–1963, 1966–1967, and 1970–1971 also showed that when new seeds became available, small-scale farmers adopted them quickly, even though no extension efforts reached them (Mencher 1974).

The coefficients of unfavorable area dummies (RF-TANK and TANK) are negative and significant in both equations. These results support the hypothesis that adoption of modern varieties is constrained by degree of water control, even though we cannot deny the possibility that those dummy variables may capture the effects of other, unspecified factors.

Land Productivity

Yield increases in rice were impressive in Tamil Nadu after the introduction of modern varieties and associated technology. Average yield increased from 2.3 t/ha to 4 t/ha between 1966 and 1987. The major contributors to the yield increase were identified as modern varieties, fertilizers, and irrigation (Hazel and Ramasamy 1991). With land area for rice fully exploited and growth of irrigated area leveling off in Tamil Nadu, the principal source of growth in rice production in the future will have to be an increase in yield per hectare. Hence, it is useful to identify the determinants of yield levels across production environments at present.

A model to explain the variations in rice yields across villages was specified to be essentially the same as the adoption function except for use of the modern variety adoption ratio as an additional explanatory variable, assuming a recursive system. The estimation results, shown in Table 10.9, demonstrate that assured irrigation is highly significant in explaining the variations in yield across villages. In fact, the results strongly suggest that degree of water control is the decisive factor influencing rice yields. The effect of modern varieties, however, cannot be distinguished from that of degree of water control, as evidenced by the insignificant coefficient of MVR, the modern varieties variable. This result is due in part to the complete adoption of modern varieties in most areas and in part to the positive correlation between modern variety adoption and irrigation intensity.

Among the regional dummy variables, RIV-CAN and RES-CAN have positive and significant coefficients, suggesting that favorable environments positively influence yield. Share tenancy, distance to the market, literacy ratio, paddy price, and farm size do not play significant roles in the yield function.

Table 10.9 also reports the results of chemical fertilizer adoption ratio and total cropping intensity functions as estimated by the Tobit method. Modern variety adoption is the most important variable accounting for intervillage variations in fertilizer use.

Somewhat unexpectedly, the coefficient of share tenancy ratio is negative and significant, a result that appears inconsistent with the nonsignificance of this variable in the yield regression. This discrepancy may be explained by the fact that organic manures, rather than chemical fertilizers, are applied in unfavorable areas, where share tenancy is common. Organic manures are used because they improve the ability of the rice crop to withstand moisture stress. The negative coefficient of SHARER, therefore, does not necessarily imply that share tenants apply less fertilizer. All other socioeconomic variables are not significant. The coefficients of the RF-TANK and TANK dummies are negative and highly significant, as there are fewer adopters of chemical fertilizer in rainfed-tank and tank areas compared with tank-well areas.

Although irrigation intensity does not have a significant coefficient in the fertilizer adoption function, it is the most significant variable explaining differences in total cropping intensity. We note that IRGR is by definition related to cropping intensity. Although not reported here, the quality of irrigation (QIRGR) has a positive and significant coefficient in the cropping intensity function.

In contrast, modern variety adoption does not significantly affect total cropping intensity. This result implies that it is irrigation quality, not the shorter growth duration or the nonphotoperiod-sensitivity of modern varieties, that critically affects cropping intensity. The coefficients of RIV-CAN and RES-CAN are highly significant because they provide assured irrigation water throughout the year.

In summary, our regression analysis indicates that degree and availability of water control, as measured by IRGR, RIV-CAN, and RES-CAN, are the decisive factors affecting rice yields and total cropping intensity, whereas modern variety adoption clearly affects the use of chemical fertilizer. Such a conclusion, however, must be qualified in view of the close association of modern variety adoption and irrigation quality.

IMPACTS ON LABOR DEMAND

Structural change in a labor market will occur as a result of changes in factors that affect supply and demand for labor. The question is: What changes have occurred in labor demand with the introduction of modern varieties? Some factors, such as modern varieties, irrigation, and fertilizer use, tend to enhance the productivity of land and the level of labor input per unit of land. But mechanization works in the opposite direction. The composition of labor use by family and hired labor may also change.

We examined the adoption of labor-saving technologies with special reference to their relationship with modern variety adoption, based on the extensive-survey data. We used intensive-survey data to estimate labor use functions and to assess the direct effects of modern varieties and other technologies on labor demand.

Labor-Saving Technology

The adoption of modern varieties and use of fertilizer have been found to increase demand for labor by increasing labor requirements for crop care, harvesting, and threshing (Barker and Cordova 1978; Chapters 4 and 6–9). It is also reported that modern variety adoption has been accompanied by adoption of machinery and other labor-displacing technology (Jayasuriya and Shand 1985). Unlike fertilizer, which is a direct technical complement to modern varieties and for which there exist limited substitutes, mechanical technology may complement, substitute for, or supplement other factors in the production relationship. Duff (1978) reports that there is little evidence to indicate a strong causal relationship between modern variety adoption and mechanization, particularly tractors.

The levels of adoption of labor-saving technology in the five Tamil Nadu areas are shown in Table 10.10. The use of tractors and threshers has considerably increased since 1970, even though the speed of adoption differed across production environments. The data indicate that tractor use tends to be more pronounced in more favorable areas, except in tank-well areas, where bullock use is still common. In contrast, the use of threshers is highest in those areas. This is a unique situation in the region and mainly attributable to the efforts of progressive farmers who adopted the technology.

It is interesting to note that a set of small entrepreneurs recently utilized the credit facilities available with the commercial banks to purchase tractors and threshers for custom services. This maneuver accelerated the use of tractors for various agricultural operations. Furthermore, frequent droughts in recent years compelled farmers to sell animals in order to cope with the sharp drop in income. They subsequently hired tractor services for land preparation.

The practice of direct seeding in the rainfed and tank areas does not seem to be aimed at saving labor. In fact, direct seeding was practiced prior to modern variety introduction in those areas, which have no stored water available at the beginning of the wet season.

Determinants of Adoption of Labor-Saving Technology

Our interest in adoption of labor-saving technology relates primarily to our concern for the employment impact of adoption of modern varieties. Table 10.11 presents the regression results of tractor and thresher adoption functions using the Tobit method.

The results clearly confirm that the adoption of modern varieties does not bear any significant relationship to adoption of tractor technology. Irrigation intensity is found to be the significant variable affecting adoption of tractors, even though its coefficient is small. All the regional dummies have positive and significant coefficients. As is evident from Table 10.10, the tank-well and rainfed-tank areas have the lowest adoption rates of tractors. The low rate of tractor adoption in the tank-well area may be attributed to the existence of a higher proportion of small and marginal farmers in the district. (With this irrigation area as a control, regional dummy variables were expected to have positive and significant coefficients.) There is, however, no indication that the shorter distance to the market town (DISTM) has encouraged tractor adoption.

The coefficient of share tenancy is not statistically significant. Although prevalence of tractor rental (TRRENT) is expected to encourage tractor use, its estimated coefficient is not significant. Neither is the coefficient of bullock rental (ANRENT).

Thresher technology has become well established in Tamil Nadu, even in areas where modern variety adoption lags behind. Threshers are typically rented on a custom-rate basis. Irrigation seems to discourage adoption of threshers, a fact that can be explained by the fact that tractors are often used for threshing operations in canal-irrigated areas, thereby reducing the use of threshers. Unfortunately, however, it was not possible to obtain reliable data on the use of tractors for threshing.

As in the case of tractor adoption, the coefficient of MVR is not significant in the thresher adoption function, which suggests that modern variety adoption does not promote mechanization. The estimation results also suggest that larger farms tend to use threshers. All the regional dummy variables are found to have negative coefficients. The share tenancy and paddy price variables are not significant.

We did not find evidence that modern rice technology induced adoption of labor-saving technology, a conclusion that runs counter to popular belief. However, tractor adoption is facilitated by the presence of irrigation.

Patterns of Labor Use

Several factors exert major influence on labor use. Irrigation intensity, modern varieties, fertilizer use, and cropping intensity, in particular, are expected to increase labor use in rice production. The descriptive statistics of these variables, based on the intensive survey, are shown in Table 10.12. Note that the tank environment shows a 100% ratio of irrigated area, even though irrigation water is available only once or twice in a growing season. Consequently, rice yields are much lower than in the favorable environments, where irrigation water is available all year.

Delayed onset of monsoon rain in the survey year (1987) is partly responsible for the low adoption of modern varieties in tank-irrigated areas, because traditional varieties are more suitable for dry seeding when rains are delayed. The use of fertilizer that year was four times larger in the most favorable environment than in the least favorable environment. It is clear that adoption of modern varieties and use of higher rates of fertilizers contribute to higher yields in the favorable production environments.

Rice cropping and total cropping intensity increase with the degree of favorableness of the production environment, a result consistent with the finding reported earlier. Rice cropping intensity is larger than total cropping intensity because the former pertains to paddy land only, whereas the latter applies to the total area, including unirrigated areas planted to other crops.

Table 10.13 presents the data on labor use per hectare in rice production for the intensive-survey villages. Labor input for land preparation is moderately higher in tank-well and river-canal areas, mainly because of the predominance of clay soils and cracking of the soil surface in the hot summer season. Labor input for crop establishment is low in rainfed-tank and tank areas, where most fields are direct seeded. Crop care, which includes weeding, water management, and chemical applications, requires more labor than any other task in all environments. Labor use for harvesting and threshing varies considerably, depending mainly on yield and on use of mechanical threshing. Total labor use per hectare varies from 153 days in the most unfavorable area, rainfed-tank, to 229 days in the tank-well area. The higher level of labor required in the tank-irrigated area as against the rainfed-tank area is due in large part to better crop care and higher rice yields, which require additional labor for harvesting and threshing.

The use of family labor is substantially smaller in more favorable environments, the river delta–canal and reservoir-canal areas. The share of hired labor ranges from 54% in the tank-irrigated village to 95% in the reservoir-canal village. These figures imply that in the more favorable areas, the larger share of labor income accrues to hired labor, which is supplied mainly by landless agricultural households. The use of hired labor in the tank-well area is low, partly because the small farm holdings there can be operated mostly by family labor.

Nonetheless, the remarkably different composition of family and hired labor among favorable and unfavorable villages suggests that modern rice technology increases hired labor demand, particularly during the peak season of crop establishment and harvesting.

Labor Use Functions

Labor use functions were estimated separately for family and hired labor using the farm household data from the intensive survey. Wage rates and other factor prices were not specified because of the limited variations within and across villages. The estimation results in Table 10.14 show the positive and significant effects of modern variety adoption on both family and hired labor use. The estimated coefficients imply that family labor use per hectare increases by about twenty-nine days, and hired labor use per hectare by about forty-three days, because of modern variety adoption. These findings are consistent with the results of Chinnappa's (1977) study in the North Arcot district in Tamil Nadu, which found that demand for family labor increased by 22% and demand for hired labor by 28% as farmers adopted modern varieties. The estimated coefficients of irrigation, however, are not significant.

As expected, farm size is inversely associated with use of family labor. RIV-CAN and RES-CAN, dummy variables representing the favorable areas, show a strong negative influence on family labor use, indicating that the family labor supply declines in those areas. Adoption of tractors and threshers show negative coefficients, but only the coefficients of tractor adoption are significant, suggesting that tractor use is particularly labor-saving.

LABOR MARKET ADJUSTMENTS
AND REGIONAL WAGE DIFFERENTIALS

Adoption of modern rice technology is expected to lead to increases in wages in the favorable areas through an effect on labor demand. In unfavorable environments, characterized by lesser degree of water control and low technology adoption, wages will not change or will decline if the output price is negatively affected by the new technology.

Higher wages resulting from modern variety adoption in favorable areas may induce labor migration from unfavorable to favorable areas. This mechanism tends to equalize wages between the environments. In the long run, an equilibrium may be established wherein the wage differential represents the long-run cost of migration.

We examined interregional labor market adjustments using the information on migration and other related variables collected from the extensive survey of fifty villages.

Labor Migration and Demographic Changes

Table 10.15 shows net permanent in-migration in different rice production areas from 1977 to 1987. The number of households that permanently in-migrated is normalized by the rice area of the village. The net seasonal in-migration given in Table 10.15 reflects the number of labor migrants relative to rice area in a normal year. It should be noted that the rate of seasonal migration will fluctuate from year to year, depending on the agricultural production in different regions. The data show that net permanent in-migration tends to be higher in the more favorable villages. This trend will result in greater incidence of landlessness in favorable villages, because permanent migrants are often landless laborers. This differential in-migration rate is consistent with our hypothesis that people tend to move into favorable villages in search of better employment opportunities.

Information on size of permanent migration of households in the villages may not be sufficiently reliable because recall data for the past ten years are subject to errors. Hence, the average annual population growth rates for the study villages were also computed using population census data for 1961–1971 and 1971–1981. The annual growth rate for 1971–1981 was 2.4% in the most favorable (reservoir-canal) village and 1.2% in the most unfavorable (rainfed-tank) village. It is remarkable that it was only during the 1970s, when modern varieties were rapidly spreading, that the population growth was clearly higher in the favorable areas.

There is also a considerable amount of seasonal migration in the study villages. Seasonal rural-to-rural migration during peak seasons is an important factor in equalizing wage rates across as well as within regions. Contrary to our expectation, however, it seems that seasonal out-migration is more important than in-migration in favorable areas, perhaps because of the increase in landless households in those areas. Landless workers move to other areas seeking jobs in the off-seasons. We point out that data on seasonal migration collected at the village level are subject to wide errors. Overall, however, there is evidence that the rural labor markets in rice-growing regions are linked by permanent and seasonal labor migrations, as is observed elsewhere in India (Misra 1970; Bardhan 1979).

Determinants of Population Growth Rate

To test the hypothesis that the adoption of modern varieties induces in-migration by increasing labor demand and wages, we estimated the population growth rate function. The dependent variable was the average annual growth rate in population between 1971–1981, and the explanatory variables considered were adoption rate of modern varieties in 1980 (MV80), irrigation intensity (IRGR), man-land ratio in 1970 (MLR70), and regional dummy variables. The estimation result is shown in Table 10.16.

Although MV80 has a positive and significant coefficient, the coefficient for IRGR is not significant. Such results are consistent with our hypothesis of interregional labor market adjustments, which asserts that population will change responding to changes in technology. Because the diffusion of modern varieties started in the late 1960s, MV80 would correspond to major technological change, calling for population adjustment in the 1970s. In contrast, irrigation quality remained largely unchanged in Tamil Nadu during the 1970s. The regression results demonstrate that it was not favorable environment per se, measured by the irrigation intensity, that brought about the population changes. This conclusion is reinforced by the nonsignificance of the coefficients of regional dummy variables. An unexpected result is that the coefficient of MLR70, which is supposed to capture the difference in initial condition, is not significant.

Regional Wage Differentials

We hypothesized that labor migration from unfavorable to favorable areas would lower the wages in the latter and increase them in the former. This process would continue until the wage differential was equated with migration costs.

We have already observed that interregional migration has taken place in response to the adoption of modern varieties. The question is: To what extent have such labor movements equalized wage rates across regions?

Table 10.17 compares the wages for different tasks in rice production for the five production areas, based on extensive-survey data. Wages are standardized to reflect compensation per eight-hour day. Male workers usually do land preparation, and female workers do transplanting. Harvesting and threshing are performed by both men and women.

The transplanting wage is particularly high in the most favorable area, about 40% higher than in the unfavorable areas (rainfed-tank and tank). A close look at Table 10.17 also reveals that differences in harvesting and land preparation wages are generally small among areas.

Differences in transplanting wage may be explained partly by the fact that the timing of transplanting activity is unpredictable because it is dependent upon the uncertain availability of canal water and rainfall. Thus, the flow of seasonal migration for transplanting activity is restricted. In contrast, seasonal migration of labor at harvesttime is a common phenomenon in Tamil Nadu, and it helps equalize wages across regions. In most locations, harvesting is done on an output-sharing basis, and we have estimated imputed daily wages by dividing total wage payments by the number of workdays for the purpose of comparison with daily wages. It is found that imputed wage rates for harvesting under output-sharing contracts are much higher than the daily wages paid for land preparation and transplanting.

We also observe that wage rates are different for different tasks. For example, harvesting wages are distinctly higher than transplanting wages. Thus, we estimated separate wage functions for different tasks. One should note, however, that as the farming activities considered here require only unskilled labor, the quality difference in labor will not substantially affect wage differential.

Average bullock rentals are similar across the areas. Even though the bullock markets are not well integrated across regions, the cost of raising a bullock may not be so different from region to region. Because the market for tractor services is well integrated in Tamil Nadu, tractor rental rates are similar across the environments. One notable exception is the river-canal area, where tractor rental costs are about three-fourths as high as in other environments. This difference is due to the recent fall in paddy production caused by the nonavailability of canal water for the first-season crop, which caused a decline in demand for tractor services in the area.

Wage Determination Functions

We estimated wage determination functions to verify the extent to which interregional labor market adjustments have contributed to the equalization of wages between favorable and unfavorable areas. After two decades of modern variety cultivation, labor markets should have almost completely adjusted. However, we expected the modern rice technology and irrigation variables to be positively associated with wage rates where migration is costly.

The wage functions included technology, irrigation intensity, socio-economic variables, and regional characteristics as explanatory variables. The technology variable was defined as the percentage of total rice area growing modern varieties during the wet season (MVR). Farm size and paddy price were included to capture the effects of village socioeconomic characteristics. Larger farm size will result in an increase in the demand for hired labor, exerting an upward pressure on wages. One can expect that paddy price, in addition to measuring the direct effect on wages, may capture regional differences in cost of living.

Distance to market center was inserted to capture, at least partially, the costs of migration between rural and urban labor markets. The rural labor markets in various areas may be indirectly linked to the unskilled urban labor markets.

Percentage of area under share tenancy was included to examine the effect of tenancy on wages because poor tenants may substitute family for hired labor, thereby depressing wage rates. Regional dummies were incorporated to examine the effect of regional characteristics on wages. The same variables were considered for bullock and tractor rental equations.

The estimation results of land preparation, transplanting, and harvesting wage functions are shown in Table 10.18. None of the estimated coefficients of MVR across the wage equations are significant. The coefficient of irrigation is significant only in land preparation wage function, but its magnitude is very small. The nonsignificant wage effect of technology can hardly be explained unless we take into account labor supply adjustments to higher labor demand through changes in landless population patterns and in-migration.

Paddy price unexpectedly shows a negative and significant influence on the land preparation wage. The coefficients of farm size, share tenancy, and distance to market center are not significant in transplanting and harvesting equations. Whereas the coefficients of regional dummy RES-CAN are statistically significant in the transplanting and harvesting equations, RIV-CAN has a significant coefficient only in the harvesting equation. Despite high rates of in-migration into these villages, migration costs may keep the wages higher in favorable areas, particularly during the peak seasons. Other regional dummies are found to have no significant effect on wage rates.

The above findings lead us to conclude that a certain degree of the integration of labor markets evolved during the era of diffusion of modern rice varieties. That integration considerably reduces regional wage differentials, a desirable feature in terms of redistribution of income between regions.

However, we have to bear in mind that equalization of wages may not be attributed entirely to the adjustment of labor markets. Tamil Nadu has diverse agricultural activities; high-value crops such as sugarcane, banana, and groundnut are being grown along with rice, particularly in unfavorable rice-production areas, causing changes in wage rates and subsequent interregional labor migration. Moreover, development of a rural transport system throughout Tamil Nadu has facilitated the integration of rural labor markets among districts.

Table 10.19 presents the estimated results of the bullock and tractor rental equations. Modern variety adoption has a positive influence on tractor rental rates, which suggests that adoption increases the demand for tractor technology. The remaining variables, with the exceptions of RIV-CAN and RES-CAN, have a negligible influence on tractor rental. RIV-CAN refers to the river-canal area, which has one of the highest tractor populations of any environment. This, coupled with the nonavailability of canal water in recent years for the first-season rice crop, has resulted in lower demand for tractor services. In the most favorable area (RES-CAN), tractor rental is somewhat lower despite the high rate of tractor adoption. There is considerable interdistrict movement of tractors in peak seasons, resulting in generally small differences in tractor rentals across the regions.

In the bullock equation, only three variables (irrigation intensity, paddy price, and distance to market) are significant. IRGR had a positive impact on bullock rental because land for grazing bullocks is limited in many favorable villages, which results in an inadequate supply of bullocks. This finding is consistent with our earlier finding that tractor adoption is positively associated with irrigation (Table 10.11). The negative coefficient of DISTM indicates that distant villages are not well integrated into the bullock labor market. The negative relationship of paddy price is unexpected.

Factor prices, as recorded in the extensive survey, do not show any major variation caused by modern rice technology, the exception being the land preparation wage. From the foregoing analysis, we believe it is fair to conclude that there were labor market adjustments during the Green Revolution that worked toward the equalization of the wages across the areas.

MODERN RICE TECHNOLOGY AND HOUSEHOLD INCOME DISTRIBUTION

Fears were expressed in the early years of modern variety cultivation that only large-scale farms would benefit from them and that the income gap between large-scale and small-scale farmers would widen.

Accumulated evidence indicates that the small-scale farmers caught up after a short time lag (Hazell and Ramasamy 1991). However, the productivity gains generated by technological change in regions endowed with better resources, such as adequate irrigation, might have resulted in regional disparities in income distribution. Although regional disparities in labor income can be reduced by labor migration, income gaps arising from the regional differences in returns to immobile factors, such as land, will persist.

Whether and how such an income gap is mitigated in practice is an issue we will examine here. We analyze functional and household income distribution using the intensive-survey data with a view to identifying the consequences of the differential adoption of modern varieties on income distribution.

Functional Income Distribution

Current inputs, capital (including bullocks, tractors, and threshers), labor, and land constitute the major categories of factor inputs to which rice income is distributed.

In the case of Tamil Nadu, since the land rental market has been inactive, reasonably accurate identification of returns to land from the land rent data was not possible. Hence, our analysis of factor shares used residual as a proxy for returns to land, which is defined as gross value of production minus both actual and imputed costs of current inputs, labor, and capital inputs. The returns to unpriced environmental and managerial factors would also be included in the residual.

Table 10.20 shows the absolute and relative factor shares in wet-season rice production across rice-production environments. It can be seen that the values of output and factor incomes are considerably different across areas. The value of output ranges from about Rs 5,700 in the tank area to about Rs 12,900 in the reservoir-canal area. Factor payments to current inputs tend to be higher in absolute terms but not in relative terms in the more favorable environments. The absolute payments to capital and labor do not vary much across the environments; hence, their factor shares tend to be lower in the more favorable environments.

Most of the production gains are captured under the residual category, which indicates that a large portion of productivity gains accrues to land. The share of residual is 32% in the most unfavorable environment, a sharp contrast to the 59% share in the most favorable environment. Insofar as this residual accrues to the landholders, it is reasonable to expect that the distribution of productivity gains associated with modern variety adoption and better irrigation facilities widens income differentials across households.

Whereas factor shares are concerned with the relative contribution of factor inputs to production, household income is more closely related with actual payments to owners of factor inputs. Thus, factor payments to labor, capital, and current inputs are divided into those accruing to hired and family labor, rented and owned capital, and owner-supplied and -purchased inputs. The sum of both actual and imputed payments to owned factors, along with residuals, constitutes the farm household income per hectare of rice production. Because the land rental market is not active, the share of rice area under tenant operation is low. The farm household income, which includes returns to land, is far above the hired labor income accrued to the agricultural landless household.

Household Income

Household income includes sources other than rice production—i.e., income from nonrice crops, livestock, and off-farm and nonfarm activities. Factor endowments, prevailing factor prices, and the availability of alternative job opportunities are the major determinants of income for both farm and landless households.

To identify the impact of modern rice technology on various sources of income, we classified farm household income into earnings from rice production, other crops, livestock, off-farm activities, and nonfarm activities. Income from rice production was further classified into returns to family labor, owned capital, and land (as measured by residuals).

For agricultural landless households, household income was divided into income from employment in rice and nonrice production and income from livestock and nonfarm sources. The annual average incomes by source of farm and agricultural landless households are presented in Tables 10.21 and 10.22.

As expected, total household income tends to be higher in more favorable rice-production environments. The difference across environments in land incomes of farm households is particularly large; the difference in land income alone between the reservoir-canal and rainfed-tank or tank areas can explain the whole difference in total income. Those observations clearly suggest that the differential adoption of modern rice technology worsens the regional income disparity by widening differences in returns to land.

This does not imply, however, that farm households in the less favorable areas do not adjust their resource allocations to improve their earnings. For example, nonrice income accounts for about 60% of total income in the rainfed-tank and tank environments, which is far greater than the contribution of nonrice income (23%) in the reservoir-canal area. The high level of nonrice income in the tank-well area results from crop diversification made possible by irrigation.

Livestock production contributes significantly to total income in the river-canal area, where the water supply is often inadequate because of upstream diversion of river water. This problem has led double-cropped lands to be converted to single-cropped wetlands and lands left fallow, increasing possibilities for livestock farming. In addition, this "rice-bowl" area offers a steady supply of rice straw, an important source of cattle feed. Similarly, contributions of off-farm and nonfarm incomes are relatively high in the rainfed-tank and tank areas.

Size of the farm households (around five persons per family) does not seem to have any relationship with production environments, so income per person varies across production environments; absolute per capita income of farm households in the most-favorable area is more than double that in the least favorable area. When rice income alone is compared, the average household income difference between the most favorable and the least favorable area is nearly fivefold. The difference is lower for total household income and for total per capita income. These findings strongly suggest that, at least in Tamil Nadu, the impact of modern varieties on household income distribution cannot be considered in isolation from nonrice earning opportunities. There seems to be judicious reallocation of labor and other resources to alternative uses wherever profitable.

Except in the case of the least favorable area, more than 85% of the total income of agricultural landless households is derived from labor earnings in rice production (Table 10.22). This ratio is expected, because landless agricultural households do not have assets or skills for profitable employment in activities other than farming. Although earnings per household and earnings per person vary across production environments, the interregional differences are not as large as in the case of farm households. This difference could be attributed to the broad geographical distribution of the areas and their widely differing socioeconomic surroundings. In fact, the reservoir-canal area is inland in Tamil Nadu (Figure 10.1), and thus the higher rice income of landless households is not necessarily inconsistent with the hypothesis of interregional labor market adjustments because of the prevalence of double cropping in the area. Thus, it could be assumed that, regional differences notwithstanding, the labor market has indeed responded and adjusted to changes brought about by the adoption of modern varieties. In fact, it is remarkable to find that total incomes of landless households in other environments are quite similar.

Determinants of Household Income

To identify the factors determining income levels from different sources, we regressed each income component on interaction terms of technology factors and farm size (MVR*FSIZE and IRGR*FSIZE), farm size, personal and family characteristics of the farmer—age of the household head, schooling, income from assets (ASSET), household size—and village dummy variables. Again, the tank-well production environment was treated as the control area. Financial assets include the interest earnings from money lending and bank deposits, dividend from shares and land rents, and earnings from fixed investments such as buildings and vehicles.

The regression results of household income determination functions for farm households by different sources of income are presented in Tables 10.23 and 10.24. The results are broadly consistent with a priori expectations and earlier observations.

It is clear that modern varieties and irrigation are major factors contributing to the higher land income in favorable areas. Both of the technology interaction variables show the expected results; estimated coefficients imply that adoption of modern varieties increases returns to land by Rs 440/ha, whereas irrigation brings about a gain of Rs 2,320/ha.

The negative coefficient of farm size is not implausible in view of the difficulty of efficiently managing large farms and the usual negative correlation between land quality and farm size for rice production. In other words, this finding is consistent with the well-known inverse relationship between farm size and productivity widely observed in India (Bhalla 1979; Verma and Bromley 1987; Bhalla and Roy 1988).

The much higher productivity of land in the most favorable area, which results from a stable supply of irrigation water, is consistent with the positive and significant coefficient of RES-CAN.

The interaction of modern variety technology with farm size has a negative and significant influence on the labor income of farm households, mainly because modern variety adoption substitutes hired labor for family labor. Thus, modern variety adoption increases income of hired labor, supplied mainly by landless households. Conversely, the interaction between irrigation and farm size has a positive and significant coefficient in the labor income regression. This is so mainly because better irrigation promotes multiple cropping of rice, providing larger annual earning opportunities for family labor.

The coefficients of farm size and assets are negative and significant in the labor income function. This result is expected because increases in nonlabor income will make family members choose more leisure, thereby reducing their labor contribution to rice production.

The regional dummy variables have negative and significant coefficients because the use of family labor is particularly high in the tank-well area, the control area. As expected, household size has a strong positive effect on the income of family labor in rice production.

Significant determinants of capital income are the rainfed-tank village dummy variable and the interaction term between irrigation intensity and farm size. The positive effect of irrigation is plausible, partly because tractor use is more common in irrigated areas where rice cropping intensity is high. The negative coefficient of RF-TANK implies that the payoff of capital investment is small in the unfavorable rice-production environment.

Modern variety technology and farm size interaction has significant effects on other crop and nonfarm income (Table 10.24). These results may be largely due to the shorter growth duration of modern varieties, which makes it possible to diversify cropping activities and allocate more time to nonfarm activities.

Income from off-farm activities increases with household size, as indicated by the positive and significant coefficient of the HSIZE variable in the third equation. Moreover, farmers who are better educated seem to have better opportunities for skilled nonfarm business activities, as seen from the positive and significant coefficient of schooling in the nonfarm income regression.

Assets are positively associated with livestock and nonfarm income. The village where conjunctive use of groundwater is practiced is most suitable for crop diversification, and because that production environment is used as a control in specifying the village dummies, there is a negative association of all the village dummy variables with other crop income.

The significant coefficient of RIV-CAN in the livestock income equation is reasonable because of a dairy development program in the canal-delta area. The significant and positive coefficient of RF-TANK in the nonfarm income equation and TANK in the off-farm income equation indicate that households in unfavorable environments allocate more time to off-farm and nonfarm activities.

The results of the landless agricultural household income determination functions are presented in Table 10.25. The household-specific rice technology variable could not be defined for this regression, so technology variables were not included in the specification of the functions. However, village dummy variables were retained to account for regional differences in the labor markets. The results of the regressions indicate that household size is the significant variable in determining labor income from rice and nonrice sources.

Neither the personal characteristics, such as age and education, nor the assets of the household have any significant effect on income from rice, probably because labor employment in rice production is an unskilled job requiring no financial and physical resources.

The reservoir-canal environment has a positive effect on rice income among landless households. The seasonality and coincidence of rice operations in this region help to keep wage rates marginally higher than in other regions during peak seasons (see Table 10.18), which is consistent with the significant coefficient of the RES-CAN dummy variable in the rice income regression.

The most unfavorable production environment, captured by the RF-TANK dummy, seems to exert pressure on agricultural landless households to seek revenue from nonrice sources, as indicated by its positive and significant coefficient. Members of landless households often supplement their earnings from rice production by entering the labor market for construction activity in neighboring urban centers during lean seasons.

Decomposition Analysis of Income Inequality of Households

The impact of the introduction of new technology should ideally be analyzed by comparing the situations before and after its introduction. Such data, however, are rarely available. For the Tamil Nadu study, we compared the Gini ratio for total income and various components of income in different production environments to examine the effects of modern rice technology on distribution of income (see Chapter 3 for methodology). It should be noted that, because we use cross-section data, some dynamic aspects of modern variety adoption (e.g., the effect on wage rate) are not properly considered.

The results of the decomposition analysis based on household income are presented in Table 10.26. The overall Gini ratios are highest in the tank-well area and lowest in the tank area. More remarkable is the fact that the Gini ratios in the favorable canal environments are relatively low and similar to that in the least favorable rainfed-tank environments. These results may imply that increased production efficiency in rice farming does not always substantially increase income inequality within a village.

Because rice is the major source of household income in the favorable rice-production environments, the contribution of rice income to total income inequality is high. For example, in the two canal-irrigated environments, the combined contribution of inequality in rice income to total income inequality amounts to more than 60%. In the tank-well area—where crop activities are diversified and, hence, the contribution of rice income to total income is relatively low—total income inequality is largely accounted for by the inequality of the distribution of income from other crops. Similarly, off-farm and/or nonfarm activities account for the major part of overall income inequality in the relatively unfavorable rainfed-tank and tank areas.

It appears that where opportunities for nonfarm employment and diversified cropping activities exist, the income shares of nonrice sources increase, which contributes to income inequality. The substitution of these sources of income in accordance with comparative advantage helps to moderate the adverse distributional consequences of the differential adoption of modern varieties. This moderating effect takes place because the distribution of rice income, particularly land income, tends to be more unequally distributed than other sources of income. If there had been no substitution of nonrice income-earning activities, the resulting income inequality would have been much higher.

The distribution of income of farmer households and agricultural landless households is shown in Table 10.27 to illustrate the frequency of various sizes of household income in the five production environments. Average household income is two to three times higher in favorable environments. In the tank-well area, there are several wealthy households earning more than Rs 50,000, which makes the income distribution in this village particularly unequal. Except for those households and the reservoir-canal area households, the income distributions are similar across environments with large concentration of households (more than two-thirds) in the lowest two income classes. These poor households are mainly dependent upon labor earnings.

Wealthier households typically receive land income in rice production, and they are found most frequently in the reservoir-canal area. Thus, it appears that although labor income tends to be equalized, income inequality arising from the differential returns to land remains critically important for overall income inequality, even though farmers in less favorable areas seek supplementary off-farm and nonfarm income-earning opportunities.

IMPLICATIONS FOR FUTURE
DEVELOPMENT OF RICE TECHNOLOGY

The spread of new rice technology—modern varieties, chemical fertilizers, tractors, and threshers—since 1970 has been impressive in Tamil Nadu. Although adoption of modern varieties is complete in favorable production areas, about 30% of the rice area is still planted to traditional varieties in unfavorable areas. There are also differential levels of adoption of fertilizer, tractors, and threshers across environments.

The econometric analysis in our study reveals that quality of irrigation is a crucial variable in influencing modern variety and tractor adoption as well as rice yields. This conclusion points to the need to improve the quality of irrigation to increase rice-production efficiency and equity in South India.

Another important finding is that the role of socioeconomic variables (literacy, market distance, tenancy, and farm size) is minor in determining the adoption of modern rice technology.

Our analysis also examines the hypothesis that labor migration, subsequent to widening of wage differentials caused by the differential adoption of modern rice technology, contributes to the equalization of wages between favorable and unfavorable areas and thus mitigates potential inequities. Results of the analysis, as in the earlier country studies in this volume, support the hypothesis.

Previous studies of the labor market in India have found a significant effect of modern variety adoption on wage rates, suggesting geographical isolation and imperfection of rural labor markets. Those studies, however, relate to the early 1970s (Johl 1975; Bardhan 1979), when modern varieties were initially spreading. Our study, conducted almost two decades later, indicates that an interregional labor market adjustment has been completed so as to equalize regional wages.

Our labor use analysis provides evidence that adoption of modern varieties increases the demand for hired labor, an increase that benefits the poorest households. However, the subsequent widespread use of labor-saving technology, particularly tractors in areas with better irrigation, has dampened potential wage increases in favorable production areas. Thus, equalization of regional wages cannot be attributed to interregional migration alone. Furthermore, because cropping patterns in Tamil Nadu are well diversified, a shift to production of nonrice crops, such as sugarcane and groundnut, would have mitigated the cost of interregional labor market adjustments.

We assessed the impacts of modern variety adoption and production environment on functional income distribution and the income levels of farm and agricultural landless households. Our analysis indicates that although modern variety adoption contributes to absolute income gains for hired labor and thereby for landless households, farm households' gains are much greater because of substantial increases in returns to land.

Although labor market adjustment through labor migration seems to have helped equalize labor earnings across the different production environments, no such adjustments have occurred in the land market. Returns to land, and thereby to landholders, have widened across production environments. Nonrice crop activities, however, contribute to a reduction in income disparities across the production environments. In the unfavorable environments, where income is inadequate, the farm and landless households engaged in nonfarm activities to earn additional income. This was often done by seasonal migration to urban areas to work in unskilled jobs. Investment in human resource development will provide more opportunities to earn additional income for these households.

Modern variety adoption has contributed to absolute income growth for all the factors of production in the favorable areas, thereby contributing to regional income inequalities. Such inequalities, however, are not as large as previously indicated in the literature because of labor and product market adjustments. Nonetheless, this should not reduce the need for increased allocation of resources for irrigation and rural infrastructure in the less favorable areas, both to increase efficiency and to ensure equity across production environments.

Given the difficulty in developing rice technology suitable for unfavorable areas, a careful reconsideration of the trade-off between efficiency and equity involved in the development of rice technology for a favorable area is required.

Figure 10.1   Location of study areas, Tamil Nadu, India, 1987

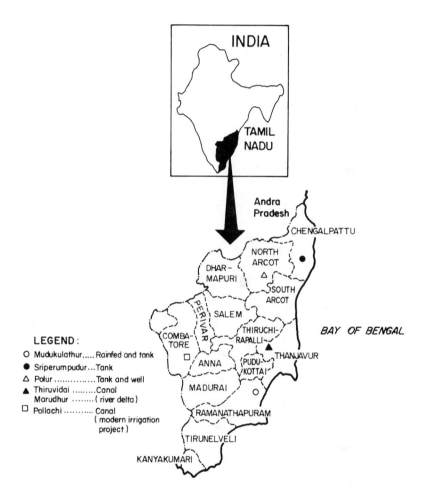

Table 10.1   Adoption of modern varieties, fertilizer (NPK) use, ratio of irrigated area, and rice yield by regions in India, 1987. Sources: Fertilizer Association of India (1985 and 1986); Ministry of Agriculture, Government of India (1988).

Regions	Modern variety adoption (% of rice area)	NPK use (kg/ha)	Rice area irrigated (%)	Yield (t/ha)
North India	92	96	88	4.6
South India	87	58	89	3.4
West India	67	35	28	3.0
East India	40	28	29	1.8
Central India	53	36	23	2.8
All India	57	31	43	2.9

Table 10.2   Selected socioeconomic characteristics of sample villages by production environment, extensive survey, Tamil Nadu, India, 1987.

	Production environments				
	Rainfed-tank	Tank	Tank-well	River-canal	Reservoir-canal
Villages (no)	10	10	10	10	10
Population[a]	1,964	2,219	2,584	4,058	8,991
Farm size (ha)[b]	1.4	1.7	0.8	1.5	1.0
Man-land ratio[c]	3.4	7.1	10.8	15.8	12.9
Ratio of landless households (%)	22	42	12	30	23
Tenure (% of farmers)					
Owner-cultivators	84	86	88	70	77
Leasehold	3	11	8	29	15
Share tenancy	13	3	4	1	8
Distance to market center (km)	14	6	9	5	10

a. 1981 census.
b. Refers only to rice lands.
c. Ratio of population to cultivated area.

Table 10.3   Selected socioeconomic characteristics of sample households by production environment, intensive survey, Tamil Nadu, India, 1987.

	Production environments				
	Rainfed-tank	Tank	Tank-well	River-canal	Reservoir-canal
Households (no)	80	90	80	90	76
Farm size (ha)[a]	5.1	2.7	3.6	2.4	4.0
Household size (no of members)	4.6	5.2	5.5	4.2	5.3
Tenancy (% of area)					
Owner-cultivators	98	73	95	88	90
Leasehold	2	1	4	12	10
Share tenancy	—	26	1	—	—

a. Refers to rice and nonrice lands.

Table 10.4   Cropping patterns (% of area) by production environment, extensive survey, Tamil Nadu, India, 1987.

	Production environments				
Cropping pattern	Rainfed-tank	Tank	Tank-well	River-canal	Reservoir-canal
Rice-rice	3	8	24	26	60
Rice-rice-rice	0	2	10	3	2
Rice-fallow	95	89	58	63	33
Rice–nonrice crops[a]	2	1	8	8	5

a. Refers to nonrice crop production in rice land (wet paddy land) only.

Table 10.5   Cropping patterns (% of area) by production environment, intensive survey, Tamil Nadu, India, 1987.

Cropping pattern	Production environments				
	Rainfed-tank	Tank	Tank-well	River-canal	Reservoir-canal
Rice land[a]					
Rice-rice	0	0	27	30	49
Rice-rice-rice	0	0	15	0	0
Rice-fallow	100	100	56	68	51
Rice–nonrice crop	0	0	2	2	0
All lands[b]					
Rice-based	64	100	66	100	95
Nonrice crop[c]	36	0	34	0	5

a. Refers to wetlands in which rice is grown at least once a year.
b. Refers to wet, garden, and dry land. In garden land, primarily nonrice irrigated crops are grown; in drylands, nonrice rainfed crops are grown.
c. Nonrice crops include sugarcane, groundnut, and vegetables in garden land, and millet, pulses, oilseed, and cotton in dry land.

Table 10.6   Sources of irrigation, irrigation intensity, and cropping intensity, extensive survey, Tamil Nadu, India, 1987.

	Production environments				
	Rainfed-tank	Tank	Tank-well	River-canal	Reservoir-canal
Sources of irrigation (% of area)					
Canal	0	0	0	86	100
Tank	90	82	31	0	0
Tank-well	8	16	52	0	0
Well	2	2	17	14[a]	0
Irrigation intensity (%)[b]	101	114	152	163	171
Total cropping intensity (%)	100	116	136	165	165
Rice crop area to total crop area (%)[c]	72	65	48	77	40

a. In this case, wells supplement canal irrigation.
b. Ratio of gross irrigated to net irrigated area.
c. Most of the fifty extensive-survey villages have a considerable amount of nonrice lands, both irrigated and nonirrigated.

Table 10.7   Technology adoption and paddy yields by production environment, extensive survey, Tamil Nadu, India, 1970–1987.

	Production environments				
	Rainfed-tank	Tank	Tank-well	River-canal	Reservoir-canal
Modern variety adoption (% of area)					
1970	21	31	32	35	31
1980	43	50	92	85	87
1987	66	72	95	100	100
Chemical fertilizer (% of farmers)					
1970	27	32	26	36	38
1980	41	44	95	79	66
1987	63	65	100	100	93
Pesticides (% of farmers)					
1970	22	21	24	15	27
1980	36	33	89	63	50
1987	62	63	100	100	79
Yield (t/ha)					
Traditional varieties					
1970	1.6	1.4	—	—	—
1980	2.1	1.8	—	—	—
1987	2.8	2.6	—	—	—
Modern varieties					
1970	2.8	3.3	3.7	4.1	4.5
1980	3.8	4.2	4.7	4.8	5.7
1987	3.9	4.3	5.0	5.6	6.0

Table 10.8   Regression results of modern variety adoption functions, extensive survey, Tamil Nadu, India, 1987.[a]

	MVR	
	(1)	(2)
Intercept	98.47**	77.93**
	(8.46)	(4.87)
IRGR	0.28	—
	(0.05)	
QIRGR	—	21.45*
		(1.93)
FSIZE	−0.58	−0.48
	(−0.47)	(−0.60)
SHARER	0.04	0.90
	(0.28)	(0.92)
PADDYP	−0.01	−0.12
	(−0.24)	(−0.26)
LIT80	0.01	−0.23
	(0.15)	(−0.35)
DISTM	0.09	0.24
	(0.17)	(0.15)
RF–TANK	−28.79**	−14.94**
	(−7.71)	(−7.96)
TANK	−22.34**	−21.36**
	(−6.04)	(−7.96)
RIV-CAN	5.12	5.68
	(0.51)	(0.56)
RES-CAN	4.34	4.15
	(0.72)	(1.04)
Log-likelihood	−144.23	−141.21
(Chi-square)	122.56	128.81

a. Numbers in parentheses are t-statistics.
** Indicates significance at 1% level; * at 5% level.

Table 10.9   Regression results of yield, fertilizer, and total cropping intensity functions, extensive survey, Tamil Nadu, India, 1987.[a]

	Yield	Chemical fertilizer	Total cropping intensity
Intercept	3.20** (2.31)	40.97* (2.11)	66.10 (0.52)
IRGR	0.96** (3.93)	–3.06 (–0.60)	67.33** (3.72)
MVR	0.17 (0.14)	56.25** (4.74)	–4.68 (–0.04)
FSIZE	–0.07 (–1.00)	1.41 (1.35)	3.05 (0.68)
SHARER	0.06 (0.72)	–51.55** (–2.96)	6.96 (1.10)
PADDYP	0.69 (0.25)	0.04 (0.68)	–0.21 (–0.81)
LIT80	–0.13 (–0.27)	0.02 (0.27)	–4.51 (–1.12)
DISTM	–0.01 (–1.01)	–0.02 (–0.12)	0.44 (0.54)
RF–TANK	–0.33 (–0.78)	–17.13** (–2.87)	–7.82 (–0.20)
TANK	0.02 (0.07)	–25.04** (–5.24)	10.88 (0.41)
RIV-CAN	0.78** (3.58)	–6.48 (–1.31)	49.08** (3.02)
RES-CAN	1.10** (6.08)	–8.96* (–2.02)	36.96** (2.54)
R^2	0.87	—	—
Log-likelihood (Chi-square)	— —	–142.07 143.51	–217.99 93.59

a. Numbers in parentheses are t-statistics.
** Indicates significance at 1% level; *at 5% level.

Table 10.10 Adoption of labor-saving technologies (% of farmers) by production environment, extensive survey, Tamil Nadu, India, 1970–1987.

Technology	Production environments				
	Rainfed-tank	Tank	Tank-well	River-canal	Reservoir-canal
Tractor					
1970	1	0	5	14	13
1980	4	19	11	51	41
1987	12	42	12	90	64
Thresher					
1970	0	4	0	0	2
1980	0	13	29	0	32
1987	0	18	77	10	66
Direct seeding					
1970	58	60	0	0	0
1980	60	60	0	0	0
1987	60	65	0	8	0

Table 10.11   Regression results of tractor and thresher adoption functions, extensive survey, Tamil Nadu, India, 1987.[a]

	Tractor	Thresher
Intercept	–5.27 (–0.10)	53.66 (0.81)
IRGR	12.81* (1.77)	–0.23* (–2.01)
MVR	0.10 (0.25)	0.03 (0.05)
FSIZE	0.62 (0.24)	7.29* (2.22)
SHARER	–0.23 (–0.58)	–0.28 (–0.74)
PADDYP	–0.03 (–0.29)	0.14 (1.06)
TRRENT	–0.04 (–0.13)	—
THRENT	—	0.50 (1.00)
ANRENT	–0.29 (–0.47)	–0.06 (–0.06)
LIT80	0.11 (0.79)	0.34* (1.70)
DISTM	0.07 (0.17)	0.40 (0.75)
RF-TANK	7.63** (3.19)	–87.55** (–4.70)
TANK	36.53** (8.47)	–70.52** (–4.46)
RIV-CAN	74.38** (7.59)	–84.62** (–8.80)
RES-CAN	48.73** (7.59)	–9.81 (–1.23)
Log-likelihood (Chi-square)	–180.77 (120.44)	–204.37 (93.88)

a. Numbers in parentheses are t-statistics.
** Indicates significance at 1% level; * at 5% level.

Table 10.12 Ratio of irrigated area, adoption of modern varieties, fertilizer use, yield, and cropping intensities by production environment, intensive survey, Tamil Nadu, India, 1987.

	Production environments				
	Rainfed-tank	Tank	Tank-well	River-canal	Reservoir-canal
Ratio of irrigated area (%)	64	100	93	100	92
Modern variety adoption (% of farmers)	83	32	94	97	100
Fertilizer use (kg NPK/ha)	70	62	158	133	288
Yield (t/ha)					
Traditional varieties	1.6	2.1	—	—	—
Modern varieties	3.1	3.4	4.1	4.2	5.8
Rice cropping intensity (%)[a]	100	100	184	151	195
Total cropping intensity (%)	100	100	139	129	160

a. Includes only cultivated rice area, whereas total cropping intensity includes nonrice cultivated land areas.

Table 10.13 Labor use (man-days/ha) and adoption of labor-saving technologies (%) in rice farming by production environment, intensive survey, Tamil Nadu, India, 1987.[a]

	Production environments				
	Rainfed-tank	Tank	Tank-well	River-canal	Reservoir-canal
Land preparation	9	16	28	22	12
(% area tractor)	(12)[b]	(51)	(24)	(90)	(68)
Crop establishment	12	10	39	42	45
(% direct seeding)	(58)	(56)	(0)	(2)	(0)
Crop care	100	94	102	74	70
Harvesting & threshing	32	78	60	53	72
(% area threshers)	(0)	(26)	(80)	(18)	(70)
Total labor	153	198	229	191	199
(% hired labor)	(66)	(54)	(60)	(88)	(95)

a. Man-day refers to eight hours of work per day for laborers during the first season.
b. Figures in parentheses indicate adoption rates.

Table 10.14 Regression results of labor use functions in rice production, intensive survey, Tamil Nadu, India, 1987.[a]

	Family labor	Hired labor
Intercept	91.69**	106.29**
	(3.54)	(4.13)
IRGR	-0.04	0.04
	(-0.73)	(0.67)
MV	28.58**	43.44**
	(3.37)	(5.16)
FSIZE	-4.05**	-0.25
	(-4.29)	(-0.27)
TRUSER	-13.90*	-16.99**
	(-2.14)	(-2.64)
THUSER	-3.77	-7.05
	(-0.25)	(-0.47)
AGE	-0.20	-0.13
	(-0.88)	(-0.54)
SCHOOL	-1.10	0.65
	(-0.38)	(0.22)
HSIZE	2.52	-2.87*
	(1.60)	(-1.83)
RF–TANK	-26.88	-26.11
	(-1.45)	(-1.43)
TANK	11.61	-0.60
	(0.62)	(-0.03)
RIV-CAN	-71.75**	28.71
	(-3.91)	(1.58)
RES-CAN	-82.18**	-17.63
	(-5.52)	(-1.19)
R^2	0.46	0.34
F-value	18.43	11.29

a. Numbers in parentheses are t-statistics.
** Indicates significance at 1% level; * at 5% level.

Table 10.15 Population growth rate, permanent and seasonal net in-migration by production environment, extensive survey, Tamil Nadu, India, 1987.[a]

	Production environments				
	Rainfed-tank	Tank	Tank-well	River-canal	Reservoir-canal
Annual population growth rate (%)					
1961–1971	2.7	3.6	1.6	3.9	2.5
1971–1981	1.2	1.5	2.1	2.1	2.4
Net permanent in-migration[b] (households/ha)	-3	-2	2	1	5
Net seasonal in-migration[c] (persons/ha)	3	-6	-2	3	-4

a. Net in-migration equals total in-migration minus out-migration.
b. Number of net in-migrated households for the last ten years normalized by rice area.
c. Number of net in-migrant workers normalized by rice area.

Table 10.16 Regression results of population growth rate functions, extensive survey, Tamil Nadu, India, 1971–1981.[a]

	Population growth rate
Intercept	–5.65 (–0.53)
IRGR	0.03 (0.98)
MVR80	0.25** (2.34)
MLR70	–0.07 (–0.73)
RF-TANK	5.00 (0.86)
TANK	7.26 (1.39)
RIV-CAN	1.18 (0.49)
RES-CAN	2.36 (1.03)
R^2	0.45
F-value	4.88

a. Numbers in parentheses are t-statistics.
** Indicates significance at 1% level; * at 5% level.

Table 10.17 Paddy price, wage rates, and rental rates by production
environment, extensive survey, Tamil Nadu, India, 1987.

	Production environments				
	Rainfed-tank	Tank	Tank-well	River-canal	Reservoir-canal
Paddy price of modern variety (Rs/kg)	1.90	2.35	2.24	2.58	2.32
Wage rates (Rs/day)					
Land preparation[a]	11	11	13	12	13
Transplanting[b]	10	10	11	11	14
Harvesting[a]	16	16	15	15	19
Bullock rental without ploughman (Rs/day)	24	22	26	25	25
Tractor rental (Rs/hour)	68	78	79	60	74

a. Refers to male wage.
b. Refers to female wage.

Table 10.18 Regression results of wage functions, extensive survey, Tamil Nadu, India, 1987.[a]

	Land preparation	Transplanting	Harvesting
Intercept	11.47* (2.11)	13.62* (2.18)	26.75** (5.74)
IRGR	0.02** (2.77)	0.001 (0.10)	−0.004 (−0.52)
MVR	0.04 (0.88)	−0.02 (−0.28)	−0.07 (−1.65)
FSIZE	−0.002 (−0.02)	0.24 (0.73)	0.46* (1.85)
SHARER	0.06 (1.34)	0.07* (1.84)	−0.02 (−0.57)
PADDYP	−0.03** (−2.52)	−0.005 (−0.39)	−0.01 (−1.34)
DISTM	−0.08* (−1.84)	−0.04 (−0.68)	0.03 (0.77)
RF–TANK	−0.41 (−0.24)	−2.87 (−1.49)	−1.95 (−1.36)
TANK	0.52 (0.37)	−2.00 (−1.25)	0.88 (0.74)
RIV–CAN	−0.57 (−0.69)	0.07 (0.07)	2.73** (3.66)
RES–CAN	−0.43 (−0.59)	2.69** (3.25)	5.13** (8.30)
R^2	0.43	0.53	0.71
F-value	2.94	4.47	9.61

a. Numbers in parentheses are t-statistics.
** Indicates significance at 1% level; * at 5% level.

Table 10.19 Regression results of tractor and bullock rental functions, extensive survey, Tamil Nadu, India, 1987.[a]

	Tractor rental	Bullock rental
Intercept	43.89*	29.84**
	(1.93)	(2.76)
IRGR	–0.03	0.04*
	(–0.92)	(1.90)
MVR	0.42*	0.04
	(2.10)	(0.46)
FSIZE	0.87	–0.83
	(0.72)	(–1.45)
SHARER	0.90	0.07
	(0.20)	(1.00)
PADDYP	–0.005	–0.05**
	(–0.10)	(–2.39)
DISTM	–0.02	–0.22**
	(–0.09)	(–2.46)
RF-TANK	–0.81	0.39
	(–0.12)	(0.12)
TANK	7.37	–0.11
	(1.27)	(–0.04)
RIV-CAN	–20.27**	0.15
	(–5.59)	(0.09)
RES-CAN	–5.30*	–0.70
	(–1.76)	(–0.49)
R^2	0.64	0.35
F-value	6.87	2.07

a. Numbers in parentheses are t-statistics.
** Indicates significance at 1% level; * at 5% level.

Table 10.20 Factor payments (thou Rs/ha) and factor shares (%) in rice
farming by production environment, intensive survey, Tamil
Nadu, India, wet season, 1987.[a]

| | Production environments | | | | |
	Rainfed-tank	Tank	Tank-well	River-canal	Reservoir-canal
Gross value of output	6.1	5.7	7.3	8.2	12.9
	(100)	(100)	(100)	(100)	(100)
Current inputs	1.4	1.1	1.9	1.5	2.5
	(23)	(20)	(26)	(19)	(16)
Owner-supplied	0.3	0.5	0.6	0.5	0.8
Purchased	1.1	0.6	1.3	1.0	1.7
Capital	0.7	0.4	0.6	0.6	0.7
	(11)	(7)	(7)	(8)	(6)
Owned	0.1	0.1	0.3	0.1	0.3
Hired	0.6	0.3	0.3	0.5	0.4
Labor	2.1	2.3	2.0	2.5	2.4
	(34)	(40)	(27)	(30)	(19)
Family	0.6	1.0	0.9	0.3	0.1
Hired	1.5	1.3	1.1	2.2	2.3
Land[b]	2.0	1.9	2.9	3.5	7.7
	(32)	(33)	(40)	(43)	(59)

a. Numbers in parentheses are the relative factor shares.
b. Estimated as residual.

Table 10.21.   Average annual income (thou Rs) of farm households by source and production environment, intensive survey, Tamil Nadu, India, 1987.

	Production environments				
	Rainfed-tank	Tank	Tank-well	River-canal	Reservoir-canal
Rice production	3.8	2.5	7.1	5.3	17.8
Labor[a]	0.6	0.6	1.0	0.4	0.3
Capital[b]	0.5	0.5	0.8	0.5	0.9
Land[c]	2.7	1.4	5.3	4.4	16.6
Nonrice income	5.2	4.9	11.6	5.1	5.4
Other crops	0.7	0	8.3	1.0	0.9
Livestock	1.2	0.5	1.4	3.5	1.7
Off-farm[d]	0.4	3.5	0.4	0.2	0.3
Nonfarm[e]	2.9	0.9	1.5	0.4	2.5
Total income	9.0	7.4	18.7	10.4	23.2
Household size	4.6	5.2	5.5	4.2	5.3
Income per person	2.0	1.4	3.4	2.5	4.4

a. Imputed family labor income in owned farm.
b. Imputed returns to owned machineries, bullocks, and other productive capital used in owned farm.
c. Residual in rice production.
d. Labor earnings by working in other farms.
e. Includes labor earnings from nonfarm employment, pensions, actual rental earnings, interest earnings, etc., from nonfarm sources.

Table 10.22 Annual average income (thou Rs) of landless households by source and production environment, intensive survey, Tamil Nadu, India, 1987.

	Production environments				
	Rainfed-tank	Tank	Tank-well	River-canal	Reservoir-canal
Rice production[a]	4.8	3.5	3.7	4.3	8.0
Nonrice production	2.0	0.6	0.6	0.3	1.0
Livestock[b]	—	0.2	0.5	0.3	0.5
Nonfarm[c]	2.0	0.4	0.1	—	0.5
Total income	6.8	4.1	4.3	4.6	9.0
Household size	4.6	3.7	3.5	4.6	4.3
Income per person	1.5	1.1	1.2	1.0	2.1

a. Labor earnings from rice production.
b. Income from sale of livestock products and bullock rentals.
c. Labor earnings from nonfarm employment, pensions, and remittances.

Table 10.23 Regression results of farm household rice income determination functions, intensive survey, Tamil Nadu, India, 1987.[a]

| | Rice income (owned farms) | | |
	Land	Labor	Capital
Intercept	–0.70	0.88**	0.54*
	(–0.41)	(6.05)	(1.70)
IRGR*FSIZE	2.32**	0.10**	0.07*
	(13.13)	(6.68)	(2.15)
MVR*FSIZE	0.44**	–0.02*	–0.04
	(3.04)	(–1.85)	(–1.46)
FSIZE	–2.07**	–0.06**	0.05
	(–8.83)	(–3.16)	(1.10)
ASSET	–0.03*	–0.00**	–0.00
	(–1.75)	(–2.79)	(–0.07)
AGE	–0.00	–0.002	–0.00
	(–0.14)	(–0.97)	(–0.94)
SCHOOL	–0.10	–0.04	0.00
	(–0.36)	(–1.54)	(0.05)
HSIZE	0.10	0.03**	–0.03
	(0.68)	(2.56)	(–0.94)
RF-TANK	0.58	–0.33**	–0.35*
	(0.64)	(–4.36)	(–2.09)
TANK	1.10	–0.43**	–0.19
	(1.20)	(–5.56)	(–1.15)
RIV-CAN	1.09	–0.51**	–0.18
	(1.15)	(–6.33)	(–1.06)
RES-CAN	6.66**	–0.88**	–0.04
	(7.14)	(–11.11)	(–0.25)
R^2	0.76	0.46	0.21
F-value	75.28	20.33	6.36

a. Numbers in parentheses are t-statistics.
** Indicates significance at 1% level; * at 5% level.

Table 10.24 Regression results of farm household nonrice income determination functions, intensive survey, Tamil Nadu, India, 1987.[a]

	Other crop income	Livestock income	Off-farm income	Nonfarm income
Intercept	3.87	1.16	0.76	−2.63*
	(1.37)	(1.21)	(1.51)	(−1.74)
IRGR*FSIZE	0.03	−0.02	−0.01	−0.09
	(0.10)	(−0.24)	(−0.22)	(−0.57)
MVR*FSIZE	0.46*	0.10	0.03	0.30**
	(1.93)	(1.28)	(0.68)	(2.39)
FSIZE	0.11	0.02	−0.08	−0.06
	(0.30)	(0.16)	(−1.19)	(−0.30)
ASSET	0.03	0.03**	−0.003	0.04**
	(1.05)	(3.00)	(−0.59)	(2.42)
AGE	0.01	−0.01	−0.007	0.05**
	(0.41)	(−1.15)	(−1.03)	(2.34)
SCHOOL	0.33	−0.05	−0.13	0.46*
	(0.69)	(−0.30)	(−1.51)	(1.82)
HSIZE	0.03	0.04	0.11**	−0.07
	(0.14)	(0.47)	(2.44)	(−0.55)
RF-TANK	−7.88**	−0.09	0.26	1.34*
	(−5.30)	(−0.19)	(0.97)	(1.69)
TANK	−6.04**	−0.25	2.99**	1.10
	(−4.01)	(−0.49)	(11.11)	(1.37)
RIV-CAN	−6.48**	2.53**	−0.06	−0.78
	(−4.17)	(4.77)	(−0.21)	(−0.94)
RES-CAN	−8.33**	0.13	0.12	0.41
	(−5.44)	(0.25)	(0.43)	(0.50)
R^2	0.23	0.23	0.56	0.14
F-value	6.97	7.26	30.13	4.02

a. Numbers in parentheses are t-statistics.
** Indicates significance at 1% level; * at 5% level.

Table 10.25 Regression results of landless household income functions, intensive survey, Tamil Nadu, India, 1987.[a]

	Rice income	Nonrice income
Intercept	0.35	–0.69
	(0.36)	(–0.73)
ASSET	0.01	0.13
	(0.11)	(1.37)
AGE	0.02	0.01
	(1.23)	(0.35)
SCHOOL	0.30	–0.04
	(1.28)	(–0.18)
HSIZE	0.60**	0.19*
	(5.58)	(1.85)
RF-TANK	0.24	1.42**
	(0.43)	(2.64)
TANK	–0.34	0.37
	(–0.63)	(0.70)
RIV-CAN	–0.15	–0.19
	(–0.28)	(–0.37)
RES-CAN	3.88**	0.60
	(7.15)	(1.15)
R^2	0.56	0.14
F-value	21.16	2.64

a. Numbers in parentheses are t-statistics.
** Indicates significance at 1% level; * at 5% level.

Table 10.26 Overall Gini ratios for all households and contribution by income components by production environment, intensive survey, Tamil Nadu, India, 1987.

| Environments | Overall Gini ratio | Rice income (owned farms) | | | Contribution by | | | | |
		Land	Labor	Capital	Other crop income	Livestock income	Off-farm income	Nonfarm income
Rainfed–tank	0.370	0.096	-0.006	0.016	0.016	0.059	0.001	0.188
Tank	0.302	0.074	-0.035	0.023	—	0.022	0.132	0.086
Tank-well	0.561	0.157	-0.013	0.016	0.323	0.026	0.003	0.049
River-canal	0.399	0.211	-0.029	0.017	0.037	0.159	-0.002	0.006
Reservoir-canal	0.405	0.319	-0.046	0.015	0.026	0.028	0.003	0.060
All	0.460	0.225	-0.009	0.017	0.099	0.053	0.005	0.070

Table 10.27 Size distribution of household income by production environment, intensive survey, Tamil Nadu, India, 1987.

Income class (thou Rs)	Production environments				
	Rainfed-tank	Tank	Tank-well	River-canal	Reservoir-canal
% of households					
< 5	29	46	38	41	4
5–10	42	43	27	33	32
10–15	20	8	12	10	29
15–20	6	3	6	6	5
20–25	1	0	4	7	7
25–30	1	0	5	2	7
30–35	0	0	0	1	4
35–40	0	0	2	0	1
40–45	0	0	1	0	5
45–50	0	0	0	0	2
>50	1	0	5	0	4
Households (no)	80	90	80	90	76
Average household income (thou Rs)	8.5	6.3	13.3	8.5	17.6

11
The Nature and Impact of Hybrid Rice In China

■

JUSTIN YIFU LIN

Feeding China's population has historically been a challenge. Since the 1950s, arable land in China has declined an estimated 10% while population has doubled to more than a billion people. China now feeds 22% of the world's population from only 7% of the world's arable land. China's agricultural sector met the challenge of feeding more than a billion people through innovative food production technology. The Chinese experience could be valuable for meeting the food needs of other developing countries.

Rice, China's most important food crop, accounted for 29% of grain crop area and 44% of grain output in 1989. China began full-scale distribution of semidwarf rice varieties with high-yield potential in 1964, two years before the International Rice Research Institute (IRRI) released IR8, the variety that launched the Green Revolution in much of Asia. By the end of the 1970s, more than 80% of China's rice-growing area was planted to the improved modern varieties. A dramatic increase in the use of chemical fertilizer—from less than 10 kg of nutrients per hectare in the early 1960s to more than 100 kg/ha in the 1980s—accompanied the diffusion of the modern varieties.

The commercial dissemination of F_1 hybrid seed in 1976 marked the second most important achievement of China's rice research. So far, China is the only country in the world where hybrids are used for large-scale rice production. F_1 hybrid rice now grows on more than one-third of the rice crop area in China. The yield advantage of F_1 hybrids over the modern semidwarf varieties is about 15%, without any significant difference in input use (He et al. 1984; He, Xigang, and Flinn 1987).

There are numerous studies about the nature and productivity impact of the modern rice varieties in other countries. The modern varieties have undisputed yield advantages over the traditional varieties. However, the modern varieties, although scale-neutral and labor-using, are best suited to

---

This chapter is based on Lin (1991a, b).

irrigated and favorable rainfed fields with adequate water control (Barker and Herdt 1985; Chapters 4–10). As a consequence, the productivity gap has widened between favorable and unfavorable rice-production environments.

With the exception of several productivity studies, little economic research has been done on the nature and impacts of new rice technology in Chinese agriculture. The change from collective farms to individual household farming in the early 1980s makes such research increasingly important for the establishment of policies for technology development and income distribution.

Rice in China is planted only in areas with adequate irrigation, which reduces the environmental barriers for new rice varieties. The uniqueness of China's rice economy, however, lies in its socioeconomic institutions. Land is collectively owned. Market-type exchanges of land and labor among different production units were not allowed in the collective system. Leasing land was, until recently, also prohibited, because rent was viewed as a form of exploitation. Therefore, channels for indirect distributional impacts of new technologies through adjustments in land and labor markets were limited.

The household responsibility system reform in 1979 modified the collective system, and individual farm households were made the basic unit of farming. Collectively owned land was leased to individual households for as long as fifteen years. In most cases, areas of land leases were made according to the size of the household. Therefore, China has no landless farmers.

More recently, there has been some relaxation of rules for land and labor market transactions. It is now legal to sublease land to other households if the original leaseholding household migrates to other areas or jobs. Households are also allowed to hire workers within a certain ceiling (Lin 1989a).

In this chapter I investigate the nature of hybrid rice technology and analyze its income distributional effects. Data for the study is taken from a survey of 500 households in five different counties in Hunan province.

HYBRID RICE DEVELOPMENT AND FARMING INSTITUTIONS IN CHINA

China moved ahead of other countries in rice research in the 1950s, emphasizing the selection and promotion of the best traditional varieties. The main production improvement was the shift from single to double cropping. Between 1952 and 1957, the rice cropping index increased from 167 to 187% in the South China rice-growing region. In comparison, Taiwan's index increased from 174 to 179% during the same period (Barker and Herdt 1985). As noted earlier, China began full-scale distribution of fertilizer-responsive, lodging-resistant modern varieties in 1964, and those modern varieties were grown on 80% of China's rice area by the late 1970s (China, Ministry of

Agriculture, Planning Bureau 1989). Commercial distribution of F_1 hybrid rice seed in 1976 marked the start of a third stage of rice breeding and production in China.

The development of hybrid maize in the 1930s in the United States provided an important impetus for breeders of other crops. Suggestions that heterosis could be commercially exploited by developing F_1 hybrid rice were made from time to time. But the rice plant, unlike corn and sorghum, self-pollinates with tiny florets, and it is impossible to produce hybrid seed in bulk by hand-emasculation. Thus, rice breeders tried exploiting the phenomenon of cytoplasmic male sterility. Commercial production of F_1 hybrid rice seed involves a complicated three-line method: 1) identifying a cytoplasmic male-sterile parent plant; 2) crossing it with a maintainer line to produce offspring with male sterility but also with desirable genetic characteristics; and 3) crossing the plants from that cross with a restorer line to produce F_1 seeds with normal self-fertilizing power (Yuan 1985). Because great difficulties are involved in working through these three steps, most breeders were discouraged from continuing their research. Breeders in China were exceptions (Virmani and Edwards 1983).

China's hybrid rice research started in Hunan Province in 1964 under the leadership of Professor Yuan Long-Ping. Yuan and his assistant had a breakthrough in 1970 when they found a cytoplasmic male-sterile rice plant. By 1971, a nationwide search for maintainer lines and restorer lines involved more than twenty research institutes in several provinces. The first maintainer line was discovered in Jiangxi Province in 1972, and the first restorer line was discovered in Guangxi Province in 1973. A hybrid combination with marked heterosis was developed in 1974. Regional production tests were conducted simultaneously in hundreds of counties in 1975. In 1976, hybrid rice was released for farmer use (Zhu 1988).

The hybrids developed by Yuan and his associates are Indica varieties adaptable to the production environments in southern China. Research work on Japonica hybrids began in 1971 by Yang Zhenyu of the Liaoning Provincial Academy of Agricultural Sciences. Japonica hybrids adaptable to the northern China production environment were released in 1975.

About 30% of China's rice area grew F_1 hybrid rice in 1987 (Figure 11.2). Rigorous household-level studies have found that the yield advantage of F_1 hybrid rice over conventional modern varieties is about 15%, without major differences in input costs and labor requirements (He et al. 1984; He, Xigang, and Flinn 1987). All fields that grow conventional modern varieties can potentially grow F_1 hybrids because of their similar environmental requirements.

The diffusion of F_1 hybrids at the initial stage, however, faced several problems. The hybrids, like any innovation, appeared risky to farmers. The range of available hybrid varieties was small and the rice-production environments were diverse; crop failures occurred in a number of areas because of the hybrids' lack of resistance to adverse environments. In addition, the hybrid breeding technology required that farmers buy F_1 seed every crop season, and a complicated seed production and distribution system was necessary for large-scale dissemination.

Producing F_1 seed requires a considerable amount of land and labor, and the productivity of hybrid seed is 10% of other rice seed production. The price of F_1 hybrid seed was officially set to be ten times that of conventional rice. That price differential is still maintained, even though technological improvements have more than doubled the yield of F_1 seed. Those technological improvements made F_1 seed production more profitable than hybrid rice production (He, Xigang, and Flinn 1987).

The problem of cost of F_1 seed was mitigated by a low seeding rate—25 to 33% of that of conventional modern varieties. Still, the cash requirement was a burden on adopters. Furthermore, most hybrids require a growing period of 125 to 140 days, longer than most conventional modern varieties. Hence, adoption of hybrids posed some difficulty for areas with two crops of rice a year. The low cooking quality of hybrid rice was also a concern at the beginning.

The problem of seed production and distribution was solved by a sophisticated three-tiered seed system—province, prefecture, and county—set up in major rice-growing provinces. A provincial seed company was responsible for the purification and rejuvenation of male-sterile seed and its distribution to prefectural seed companies. The prefectural seed companies were responsible for the multiplication of male-sterile seed. They distributed male-sterile seed and provided technical guidance to registered producers, then bought seed back from those producers, checked its quality, and sold it to county seed companies. The county seed companies arranged the multiplication, quality control, and sale of F_1 hybrid seed to farmers in a way similar to that of a prefectural company. In addition, a four-level research-extension network—county, commune, brigade, and production team—provided a mechanism for rapid evaluation and selection of adapted seed and diffusion of information about hybrids.

The above system contributed to the rapid diffusion of F_1 hybrid rice in China. Moreover, collective management facilitated the government's use of political pressure in promoting the new technology. It should be emphasized that the collective system also had disadvantages. Although an adoption decision was made by collective leaders, the potential of a new technology could not be fully exploited without the cooperation of all collective members. A collective member generally received only a small share of the marginal return for his additional effort (Lin 1988), so the incentive to learn new technology was low. Gains from economies of scale in the collective system were probably less than the losses due to such incentive problems.

The incentive issue might have contributed to China's dismal agricultural performance in the 1960s and 1970s despite rapid technological progress. Grain output grew at a rate of 2.2% annually between 1957 and 1978, whereas population grew at a rate of 1.9% (Lin 1992). Despite improvements in distribution, 10 to 20% of China's population was reported to have an insufficient amount of food grain in the 1970s (Barker and Herdt 1985).

After the death of Chairman Mao, government policy changed to stress individual incentives and gave producers more flexibility in decisionmaking. By the end of 1983, more than 97% of the collectives in China had begun using individual households as the basic unit of farm operation. The "household responsibility system" allowed a household to lease a plot of land from the collective under a fifteen-year contract. The leasing household, after fulfilling a state grain-procurement quota and making certain contributions to collective funds, could retain the rest of its production. In addition, land use plans became indicative, and individual households had more autonomy in selecting their crop mix. A 20% increase in the price of grain procured under quota was introduced in 1979, and the premium paid for grain above the quota was raised from 30% to 50% of quota prices.

These reforms resulted in unprecedented success in agricultural production. Agricultural output, measured at constant prices, grew 7.4% annually between 1978 and 1984, and grain output grew 4.8% annually in the same period. The improvement in incentives resulting from the shift to the household-based farming system was found to be the main source of the unprecedented output growth (Lin 1992). Institutional reform should have also accelerated diffusion of hybrid rice in China (Lin 1991a).

THE SURVEY AND STUDY AREAS

The study data are from a survey of 500 households taken from December 1988 to January 1989 in five counties in Hunan Province (Figure 11.1). The province is semitropical and has 2.56 million hectares of cultivated land, 82% of which is irrigated. Total population is 5.8 million, of which 4.8 million is agricultural. Per capita cultivated area is 0.05 ha, which is below the national average.

In terms of the ratio of agricultural to total population and per capita gross values of agricultural and industrial output, Hunan is predominantly agricultural (Table 11.1). Rice is its most important crop. In 1987, 57% of the total cultivated area (or 82% of the grain crop area) grew rice; 46% of the rice crop area grew hybrid rice.

The province has 105 counties in three types of geographic settings— lake-plain, hill, and mountain. Among the five counties surveyed, Tiaojiang (HL1) and Xiangxiang (HL2) are hill counties, Nanxian (LP1) and Anxiang (LP2) are lake-plain counties, and Zhijiang (MT1) is a mountain county.

These five counties were selected from a provincial sample of thirty-four counties surveyed annually by a state investigation team.

One hundred households from each county were surveyed. Table 11.2 summarizes the key characteristics of the households. Households in the lake-plain counties had the largest farm size because a substantial amount of cultivated land has been newly reclaimed from Dongting Lake, one of the five largest lakes in China. About 75% of the cultivated land in each of the five counties is paddy land.

Hybrid seed was released to farmers in 1976 at a price that matched the price of conventional seed. However, the price of hybrid seed was later set officially at ten times the price of conventional seed, because hybrid seed fields initially produced about 10% of the seed yield of a conventional modern variety field. The increase in the cost of seed, however, was mitigated by the lower seed requirements—hybrid rice has a high tillering rate and a seeding rate 25 to 33% of that for conventional modern varieties.

Diffusion of hybrid rice in Hunan was rapid in the first two years after its introduction but declined sharply in 1979 and stagnated until 1983 (Figure 11.2). Several factors may have contributed to the stagnation. There was substantial government intervention at the beginning stage. Crop failures occurred in a number of areas because the hybrids lacked disease resistance. In addition, the earliest hybrids released were late-maturing, and their cooking quality was unsatisfactory.

Most of the problems causing low adoption rates for hybrid rice were largely solved by 1988, the time of the survey. The shift from the collective system to the new household-based system in the early 1980s induced to some extent the wider diffusion of hybrid rice. Table 11.3 compares the percentages of households in each county that adopted hybrid rice in 1981–1982 and in 1988. The high early adoption in MT1 probably reflects the fact that most households in this county grow only one crop of rice a year. Most households in the other counties grow two crops of rice a year. The late-maturing, early-released hybrids were best suited for the cropping system in MT1.

Among the households in the sample, 78% reported to have increased their hybrid rice–planted area, whereas only 4% reported that they reduced their hybrid rice area. The main reason reported for increases in hybrid rice area was improvement in yield advantage (384 out of 390 households). Releases of new varieties with a shorter maturation period, however, could have also contributed to this increase. As indicated by Table 11.4, mountain farmers grow one middle-season crop, and farmers in the hills and lake-plain grow an early-season crop followed by a late-season crop. The survey shows that the actual growth duration in 1988 averaged 111 days for early-season, 152 days for middle-season, and 122 days for late-season hybrid varieties, compared to 109 days for early-season, 149 days for middle-season, and 125 days for late-season conventional modern varieties. Although only 13 of the

495 households planted hybrids in the early season, a majority of households adopted hybrid seed either in the middle season if only one crop of rice was grown (MT1) or in the late season if two crops of rice were grown.

The government offered support for the early adoption of hybrids. In the survey, 21% of households reported that when hybrids were first promoted chemical fertilizers were used as a reward; another 3% reported that hybrid seed was subsidized. In 1988, none of the surveyed households reported seed subsidies, and only 4% of the households reported having fertilizer support. Government support remains, but only in the form of the seed research and distribution system.

The survey also found that cooking quality of hybrid rice is no longer an issue. Among the 319 households growing both hybrids and conventional rice, 48% reported eating conventional rice for daily meals; the other 52% reported eating hybrid rice. For special occasions, 25% preferred to use conventional rice, 40% preferred hybrid rice, and the remaining 35% had no preference.

IMPACT ON INPUT DEMANDS

Hybrid rice changes the combination of inputs and the optimal amount of their applications, which has implications for the profitability and acceptance of the new technology. It is noteworthy that the rice varieties currently used in China are all modern varieties, either conventional modern varieties or hybrids, which could be termed the most modern of all. Input and output comparisons in this study are between hybrid and conventional modern varieties.

Table 11.5 compares the use of seeds, labor, animal power, mechanical power, and chemical fertilizers for hybrid and conventional modern varieties. As expected, seed requirements are much lower for hybrid varieties—about one-third of the amount used for conventional varieties. Seeding rate for the early-season hybrids is about 50% higher than for the middle- and late-season hybrids because of cold weather at seeding time. Seeding rate for the early-season conventional modern rice is also much higher.

The difference between hybrid and conventional modern varieties in use of inputs other than seeds is not significant, except that more mechanical power is used for early-season hybrids and more animal power is used for middle-season hybrids.

The information presented in Table 11.5, however, may be misleading. The application level of an input is itself a choice variable. In addition to the technical nature of a variety, a household's optimal use of an input also depends on the relative prices of inputs, a household's resources, and region-specific exogenous variables such as temperature and topography. For example, Table 11.6 shows dramatic cross-county variations in the mean labor input of sample households. The mean labor input in MT1 is almost twice that of LP2. Moreover, significantly less labor is used for hybrid varieties than for conventional modern varieties in HL1 and MT1. Thus, in the investigation of the technical nature of hybrid rice, especially the levels of input use, it is important to control for the potential impacts of other variables. Therefore, the appropriate method for analyzing the impact of hybrid seeds on input use is regression analysis, in which the effects of other variables can be isolated.

In an income-maximization model, the application level of an input relative to a unit of land is a function of several groups of exogenous variables: the technical nature of the seed, the prices of various inputs, the personal characteristics of the decisionmaker (which affect the efficiency and opportunity cost of input use), the household endowments (which influence the income as well as opportunity costs of land and labor), and other unobservable regional characteristics. Such a model provides a basis for estimation of input demand functions.

The estimated functions are reduced-form equations. The explanatory variables include 1) a dummy variable for hybrid rice adoption (HYBRID); 2) county dummy variables representing environmental and other county-specific factors such as topology, frost-free period, and temperature (HL2, LP1, LP2, MT1, with HL1 as control variable) as well as season dummy variables (MIDDLE and LATE, with EARLY as control variable); 3) measures of economic environment, such as village-specific wages (WAGE), tractor rental (TRRENT), animal rental (ANRENT), and fertilizer price (FERTP), as shown in Table 11.7; 4) personal characteristics of the household head (SCHOOL, AGE, FEMALE) that may influence the level of input use through the allocative ability and the opportunity cost of labor of the household head; and 5) household resource endowments, such as farm size (FSIZE), labor-land ratio (LABFR), and capital-land ratio (CAPFR). Capital refers to the aggregate value of farm implements, machinery, and draft animals. Different items of farm capital may have different technical properties; some are labor substitutes and others are labor complements. An alternative way to estimate the impact of capital endowment on input use is to include the dummy variables for the various items of farm capital—i.e., tractors with more than 12 horsepower (TROWNER), hand tractors with less than 12 horsepower (HTOWNER), threshers (THOWNER), and draft animals (ANOWNER). Except for dummy variables, all variables are in logarithmic form (1 is added to the variable if some observations are 0). The estimated input use functions, based on the plot-level information in the data set, are reported in Tables 11.8 and 11.9.

Equations (1) and (2) of Table 11.8 report alternative estimates of the labor demand function. In both estimates, the coefficients of hybrid rice adoption are negative, and one of them is significant. This result implies that compared to conventional modern varieties, hybrid rice reduces labor use by about 4%. The estimates also indicate that regional variations in labor use are substantial, but differences among early-, middle-, and late-season rice are not significant. Wage rate has the expected significant negative effect on labor use.

Labor use is also affected by the age and sex of a household head. Thus, an older, female household head tends to use more labor per unit of land than a younger, male household head. This tendency may be a result of the difference in opportunity costs due to the difference in off-farm and nonfarm job opportunities. Farm size has a significantly negative impact on labor use, whereas other household variables do not have significant effects.

Equations (3) and (4) of Table 11.8 report the estimates for the use of draft animals. The coefficients of hybrid rice adoption are negative and significant. The estimates indicate that use of draft animals for hybrid rice is about 2% less than for conventional modern rice. As in labor use, there are large variations in the use of animal power across regions, as suggested by the estimated coefficients of the regional dummy variables. Compared to early-season rice, significantly more animal power is used for middle-season rice, but significantly less is used for late-season rice. Draft animal rental rate has the expected negative impact on use of draft animals. The estimate for draft animal use is significantly different from zero in a two-tailed t-test in equation (4) but not in equation (3). However, if a one-tailed test is used, the estimate in equation (3) is also significantly different from zero at the 10% level.

The estimates in equations (3) and (4) indicate that the household head's personal characteristics, farm size, and labor-land ratio do not have significant impacts on the use of animal power. Neither does the capital-land ratio. However, in equation (4), where capital-land ratio is replaced by dummy variables for various forms of farm capital, it is found that a household uses significantly less draft animal power if it owns a hand tractor and significantly more if it owns a draft animal. If a household owns a draft animal, the opportunity cost for using draft animal power is reduced, and the draft animal is substituted for a hand tractor. It is interesting to note that the dummy variable for the large-size tractor has no significant effect on the use of draft animal power. This result confirms a casual observation that, in southern China, the large-size tractor is used mainly as a transportation vehicle and not for paddy work.

Table 11.9 reports the estimates of the demand for mechanical power and chemical fertilizers in rice production. Demand for mechanical power does not seem to be affected by the hybrid rice technology, but hybrid rice has a significantly positive effect on demand for chemical fertilizers. From the estimated coefficients, a household uses about 6% more chemical fertilizers in hybrid rice than in conventional modern rice.

The coefficient of tractor rental in the demand function of mechanical power and the coefficient of fertilizer price in the demand function for chemical fertilizer both have the expected significantly negative signs. In the mechanical power demand function, the coefficient of ownership of hand tractor is significantly positive and the coefficient of ownership of draft animal is significantly negative, the opposite of the results in the animal power function in Table 11.8. This result clearly indicates that mechanical power is a substitute for animal power. The coefficient of large-size tractor ownership in the mechanical power demand function is not significantly different from zero, confirming once again the observation that tractors are not used in paddies.

The coefficient of farm size is negative and highly significant in the chemical fertilizer demand function, indicating that increases in farm size reduce the use of chemical fertilizers per unit of land. It is interesting to note that the education level of the household head has a significantly positive effect on the level of application of chemical fertilizers. This result is consistent with the empirical evidence in other developing countries (Jamison and Lau 1982).

A final note is that the coefficients of the regional dummies in equations (1) to (4) indicate significant variations across regions in the use of mechanical power and chemical fertilizers.

In summary, the regression analysis in Tables 11.8 and 11.9 suggests that, compared to conventional modern varieties, hybrid rice is labor-saving. It requires less labor and animal inputs per unit of crop area and does not require more mechanical input, which may arise from the fact that seed use in the production of hybrid rice is one-third or less of seed use for the conventional modern varieties. Therefore, less labor and animal power are needed for seedbed preparation and transplanting. The opposite is true of conventional modern varieties, which increase the labor requirement for crop care and harvesting (see Chapters 4 and 6–10). Hybrid rice, however, yields best with somewhat higher rates of chemical fertilizers than the conventional modern varieties. The same phenomenon is also found in the comparison between modern varieties and traditional varieties.

THE IMPACT ON PRODUCTIVITY

China is committed to a policy of self-sufficiency in food grain, but it is an extremely land-scarce country, and the potential for increasing cultivated land area is low. Therefore, one of the desirable properties of new agricultural technology is to raise yield in order to meet the ever-increasing demand for grain.

A new agricultural technology will not be acceptable to farmers, however, unless it raises total productivity. I estimated a production function to see to what extent the total factor productivity is increased by the introduction of hybrid rice, and then I analyzed the marginal productivity of land, labor, and other inputs.

Table 11.10 reports the tabulation of average yields of hybrid and conventional rice in each county's samples. The average yield of hybrid rice is higher than that of conventional rice in each of these counties. However, because more chemical fertilizers are used in the production of hybrid rice, it is impossible to decide whether the yield advantage of hybrid rice simply reflects the impact of differences in the level of chemical fertilizer application or the technical property of hybrid rice itself. An appropriate technique for determining the impact of hybrid rice technology on productivity is the regression analysis.

A frequently used method of estimating the productivity impact of a new technology is the Cobb-Douglas function, which makes it possible to estimate the production elasticity and the marginal productivity of the input. The sum of the coefficients of inputs also indicates the degree of returns to scale in production.

Plot-level data from the household survey were used to estimate the production functions in log-linear form. Several group of variables were included as independent variables: 1) county dummies; 2) dummy variables for the incidence of natural calamities (DISASTER), middle-season rice (MIDDLE), and late-season rice (LATE); 3) inputs, including the sown area measured by hectare (FSIZE), labor input measured by day (LABORQ), chemical fertilizers measured by quantity (FERTQ), and machinery service (MECHQ) as well as draft animal service (ANIMQ), both measured by day; and 4) personal characteristics of the household head, including years of school (SCHOOL), age (AGE), and sex (FEMALE).

Two variants of production function were estimated. The first included a dummy for hybrid rice in the regression equation. This method, assuming the elasticities of each variable unaltered, estimated the shift in the intercept. The second variant introduced an interaction term to each variable assuming shifts in both intercept and slopes. From the coefficients and the t-statistics of each interaction term, the impact of hybrid rice technology on each variable could be measured separately.

The results of fitting the production function by OLS are presented in Table 11.11. Equation (1) reports the estimates of the first variant. Except for the coefficients of machine service, draft animal service, and the three variables representing the household head's personal characteristics, all the variables' coefficients are significantly different from zero. The F-statistic for the null hypothesis that the coefficients of the above five variables are jointly zero is 0.262. With degrees of freedom 5 and 1,045, the null hypothesis cannot be rejected. Therefore, these five variables can be excluded from the regression function. Equation (2) reports the re-estimates.

The results of fitting the second variant are reported in equation (3). For the same reason as in estimating the first variant, the five insignificant variables were dropped.

The estimated coefficient of the hybrid rice dummy in equation (2) measures the shift in the intercept of production function, assuming the coefficients of parameters in the production function are invariant for the hybrid rice and conventional rice. The shift captures the net impact of hybrid rice technology on total factor productivity. From the estimated coefficient of 0.17 for the hybrid rice dummy, it can be inferred that the total factor productivity of hybrid rice is nearly 19% higher than that of conventional rice.

Although the simple hybrid rice dummy would reflect the "average" impact of hybrid rice on total factor productivity, hybrid rice technology may change the coefficients of individual parameters of the production function. Equation (3) presents the results of attempts to estimate these two types of changes simultaneously. From the estimates of the interaction terms in equation (3), one can infer that, except for the impact on regional dummies, hybrid rice's main impact on the production function comes from the increase in the elasticity of labor. The estimated coefficient of the interaction of the hybrid rice dummy with labor is positive and significant. The coefficient suggests that hybrid rice is about 150% more responsive to labor input than conventional rice.

The interactions of the hybrid rice dummy with land (FSIZE*HYBRID) and chemical fertilizers (FERTQ*HYBRID) are negative but not statistically significant. The hybrid rice dummy in equation (3) is negative but not statistically significant, although it indicates that the hybrid rice production function probably has a lower intercept than the function for conventional rice. This result implies that the hybrid rice production function may not globally dominate the conventional rice function. Conventional rice may have a higher productivity than hybrid rice at a low input level.

Table 11.12 reports the estimates of marginal productivity at the mean level of application of labor, land, and chemical fertilizers for conventional rice and hybrid rice, based on the elasticities in equation (3) of Table 11.11. The following major points can be noted. Compared with the conventional rice's marginal productivity of labor, land, and chemical fertilizers, hybrid rice's marginal productivity is about 182% higher for labor, about 15% higher for land, and about 14% higher for fertilizers. Because hybrid rice's elasticities of land and chemical fertilizers do not differ significantly from those of conventional rice (as seen in equation (3) of Table 11.11), the 14 to 15% difference in the marginal productivity of land and chemical fertilizers between these two types of rice varieties may not be important.

If the production function is continuous with respect to its inputs, the following principles should be observed for optimal resource allocation: 1) when an input is used in the production of several crops, the value of marginal product of this input should be equalized across crops; and 2) the value of the marginal product of an input should be equal to the market price of that input.

If the first condition does not hold, efficiency can be improved by shifting part of the input from one crop to another. In a case where the second condition does not hold, efficiency can be improved by increasing or decreasing the application of the input, depending on whether the value of marginal product is larger or smaller than the price of the input.

The estimated marginal productivity of land and fertilizers for hybrid rice and conventional rice are nearly the same. The values of marginal product of fertilizers, estimated by applying average rice price of ¥0.61 per kg, are almost in line with the reported market price listed in Table 11.7. This similarity suggests that farmers have allocated chemical fertilizers efficiently.

Information on the prevailing rent for subleased land is not available. However, judging from the marginal product of land in Table 11.12, the rent should be around 4,500 kg/ha.

The estimated value of marginal products of labor is substantially lower than the wage rate reported in Table 11.7. This difference may arise from the fact that, as shown in Table 11.13, more than 90% of labor hiring occurs during the three peak labor seasons—seedbed preparation, plowing, and harvesting. Labor has the greatest marginal value at those times.

Because marginal productivity of labor is significantly higher for hybrid rice than for conventional rice, a shift of labor input from conventional rice production to hybrid rice production may improve resource allocation. In fact, judging from the estimated labor demand function in Table 11.8, which indicates a labor-saving effect for hybrid rice, it may well be that excessive labor input is allocated to the production of conventional modern varieties. This conclusion presupposes, however, that the production elasticity of labor input decreases with its application, unlike the basic assumption of constant production elasticities of inputs in a Cobb-Douglas production function.

DETERMINANTS OF HYBRID RICE ADOPTION

Although hybrid rice is a labor-saving technology and significantly increases total factor productivity, its equity implication further depends on:

- the extent and intensity of adoption of hybrid rice among households with different characteristics;
- the scope of factor market adjustments in response to the adoption; and
- adjustments in cropping pattern, farm activities, and household members' employment patterns.

The first analysis concerns the direct impact of hybrid rice technology on household income distribution; the latter two analyses concern the indirect effects.

Several groups of variables may affect the probability of a household's adoption of hybrid rice and the intensity of that adoption. First, adoption of a new technology poses risks for farmers because of imperfect information and the possibility of errors. Therefore, the decision to adopt may be affected by a household head's personal characteristics, such as education, farming experience, and sex. It may be hypothesized that the level of education contributes positively to adoption of hybrid rice. Second, because hybrid rice is a new technology, adoption of hybrid rice may involve some fixed costs. Therefore, farm size and other farm-specific characteristics may have an impact on adoption decisions. Third, input requirements for the cultivation of hybrid rice are different from those of conventional rice. The costs, and thus the profitability, of cultivating hybrid rice also depend on the prices of various inputs. Because production of hybrid rice uses more purchased inputs, including fertilizers and seed, availability of credit may affect the adoption decision. Fourth, the yield advantage of hybrid rice may be sensitive to local ecological conditions. Therefore, some region-specific variables may affect the adoption decision. Finally, some households are obliged to sell certain amounts of grain to the government, and they may adopt hybrid rice for its higher yield, which helps fulfill the quota obligation.

Adoption of hybrid rice involves two separate decisions: whether or not to adopt hybrid rice and the optimal rate of adoption. The first decision is a dichotomous choice. If it is assumed that the residual variable of the adoption decision function is identically and independently distributed as a normal distribution over the population, then the probit is the appropriate method for estimating the unknown parameters in the dichotomous choice model. The second decision variable is censored, as it ranges between 0 and 1. Again, if the explanatory variables are linear and the residual term has a normal distribution, then the two-limit Tobit is the appropriate method for estimating the unknown parameters in the optimal rate of adoption decision.

The results of estimating the decision functions are reported in Table 11.14. For the dependent variables in the analysis, only the adoption decision with respect to middle-season rice and late-season rice was considered. Early-season rice was excluded because of limited adoption of hybrids for that season. In the dichotomous choice model, a household was considered an adopter if it grew hybrid rice in either the middle or the late seasons. In the model of optimal rate of adoption decisions, the dependent variable was the percentage of total rice area planted with hybrids in both seasons.

The explanatory variables included county dummy variables, head of household's personal characteristics, and prices of various inputs, as in the input demand functions. However, two other variables were added, namely, the household's quota obligation (QUOTA) and its credit experience (CREDIT), where the value of 1 was assigned when the household took at least one loan in the past two years and 0 was assigned otherwise. Except for the dummy variables, the explanatory variables are specified in logarithms.

From the results of fitting the dichotomous decision model in equation

(1) of Table 11.14, it is seen that the adoption decision is positively and significantly affected by farm size, quota obligation, and years of schooling. The positive effect of farm size on the adoption decision is probably due to the economies of scale in hybrid rice production and better access to information. The existence of a quota obligation contributes positively to the likelihood of adoption, probably because of the higher yield of hybrid rice. Education's positive effect may derive from its effect on a household head's ability to deal with new information, which reduces the risk of adopting hybrid rice.

The coefficient of seed price is negative but not significant, mainly because of limited price variation across the sample counties. As for the optimal rate of adoption, equation (2) of Table 11.14 indicates that besides the regional dummy variable, both the household head's education and the household's capital endowment have positive and significant effects.

IMPACT ON HOUSEHOLD INCOME

Although hybrid rice technology increases yield significantly, the seed costs and fertilizer requirement of hybrid rice are higher than those of conventional modern varieties. The degree to which household income from rice cultivation is increased by the adoption of hybrid rice depends on the price of seed and other inputs. Because an agricultural household in China is obliged to be self-sufficient in rice and also meet a delivery quota, a household may adopt hybrid rice for its higher yield without considering the profitability of its production. In addition, because hybrid rice requires less labor per unit of land, the adoption of hybrid rice will affect a household's allocation of labor for different crops and different jobs. Moreover, even if hybrid rice is found to have a positive impact on rice income, its impact on the relative income position of adopting households vis-à-vis nonadopting households cannot be predicted directly.

Households in areas for which there are no suitable hybrid varieties may increase the cultivation of other crops for which the area has comparative advantages. The potentially adverse effect of hybrid rice innovation on relative income position can thus be mitigated. To investigate the impacts of hybrid rice innovation on household income, one needs to examine both their direct effect on rice income and their indirect effect on nonrice income.

Table 11.15 reports the average annual income per household for the five Hunan production environments. Household income essentially represents returns to family labor, owned capital, and land. Rice is clearly the most important source of income. MT1 has the highest ratio of land planted to hybrid rice (Table 11.4), but the contribution of rice income to total household income is small because only a single rice crop is grown. Although the proportion of rice area planted to hybrid rice in HL1 is about the same as that in LP2, average rice income per household in HL1 is 61% of that in LP2. Nevertheless, total household income in LP2 is almost the same as that in HL1. The substitution of income sources seems to have taken place in accordance with the comparative advantage of rice and nonrice activities.

A host of factors other than hybrid rice technology determine rice income and household income, and simple tabulations will not dissociate hybrid rice from the effects of other factors. A more appropriate method of measuring the income effect of hybrid rice technology would be to fit a regression model relating income to its determinants and incorporating hybrid rice technology as an explanatory variable.

Table 11.16 reports the results. I estimated the income determination functions by including a dummy in the regressor indicating whether a household is an adopter of hybrid rice. To show the differences in the impact of the adoption of hybrid rice on various sources of income, the determination functions of rice income, nonrice agricultural income, and nonfarm income were estimated separately. Aside from the technology and county dummy variables, the explanatory variables in the income determination functions included the household's endowments of labor and capital stock and the personal characteristics of the household head.

If the adoption of hybrid rice were an exogenous variable, OLS would be the appropriate method for fitting the regression functions. However, as argued in previous sections, adoption of hybrid rice is an endogenous variable. Predicted values of hybrid rice adoption, based on the adoption function estimated by probit procedures shown in Table 11.14, were used to provide consistent estimates of the parameters.

The regression indicates that adoption of hybrid rice technology significantly increases rice income, as expected. However, hybrid rice adoption significantly lowers nonrice agricultural income and nonfarm income. This evidence indicates that households with comparative advantage in the cultivation of hybrid rice allocate more resources for rice production, whereas households without comparative advantage shift their resources to nonrice agricultural production and nonfarm activities. That shift mitigates the potentially adverse effects of hybrid rice technology on their income. Though not reported here, it has been found that hybrid rice technology has no significant effect on total household income.

A similar adjustment process is also observed in the case of a household's landholding. The size of a household's landholding is the most important factor determining a household's income from rice. The estimated coefficient of landholding indicates that a 10% difference in the size of landholding results in a 6% difference in the household's rice income. However, the size of a household's landholding has a significantly negative effect on the household's nonfarm income. This relationship suggests that households with small landholdings shift labor from land-intensive rice cultivation to more labor-intensive nonfarm activities. The estimated elasticity of labor in the nonfarm income determination function is 0.95, which is much larger than the elasticities of 0.23 in the rice and nonrice income regressions. Given limited employment opportunities in agriculture, additional family labor tends to be allocated more to nonfarm jobs.

The signs and magnitudes of the coefficients of the other explanatory variables in Table 11.16 also provide interesting information about the determinants of household income. Capital contributes positively and significantly to nonrice agricultural income and nonfarm income. The effect of capital stock on rice income, however, is insignificant. The female dummy variable has a positive and significant impact on nonfarm income mainly because female-headed households obtain significantly more remittance than male-headed households. A female-headed household receives an average of 840 yuan annually, compared to 260 yuan for the male household head. Age of the household head also contributes positively to nonfarm income.

The effects of education on rice income and nonrice agricultural income are not significant. However, its effect on nonfarm income is highly significant. A 10% increase in a household head's years of schooling contributes a 5.6% increase in household nonfarm income. This evidence suggests that farmers with higher education have better opportunities for nonfarm employment.

A question frequently asked about a new technology concerns its distributional implication. As shown earlier, hybrid rice technology significantly increases labor productivity. In a market economy where land is unequally distributed and landless households are poor, this property of technological change will have an equalizing effect on the income distribution, especially by increasing the income of landless households. However, it was also shown earlier that hybrid rice is a labor-saving technology. This property will have a negative effect on the income position of landless households, whose incomes are dependent on seasonal or permanent employment in rice cultivation. The net impact on income distribution will thus depend on which effect is more important.

China has no landless labor. Moreover, in the face of the introduction of a new technology, the mechanism of reallocation of household resources among different crops and jobs according to a household's comparative advantages seems to work reasonably well. Households adopting hybrid rice reduce time, land, and capital allocated to nonrice production and nonfarm activities, and the opposite is true for nonadopting households. Therefore, the adoption of hybrid rice technology will not significantly widen differences in total income across households, as is evident from the estimations in Table 11.16. It is thus concluded that the impact of hybrid rice technology on the distribution of household income tends to be small.

Rice production is the most important source of income in the sample households. In turn, one estimation result of the rice income determination function in Table 11.16 indicates that land is the most important determinant of rice income. Because of the household responsibility system reform of 1979, land is fairly equally distributed in China. Moreover, households with unfavorable land endowments shift their activities to labor-intensive nonfarm business and employment and thereby mitigate their unfavorable position. Thus, it is expected that household income in China will be fairly equally distributed.

Table 11.17 reports the overall Gini ratios of household income and its decomposition into different sources (see Chapter 3 for methodology). The total household income Gini ratio ranges from .21 to .25 (see column 4). Except for the Gini ratio of rice income in HL2, the total household income Gini ratio is substantially lower than the Gini ratios of rice income, nonrice agricultural income, and nonfarm income in each of the five counties (see column 1). The same observation holds when the data of these five counties are pooled together. The Gini ratio of household income is .234, compared to .322 for rice income, .304 for nonrice agricultural income, and .552 for nonfarm income. These figures further confirm the existence of job specialization in response to households' comparative advantages.

The last column of Table 11.17 shows that the Gini ratio of per capita income in a county is lower than the corresponding household income Gini. However, it is higher than the household income Gini ratio when the data from the five counties are pooled. Moreover, the Gini ratio of the pooled data is substantially higher than the Gini ratio of each individual county. This result suggests that the major source of personal income inequality in the areas studied arises from the interregional disparities in income opportunities.

THE IMPACT OF HYBRID RICE: A SUMMARY

Hybrid rice is a labor-saving technology. The labor input per unit of cultivated land of hybrid rice is about 4% less than that of conventional rice. Although the difference is small, it is statistically significant. Hybrid rice production uses less labor than conventional rice production because of the former's lower labor requirement for seedbed preparation and transplanting. Conversely, conventional modern varieties use more labor compared to traditional varieties.

Hybrid rice also significantly reduces the demand for draft animals, and its effect on demand for tractors is insignificant. Draft animals are more likely to be used in seedbed preparation, and there is less need for seedbed preparation for hybrid rice.

Hybrid rice, like conventional modern varieties, significantly increases use of fertilizers. This study indicates that hybrid rice uses about 6% more chemical fertilizers than the conventional modern varieties and that the yield advantage of hybrid rice is about 17%, given the same level of inputs. The major source of the productivity increase in hybrid rice comes from its higher responsiveness to labor inputs. The production elasticity of labor input in the hybrid rice production function is 0.16, compared to 0.06 in the conventional rice production function.

The study also found that farm size, the existence of a quota obligation, and the years of schooling of the household head contribute positively to the likelihood of hybrid rice adoption. Moreover, a household's capital endowment has a positive and significant effect on the rate of adoption.

Differential adoption of hybrid rice does not have a significant effect on the difference in overall household income, even though it significantly increases income from rice. This effect occurs because adoption of hybrid rice has a significantly negative impact on nonrice agricultural income and nonfarm income. We may conclude that households with favorable production environments for hybrid rice production increase their income by adopting hybrid rice, whereas households with unfavorable environments allocate their resources to nonrice crops, or to nonfarm jobs in which they have a comparative advantage. Because of the existence of this readjustment process, hybrid rice adoption does not have a significant cross-sectional effect on differences in household income.

A similar adjustment process is observed for differences in household endowments. A household with a relatively more abundant land endowment tends to specialize in land-intensive rice cropping, whereas a household with a relatively more abundant labor endowment tends to specialize in nonfarm employment. As a result of this adjustment process, the income distribution is fairly equal in the study areas.

Figure 11.1 Location of Study areas, intensive survey, Hunan Province, China, 1988

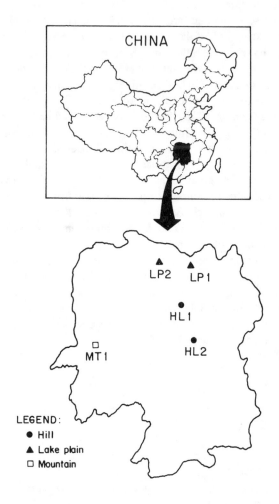

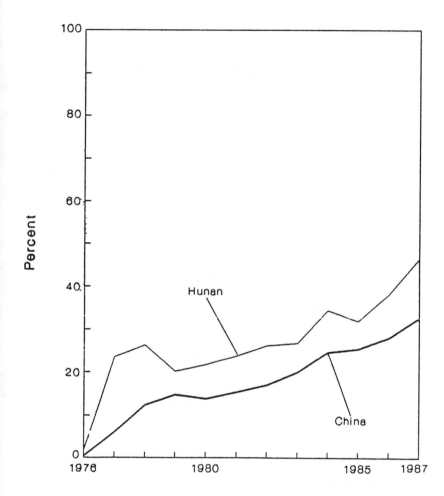

Figure 11.2   Adoption rate of hybrid rice in China, 1976–1987.
    Source: Ministry of Agriculture, Animal Husbandry, and
    Fisheries.

Table 11.1   Economic profile of sample counties, Hunan, China, 1988.
Sources: China Statistical Yearbook, 1989; Hunan Statistical
Yearbook, 1989.

| | Population (thou) | | Gross value added per capita (¥)[a] | |
	Total	Agricultural	Agricultural	Industrial
China	1,096,140	552,450	535	1,662
Hunan	59,157	50,356	512	983
County (HL1)	765	699	701	494
County (HL2)	843	761	631	851
County (LP1)	678	573	742	723
County (LP2)	522	429	660	515
County (MT1)	316	286	621	479

a. 3.7 yuan (¥) = US$1 in 1988.

Table 11.2   Socioeconomic characteristics of sample households by production environment, Hunan, China, 1988.

| | Hills | | Lake-plain | | Mountain |
	HL1	HL2	LP1	LP2	MT1
Sample households (no)	100	100	100	100	100
Farm size (ha)	0.33	0.31	0.54	0.56	0.40
Rice farm size (ha)	0.26	0.26	0.39	0.41	0.31
Household size (persons)	4.3	4.3	4.6	4.6	4.2
Family workers (no)	3.1	3.3	3.4	3.6	3.3
Topography (% of area)					
Flat	83	64	99	99	21
Steep	11	29	0	1	56
Very steep	4	5	0	0	20
Mixed	2	2	1	0	3

Table 11.3   Changes in the adoption rate (% of area) of hybrid rice by production environment, Hunan, China, 1981–1988.

	Hills		Lake-plain		Mountain
	HL1	HL2	LP1	LP2	MT1
Adopter					
1981–1982	27	10	4	20	52
1988	78	67	64	93	99
Nonadopter					
1981–1982	63	90	96	80	48
1988	22	23	36	7	1

Table 11.4   Adoption of hybrid and conventional modern rice varieties (no of households) by production environment, Hunan, China, 1988.

	Hills		Lake-plain		Mountain
	HL1	HL2	LP1	LP2	MT1
Sample households (no)	100	100	97	99	99
Early-season rice					
Hybrid	4	7	0	0	2
Conventional	98	98	92	98	6
Both	2	5	0	0	0
Middle-season rice					
Hybrid	0	1	8	8	99
Conventional	0	0	11	9	14
Both	0	0	0	2	14
Late-season rice					
Hybrid	79	67	63	90	9
Conventional	35	49	78	51	0
Both	14	18	46	43	0
Intensity of hybrid rice					
Percent of total rice crop area	40	33	26	40	96
Percent of middle-season and late-season rice crop area	71	60	45	73	97

Table 11.5   Current inputs and draft animal and machine adoption between hybrid and conventional modern rice, Hunan, China, 1988.[a]

	Early Rice		Middle Rice		Late Rice	
	Conventional	Hybrid	Conventional	Hybrid	Conventional	Hybrid
Samples (no)	390	12	32	116	204	308
Seed (kg/ha)	176	47***	104	31***	93	30***
	(63.8)	(33.2)	(46.8)	(13.5)	(49.5)	(35.0)
Fertilizer (kg/ha)[b]	901	876	727	832	860	894
	(473.3)	(218.6)	(586.5)	(447.0)	(374.2)	(334.8)
Labor (days/ha)	238	264	351	331	217	223
	(93.7)	(60.3)	(200.3)	(114.6)	(78.3)	(74.2)
Draft animal	18	27	38	55	12	13
(days/ha)	(17.5)	(16.7)	(44.3)	(37.2)	(14.0)	(11.8)
Machine (days/ha)	8	20***	20	9*	9	9
	(13.2)	(20.4)	(103.2)	(4.6)	(13.6)	(15.0)

a. Numbers in parentheses are standard errors.
b. Material weight of chemical fertilizer.
* Indicates significant differences in means between conventional and hybrid rice production at 5% level; ** at 1%; *** at 0.1%.

Table 11.6   Labor use (man-days/ha) in rice farming by type of variety and by production environment, Hunan, China, 1988.[a]

	Hills		Lake-plain		Mountain
	HL1	HL2	LP1	LP2	MT1
Hybrid	256	214	214	194	355
	(65.3)	(62.3)	(53.3)	(64.5)	(108.4)
Conventional	281	220	216	207	488
	(85.3)	(61.8)	(79.6)	(96.0)	(196.5)
Average	272	218	215	202	375
	(79.1)	(61.9)	(73.0)	(85.6)	(133.9)

a. Numbers in parentheses are standard errors.

Table 11.7   Fertilizer price, wage rate, and custom rental rate by production environment, Hunan, China, 1988.[a]

	Hills		Lake-plain		Mountain
	HL1	HL2	LP1	LP2	MT1
Fertilizer price (¥/kg)[b]	0.5	0.4	0.5	0.3	0.4
	(0.04)	(0.09)	(0.05)	(0.01)	(0.04)
Wage rate (¥/day)	9.8	5.5	7.4	8.9	7.8
	(4.99)	(3.53)	(4.84)	(6.28)	(4.51)
Custom rental (¥/day)					
Animal	8.9	8.9	5.6	11.3	9.4
	(9.69)	(4.10)	(2.94)	(7.89)	(1.77)
Tractor	15.9	7.7	10.3	12.3	—
	(17.91)	(8.07)	(6.72)	(10.26)	

a. Numbers in parentheses are standard errors.
b. Average price of chemical fertilizer per kg of material.

Table 11.8   Regression results of the demand for labor and draft animal inputs, Hunan, China, 1988.[a]

	Ln labor		Ln draft animal	
	(1)	(2)	(3)	(4)
Intercept	1.06**	1.12**	0.13*	0.15**
	(4.30)	(4.54)	(2.02)	(2.51)
HL2	−0.27**	−0.26**	−0.03**	−0.02*
	(−6.09)	(−5.90)	(−2.52)	(−1.94)
LP1	−0.27**	−0.26**	−0.17**	−0.10**
	(−5.35)	(−4.58)	(−12.79)	(−7.31)
LP2	−0.28**	−0.29**	−0.11**	−0.09**
	(−6.27)	(−6.45)	(−9.71)	(−8.61)
MT1	0.25**	0.26**	0.13**	0.14**
	(4.49)	(4.57)	(8.62)	(9.98)
TROWNER	—	0.09	—	0.003
		(1.22)		(0.18)
HTOWNER	—	0.001	—	−0.04**
		(0.02)		(−3.51)
THOWNER	—	−0.002	—	−0.009
		(−0.06)		(−1.05)
ANOWNER	—	0.03	—	0.04**
		(1.13)		(6.86)
Ln FSIZE	−0.19**	−0.19**	−0.008	−0.01
	(−5.97)	(−5.87)	(−0.95)	(−1.47)
Ln CAPFR	0.02	—	0.001	—
	(1.47)		(0.24)	
Ln LABFR	0.01	0.01	0.004	0.008
	(0.19)	(0.36)	(0.49)	(1.02)
Ln WAGE	−0.12**	−0.13**	−0.003	−0.001
	(−3.42)	(−3.63)	(−0.31)	(−0.16)
Ln FERTP	−0.30**	−0.30**	−0.14**	−0.11**
	(−3.52)	(−3.47)	(−6.48)	(−5.06)
Ln TRRENT	−0.03	−0.03	0.003	0.01*
	(−1.26)	(−1.28)	(0.57)	(1.84)
Ln ANRENT	0.01	−0.003	−0.02	−0.02*
	(0.02)	(−0.06)	(−1.51)	(−1.76)
Ln AGE	0.07	0.07	0.002	−0.003
	(1.64)	(1.59)	(0.18)	(−0.26)
Ln SCHOOL	0.02	0.02	−0.0002	−0.004
	(1.00)	(0.81)	(−0.03)	(−0.67)
FEMALE	0.10*	0.10*	0.01	0.01
	(1.86)	(1.89)	(1.11)	(1.00)
HYBRID	−0.04*	−0.04	−0.02**	−0.02**
	(−1.66)	(−1.62)	(−2.47)	(−2.37)
MIDDLE	0.03	0.03	0.02*	0.02
	(0.71)	(0.70)	(1.88)	(1.61)
LATE	−0.02	−0.02	−0.02**	−0.01**
	(−0.81)	(−0.84)	(−2.37)	(−2.39)
R^2	0.35	0.34	0.59	0.62

a. Numbers in parentheses are t-statistics.
** Indicates significance at 1% level; * at 5% level.

Table 11.9   Regression results of the demand for mechanical and fertilizer inputs, Hunan, China, 1988.[a]

	Ln Mechanical power		Ln Fertilizer	
	(1)	(2)	(3)	(4)
Intercept	0.17**	0.16*	2.04**	2.16**
	(2.95)	(2.79)	(7.04)	(7.49)
HL2	0.13**	0.13**	-0.10*	-0.09*
	(13.04)	(12.61)	(-2.02)	(-1.82)
LP1	0.04**	-0.001	-0.10*	0.02
	(3.08)	(-0.11)	(-1.71)	(0.24)
LP2	0.006	-0.006	-0.09*	-0.06
	(0.60)	(-0.61)	(-1.76)	(-1.25)
MT1	-0.005	-0.01	-0.11*	-0.09
	(-0.39)	(-0.94)	(-1.71)	(-1.35)
TROWNER	–	0.003	–	0.07
		(0.17)		(0.81)
HTOWNER	–	0.04**	–	-0.20**
		(3.82)		(-3.92)
THOWNER	–	0.009		0.56
		(1.11)		(1.34)
ANOWNER	–	-0.01*	–	0.04
		(-1.98)		(1.55)
Ln FSIZE	-0.011	-0.01	-0.16**	-0.16**
	(-1.51)	(-1.50)	(-4.41)	(-4.21)
Ln CAPFR	0.002*	–	0.003	–
	(1.70)		(0.16)	
Ln LABFR	0.02*	0.01*	-0.03	-0.01
	(2.20)	(2.02)	(-0.77)	(-0.30)
Ln WAGE	-0.01*	-0.02*	0.001	-0.002
	(-1.71)	(-1.86)	(0.03)	(-0.05)
Ln FERTP	-0.02	-0.04*	-0.37**	-0.32**
	(-1.18)	(-2.05)	(-3.61)	(-3.17)
Ln TRRENT	-0.02**	-0.02**	-0.15**	-0.14**
	(-3.22)	(-4.16)	(-5.59)	(-5.23)
Ln ANRENT	0.002	0.005	0.089	0.08
	(0.18)	(0.47)	(1.62)	(1.40)
Ln AGE	-0.008	-0.003	0.06	0.04
	(-0.75)	(-0.26)	(1.12)	(0.69)
Ln SCHOOL	-0.001	0.01	0.06**	0.06*
	(-0.13)	(0.17)	(2.38)	(2.19)
FEMALE	-0.003	-0.001	0.18**	0.18**
	(-0.22)	(-0.06)	(2.99)	(2.94)
HYBRID	-0.001	-0.002	0.06*	0.06*
	(-0.18)	(-0.35)	(1.89)	(2.05)
MIDDLE	0.10	0.01	-0.17**	-0.18**
	(0.89)	(1.10)	(-3.09)	(-3.21)
LATE	0.006	0.005	-0.02	-0.02
	(1.03)	(0.98)	(-0.84)	(-0.85)
R^{-2}	0.43	0.44	0.08	0.09

a. Numbers in parentheses are t-statistics.
** Indicates significance at 1% level; * at 5% level.

Table 11.10 Yields (t/ha) of hybrid and conventional modern rice by production environment, Hunan, China, 1988.[a]

	Hills		Lake-plain		Mountain
	HL1	HL2	LP1	LP2	MT1
Hybrid rice	5.2	6.8	5.5	5.8	6.5
	(1.1)	(1.1)	(1.4)	(1.0)	(2.0)
Conventional rice	5.1	6.0	4.7	4.5	5.4
	(1.2)	(1.0)	(1.6)	(0.9)	(2.7)

a. Numbers in parentheses are standard errors.

Table 11.11 Regression results of rice-production functions, Hunan, China, 1988.[a]

	(1)	(2)	(3)
Intercept	3.27**	3.27**	3.46**
	(24.03)	(24.03)	(42.03)
HL2	0.21**	0.21**	0.17**
	(5.98)	(5.93)	(6.65)
LP1	0.04	0.05*	0.02
	(1.45)	(2.24)	(0.57)
LP2	0.05*	0.06**	−0.02
	(2.16)	(2.53)	(−0.80)
MT1	0.17**	0.17**	0.16**
	(4.41)	(4.53)	(2.51)
HL2*HYBRID	—	—	0.10*
			(2.20)
LP1*HYBRID	—	—	0.08*
			(1.70)
LP2*HYBRID	—	—	0.21**
			(4.43)
MT1*HYBRID	—	—	−0.03
			(−0.40)
Ln FSIZE	0.81**	0.81**	0.81**
	(33.56)	(33.94)	(27.87)
FSIZE*HYBRID	—	—	−0.008
			(−0.16)
LABORQ	0.12**	0.11**	0.06*
	(4.59)	(4.68)	(1.97)
LABORQ*HYBRID	—	—	0.10*
			(1.98)
FERTQ	0.10**	0.10**	0.09**
	(6.25)	(6.18)	(4.83)
FERTQ*HYBRID	—	—	−0.02
			(−0.77)
MIDDLE	−0.08*	−0.08**	−0.26**
	(−2.24)	(−2.41)	(−5.50)
MIDDLE*HYBRID	—	—	0.33**
			(3.72)
LATE	−0.04*	−0.04*	−0.04*
	(−2.14)	(−2.11)	(−2.10)
LATE*HYBRID	—	—	0.04
			(0.56)
DISASTER	−0.10**	−0.10**	−0.08**
	(−5.85)	(−5.86)	(−3.63)
DISASTER*HYBRID	—	—	−0.03
			(−1.04)
HYBRID	0.17**	0.17**	−0.18
	(9.39)	(9.43)	(−1.38)
Ln MECHQ	0.002	—	—
	(0.12)		

(continues)

Table 11.11 *(continued)*

Ln ANIMQ	–0.008	—	—
	(–0.58)		
Ln SCHOOL	–0.01	—	—
	(–0.79)		
Ln AGE	–0.005	—	—
	(–0.17)		
FEMALE	0.003	—	—
	(0.08)		
R^{-2}	0.90	0.90	0.91

a. Numbers in parentheses are t-statistics.
** Indicates significance at 1% level; * at 5% level.

Table 11.12 Estimates of average and marginal products of labor, land, and fertilizer, Hunan, China, 1988.

	Labor (kg/day)		Land (kg/ha)		Fertilizer (kg/kg)	
	Average	Marginal	Average	Marginal	Average	Marginal
Conventional rice	24.7	1.6	5,164.5	4,273.7	7.1	0.5
Hybrid rice	26.6	4.9	6,002.0	4,837.5	8.2	0.6

Table 11.13 Incidence of labor hiring arrangements, Hunan, China, 1988.

	Frequency	Percent
Clearing of field	2	1
Seedbed preparation	44	18
Plowing	150	62
Transplanting	6	2
Weeding	2	1
Fertilizer application	4	2
Pesticide application	2	1
Harvesting	27	11
Drying	2	1
Total	239	100

Table 11.14 Regression results of hybrid rice adoption functions, Hunan, China, 1988.[a]

	Probit (1)	Two-limit Tobit (2)
Intercept	–3.34	–1.41
	(–1.36)	(–0.82)
HL2	–0.41	–0.17
	(–1.25)	(–0.75)
LP1	–0.79	–0.75*
	(–1.42)	(–2.20)
LP2	0.68	–0.02
	(1.54)	(–0.08)
MT1	5.98	1.05**
	(0.02)	(2.95)
Ln FSIZE	0.77**	0.08
	(3.22)	(0.51)
Ln WAGE	–0.58	–0.13
	(–1.57)	(–0.52)
Ln SEEDP	–0.95	0.24
	(–1.55)	(0.54)
Ln FERTP	–0.20	–0.07
	(–0.18)	(–0.11)
Ln PESTP	0.41	0.17
	(1.23)	(0.67)
Ln LABORQ	–0.35	–0.22
	(–1.31)	(–1.19)
Ln CAPITALQ	0.06	0.08*
	(1.03)	(2.06)
Ln TRRENT	0.04	0.19
	(0.24)	(1.56)
Ln ANRENT	–0.09	–0.08
	(–0.21)	(–0.24)
Ln AGE	0.22	0.07
	(0.60)	(0.29)
Ln SCHOOL	0.57**	0.21*
	(2.94)	(1.65)
FEMALE	0.39	0.44
	(0.95)	(1.57)
CREDIT	0.18	–0.10
	(1.12)	(–0.87)
QUOTA	0.81*	0.52
	(2.03)	(1.53)
Log-likelihood	–177.64	–425.30

a. Numbers in parentheses are t-statistics.
** Indicates significance at 1% level; * at 5% level.

Table 11.15 Average annual income (¥) of farm households by source
and production environment, Hunan, China, 1988.

	Hills		Lake-plain		Mountain
	HL1	HL2	LP1	LP2	MT1
Agricultural income	2,233	2,350	2,481	2,918	1,900
Rice[a]	1,187	1,485	1,547	1,943	826
Cash crop	272	191	565	504	436
Forestry	34	50	0	0	180
Husbandry + sidelines	736	608	346	471	448
Off-farm agricultural employment	4	16	23	0	10
Nonfarm income	1,352	984	583	743	644
Nonfarm employment	154	94	64	73	90
Nonfarm business	792	521	285	366	483
Transfer	406	369	234	304	71
Total income	3,585	3,334	3,064	3,661	2,544
Household size	4.3	4.3	4.6	4.6	4.2
(no of working members)	(3.1)	(3.3)	(3.4)	(3.6)	(3.3)
Income per person	834	775	666	796	606
(per working member)	(1,156)	(1,010)	(901)	(1,017)	(771)

a. The price used to calculate income from rice is the weighted average price
received by the agricultural households in 1988 (0.611 ¥/kg).

Table 11.16 Instrumental variable estimates of the impact of hybrid rice
adoption on income distribution, Hunan, China, 1988.[a]

	Ln Rice income	Ln Nonrice agricultural income	Ln Nonfarm income
Intercept	4.05**	5.01**	4.73**
	(7.37)	(8.02)	(3.20)
HL2	0.39**	−0.24**	−1.10**
	(4.41)	(−2.39)	(−4.65)
LP1	−0.04	−0.41**	−1.10**
	(−0.43)	(−3.52)	(−4.01)
LP2	−0.06	−0.15	−0.63**
	(−0.62)	(−1.35)	(−2.48)
MT1	−0.86**	0.09	−0.65**
	(−8.43)	(0.74)	(−2.38)
Ln FSIZE	0.60**	0.38**	−0.38*
	(7.41)	(4.11)	(−1.75)
Ln WORKER	0.23**	0.23**	0.95**
	(2.62)	(2.33)	(4.07)
Ln CAPITALQ	−0.002	0.05*	0.10*
	(−0.07)	(1.98)	(1.73)
FEMALE	−0.11	0.03	0.77*
	(−0.74)	(0.19)	(1.98)
Ln AGE	−0.14	0.04	0.65*
	(−1.12)	(0.31)	(1.96)
Ln SCHOOL	−0.06	0.07	0.56**
	(−0.90)	(0.98)	(3.39)
HYBRID	1.32**	−0.58*	−1.83**
	(4.70)	(−1.81)	(−2.42)

a. Numbers in parentheses are t-statistics.
** Indicates significance at 1% level; * at 5% level.

Table 11.17 Overall Gini ratios of farm household income and contributions by income component, Hunan, China, 1988.

	Factor Gini	Income share	Rank correlation	Gini Decomposition	Gini ratio of per capita income
	(1)	(2)	(3)	(4)= (1)x(2)x(3)	(5)
HL1					
Rice	.226	.331	.620	.046	
Nonrice agricultural	.317	.292	.509	.047	
Nonfarm	.456	.377	.721	.124	
Total income	—	1.000	—	.217	.190
HL2					
Rice	.232	.445	.679	.070	
Nonrice agricultural	.299	.260	.455	.035	
Nonfarm	.558	.295	.772	.128	
Total income	—	1.000	—	.234	.178
LP1					
Rice	.367	.505	.755	.140	
Nonrice agricultural	.283	.305	.335	.029	
Nonfarm	.516	.190	.419	.040	
Total income	—	1.000	—	.209	.204
LP2					
Rice	.246	.531	.736	.096	
Nonrice agricultural	.275	.267	.512	.038	
Nonfarm	.570	.202	.617	.071	
Total income	—	1.000	—	.205	.196
MT1					
Rice	.335	.325	.653	.071	
Nonrice agricultural	.326	.421	.609	.083	
Nonfarm	.574	.253	.688	.100	
Total income	—	1.000	—	.254	.222
Total					
Rice	.322	.432	.687	.096	
Nonrice agricultural	.304	.302	.455	.042	
Nonfarm	.552	.266	.656	.096	
Total income	—	1.000	—	.234	.291

PART 3

■

Technology and Income in Asian Rice Farming

12
Modern Rice Technology: Emerging Views and Policy Implications
■

CRISTINA C. DAVID AND KEIJIRO OTSUKA

In the preceding eight chapters, the impact of differential modern rice variety adoption across production environments has been examined for seven countries. The focus has been on the issue of regional income distribution, because the main, unresolved equity question of the Green Revolution involves its effects in favorable versus unfavorable rice-growing regions. Although partial equilibrium analysis was used, attempts were made to investigate not only the direct effects of differential technology adoption on productivity and factor use but also the indirect effects on factor prices and income through labor, land, and product market adjustments. The latter analysis enabled us to draw some general equilibrium implications.

The case studies covered different rice-production environments, agrarian structures, and policy frameworks. The analysis of each country study was based on cross-section village- and household-level data gathered during 1985–1988.

The extensive village-level survey covered a wide range of production environments, whereas the intensive household-level survey focused on representative villages. Because the survey data were collected in a limited number of areas, the paucity of exogenous variables confined analyses to estimation of reduced-form rather than simultaneous-equation systems. Although it is difficult to statistically identify the structures of causes and effects from the estimation of reduced-form equations, cross-country comparisons, combined with theoretical reasoning, helped us make useful inferences on underlying causal relations.

MAJOR FINDINGS

In this section we summarize the major general findings of the case studies and highlight differences and similarities across countries.

Modern Variety Adoption and Regional Productivity Differential

The country studies identified the determinants of modern variety adoption and the modern varieties' impact on rice yield. They also shed light on the importance of environmental and technological factors vis-à-vis socioeconomic factors in determining the productivity in rice farming.

Determinants of Modern Variety Adoption. The studies consistently found, despite data from widely varying agrarian structures, that environmental factors, particularly degree of water control, are the decisive factors affecting modern variety adoption. Table 12.1 compares adoption rates of modern varieties in Southeast Asian and South Asian countries, along with hybrid rice in China, across production environments. Note that the environmental classifications vary somewhat among countries. It is clear that modern variety adoption is almost complete in irrigated and favorable rainfed areas, but there has been little adoption in uplands, tidal swamps, deepwater areas, and drought- and submergence-prone rainfed lowlands. An exception is the relatively low rate of modern variety adoption in irrigated areas of Thailand because of the high-quality grain required for export. Another exception is in Bangladesh, where modern varieties have been adopted in deepwater rice areas. In those areas, modern varieties increase economic returns from investments in tubewell pumps, inducing farmers to shift from traditional deepwater rice in the wet season to modern varieties in the dry season.

In China, where all rice is grown in irrigated areas, hybrid rice is adopted most widely in the relatively unfavorable mountainous region, because the longer-growth-duration hybrid rice best fits the pattern of single cropping.

Table 12.2 summarizes the estimated coefficients of the modern variety (and hybrid rice) adoption function. The coefficient of irrigation (IRGR) indicates an increase in the ratio of modern variety adoption area when the ratio of irrigated area increases from zero to one. Coefficients of farm size (FSIZE) and schooling of household head (SCHOOL) show change in modern variety adoption ratio in response to 100% increase in farm size or schooling. Zero implies that a coefficient is statistically insignificant.

Irrigation consistently has a significant effect on the adoption of modern varieties. Although not reported in Table 12.2, it was also found that the coefficient of the dummy for the favorable rainfed environment is positive and significant for the Philippines and Indonesia, where most rainfed areas are favorable production environments.

Furthermore, the regression results consistently indicate that neither farm size nor tenure significantly affects modern variety adoption. These findings refute the opinions widely expressed in the rice literature that large-scale farmers adopt modern varieties more rapidly than small-scale farmers and that tenants, particularly share tenants, adopt modern varieties more slowly than owner-cultivators. Adoption of modern varieties by small-scale farmers and share tenants may have been equally rapid because farmers are not generally inefficient in Asia, as argued by Hayami and Otsuka (1993). In fact, small farms in Bangladesh and Thailand have significantly high rates of modern variety adoption, which is not surprising because modern varieties are part of a land-augmenting and care-intensive technology. In contrast, larger farms in China adopt hybrid rice more frequently than conventional modern varieties, which is consistent with estimates of labor use function that show hybrid rice to be a labor-saving technology.

Although cash requirements increase with modern variety adoption, government-supervised credit programs and the emergence of trader-lenders in the informal credit market seem to have reduced the credit constraints of small-scale farmers. Furthermore, ongoing introduction of modern varieties with increased disease resistance, improved drought tolerance, shorter growth duration, and better grain quality leads to their wider diffusion.

We note that farm household–level data show education to be significantly associated with differences in adoption of hybrid rice in China.

In summary, the country studies consistently found that environmental factors—especially the degree of water control—rather than socioeconomic factors such as farm size and tenure, are the decisive factors affecting modern variety adoption. These findings are consistent with accumulated evidence on adoption of modern rice varieties in Asia (Ruttan 1977; Barker and Herdt 1985).

Productivity differentials. Modern varieties increase land productivity by increasing yields and cropping intensity. Table 12.3 summarizes patterns of yield per hectare and cropping intensity across production environments and countries. Average yields are clearly higher in favorable areas, which reflects partly the effect of differential adoption of modern varieties and partly the effect of differences in production environments. Yields, other than for hybrid rice, range from 2.8 to 5.8 t/ha in irrigated areas, 2.7 to 5 t/ha in favorable rainfed areas, and 1.7 to 3.4 t/ha in unfavorable areas. Yields are particularly high in India (Tamil Nadu), Indonesia (mostly Java), and China (Hunan Province) because of high rates of adoption of modern varieties (hybrid rice in China), high levels of fertilizer use, and well-maintained gravity irrigation systems.

In Nepal, yields in irrigated areas are lowest among the seven countries because Mahsuri rice, which is lower-yielding but more drought-tolerant than IRRI-type modern varieties, is preferred by farmers there.

Regression analysis indicates that modern variety (and hybrid rice) adoption has a statistically positive effect on yields, not to mention production environments (Table 12.4). The estimated coefficients imply that the adoption of modern varieties increases yield per hectare 25 to 70% or more, whereas irrigation increases yield per hectare 13 to 40%. It is only for Tamil Nadu, India, that the effect of modern varieties cannot be distinguished from degree of water control. There is complete adoption of modern varieties in most areas and a strong positive correlation between modern variety adoption and quality of irrigation in Tamil Nadu.

Hybrid rice yields in China are about 17% higher than those of conventional modern varieties, as reflected in the coefficient of the hybrid rice variety dummy variable.

We have yields of traditional varieties have been essentially unchanged over time and are largely similar across production environments. Thus, we conclude that adoption of modern, as well as hybrid, varieties clearly widens the yield gap across production environments.

Cropping intensity tends to be highest in more favorable environments, particularly in irrigated areas (Table 12.3). An exception is Bangladesh, where nonrice crops are generally grown, even during the dry season, in rainfed areas.

Because modern varieties have a shorter growth duration than traditional varieties and are not photoperiod-sensitive, double cropping with rice or another crop may increase. However, adequate water supply from irrigation during the dry season, or even distribution of rainfall throughout the year in the rainfed lowlands, would still be required to grow a second crop. Moreover, because rice requires more water than nonrice crops, sufficient dry-season irrigation water is critically important to double rice cropping.

The studies did not find a statistically significant effect of modern varieties on total cropping or rice cropping intensity separate from the effect of irrigation in Thailand, Nepal, India (Tamil Nadu), or Indonesia (Table 12.5). It may well be that the effect of modern varieties on cropping intensity is relatively modest. In the Philippines, where the sample villages included rainfed areas with relatively even rainfall distribution, a statistically significant coefficient of modern varieties was obtained in the rice cropping intensity function.

Irrigation has, in general, a highly significant effect on cropping intensity. Because modern varieties were fully adopted in most irrigated areas by the late 1980s, time series data may be required to identify the effect of modern varieties on total cropping intensity. This seems to be particularly the case in Indonesia. In Bangladesh, where modern variety adoption affects rice cropping intensity, no significant difference in total cropping intensity was observed between irrigated and nonirrigated environments. When modern varieties are adopted, rice cropping intensity increases partly at the expense of other dry-season crops, such as the low-yielding pulses and oilseeds.

Socioeconomic factors have essentially no effects on cropping intensity. We conclude that it is physical environments, particularly the presence of irrigation and to a lesser extent the adoption of modern varieties, that determines cropping intensity.

Labor Market Adjustment

The survey data were used to examine the impact of modern rice technology on labor demand, interregional migration, and regional wage differential across production environments and to assess the role of labor markets in equalizing regional wages as a response to differential technology adoption.

Patterns of labor use. Except in the case of hybrid rice in China, the country studies generally found that adoption of modern varieties in favorable environments significantly increases labor use per hectare by raising the labor requirement for crop care, harvesting, and threshing (Table 12.6). In general, there is a positive association between production environments and days of labor use per hectare per season. It is also interesting to note that labor use tends to be high in low-income countries, such as Bangladesh, India, and China, which indicates a high degree of substitutability among factor inputs in rice production.

The greater use of hired labor in more favorable environments, which in some cases leads to an absolute decline in the use of family labor, is particularly pronounced. An exception is the case of deepwater rice areas in Thailand, where, because of relatively large farm size, the proportion of hired labor is even higher than in irrigated areas with high adoption of modern varieties.

In irrigated areas of Nepal, India, Indonesia, and the Philippines, well over half of labor input depends on hired labor. This proportion is due partly to a sharper peak-season demand for labor associated with the shorter growth duration of modern varieties, and partly to the negative income effect on family labor use generated by the adoption of modern varieties. To the extent that modern varieties increase total cropping or rice cropping intensity, labor use per hectare per year is further increased. Even if rice merely replaces other crops in the dry season, as in Bangladesh, labor use will increase, because the labor requirement for rice cultivation is typically higher than for other crops.

Because the major source of hired labor is poor landless laborers and marginal farmers, modern rice technology's high use of hired labor ought to have a desirable impact on income distribution. Though not a subject of analysis in this book, rapid growth in farm income due to modern variety adoption in the favorable areas would have induced growth linkage effects in the rest of the economy through greater employment in the nonfarm sector, as the bulk of expenditures in the rural sector are spent on food and labor-intensive industrial goods (Hazell and Roell 1983; Gibbs 1974; Bell, Hazell, and Slade 1982; Hazell and Ramasamy 1991).

The greater labor demand from modern rice technology should increase wage rates in the favorable areas faster than in the unfavorable areas, unless interregional labor migration from unfavorable to favorable areas takes place or labor-saving technologies are adopted in favorable areas. If a labor market adjusts through interregional permanent or seasonal migration, wages will tend to equalize across production environments. In such a case, benefits from technical change in the favorable areas will be shared with people in the unfavorable areas, particularly with landless workers, who tend to be more geographically mobile than farmers. If mechanization or direct seeding is adopted, wages will equalize, but they will do so at a lower level, adversely affecting the welfare of landless households.

Modern varieties and adoption of labor-saving technology. There is a common belief that diffusion of modern varieties promotes adoption of threshers, tractors, and other labor-saving technology. Table 12.7 presents adoption rates of labor-saving technologies by production environments in five countries. Bangladesh and China are not included because adoption of labor-saving technology is negligible in those countries, except for the practice of direct seeding of traditional varieties in deepwater areas in Bangladesh.

Thailand, India, and the Philippines have relatively high adoption rates of labor-saving technologies. In contrast, the rates of mechanization and direct seeding are low or nonexistent in Indonesia and Nepal, except for direct seeding of traditional varieties in upland areas of Indonesia, shown in the category labeled "others" in Table 12.7.

Intercountry comparison suggests that farm size and relative factor prices are more important factors than modern variety adoption in explaining differential adoption of labor-saving technologies. This is evidenced by the fact that adoption rates of tractors, threshers, and direct seeding are notably high in Thailand, where modern variety adoption is lowest but farm size and wages are highest among the countries under study. Contrast that with Indonesia, where more than 80% of crop area is planted with modern varieties and farm size is lowest.

When adoption rates are compared across production environments, use of tractors appears higher in the more favorable environments with relatively high adoption of modern varieties. As is shown in Table 12.8, however, regression analysis consistently indicated that it is not modern varieties but irrigation (or more specifically double cropping) that induces wider adoption of tractors. Double cropping of rice increases the cost of maintaining draft animals, primarily because of the lack of grazing land during the dry season.

It is obvious from the data in Table 12.7 that the adoption of threshers is largely unrelated to production environments and modern variety adoption. In Thailand, threshers have been adopted completely in deepwater areas, where farm size is largest. In the Philippines, thresher adoption is lower in the unfavorable rainfed areas, primarily because of difficulties in moving machines in hilly and mountainous environments.

Direct seeding also does not appear to be related to modern variety adoption. It is mainly practiced in the unfavorable areas that grow traditional varieties, where the crop has to be established before flooding (deepwater areas), where there is no standing water in the field (upland), or where rainfall is so uncertain that seeding has to be done immediately after the first onset of rains (unfavorable rainfed lowland).

In the Philippines, however, the reasons behind the spread of direct seeding in favorable areas, where modern varieties have been completely adopted, need to be explored further. In the favorable rainfed lowlands, direct seeding seems to be practiced with modern varieties in order to increase cropping intensity (Barlow, Jayasuriya, and Price 1983).

In short, there is no strong evidence that adoption of modern varieties induces adoption of labor-saving technologies. As long as adoption of the modern varieties increases labor demand, it must have desirable effects on income distribution.

Interregional migration and wage differential. Although village-level migration data were not available, the hypothesis that interregional migration occurs in response to differential technology adoption was tested empirically by examining trends in village population growth rates, patterns of man-land ratio, and proportion of landless households across production environments (Table 12.9). Higher population growth rates in the more favorable areas (observed in countries where data are available) conform with the hypothesis that the direction of net migration is from unfavorable to irrigated or favorable rainfed areas.

The Philippine and Indian studies showed that modern variety adoption is significantly and positively associated with population growth (Chapters 4 and 10). In the case of Indonesia, the effect of modern varieties on population growth rates cannot be distinguished from the effect of irrigation, which is positive and significant (Chapter 5).

The relatively high man-land and landless household ratios in the favorable production environments in most countries strongly suggest that interregional migration from unfavorable to favorable areas corresponds to increased employment opportunities in favorable areas. Furthermore, the Nepal study showed statistically that there is substantial flow of seasonal migration from unfavorable to favorable areas (Chapter 9).

Thus, the available evidence strongly indicates that rural labor markets are closely integrated through interregional migration.

Interregional migration contributes significantly to the equalization of wage rates across production environments. Table 12.10 shows the pattern of transplanting and harvesting wages across production environments in the different countries. Wages in Table 12.10 are expressed in terms of U.S. dollars, using the prevailing official exchange rates in survey years for each country. Because survey years vary slightly and because official exchange rates do not necessarily reflect differences in the purchasing power of local currencies, caution must be used in making comparisons across countries.

Consistent with levels of economic development, average wages tend to be lower in South Asia than in Southeast Asia. Harvesting wage tends to be significantly higher than transplanting wage in most countries, primarily because harvesting is usually performed under output-sharing or piece-rate contracts involving mostly male labor. In contrast, transplanting is based mostly on daily-wage contracts and performed mainly by female labor, both of which involve lower wages.

Wages across production environments within a country and task are more similar, and with a few exceptions no systematic patterns are observed. In fact, according to the estimation results of wage functions summarized in Tables 12.11 and 12.12, neither modern variety adoption nor irrigation is associated with interregional wage differences in Indonesia, Nepal, India, and the Philippines.

Regional wage difference is significantly associated with irrigation in Thailand, but the estimated coefficient indicates only a 7% difference in wages between irrigated and nonirrigated areas. The adoption rate of modern varieties in Thailand, even in the irrigated villages, is relatively low. In any case, such wage differences may well be explained by the cost of migration rather than lack of interregional labor market adjustments. In fact, the distance to the market town (DISTM), which is supposed to measure the cost of migration, has generally negative effects on wage rates.

The coefficient of modern variety ratio for transplanting wage in Bangladesh is significant and positive (Table 12.11) because transplanting of the modern variety *boro* crop coincides with the peak harvesting season of the local *aus* and broadcast *amon* crop. In contrast, the harvest of the modern variety *boro* crop in irrigated environments takes place in a slack season, which explains the negative coefficient of IRGR in the harvesting wage equation (Table 12.12).

Those who remain in unfavorable areas, as well as migrant workers, benefit from modern variety adoption in the favorable areas because wage rates increase in unfavorable areas as a result of out-migration. In this way, income gains from technological change in the favorable areas are shared by landless laborers at large. We also note that although rural-to-rural migration is primarily from unfavorable to favorable areas, interregional labor market adjustments in the form of higher rural-to-urban migration from the less favorable areas also play an important role.

Therefore, because of interregional migration, differential technology adoption across production environments does not cause significant regional wage differential. As far as the well-being of poor landless laborers is concerned, the impact of modern rice technology does not seem to be as inequitable as generally believed.

Land Market Adjustments

Unlike labor, land is immobile, and hence supply is much more inelastic. Differential technology adoption across production environments is therefore expected to widen regional differences in returns to land, as well as in land prices, as productivity gains are capitalized into land values.

Modern varieties and land rent differentials. Factor-share analysis based on the intensive-survey data showed that the residual return to land (estimated by subtracting actual and imputed costs of current inputs, capital inputs, and labor from the gross value of production) is far larger in favorable than in unfavorable areas (Table 12.13). Factor shares of land in the irrigated and favorable rainfed areas range from 33 to 56%, whereas its share ranges from 19 to 51% in the unfavorable areas. The absolute difference in the estimated returns to land per hectare is as much as threefold between the most and least favorable production environments.

The contribution of varietal difference to this gap, however, is substantially smaller when there is control for difference in production environment. For example, absolute returns to irrigated and favorable rainfed land in the Philippines, where adoption rates of modern varieties are similar across regions, do not substantially differ. In contrast, the difference between irrigated and unfavorable rainfed areas, where no modern varieties are grown, is at least twofold in other countries.

As the returns to land, in absolute and relative terms, increase with modern variety adoption in the favorable areas, the factor share of labor (except in the case of Indonesia) declines significantly (Table 12.13). It should be noted, however, that the absolute return to labor per hectare increases substantially in the favorable areas—as much as 60% in Thailand and in Indonesia.

The gains in labor income for landless households and small-scale farmers are even greater, as modern variety adoption increases demand for hired labor more than it increases the use of family labor. Furthermore, in Bangladesh, and possibly in other countries, increased labor demand was accompanied by change in labor contract from the relatively low wage of attached labor to the higher wage of casual labor. Note, however, that wages tend to be lower for attached labor because it has more employment security than casual labor.

The impact of modern variety adoption on land rents and land prices was estimated econometrically in Thailand and Indonesia (Table 12.14). The Thailand study found statistically significant effects of modern variety adoption and ratio of irrigated area on regional differences in land rents. The estimated coefficients indicate that land rents are 32% higher in areas planted to modern varieties than in areas planted to traditional varieties and 51% higher in irrigated areas than in rainfed areas. Conversely, the Indonesian study could not distinguish the separate effect of modern variety adoption and irrigation because of problems of multicollinearity. However, regression analysis using a unique set of time series–transacted land prices collected by farmers' recall for Lampung, Indonesia, convincingly demonstrated that modern variety adoption significantly and substantially increases land prices

(Table 12.14). The Lampung study also found that adoption of more productive, newer-generation modern varieties progressively increases land prices.

Thus, differential adoption of the modern rice technology may worsen the regional income distribution by widening the returns to land.

The income gap potentially arising from the widening returns to land between favorable and unfavorable areas, however, may be mitigated by adjustments to land and product markets. Specifically, changes in demand for land may trigger changes in farm size and tenancy structure—i.e., decrease in farm size and increase in the incidence of land renting in favorable areas—leading to wider sharing of gains from the higher land rental resulting from technical change.

Farm size and tenure structure. Table 12.15 compares farm size and ratio of owner-cultivators by production environment. Farm size differs markedly across countries according to the endowment of cultivable land relative to rural population.

Land allocation in China is based on the number of working household members rather than on market transactions. Average farm size is relatively higher in the lake-plain area (included in the "irrigated" environment category), a newly reclaimed area where productivity is relatively low, reflecting the fact that land distribution by the state also considers land quality factors.

In Thailand and Indonesia, farm sizes are significantly larger (as much as two to four times) in the unfavorable areas than in irrigated and favorable rainfed areas. In contrast, farm size is largely similar across production environments in the Philippines, Bangladesh, India, and Nepal.

In many cases, farm size has not adjusted to modern variety adoption, partly because land reform laws prohibit the transfer of cultivation and ownership rights. In the Philippines, for example, the land reform law has been effectively implemented in favorable rice-growing areas, preventing farm size adjustment to a considerable extent (Otsuka 1991). In Nepal, conversely, farm size is smaller in the hills than in the *tarai* region partly because of a larger landownership ceiling in the *tarai*.

Farmers' income depends not only on farm size but also on tenure status. With a few exceptions, tenancy patterns are consistent with the expectation that favorable regions will have a higher incidence of tenancy, given the somewhat inactive land market and greater demand for land. Moreover, the Bangladesh study found that modern variety adoption shifts rental contracts from sharecropping to fixed rents, increasing the proportion of land income accruing to tenants. Land reform in the Philippines, implemented at the time modern varieties were rapidly spreading, distributed the benefits from higher land rental from landowners to former share tenants.

Adjustments in farm size and tenancy markets seem to have helped reduce the potentially inequitable effects of differential technology adoption.

Differential Modern Variety Adoption and Income Distribution

Farmers may adjust to the changing profitability of rice farming across production environments by altering patterns of land use and time allocation. As modern varieties increase the profitability of rice relative to other enterprises in the favorable areas, farmers consequently allocate more land and time to rice production. In contrast, if real rice price declines as a result of technical change, farmers in the unfavorable areas will tend to plant other crops or increase nonfarm employment in accordance with their comparative disadvantage in rice production. Such adjustments will mitigate the potentially inequitable effects of differential modern variety adoption on the income of farm households in the unfavorable areas.

Sources of household income. Table 12.16 presents the contribution of income from rice farming to total income of farm and landless labor households. The share of rice income is generally less than 50%, even in the favorable rainfed areas, implying that income from nonrice and nonfarm sources is generally important, even though the surveys covered typical rice-dependent villages commonly observed in Asia.

The importance of rice production as a source of income tends to be lower in less favorable areas. Depending on the availability of alternative crops and nonfarm employment opportunities, farmers and landless laborers in the unfavorable areas allocate more resources to nonrice activities. Such allocation is generally in accordance with the regional comparative advantage of rice production and nonrice activities.

The extent to which total household income differs across favorable and unfavorable areas is reported in U.S. dollars in Table 12.17. As noted earlier, because survey years vary slightly and because official exchange rates do not necessarily reflect differences in the purchasing power of local currencies, caution must be used in making comparisons across countries.

Average incomes of farm households clearly are much higher in irrigated and favorable rainfed areas than in unfavorable areas. However, in Bangladesh, where farm size across households is small and not widely different, average incomes of farm households with varying degrees of modern variety adoption are largely similar. In Indonesia, Nepal, and China, differences in per capita farm household income between the most favorable and least favorable areas are remarkably small. This finding is not unexpected in China, where access to land is equitably distributed and all rice farms are irrigated. Indeed, hybrid rice adoption in China reduces income inequality directly because it has been adopted most in the less favorable mountainous regions, where average incomes are lower than in the hills or lake-plain regions.

In the other countries, the profitable opportunities for planting other crops and finding employment in the nonfarm sector greatly reduce the income gap across production environments. In Indonesia, this gap reduction is helped by the larger farm size in the upland areas. In Thailand, farmers in deepwater areas are not much worse off than those in irrigated areas because of larger farm size and proximity to Bangkok, where nonfarm employment opportunities are plentiful. However, farmers in the unfavorable rainfed lowland areas in northeast Thailand, where nonfarm employment opportunities are scarce, are at a disadvantage.

It is ironic that the Philippines and India, with stronger land reform programs, have the widest divergence of per capita income across production environments. The nature of production environments, as well as the relatively more remote location of the unfavorable villages sampled in these countries, undoubtedly explains a major part of that difference. However, land reform legislation itself, by prohibiting share tenancy and land sales, contributes to this wide disparity. In the Philippines, this tendency has been exacerbated by the fact that land reform—in terms of converting share tenants to leasehold and amortizing owners—has been successfully implemented in the favorable areas, but a significant proportion of farmers remain as share tenants in the unfavorable areas.

Although not reported here, the regression analysis of the determinants of farm household income by source commonly and consistently found that modern varieties and irrigation strongly increased the land income from rice production but not necessarily labor incomes from rice production and other sources.

Thus, intervillage income differences can be explained largely by differences between favorable and unfavorable areas in returns to land associated with differential technology adoption, as well as by differences in average farm size and tenure patterns. Farmers in less favorable areas, however, earn larger shares of income from nonrice sources, which must mitigate the potentially inequitable effects of the differential technology adoption across production environments.

Landless households are generally poorer than farm households in the same production environment, mainly because of lack of access to land. In fact, in unfavorable rainfed areas of Thailand, Bangladesh, India, and the Philippines, where the return to land is relatively low, the difference in income between farm and landless households is also low. Income disparities across production environments are much lower among landless than among farm households, which is consistent with the findings of wage equalization across production environments through labor migration. Furthermore, it is interesting to observe that per capita income of the landless in the irrigated areas is sometimes even higher than that of farm households in the unfavorable areas. It seems clear that regional productivity differentials associated with differential technology adoption do not significantly widen income inequality among the landless poor across production environments.

As the studies have shown, the poor actively seek better farm employment opportunities through migration from unfavorable to favorable areas. They also actively engage in nonfarm activities, particularly in less favorable rice-production areas. Yet the fact remains that it is primarily landless laborers who suffer most from poverty.

An important finding from the country studies is that schooling is a major determinant of nonfarm income of the poor. Thus, rural poverty is caused not only by lack of access to land but also by lack of human capital on the part of the poor.

Income Distribution. Table 12.18 summarizes the Gini ratios of household income by production environment. It is not surprising that household income is most equally distributed in China, where rural households have generally equal access to land. Household incomes in Nepal, India, and the Philippines are generally more unequal than in Bangladesh, Thailand, and Indonesia. It is important to note that differences in the Gini ratios across production environments are slight and do not follow any clear pattern, which suggests that higher productivity in rice farming does not necessarily result in larger intravillage income inequality.

The overall income inequality across all households in each country is also indicated in Table 12.18. The magnitude of overall Gini ratios is similar to that of the Gini ratios for each village, which implies that differential technology adoption across production environments does not significantly worsen interregional income inequality. Studies in the Philippines (Otsuka, Cordova, and David 1992) and Nepal (Thapa, Otsuka, and Barker 1992) did counterfactual analysis of income distribution, to learn what income distribution would have been if there had been no technological change in rice farming. The estimated counterfactual Gini ratios were largely similar to those based on actual data.

Because differential technology adoption across production environments worsens land income distribution, its contribution to the Gini ratio for all villages is shown for each country. Inequality in land income is most important in India, accounting for nearly half of the Gini ratio. It is least important in Indonesia, where average farm size in the unfavorable areas is nearly four times that in the irrigated areas. It should be noted that not only modern variety adoption but also differences in tenure structure, landlessness, and quality of production environment account for differences in land income. It is also important to note that because of the substantial contribution of income outside rice farming, accounting for 40 to 65% of total household income, relative contribution of the distribution of nonrice income to overall Gini ratio ranges from about 45 to 70%.

We conclude that although modern rice technology has brought about large income gains to landholders in favorable areas, which tends to worsen income distribution, market adjustments through labor migration, allocation of resources away from rice in unfavorable areas, and farm size and tenure changes have mitigated the potentially inequitable distributional consequences.

TRENDS IN INCOME DISTRIBUTION
AND THE OVERALL ECONOMY

Technological change in rice farming reduces rice prices by shifting the supply curve of rice to the right. As has been indicated by the literature dealing with the Green Revolution (Hayami and Herdt 1977; Barker and Herdt 1985), the most significant way by which technological change in agriculture improves income distribution and the well-being of the poor is through the reduction of output prices. Also important, in our view, is the effect of technological change on rural wages and employment opportunities. Because of the cross-sectional nature of the data available for the seven countries, however, analysis of price and wage effects on overall income distribution could not be incorporated into this study. Nonetheless, we attempted to examine trends in real wages and real rice price to obtain broader perspectives on the overall impact of modern rice technology in Asia.

Trends in Real Wages and Gross Domestic Product

Labor is the main resource of the poor. Hence, trends in real rural wages are an important indicator of the welfare of the rural poor. A major factor affecting returns to labor is high population growth rate, averaging 2.5% per annum in recent decades, in South and Southeast Asia. If technology is constant, marginal returns to additional labor input on a constant supply of land lead to declining real wages relative to land rental (Hayami and Kikuchi 1982). Whether or not real wages increase depends on the rate of technical change in agriculture, population growth, and growth in labor demand in nonfarm sectors.

Figure 12.1 depicts trends in real wages in five countries, estimated by using rice price and the consumer price index as deflators. No wage data were available for China and Nepal. Real wages have increased steadily in Thailand and Indonesia, remained largely unchanged in India and the Philippines, and declined in Bangladesh. Such diverse trends in real wages do not seem to be well explained by the varying success of modern rice technology in these countries. A good example is Thailand, where modern varieties have been adopted in limited areas. Judging from our findings that rural labor markets function effectively and that the rural population actively seeks nonfarm employment, it seems reasonable to hypothesize that rural wages are critically determined by growth in the overall economy and population rather than growth in the rice sector.

The patterns of average annual growth rates in gross domestic product (GDP) by major sectors and population for 1965–1988 are shown in Table 12.19. Thailand and Indonesia have the most rapid growth rate in per capita GDP, mainly because of the remarkable performance of the nonagricultural sector. Indonesia also has the highest growth rate in the rice and nonagriculture sectors. It is therefore not surprising that growth rates of farm wages are highest in those countries. In contrast, growth rate of per capita GDP is lowest in Bangladesh, where real farm wage rate has declined.

Despite the relatively rapid growth of the rice and agricultural sectors in the Philippines, growth in farm wages has been low, presumably because of the poor record of the nonagriculture sector and the high growth rate of the population. Real farm wages also have stagnated in India, where per capita GDP has grown slowly.

Thus, it seems clear that growth in farm wages is largely determined by growth in the overall economy. If so, farm wages would have grown significantly in China, which experienced remarkable growth both in the farm and nonfarm sectors, and stagnated in Nepal, whose economy recorded the poorest performance among the seven countries in the study.

Our argument does not imply, however, that the Green Revolution has not significantly affected the welfare of the poor. To the extent that the poor's welfare critically depends on the price of rice, a main staple food for the poor in Asia, it is appropriate to examine the trend of wages deflated by rice prices as an indicator of the poor's well-being. As shown in Figure 12.1, real wages deflated by rice prices have become higher than those deflated by consumer price index since the late 1970s in India, Bangladesh, and the Philippines. Such differences in wage trends are likely to be at least partly the result of technological change in the rice sector, which has reduced prices of rice relative to other commodities.

Trends in Real Rice Price and Income Distribution

Although rice is internationally tradable, government intervention has often insulated domestic rice markets from world price trends to achieve price stability in the domestic rice market. When rice trade is restricted, adoption of modern varieties will reduce domestic rice prices. Although the reduction in rice prices adversely affects real income of farmers unable to adopt modern varieties, it accrues large benefits to rice consumers, including landless agricultural laborers and the urban poor, who spend a greater proportion of their income on rice than the rich. Indeed, recent studies in the Philippines and India indicate that even though modern variety adoption is limited to favorable areas, its impact on overall income distribution is clearly progressive (Quizon and Binswanger 1986; Binswanger and Quizon 1989; Coxhead and Warr 1991).

Differences in trends in the wholesale rice price deflated by the consumer price index (Figure 12.2) indicate the varying nature of government interventions and trade balance in the different countries. It is noteworthy, however, to observe similar declining trends in domestic rice prices since the early 1970s. Without the Green Revolution, such a trend would not have been realized (David 1990).

The greater degree in decline of real rice prices in the Philippines and India, both of which have relatively high adoption rates of modern varieties, has clearly been influenced by the rapid growth in productivity and achievement of rice self-sufficiency in the late 1970s. Real rice price did not drop in Indonesia, despite similar productivity performance, mainly because of government efforts to protect farmers' income against the downward trend in world prices.

In Thailand, where rice is a major export, and Bangladesh, where rice is a major import and where modern variety adoption is relatively low, divergence from the price trends of other countries is mainly a result of trade policy.

Because of unlimited border trade between India and Nepal, which is a net exporter of rice solely to India, the domestic price of rice in Nepal is essentially determined by trends in domestic price in India. Given Nepal's low rate of adoption of modern varieties, the decline in export demand for rice resulting from the success of modern rice technology in India has negatively affected Nepal's real rice price.

Thai farmers could have been penalized by the decline in world rice prices in the 1980s, which was partly caused by the attainment of self-sufficiency in rice by a number of traditionally importing countries. Domestic rice price in Thailand, however, did not decrease to the same extent, because the government phased out the rice export premium tax, which was as high as 30% in the 1950s and 1960s. The tax phase-out was a response to the drop in world rice price and the declining importance of the rice sector as a source of government revenue. Moreover, strong world commodity prices in the 1970s facilitated diversification in Thai agriculture, as the share of rice in agriculture dropped substantially (Siamwalla and Setboonsarng 1991).

The above trends strongly indicate that the widespread adoption of modern varieties in the Asian rice economy has significantly contributed to the generally declining trend of real rice prices. The major beneficiaries of the decreases in real rice prices are the poor, who spend well more than half of their income on food (Lipton and Longhurst 1989). Consistent with such an expectation, a recent collaborative research on poverty organized by the Asian Development Bank found that the incidence of absolute poverty has significantly declined over the last two decades in Thailand, Bangladesh, India, Indonesia, and the Philippines (Krongkaew and Tinakon 1993; Hossain et al. 1993; Dev, Parakh, and Surnaraya 1993; Tjondronegoro, Soejono, and Hardjono 1993; and Balisacan 1993). The proportion of the population below the poverty line has declined more significantly in Thailand and Indonesia, where the economy has grown more rapidly.

SUMMARY AND POLICY IMPLICATIONS

The country studies confirm earlier findings that neither farm size nor tenure significantly affects modern variety adoption. It is limited to irrigated and favorable rainfed environments, and thus the yield gap between favorable and unfavorable rice-growing areas has widened. The country studies also show, however, that when the indirect effects through labor, land, and product market adjustments are accounted for, differential adoption of modern varieties across production environments does not significantly worsen income distribution.

As modern variety adoption increases labor demand in the favorable areas, wage rate as well as employment opportunities in those areas also increase. In the longer run, interregional permanent and seasonal labor migration from unfavorable to favorable rice-growing regions takes place. That migration tends to equalize wages, enabling people in the unfavorable areas, mainly landless workers and marginal farmers, to share the benefits from higher labor income.

The country studies also demonstrate that mechanization, which could equalize wages at a lower level, is not induced by modern variety adoption. Nor is direct seeding generally induced by modern variety adoption.

As far as the income of landless laborers is concerned, therefore, there is no evidence that differential modern variety adoption significantly worsens regional income distribution. It seems fair to conclude that the distribution of increased labor income resulting from modern rice technology is not inequitable.

The adoption of modern rice technology does, however, widen regional differences in returns to land, conferring larger economic gains upon landholders in favorable rice-growing areas, thereby aggravating inequalities in income distribution. The income gap potentially arising from the widening returns to land between favorable and unfavorable areas, however, is significantly mitigated by changing farm size and tenure and by shifts in land use and time allocation to alternative crops and nonfarm employment.

Farm size tends to be larger in unfavorable areas than in irrigated areas, particularly in Indonesia and Thailand. The proportion of household income originating from nonrice crops and nonfarm income is higher in the unfavorable areas than in favorable areas in nearly all countries.

In China, where migration and land market transactions are restricted, changes in family labor and capital allocation across farm and nonfarm enterprises within a small locality are the main adjustment mechanisms to differential rates of hybrid rice adoption. It turns out, however, that adoption of hybrid rice, which is highest in the poorer, mountain regions, in fact directly improves income distribution.

In Bangladesh, many farmers in deepwater areas believed to have been bypassed by modern rice technology actually benefit from modern varieties by growing them as a dry-season crop with pump irrigation (Figure 12.3).

Policy Implications

What policy implications can we draw from this seven-country study? One of the key issues in the Asian rice economy is the allocation of research resources for favorable and unfavorable areas. Rice research has historically focused on favorable environments because of the higher probability of scientific success. The homogeneous nature of the irrigated areas also implies wide adaptability of new technologies, ensuring a high research payoff. National and international rice research institutions, however, have been under pressure to shift research priorities toward the unfavorable rice-production environments as a way to improve income distribution and alleviate poverty. Yet this multicountry study shows that factor- and product-market adjustments largely counteract the potentially adverse effects of differential modern variety adoption across production environments.

It is scientifically much more difficult to develop new varieties for unfavorable production environments. Moreover, unfavorable environments are highly heterogeneous, so that superior varieties, even if successfully developed, can be diffused only in limited areas. Targeting rice research toward unfavorable rice-growing environments, therefore, will not be an efficient means of improving income distribution. Furthermore, the potential gain in production efficiency in the rice economy as a whole is largely sacrificed under such a strategy, and that would have undesirable consequences on the welfare of the poor rice consumers.

In countries (such as those in South Asia) where a large proportion of the rice-growing area is in unfavorable environments, some allocation of rice research in those environments, particularly where few alternative crops can be profitably grown, can be justified. As we pointed out in Chapter 2, both modern variety adoption and rice yield continued to grow in the less favorable regions of South Asia, such as East India, during the 1980s. As a result, the average annual growth rate of rice yield in South Asia accelerated significantly, from 1.4% in the 1970s to 2.9% in the 1980s. There may be further technological potential to exploit through adaptive research for these areas (Rao 1989).

It is necessary to evaluate the relative economic payoff between investments in land development and rice research for the unfavorable environment. As the experience of Bangladesh indicates, the payoff from converting deepwater rice areas for cultivation of irrigated modern varieties may be higher than the payoff from greater research investments for improving deepwater rice. Also relevant is the relative economic payoff for research investments in crops more suitable to unfavorable areas.

In countries where the proportion of favorable rice areas is relatively high, such as the Philippines and Indonesia, rice researchers may well spend their major efforts in further improving the technology for the favorable areas. At the same time, the public sector can invest in research, and in production and marketing infrastructure, to introduce alternative crops in unfavorable areas and reduce the cost of interregional migration. In fact, the cultivation of perennial tree crops instead of rice in ecologically fragile environments such as sloping upland will improve agricultural sustainability.

Growth in rice yields in Southeast Asia has recently tended to level off (David 1991; Hayami and Otsuka 1994). To support agricultural as well as overall economic development in these countries, the maintenance of growth in rice yields through intensified research and irrigation investments is critically important. Otherwise, rice prices will begin to increase, which will adversely affect not only the welfare of the poor but also the pace of overall economic development. Furthermore, high rice prices relative to prices of other crops may deter the diversification of resources to nonrice crops in less favorable environments, which may be counterproductive to the development strategy to raise income of farmers in these environments.

It should be stressed that agricultural research is a highly effective policy instrument for raising productivity but a very blunt one to be used specifically for improving income distribution. Because of the nature of rice as a staple food and because of factor-market adjustments, rice research allocation by production environment based on efficiency goals will generally satisfy equity objectives as well. In short, the trade-off between efficiency and equity in rice research is not sharp.

For the sake of distributional justice consistent with efficiency goals, other, more effective policy instruments should be considered. A good example is investment in human capital, particularly in unfavorable areas. Because human capital improvement, as measured by schooling in the country studies, is generally an important determinant of labor earnings from nonfarm sources, public investment in human capital development should be strengthened. We must clearly recognize that, after all, rice research is merely one of the policy instruments for facilitating agricultural as well as overall economic development.

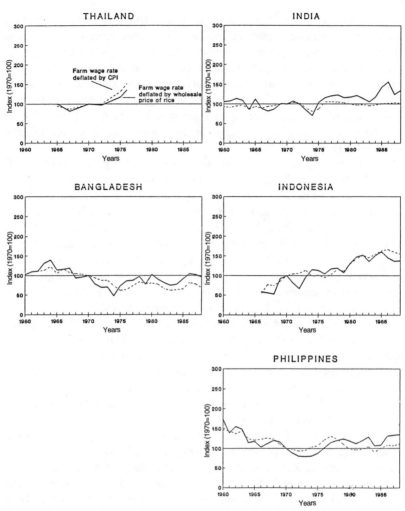

Figure 12.1   Trends in real farm wage rates deflated by rice price and consumer price index (CPI). *Source*: IRRI (1991)

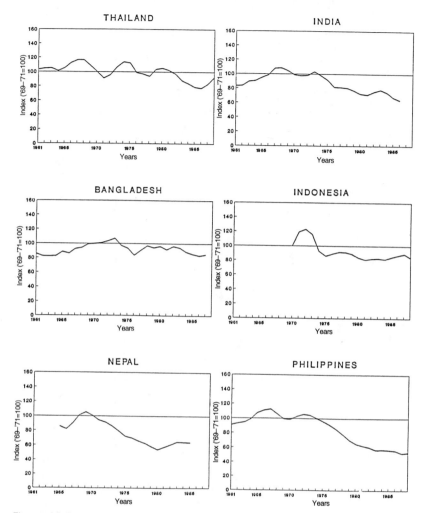

Figure 12.2 Trends in wholesale price of rice deflated by the consumer price index. *Source*: IRRI (1991)

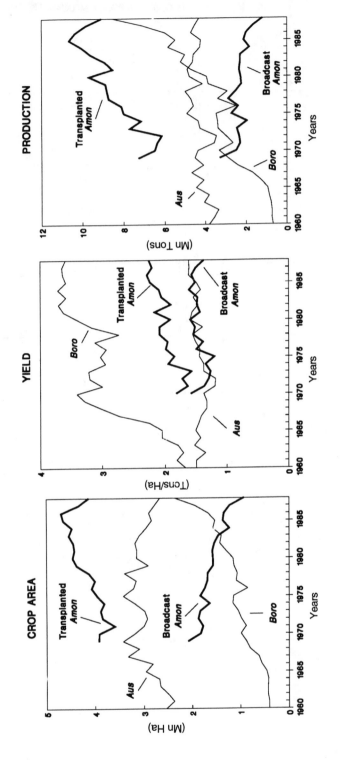

Figure 12.3   Trends in rice production, crop area, and yield, Bangladesh, 1960–1988.
Source : IRRI (1991)

Table 12.1   Patterns of modern variety adoption (% of area) in selected Asian countries by production environment, extensive survey.

	Thailand	Bangladesh	Nepal	India[a]	Indonesia	Philippines	China[b]
Irrigated	30	51	74	100	98	97	79
Favorable rainfed	—	23	—	95	81	99	73
Unfavorable rainfed[c]	6	21	35	69	—	41	99
Deepwater	0	10	—	—	0[d]	—	—
Others	—	15[e]	—	—	0[f]	—	—

a. Refers to Tamil Nadu only. Figure in irrigated environment pertains to canal-irrigated areas, in favorable rainfed environment to tank-well area, and in unfavorable environment to tank area.

b. Refers to adoption of hybrid rice in Hunan province only. Figure in irrigated environment pertains to lake-plain area, in favorable rainfed environment to hills area, and in unfavorable rainfed environment to mountain area.

c. Mainly drought-prone rainfed lowland areas, except in India and China.

d. Swampy area.

e. Saline area.

f. Upland area in Lampung based on intensive survey.

Table 12.2   Summary results of modern variety adoption function in selected Asian countries, extensive survey.[a]

	Thailand	Bangladesh	Nepal	India	Indonesia	Philippines	China
IRGR[b]	0.50**	0.96**	0.79**	0.21*[c]	0.10*	0.47**	—
FSIZE[d]	-0.06*	-0.54**	0	0	0	0	0.77**
TENANCY	0	0	0	0	0	0	—
FPPRICE[d]	0	-0.19**	—	—	0	0	0
SCHOOL[d]	—	0	—	—	—	—	0.57**

a. "0" indicates that the estimated coefficient is not significant, and "—" means not applicable. ** indicates that the coefficient is significant at 1% level; * at 5% level.

b. Numbers indicate an increase in ratio of modern variety adoption area when ratio of irrigated area increases from zero to one.

c. Refers to the impact of changes in quality of irrigation (i.e., proportion of area where irrigation water is available at the time of planting).

d. Numbers indicate change in ratio of modern variety adoption area in response to 100% increase in farm size or schooling of household head or fertilizer paddy price ratio.

Table 12.3   Patterns of paddy yields and total cropping intensity in selected Asian countries by production environment, extensive survey.[a]

	Thailand	Bangladesh	Nepal	India	Indonesia	Philippines	China
Average yield (t/ha)							
Irrigated	3.4	3.6	2.8	5.8	4.3	3.6	5.1
Favorable rainfed	—	2.7	—	5.0	3.5	3.3	5.8
Unfavorable rainfed	2.7	2.2	2.1	3.4	—	2.6	6.0
Deepwater	1.9	3.2	—	—	1.7	—	—
Others	—	2.4	—	—	1.8	—	—
Cropping intensity (%)							
Irrigated	183	170	217	165	181[b]	195	—
Favorable rainfed	—	180	—	136	117[b]	123	—
Unfavorable rainfed	110	163	192	108	—	98	—
Deepwater	132	182	—	—	106[b]	—	—
Others	—	175	—	—	100[b]	—	—

a. See footnotes a to f in Table 12.1 for the environmental classification and other remarks.
b. Refers to rice cropping intensity.

Table 12.4   Summary results of yield functions in selected Asian countries, extensive survey.[a]

	Thailand	Bangladesh	Nepal	India	Indonesia	Philippines	China
MVR	0.39**	0.25**	0.40**	0	0.71**	0.48**	0.17**[b]
IRGR	0.30**	0.21**[c]	0.39*	0.19**	0.26*	0.13*	—
FSIZE	—	-0.07*	0	0	0	0	0.81**
TENANCY	0	-0.20**[d]	0	0	0	-0.30**[e]	—
FPPRICE	—	—	—	—	0	0	—
SCHOOL	—	0	—	—	—	—	0

a. Numbers indicate rate of change in yield, when modern variety adoption, irrigation, or tenancy area ratio increases from zero to one, and an elasticity for the case of farm size (FSIZE). "0" indicates that the estimated coefficient is insignificant and "—" means not applicable. ** indicates that the coefficient is significant at 1% level * at 5% level.
b. Coefficient of hybrid rice adoption dummy.
c. Coefficient of interaction term between modern variety adoption and irrigation ratios, which indicates combined effects of modern varieties and irrigation.
d. Leasehold tenancy area ratio.
e. Share tenancy area ratio.

Table 12.5   Summary results of cropping intensity functions in selected Asian countries, extensive survey.[a]

	Thailand (Total)	Bangladesh (Total)	Nepal (Rice)	India (Total)	Indonesia (Total)	Indonesia (Rice)	Philippines (Total)	Philippines (Rice)
MVR	0	0.30**	0.33**	0	0	0	0	0.34*
IRGR	0.85**	0[b]	0.31**[b]	0.50**	0.67**	0.56**	0.70**	0.79**
FSIZE	0	0	0	0	0	–0.34*	0	0
TENANCY	0	–0.16**	0	0	0	0	0	0
FPPRICE	—	—	0	—	—	0	0	0
SCHOOL	—	0	0	—	—	—	—	—

a. Numbers indicate change in cropping intensity, expressed in ratio, when modern variety adoption, irrigation, or tenancy area ratio increases from zero to one, and when farm size increases by 100%. "0" indicates that the estimated coefficient is insignificant and "—" means not applicable. ** indicates that the coefficient is significant at 1% level; * at 5% level.
b. Coefficient of interaction term between modern variety adoption and irrigation ratios, which indicates combined effects of modern varieties and irrigation.

Table 12.6   Patterns of labor use and proportion of hired labor in selected Asian countries by production environment, intensive survey.[a]

	Thailand	Bangladesh	Nepal	India	Indonesia	Philippines	China
Labor use (man-days/ha)							
Irrigated	64	243	144	195	156	82	209
Favorable rainfed	—	209	—	229	174	71	245
Unfavorable rainfed	62	239	132	176	—	91	375
Deepwater	37	226	—	—	—	—	—
Others	—	209	—	—	70	—	—
Hired labor (%)							
Irrigated	41	35	69	92	60	73	—
Favorable rainfed	—	35	—	60	52	59	—
Unfavorable rainfed	15	32	57	60	—	37	—
Deepwater	50	37	—	—	—	—	—
Others	—	36	—	—	49	—	—

a. See footnotes a to f in Table 12.1 for environmental classification and other remarks.

Table 12.7   Adoption rate of labor-saving technologies (% of area) by production environment in selected Asian countries, extensive survey.[a]

	Thailand	Nepal	India	Indonesia	Philippines
Tractors					
Irrigated	90	15	77	27	76
Favorable rainfed	—	—	12	2	56
Unfavorable rainfed	62	15	27	—	42
Deepwater	100	—	—	0	—
Others	—	—	—	0	—
Threshers					
Irrigated	65	0	38	12	94
Favorable rainfed	—	—	77	32	95
Unfavorable rainfed	35	0	9	—	72
Deepwater	100	—	—	0	—
Others	—	—	—	0	—
Direct seeding					
Irrigated	34	0	4	0	33
Favorable rainfed	—	—	0	0	51
Unfavorable rainfed	29	0	63	—	20
Deepwater	100	—	—	0	—
Others	—	—	—	100	—

a. See footnotes a to f in Table 12.1 for environmental classification and other remarks.

Table 12.8   Summary results of tractor adoption functions in selected Asian countries, extensive survey.[a]

	Thailand	India	Philippines
MVR[b]	0	0	0
IRGR[b]	0.87**	0.13*	0.57*
FSIZE[c]	0	0	0.49**
TENANCY	0	0	0
DIST[c]	0	0	–0.25**

a. "0" indicates that the estimated coefficient is insignificant and "-" means not applicable. ** indicates that the coefficient is significant at 1% level; * at 5% level.
b. Numbers indicate an increase in ratio of tractor adoption when ratio of modern variety adoption or irrigated area increases from zero to one.
c. Numbers indicate change in ratio of tractor adoption in response to 100% increase in farm size or distance from the major city (DIST).

Table 12.9 Population growth, man-land ratio, and proportion of land-less households by production environment in selected Asian countries, extensive survey.[a]

	Thailand	Bangladesh	Nepal	India	Indonesia	Philippines
Population growth (%)				(1971–1981)	(1980–1987)	(1970–(1986)
Irrigated	—	—	—	2.3	1.7	2.5
Favorable rainfed	—	—	—	2.1	1.4	1.9
Unfavorable rainfed	—	—	—	1.4	—	1.5
Deepwater	—	—	—	—	0.8	—
Others	—	—	—	—	—	—
Man-land ratio[b]						
Irrigated	4.4	—	—	14.4	14.6	6.3
Favorable rainfed	—	—	—	10.8	5.8	5.1
Unfavorable rainfed	2.6	—	—	5.3	—	4.7
Deepwater	1.7	—	—	—	1.6	—
Others	—	—	—	—	—	—
Landless ratio (%)						
Irrigated	12	37	30[c]	27	26	31
Favorable rainfed	—	42	19[c]	12	11	18
Unfavorable rainfed	7	36	—	32	—	15
Deepwater	9	36	—	—	8	—
Others	—	27	—	—	—	—

a. See footnotes a to f in Table 12.1 for environmental classification and other remarks.
b. Ratio of village population to cultivated area.
c. Pertains to *tarai* region. In the hills, ratio of agricultural landless ratio is 5% in the irrigated villages and 2% in favorable rainfed villages.

Table 12.10 Patterns of transplanting and harvesting wage (US$/day) in selected Asian countries by production environment, extensive survey.[a]

	Thailand	Bangladesh	Nepal	India	Indonesia	Philippines
Transplanting wage						
Irrigated	1.44	1.20	1.01[b]	0.96[b]	1.11	1.18
Favorable rainfed	—	0.97	—	0.85[b]	0.73	1.34
Unfavorable rainfed	1.31	1.07	1.05[b]	0.77[b]	—	1.56
Deepwater	—	—	—	—	1.52[c]	—
Others	—	—	—	—	—	—
Harvesting wage						
Irrigated	2.14[c]	1.16	0.92[b]	1.31	1.73[c]	2.90[c]
Favorable rainfed	—	0.94	—	1.16	1.82[c]	3.06[c]
Unfavorable rainfed	1.87	1.07	1.05[b]	1.23	—	2.69[c]
Deepwater	2.14[c]	—	—	—	2.28[c]	—
Others	—	—	—	—	—	—

a. See footnotes a to f in Table 12.1 for environmental classification and other remarks, except for Bangladesh. Classification for Bangladesh is based on the rate of modern variety adoption (i.e., high-adopter, medium-adopter, and low-adopter villages). Except as otherwise indicated, wage refers to daily wage contract of casual labor.
b. Refers to female wage.
c. Refers to imputed wage based on piece-rate or output-sharing contract.

Table 12.11 Summary results of transplanting wage functions in selected Asian countries, extensive survey.[a]

	Thailand	Bangladesh	Nepal	India	Indonesia	Philippines
MVR[b]	0	0.38**	—	0	0	0
IRGR[b]	0.07**	0	0	0	0	–0.34**
FSIZE[c]	0	0.28*[f]	0	0	—	0
TENANCY[b]	0	—	0.37*[d]	0.006**[e]	—	—
FPPRICE[c]	—	—	—	—	0	—
DISTM[c]	-0.06**	—	-0.04**	0	0.17**	0

a. "0" indicates that the estimated coefficient is insignificant and "—" means not applicable. ** indicates that the coefficient is significant at 1% level; * at 5% level.
b. Numbers indicate rate of change in wage rate when modern variety adoption, irrigation, or tenancy area ratio increases from zero to one, except in Bangladesh, where IRGR refers to the combined effect of irrigation and modern varieties captured by interaction term between irrigation and modern variety adoption ratios.
c. Numbers show elasticity with respect to changes in farm size, fertilizer-paddy price ratio, and distance to the market town.
d. Owner-area ratio.
e. Share tenancy ratio.
f. Refers to the effect of land-man ratio.

Table 12.12 Summary results of harvesting wage functions in selected Asian countries, extensive survey.[a]

	Thailand	Bangladesh	Nepal	India	Indonesia	Philippines
MVR[b]	0	0	—	0	0	0
IRGR[b]	0.07**	–0.23*	0	0	0	0
FSIZE[c]	0	0.24*[d]	0	0.03*	—	0
TENANCY[b]	0	—	0	0	—	—
FPPRICE[c]	—	—	—	—	0	—
DISTM[c]	–0.04*	0.22**	–0.02*	0	0	–0.15*

a. "0" indicates that the estimated coefficient is insignificant and "—" means not applicable. ** indicates that the coefficient is significant at 1% level; * at 5% level.
b. Numbers indicate rate of change in wage rate when modern variety adoption, irrigation, or tenancy area ratio increases from zero to one, except in Bangladesh, where IRGR refers to the combined effect of irrigation and modern varieties captured by interaction term between irrigation and modern variety adoption ratios.
c. Numbers show elasticity with respect to changes in farm size, fertilizer-paddy price ratio, and distance to the market town.
d. Refers to the effect of land-man ratio.

Table 12.13 Factor shares of land and labor in rice cultivation in selected Asian countries by production environment, intensive survey.[a]

	Thailand (thou B)	Bangladesh[b] (thou Tk)	Nepal (thou Rs)	India (thou Rs)	Indonesia (thou Rp)	Philippines (thou P)
Land						
Irrigated	46 (5.8)	43 (11.2)	56 (5.4)	51(5.6)	36 (285)	33 (4.2)
Favorable rainfed	—	—	—	40 (2.9)	36 (212)	40 (3.9)
Unfavorable rainfed	34 (1.6)	47 (6.3)	51 (3.6)	33 (2.0)	—	19 (1.0)
Deepwater	43 (3.2)	—	—	—	—	—
Others	—	—	—	—	28 (90)	—
Labor						
Irrigated	28 (3.2)	22 (5.8)	28 (2.7)	25 (2.5)	39 (310)	28 (3.4)
Favorable rainfed	—	—	—	27 (2.0)	40 (246)	26 (2.6)
Unfavorable rainfed	43 (2.1)	31 (4.2)	34 (2.4)	37 (2.2)	—	46 (2.5)
Deepwater	27 (2.0)	—	—	—	—	—
Others	—	—	—	—	38 (121)	—

a. Figures without parentheses show percentage shares, whereas figures with parentheses show absolute values of factor income per hectare in domestic currency. See appendix for currency exchange rates. See footnotes in Table 12.1 for environmental classification and other remarks.

b. Irrigated row refers to factor shares of modern varieties (weighted average of *boro*, *aus*, and *amon* crops); unfavorable rainfed row to factor share of traditional varieties (weighted average of *aus*, broadcast *amon*, and transplanted *amon* crops).

Table 12.14 Summary results of land rent and land price functions in selected Asian countries.[a]

	Land rent		Land price	
	Thailand	Indonesia	Indonesia	Innonesia (Lampung)
MVR[b]	0.32*	0	0	0.42**
MVR*IRGR[b]	—	—	—	0.67**
IRGR[b]	0.51**	0.46**	0.69**	0.39*
FSIZE[c]	0	—	—	—
FPPRICE[c]	0	0	-0.03**	-1.002**
TENANCY[b]	0	—	—	—
MLR[c]	—	0	0	0.14*
DISTC[c]	-0.08*	0	0	0

a. "0" indicates that the estimated coefficient is insignificant and "—" means not applicable. ** indicates that the coefficient is significant at 1% level; * at 5% level.
b. Numbers indicate rate of change in land rent or land price when modern variety adoption ratio, irrigation ratio, interaction term between modern variety adoption and irrigation ratios (MVR*IRGR), or tenancy area ratio increases from zero to one.
c. Numbers show elasticity with respect to changes in farm size, fertilizer-paddy price ratio, man-land ratio, and distance to market.

Table 12.15 Patterns of farm size and tenure by production environment in selected Asian countries, extensive survey.[a]

	Thailand	Bangladesh	Nepal	India	Indonesia	Philippines	China
Farm size (ha)							
Irrigated	2.2	0.6	1.5	1.3	0.5	1.7	0.6
Favorable rainfed	—	0.6	—	0.8	0.5	1.7	0.3
Unfavorable rainfed	3.4	0.7	1.4	1.6	—	1.6	0.4
Deepwater	5.3	0.6	—	—	2.4	—	—
Others	—	0.8	—	—	1.9	—	—
Tenure							
(% of owner)							
Irrigated	69	—	70	74	77	22	100
Favorable rainfed	—	—	—	88	86	19	100
Unfavorable rainfed	70	—	80	85	—	43	100
Deepwater	49	—	—	—	74	—	—
Others	—	—	—	—	98	—	—

a. See footnotes a to f in Table 12.1 for environmental classification and other remarks.

Table 12.16 Contribution of rice income to total income by production environment in selected Asian countries (%), intensive survey.[a]

| | | Bangladesh[b] | | | | Indonesia | | |
	Thailand	(1)	(2)	Nepal	India	(Lampung)	Philippines	China
Farm household								
Irrigated	53	49	52	45	69	51	53	52
Favorable rainfed	—	41	39	—	38	36	44	39
Unfavorable rainfed	38	36	36	39	38	—	14	32
Deepwater	52	—	36	—	—	—	—	—
Others	—	—	47	—	—	24	—	—
Landless household								
Irrigated	76	—	—	48	91	—	30	—
Favorable rainfed	—	—	—	—	86	—	28	—
Unfavorable rainfed	45	—	—	29	76	—	52	—
Deepwater	28	—	—	—	—	—	—	—
Others	—	—	—	—	—	—	—	—

a. See footnotes a to f in Table 12.1 for environmental classification and other remarks.

b. Classification in column (1) is based on the rate of modern variety adoption (i.e., high-adopter, medium-adopter, and low-adopter villages), whereas the classification in column (2) is the same as in Table 12.1.

Table 12.17 Annual income per capita (US$) of farm and landless households by production environment in selected Asian countries, intensive survey.[a]

	Thailand	Bangladesh[b] (1)	Bangladesh[b] (2)	Nepal	India	Indonesia (Lampung)	Philippines	China
Farm households								
Irrigated	437	146	163	174	266	150	258	197
Favorable rainfed	—	137	135	—	262	119	201	216
Unfavorable rainfed	198	145	121	149	131	—	86	163
Deepwater	373	—	145	—	—	—	—	—
Others	—	—	154	—	—	116	—	—
Landless households								
Irrigated	245	—	114	64	120	—	126	—
Favorable rainfed	—	—	115	—	92	—	121	—
Unfavorable rainfed	115	—	96	54	100	—	75	—
Deepwater	120	—	138	—	—	—	—	—
Others	—	—	154	—	—	—	—	—

a. See footnotes a to f in Table 12.1 for environmental classification and other remarks.

b. Classification in column (1) is based on the rate of modern variety adoption (i.e., high-adopter, medium-adopter, and low-adopter villages), whereas the classification in column (2) is the same as in Table 12.1.

Table 12.18 Gini ratio of representative villages by production environment in selected Asian countries, intensive survey.[a]

	Thailand	Bangladesh[b] (1)	(2)	Nepal	India	Indonesia (Lampung)	Philippines	China
Irrigated	0.28	0.34	0.36	0.46	0.40	0.35	0.44	0.21
Favorable rainfed	—	0.36	0.36	—	0.56	0.36	0.40	0.23
Unfavorable rainfed	0.34	0.34	0.30	0.48	0.34	—	0.39	0.25
Deepwater	0.41	—	0.36	—	—	—	—	—
Others	—	—	0.39	—	—	0.38	—	—
All	0.40	—	0.36	0.48	0.46	0.37	0.44	0.23
(% of land income)[c]	(35)	—	(na)	(33)	(50)	(16)	(39)	(na)

a. See footnotes a to f in Table 12.1 for environmental classification and other remarks.
b. Classification in column (1) is based on the rate of modern variety adoption (i.e., high-adopter, medium-adopter, and low-adopter villages), whereas the classification in column (2) is the same as in Table 12.1.
c. Refers to percentage contribution of land income distribution to overall Gini ratio.

Table 12.19 Annual growth rate (%) of gross domestic product (GDP) and population, 1965–1988. Sources: United Nations 1990, *1990 Revision World Population Prospects;* Asian Development Bank 1973–1990, *Key Indicators of Developing Member Countries of ADB* (various issues).

	Thailand	Bangladesh	Nepal	India	Indonesia	Philippines	China
GDP							
Total	7.1	3.6	2.5	4.6	6.8	4.4	8.5
Agriculture	3.3	1.3	1.5	2.5	2.7	3.5	8.1
(rice)	(2.5)	(2.0)	(1.2)	(2.8)	(4.9)	(3.6)	(3.1)
Non-agriculture	8.3	5.9	4.2	5.9	8.8	4.7	8.8
Population	2.5	2.5	2.6	2.2	2.2	2.7	1.7
GDP/capita	4.3	0.9	0.4	2.0	4.6	1.7	5.5

Appendix

Exchange rates, selected Asian countries.

Country	Year	Currency	Exchange rate to US $
Bangladesh	1987	Taka	30.95
China	1988	Yuan	3.72
India	1987	Rupees	12.96
Indonesia	1987	Rupiah	1,643.8
Nepal	1987	Rupees	21.82
Philippines	1985	Peso	18.61
Thailand	1987	Baht	25.72

References

Ahluwalia, Montek S. D. 1978. Rural poverty and agricultural performance in India. *Journal of Development Studies* 14(3): 298–323.

Ahmed, Q. K., and M. Hossain. 1984. *Rural poverty alleviation in Bangladesh: experiences and policies.* World Conference on Agrarian Reform and Rural Development follow-up study series. Rome: Food and Agriculture Organization.

Alston, J. M. 1986. An analysis of growth of U.S. farmland prices, 1963–82. *American Journal of Agricultural Economics* 68(1): 1–18.

Anden-Lacsina, T., and R. Barker. 1978. The adoption of modern varieties. In *Interpretive analysis of selected papers from changes in rice farming in selected areas of Asia.* Los Baños: International Rice Research Institute.

Anderson, D., and M. Leiserson. 1980. Rural non-farm employment in developing countries. *Economic Development and Cultural Change* 28(2): 227–248.

Anitawati, M. T., and C. A. Rasahan. 1986. Analisa pendapatan migran dan faktor-faktor yang mempengaruhi peluang bermigras (Income analysis of migrants and factors affecting the probability to migrate). *Forum Agro Ekonomi* 4(2): 17–23.

Asaduzzaman, M. 1979. Adoption of HYV rice in Bangladesh. *Bangladesh Development Studies* 7(3): 23–29.

Asian Development Bank. 1973–1990. Key indicators of Developing Member Countries of ADB. Manila, Philippines.

Bagchi, A. 1982. *The political economy of under-development.* Modern Cambridge Economics Series. Cambridge: Cambridge University Press.

Balisacan, A. M. 1993. Rural poverty in the Philippines: incidence, issues, and policies. In *Rural Poverty in Asia*, edited by M. G. Quibria and T. N. Srinivasan. Oxford: Oxford University Press.

Bangladesh, Bureau of Statistics. 1986. *The Bangladesh Census of Agriculture and Livestock:* 1983–84, Vols. 1 and 4, Dhaka.

Bangladesh, *Statistical Yearbook 1991.* Dhaka.

―――. 1988. *Report of the household expenditure survey 1985–86.* Dhaka.

Bangladesh, Ministry of Irrigation. 1986. *The National Water Plan*, Vol. 1. Dhaka.

Bardhan, P. K. 1974. Inequality of farm income: a study of four districts. *Economic and Political Weekly* 9(6–8): 301–307.

―――. 1979. Wages and unemployment in poor agrarian economy: a theoretical and empirical analysis. *Journal of Political Economy* 87(3): 479–500.

Barker, R., and V. Cordova. 1978. Labor utilization in rice production. In

453

Economic consequences of the new rice technology. Los Baños: International Rice Research Institute.

Barker, R., and R. W. Herdt. 1985. *The rice economy of Asia.* Washington, DC: Resources for the Future.

Barlow, C., S. Jayasuriya, and E. C. Price. 1983. *Evaluating technology for new farming systems: case studies from Philippine rice farms.* Los Baños: International Rice Research Institute.

Bartsch, W. H. 1977. *Employment and technology choice in Asian agriculture.* New York: Praeger Publishers.

Bautista, E. D. 1988. Rural labor market adjustment to differential technical change. Ph.D. dissertation, University of the Philippines, Quezon City.

Bell, C., P. Hazell, and R. Slade. 1982. *Project evaluation in regional perspective.* Baltimore and London: Johns Hopkins University Press.

Bernsten, R. H., B. H. Siwi, and H. M. Beachell. 1982. The development and diffusion of rice varieties in Indonesia. IRRI Research Paper Series, No. 71. Los Baños: International Rice Research Institute.

Berry, A. R., and W. R. Cline. 1979. *Agrarian structure and productivity in developing countries.* Baltimore: Johns Hopkins University Press.

Bhaduri, A. 1973. A study of agricultural backwardness under semi-feudalism. *Economic Journal* 83(329): 120–137.

Bhalla, S. S. 1976. New relations of production in Haryana agriculture. *Economic and Political Weekly* 11(13): 23–30.

_____. 1979. Farm structure and technical changes in Indian agriculture. In *Agrarian structure and productivity in developing countries,* edited by R. Berry and W. R. Cline. Baltimore: Johns Hopkins University Press.

Bhalla, S. S., and P. Roy. 1988. Mis-specification in farm productivity analysis: the role of land quality. *Oxford Economic Papers* 40(1): 55–73.

Binswanger, H. P. 1974. The measurement of technical change biases with many factors of production. *American Economic Review* 64(6): 964–976.

_____. 1978. *The economics of tractors in South Asia.* New York: Agricultural Development Council.

_____. 1980. Income distribution effects of technical change: some analytical issues. *Southeast Asian Economic Review* 1(3): 179–218.

Binswanger, H. P., Y. Mundlak, M. Yong, and A. Bovers. 1986. On the determinants of cross-country aggregate supply. Report No. ARU56, Washington, DC: World Bank.

Binswanger, H. P., and J. B. Quizon. 1989. What can agriculture do for the poorest rural group? In *The balance between industry and agriculture in economic development, Vol. 4, Social effects,* edited by I. Adelman and S. Lane. Basingstoke, Hampshire, UK: Macmillan Press Ltd.

Binswanger, H. P., and M. R. Rosenzweig. 1984. Contractual arrangements, employments, and wages in rural labor markets: a critical review. In *Contractual arrangements, employment and wages in rural labor markets in Asia,* edited by H. Binswanger and M. Rosenzweig. New Haven: Yale University Press.

_____. 1986. Behavioral and material determinants of production relations in agriculture. *Journal of Development Studies* 22(3): 503–539.

Binswanger, H. P., and V. W. Ruttan. 1978. *Induced innovation: technology, institutions and development.* Baltimore: Johns Hopkins University Press.

Bliss, C. K., and N. H. Stern. 1982. *Palanpur: The Economy of an Indian Village.* Oxford: Clarendon Press.

Boserup, E. 1965. *The conditions of agricultural growth: the economics of agrarian change under population pressure.* London: George Allen and Unwin Ltd.

Braverman, A., and J. E. Stiglitz. 1986. Landlords, tenants and technological innovations. *Journal of Development Economics* 23(2): 313–332.

Burt, O. R. 1986. Econometric modelling of the capitalization formula for farmland price. *American Journal of Agricultural Economics* 68(1): 10–26.

Castle, E. N., and I. Hoch. 1982. Farm real estate price components, 1920–78. *American Journal of Agricultural Economics* 64(1): 8–18.

Chandler, R. E., Jr. 1982. *An adventure in applied science: a history of the International Rice Research Institute.* Los Baños: International Rice Research Institute.

Chattopadhyay, A. 1986. The new rice technology in West Bengal. *Indian Journal of Agricultural Economics* 41(4): 471–478.

Chayanov, A. V. 1966. *The theory of peasant economy,* edited by Daniel Thorner. Home Wood, IL: Richard D. Irwin.

China, Ministry of Agriculture, Planning Bureau. 1989. *Zhongguo Nongcun Jinggi Tongji Daquan, 1949–1986* (Report of rural economic statistics in China). Beijing: Agricultural Press.

China, Hunan Statistical Bureau. 1989. *Hunan statistical yearbook.* Beijing.

Chinn, D. L. 1979. Rural poverty and the structure of farm household income in developing countries: evidence from Taiwan. *Economic Development and Cultural Change* 27(2): 283–301.

Chinnappa, B. N. 1977. Adoption of the new technology in North Arcot district. In *Green Revolution: technology and change in rice growing areas of Tamil Nadu and Sri Lanka,* edited by B. H. Farmer. London: MacMillan.

Cleaver, Harry M. 1972. The contributions of the Green Revolution. *American Economic Review* 72(May): 177–188.

Collier, W. L. 1978. Declining labor absorption (1978–1980) in Javanese rice production. Paper presented at the Agricultural Economic Society of South East Asia's Third Biennial Meeting, November 27–29, Kuala Lumpur, Malaysia.

Collier, W. L., G. Wiradi, and Soentoro. 1973. Recent changes in rice harvesting method. *Bulletin of Indonesian Economic Studies* 9(2): 36–45.

Collier, W. L., Soentoro, G. Wiradi, and Makali. 1974. Agricultural technology and institutional change in Java. *Food Research Institute Studies* 13(2): 169–184.

Collier, W. L., G. Wiradi, Soentoro, Makali, K. Santoso. 1988. A preliminary study of employment trends in lowland Javanese village. Research report submitted to the United States Agency for International Development.

Connel, J. Biplap, R. L. Dasgupta, and M. Lipton. 1976. *Migration from rural areas: the evidences from villages studies.* Delhi: Oxford University Press.

Cordova, V. 1987. Rice technology, productivity and economic return between favorable and unfavorable villages in the Philippines. Paper presented at the First Differential Impact Study Workshop, March, International Rice Research Institute, Los Baños, Philippines.

Coxhead, I. A. 1984. The economics of wet seeding: inducements to and consequences of some recent changes in Philippine rice cultivation. M.A. thesis, Australian National University.

Coxhead, I. A., and P. Warr. 1991. Technical change, land quality, and income distribution: a general equilibrium analysis. *American Journal of Agricultural Economics* 73(2): 345–360.

Cruz, C., I. Z. Feranil, and C. L. Goce. 1986. Population pressure and migration: implications for upland development in the Philippines. CPDS Working Paper 86–06, University of the Philippines at Los Baños.

Dahal, D. R., N. K. Raj, and A. E. Manzando. 1977. Land and migration in Far-western Nepal. Kathmandu: Tribhuvan University, mimeo.

David, C. C. 1976. Fertilizer demand in the Asian rice economy. *Food Research Institute Studies* 5(1): 109–124.

_____. 1990. The political economy of rice price protection, Division of Social Sciences paper 90–22. Los Baños: International Rice Research Institute.

_____. 1991. The World Rice Economy: Challenges Ahead. In *Rice Biotechnology*, edited by Gurdev S. Khush and Gary H. Toenniessen. CAB International in association with the International Rice Research Institute.

David, C. C., and K. Otsuka. 1990. The modern seed-fertiliser technology and adoption of labour-saving technologies: the Philippine case. *Australian Journal of Agricultural Economics* 34(2): 132–146.

Day, R. H., and I. Singh. 1977. *Economic development as an adaptive process: the Green Revolution in Indian Punjab*. Cambridge: Cambridge University Press.

Deaton, A. 1988. Quality, quantity, and spatial variation of prices. *American Economic Review* 78(3): 418–430.

De Datta, S. K. 1980. Weed control in rice in South and Southeast Asia. Food and Fertilizer Technology Centre Extension Bulletin 156. Taipei, Taiwan.

Dev, S. M., K. S. Parakh, and M. H. Surnaraya. 1993. Rural poverty in India: incidence, issues and policies. In *Rural Poverty in Asia*, edited by M. G. Quibria and T. N. Srinivasan. Oxford: Oxford University Press.

Dhanagare, D. N. 1987. Green Revolution and social inequalities in rural India. *Economic and Political Weekly* 22(1a): 137–144.

Dhar, S. 1984. Interstate and within-state migration in India. In *Contractual arrangements, employment, and wages in rural labor market in Asia*, edited by H. Binswanger and M. Rosenzweig. New Haven: Yale University Press.

Duff, J. B. 1978. Mechanization and use of modern rice varieties. In *Economic Consequences of the New Rice Technology*. Los Baños: International Rice Research Institute.

Evenson, R. E. 1975. Gains and losses from agricultural technology. *Philippine Economic Journal* 14(3): 363–379.

Falcon, W. P. 1970. The Green Revolution: generations of problems. *American Journal of Agricultural Economics* 52(5): 698–710.

Farmer, B. H., ed. 1977. *Green Revolution: technology and change in rice growing areas of Tamil Nadu and Sri Lanka*. London: Macmillan.

Feder, G., R. E. Just, and D. Zilberman. 1985. Adoption of agricultural innovations in developing countries: a survey. *Economic Development and Cultural Change* 33(2): 255–298.

Fei, J.C.H., G. Ranis, and S.W.Y. Kuo. 1978. Growth and family distribution of income by factor components. *Quarterly Journal of Economics* 92(1): 17–53.

Fertilizer Association of India. 1985. *Fertilizer statistics*. New Delhi.

Fertilizer Association of India. 1986. *Fertilizer statistics*. New Delhi.

Flinn, J., B. B. Karki, T. Rawal, P. Masicat, and K. Kalirajan. 1980. Rice production in the tarai of Kosi Zone, Nepal. IRRI Research Paper Series No. 65. Los Baños: International Rice Research Institute.

Floyd, J. 1965. The effects of farm price supports on the returns to land and labor in agriculture. *Journal of Political Economy* 73(1): 148–158.

Frankel, F. R. 1971. *India's Green Revolution: economic gains and political costs*. Princeton: Princeton University Press.

Fuller, W., and G. Battese. 1974. Estimation of linear models with crossed-error structure. *Journal of Econometrics* 2(1): 67–78.

Garrity, D., L. R. Oldeman, R. A. Morris, and D. Lenke. 1986. Rainfed lowland rice ecosystems: characterization and distribution. In *Progress in Rainfed Lowland Rice*. Los Baños: International Rice Research Institute.

Gibbs, A. 1974. Agricultural modernization, non-farm employment and low-level urbanization: a case study of a Central Luzon sub-region. Ph.D. dissertation, University of Michigan.

Goldman, R. H., and L. Squire. 1982. Technical change, labor use, and income distribution in the Muda Irrigation Project. *Economic Development and Cultural Change* 30(4): 753–775.

Griffin, K. 1974. *The political economy of agrarian change: an essay on the Green Revolution.* Cambridge: Harvard University Press.

Griliches, Z. 1957. Hybrid corn: an exploration in the economics of technical change. *Econometrica* 25(4): 501–522.

Hart, G., and D. Sisler. 1978. Aspects of rural labor market operation: A Javanese case study. *American Journal of Agricultural Economics* 60(5): 821–826.

Hayami, Y., and R. W. Herdt. 1977. Market price effects of technological change on income distribution in semisubsistence agriculture. *American Journal of Agricultural Economics* 59(2): 245–256.

Hayami, Y., and M. Kikuchi. 1978. Investment inducements to public infrastracture: irrigation in the Philippines. *Review of Economics and Statistics* 60(1): 70–77.

_____. 1982. *Asian village economy at the crossroads.* Tokyo: University of Tokyo Press, and Baltimore: Johns Hopkins University Press.

Hayami, Y., M. A. Quisumbing, and L. Adriano. 1990. *Towards an alternative land reform paradigm: a Philippine perspective.* Quezon City, Philippines: Ateneo de Manila University Press.

Hayami, Y., and K. Otsuka. 1994. Beyond the green revolution: agricultural development strategy into the new century. In *Agricultural technology: policy issues for the international community,* edited by J. Anderson. CAB International.

_____. 1993. *The economics of contract choice: an agrarian perspective.* Oxford: Clarendon Press.

Hayami, Y., and V. W. Ruttan. 1985. *Agricultural development: an international perspective.* Baltimore: Johns Hopkins University Press.

Hazell, P. B., and A. Roell. 1983. Rural growth linkage: household expenditure patterns in Malaysia and Nigeria. IFPRI Research Report No. 41. Washington, DC: International Food Policy Research Institute.

Hazell, P. B., and C. Ramasamy. 1991. *Green Revolution reconsidered: The impact of high yielding rice varieties in South India.* Baltimore and London: Johns Hopkins University Press.

He, Guiting, A. Te, Zhu Xigang, S. L. Travers, Lai Xiugang, and R. W. Herdt. 1984. The economics of hybrid rice production in China. IRRI Research Paper Series No. 101. Los Baños: International Rice Research Institute.

He, Guiting, Zhu Xigang, and J. C. Flinn. 1987. A comparative study of economic efficiency of hybrid and conventional rice production in Jiangsu Province, China. *Oryza* 24(4): 285–296.

Herdt, R. W. 1978. Costs and returns for rice production. In *Economic consequences of the new rice technology.* Los Baños: International Rice Research Institute.

_____. 1987. A retrospective view of technological and other changes in Philippine rice farming, 1965–1982. *Economic Development and Cultural Change* 35(2): 329–349.

Herdt, Robert W., and W. W. Cochrane. 1966. Farm land prices and farm technological advance. *Journal of Farm Economics* 48(2): 243–263.

Heytens, P. 1991a. Policy alternatives for future rice production growth. In *Rice policy in Indonesia*, edited by S. Pearson, W. Falcon, P. Heytens, E. Monke, and R. Naylor. Ithaca: Cornell University Press.

_____. 1991b. Rice production systems. In *Rice policy in Indonesia*, edited by S. Pearson, W. Falcon, P. Heytens, E. Monke, and R. Naylor. Ithaca: Cornell University Press.

_____. 1991c. Technical change in wetland rice agriculture. In *Rice policy in Indonesia*, edited by S. Pearson, W. Falcon, P. Heytens, E. Monke, and R. Naylor. Ithaca: Cornell University Press.

Hossain, M. 1977. Farm size, tenancy and land productivity: an analysis of farm level data in Bangladesh agriculture. *Bangladesh Development Studies* 5(3): 285–348.

_____. 1988. Nature and impact of Green Revolution in Bangladesh, IFPRI and BIDS Research Report No. 67. Washington, DC: International Food Policy Research Institute, and Dhaka: Bangladesh Institute of Development Studies.

_____. 1990. Returns from education in rural Bangladesh. In *Trade, planning and rural development: essays in honor of Nurul Islam*, edited by A. R. Khan and R. Sobhan. London: Macmillan.

Hossain, M., R. Mannar, H. Z. Rahman, and B. Sen. 1993. Priority issues in rural poverty alleviation in Bangladesh. In *Rural Poverty in Asia*, edited by M. G. Quibria and T. N. Srinivasan. Oxford: Oxford University Press.

Ihalauw, J., and W. Utami. 1975. Indonesia: Klaten, Central Java. In *Changes in rice farming in selected areas of Asia*. Los Baños: International Rice Research Institute.

Imperial, E. M. 1980. Chemical weed control in direct seeded rice (*Oryza sativa* L.) grown under puddled conditions. *Philippine Journal of Weed Science* 7(1): 70–75.

India, Ministry of Agriculture. 1988. *Indian agriculture in brief, 22d edition*. New Delhi.

Indonesia, Central Bureau of Statistics. 1989. *Luas penggunaan tanah di Jawa dan di luar Jawa* (Land utilization in Java and in other islands of Indonesia), Jakarta.

Indonesia, *Statistical yearbook* 1975. Jakarta.

Indonesia, *Statistical yearbook* 1983. Jakarta.

Indonesia, *Statistical yearbook* 1989. Jakarta.

International Rice Research Institute. 1991. *World rice statistics, 1990*. Los Baños, Philippines.

Ishikawa, S. 1978. Labor absorption in Asian agriculture. International Labor Organization, Bangkok.

Islam, R. 1984. Poverty and income distribution in rural Nepal. In *Poverty in rural Asia*. Bangkok: International Labor Organization.

Isvilanonda, S. 1990. Effect of pregerminated direct seeding on factor use and performance of rice farming: a case study in the irrigated area of Suphan Buri. In *Rice farming in transition*, edited by A. Fujimoto, K. Adulavidhaya, and T. Matsuda. Tokyo: World Planning.

Isvilanonda, S., S. Wattanutchariya, and K. Otsuka. 1992. Modern rice technology and regional factor price differential in Thailand. *Southeast Asian Journal of Agricultural Economics* 1(2): 137–150.

Jackson, B. R., W. Panichapat, and S. Awakul. 1969. Breeding performance and characteristics of dwarf, photoperiod non-sensitive varieties for Thailand. *Thai Journal of Agricultural Science* 2(2): 83–92.

Jamison, D. T., and L. J. Lau. 1982. *Farmer education and farm efficiency*. Baltimore: Johns Hopkins University Press.

Jatileksono, T. 1987. *Equity achievement in the Indonesian rice economy.* Yogyakarta: Gadjah Mada University Press.

Jatileksono, T., and K. Otsuka. 1993. Impact of modern rice technology on land prices: The case of Lampung in Indonesia. *American Journal of Agricultural Economics* 75(3): 652–665.

Jayasuriya, S. K., and R. T. Shand. 1985. Technical change and labor absorption in Asian agriculture: some emerging trends. *World Development* 14(3): 415–428.

Johl, S. 1975. Gains of the Green Revolution: how they have been shared in Punjab. *Journal of Development Studies* 11(3): 178–189.

Johnston, J. 1984. *Econometric methods*, 3rd ed. New York: McGraw-Hill.

Johnston, B. F., and J. Cownie. 1969. The seed-fertilizer revolution and labor force absorption. *American Economic Review* 59, 4: 569–582.

Junankar, P. N. 1975. Green Revolution and inequality. *Economic and Political Weekly* 10(13): A15–A18.

Kasryno, F. 1988. Pola penyerapan tenaga kerja pedesaan di Indonesia (Labor absorption in rural Indonesia). In *Perubahan ekonomi pedesaan menuju struktur ekonom berimbang* (Towards a balanced structure of rural economic development), edited by F. Kasryno, A. Suryana, A. Djauhari, P. Simatupang, B. Hutabarat, and C. A. Rasahan. Bogor: Center for Agro Economic Research.

Kawagoe, T., K. Otsuka, and Y. Hayami. 1986. Induced bias of technical change in agriculture: the United States and Japan, 1880–1980. *Journal of Political Economy* 94(3): 523–544.

Kawakami, J. 1983. Ine Mahsuri: nihongata riyo niyoru indogata hinshu no ikushu (Rice cultivar Mahsuri: development of Indica based on Japonica). In *Sakumotsu hinshu no riron to hoho* (Methodology and theory of plant breeding), edited by Kanichi Murakami, et al. Tokyo: Yokendo.

Khadka, K. R. 1977. An analysis of the factors of migration in Chitwan District, Nepal. M.S. thesis, University of the Philippines, Diliman, Quezon City.

Khush, G. S. 1984. *Terminology for rice growing environments.* Los Baños: International Rice Research Institute.

Kikuchi, M., A. Huysman, and L. Res. 1983. New rice technology and labor absorption: comparative history of two Philippine rice villages. IRRI Research Paper Series No. 90. Los Baños: International Rice Research Institute.

Krongkaew, M., and P. Tinakon. 1993. Poverty issues and policy measures to alleviate rural poverty: the case of Thailand. In *Rural Poverty in Asia*, edited by M. G. Quibria and T. N. Srinivasan. Oxford: Oxford University Press.

Ladejinsky, W. 1977. *Agrarian reform as unfinished business: the selected papers of Wolf Ladejinsky*, edited by L. J. Walinsky. Oxford: Oxford University Press.

Lal, D. 1976. Agricultural growth, real wages, and the rural poor in India. *Economic and Political Weekly* 11(26): A47–A61.

Liao, S. H. 1968. Factors affecting productivity and adoption of improved farm practices in rice farms. M.S. thesis, University of the Philippines, Los Baños, Philippines.

Lin, J. Y. 1988. The household responsibility system in China's agricultural reform: a theoretical and empirical study. *Economic Development and Cultural Change* 36(3): S199–S224.

_____. 1989a. Rural factor markets in China after the household responsibility reform. In *Chinese Economic Policy*, edited by Bruce Reynolds. New York: Paragon.

_____. 1991a. Education and innovation adoption in agriculture: evidence from hybrid rice in China. *American Journal of Agricultural Economics* 73(3): 713–723.

_____. 1991b. The household responsibility system reform and the adoption of hybrid rice in China. *Journal of Development Economics* 36: 353–372.

_____. 1992. Rural reforms and agricultural growth in China. *American Economic Review* 82(1): 34–51.

Lipton, M., and R. Longhurst. 1989. *New seeds and poor people*. London: Unwin Hyman.

Mandal, G. C., and M. G. Ghosh. 1976. *Economics of the Green Revolution: a study in East India*. New York: Asia Publishing House.

Mandal, M.A.S. 1980. Farm size, tenancy and productivity in an area of Bangladesh. *Bangladesh Journal of Agricultural Economics* 3(2): 21–42.

Mangahas, M. 1970. An economic analysis of diffusion of new rice varieties in Central Luzon. Ph.D. dissertation, University of Chicago.

Manning, C. 1988. The Green Revolution, employment, and economic change in rural Java. Occasional Paper No. 84. Institute of Southeast Asia Studies.

Melichar, E. 1979. Capital gains versus current income in the farming sector. *American Journal of Agricultural Economics* 61(5): 1085–1092.

Mencher, J. P. 1974. Conflicts and contradictions in the Green Revolution: the case of Tamil Nadu. *Economic and Political Weekly* 9(6–8): 309–322.

Misra, V. N. 1970. Labor market in agriculture: a study of Gujarat districts. *Indian Journal of Agricultural Economics* 25(3): 8–15.

Moody, K. 1982. Weed control in sequential cropping in rainfed lowland rice growing areas in tropical Asia. In *Weed control in small farms*, edited by M. Soerjani, D. E. Barnes, and T. O. Robson. Honolulu, Hawaii: Asian-Pacific Weed Science Society.

Moody, K., and V. Cordova. 1983. Wet seeded rice. In *Women in rice farming*. England: Gower Publishing Company Ltd.

Muqtada, M. 1986. Poverty and inequality: trends and causes. In *Bangladesh: selected issues in employment and development*, edited by R. Islam. New Delhi: International Labor Organization.

Naylor, R. 1991a. Equity effects of rice strategies. In *Rice policy in Indonesia*, edited by S. Pearson, W. Falcon, P. Heytens, E. Monke, and R. Naylor. Ithaca: Cornell University Press.

_____. 1991b. The rural labor market in Indonesia. In *Rice policy in Indonesia*, edited by S. Pearson, W. Falcon, P. Heytens, E. Monke, and R. Naylor. Ithaca: Cornell University Press.

Nepal, Central Bureau of Statistics. 1985. *National sample census of agriculture*. Kathmandu.

_____. 1987. *Statistical year book of Nepal*. Kathmandu.

New Era. 1981. Study on inter-regional migration in Nepal. Report submitted to National Commission on Population, Kathmandu, Nepal.

Newberry, D. 1975. Tenurial obstacles to innovations. *Journal of Development Studies* 11(4): 263–277.

Oberai, A. S., and H.K.M. Singh. 1980. Migration flows in Punjab's Green Revolution belt. *Economic and Political Weekly* 15(13): A2–A12.

Onchan, T. 1983. Farm mechanization policy in Thailand. Staff Paper No. 51, Department of Agricultural Economics, Kasetsart University.

Otsuka, K. 1991. Determinants and consequences of land reform implementation in the Philippines. *Journal of Development Economics* 35(1): 339–355.

Otsuka, K., and Y. Hayami. 1988. Theories of share tenancy: A critical survey. *Economic Development and Cultural Change* 37(1): 31–68.

Otsuka, K., H. Chuma, and Y. Hayami. 1992. Land and labor contracts in agrarian

economics: theories and facts. *Journal of Economic Literature* 30(4): 1965–
2018.

_____. 1993. Permanent labor and land tenancy contracts in agrarian economies:
An integrated analysis. *Economica* 60 (237): 57–77..

Otsuka, K., V. Cordova, and C. C. David. 1990. Modern rice technology and
regional wage differentials in the Philippines. *Agricultural Economics* 4(4):
297–314.

_____. 1992. Green Revolution, land reform, and household income distribution
in the Philippines. *Economic Development and Cultural Change* 40(4): 719–
741.

Otsuka, K., F. Gascon, and S. Asano. 1994a. "Second-generation MVs" and the
Evolution of the Green Revolution: the case of Central Luzon, 1966–1990.
Agricultural Economics, forthcoming.

_____. 1994b. Green Revolution and labour demand in rice farming: the case of
Central Luzon, 1966–1990. *Journal of Development Studies*, forthcoming.

Panpiemras, K., and S. Krusuansombat. 1985. Seasonal migration and
employment in Thailand. In *Food policy analysis in Thailand*, edited by T.
Panayotou. New York: Agricultural Development Council.

Pears, A. 1980. *Seeds of plenty, seeds of want: social and economic implications
of the Green Revolution*. Oxford: Clarendon Press.

Pearson, S., W. Falcon, P. Heytens, E. Monke, and R. Naylor, eds. 1991. *Rice
policy in Indonesia*. Ithaca: Cornell University Press.

Prabowo, D., and P. Sajogyo. 1975. Indonesia: Sidoarjo, East Java and Subang,
West Java. In *Changes in rice farming in selected areas of Asia*. Los Baños:
International Rice Research Institute.

Prahladachar, M. 1983. Income distribution effects of the Green Revolution in
India: a review of empirical evidence. *World Development* 11(11): 927–944.

Pyatt, G., C. Chen, and J. C. Fei. 1980. The distribution of income by factor
components. *Quarterly Journal of Economics* 95(3): 451–473.

Quizon, J. B., and H. P. Binswanger. 1983. Income distribution in agriculture : a
unified approach. *American Journal of Agricultural Economics* 65(4): 526–
538.

_____. 1986. Modelling the impact of agricultural growth and government
policy on income distribution in India. *The World Bank Economic Review*
1(1): 103–148.

Rahman, A., and T. Haque. 1988. Poverty and inequality in Bangladesh in the
eighties: an analysis of some recent evidence. Research Report No. 91. Dhaka:
Bangladesh Institute of Development Studies.

Raju, V. T. 1976. Impact of new agricultural technology on farm income
distribution in West Godavari District, India. *American Journal of Agricultural
Economics* 58(2): 346–350.

Ramasamy, C., and V. Rajagopalan. 1973. Impact of new technology on the
pattern of income distribution among farmers. *Southern Economic Review*
2(3): 225–236.

Ramasamy, C., and K. Otsuka. 1992. Differential adoption of modern rice
technology and labor market adjustments in South India. *Bangladesh
Development Studies* 30(1): 93–107.

Ramasamy, C., P. Paramasivam, and K. Otsuka. 1992. The modern rice
technology and adoption of labor saving technology in rice production: The
Tamil Nadu case. *Indian Journal of Agricultural Economics* 47(1): 35–47.

Ranade, C. G. 1977. Distribution of benefits from new agricultural technologies:
a study at farm level. Ph.D. dissertation, Cornell University.

Ranade, C. G., and R. W. Herdt. 1978. Shares of farm earnings from rice production. In *Economic consequences of the new rice technology*. Los Baños: International Rice Research Institute.

Rao, C.H.H. 1975. *Technological change and distribution in Indian agriculture*. New Delhi: MacMillan Company.

———. 1989. Technological change in Indian agriculture: emerging trends and perspectives. *Indian Journal of Agricultural Economics* 44 (4): 385–398.

Rao, Mohan J. 1989. Agricultural supply response: a survey. *Agricultural Economics* 3(1): 1–22.

Rawal, T. 1981. An analysis of factors affecting the adoption of modern varieties in Eastern Nepal. HMG-USAID-ADB Project Research Paper Series No. 11. Kathmandu: Winrock International.

Reinsel, R. D., and E. I. Reinsel. 1979. The economics of asset values and current income in farming. *American Journal of Agricultural Economics* 61(5): 1093–1097.

Renkow, M. 1993. Differential technology adoption and income distribution in Pakistan: implications for research resource allocation. *American Journal of Agricultural Economics* 75(1): 33–43.

Robison, L. J., D. A. Lins, and R. Venkataraman. 1985. Cash rents and land values in U.S. agriculture. *American Journal of Agricultural Economics* 67(4): 794–804.

Rosenzweig, M. R. 1984. Determinants of wage rates and labor supply behaviour in the rural sector of a developing country. In *Contractual arrangements, employment and wages in rural labor markets in Asia*, edited by Hans P. Binswanger and M. R. Rosenzweig. New Haven: Yale University Press.

Rosett, R. N., and F. O. Nelson. 1975. Estimation of the two-limit Tobit regression model. *Econometrica* 43(1): 141–46.

Roumasset, J. A., and J. Smith. 1981. Population, technological change and the evolution of labor markets. *Population and Development Review* 7(3): 401–419.

Roumasset, J. A., and M. Uy. 1980. Piece rates, time rates, and teams: explaining patterns in employment relation. *Journal of Economic Behaviour and Organization* 1(1): 343–360.

Ruttan, V. W. 1977. The Green Revolution: seven generalizations. *International Development Review* 19(1): 16–23.

Schultz, T. W. 1964. *Transforming traditional agriculture*. New Haven: Yale University Press.

———. 1975. The value of the ability to deal with disequilibria. *Journal of Economic Literature* 13(3): 827–846.

Setboonsarng, S., S. Wattanutchariya, and B. Puthigorn. 1988. Seed industry in Thailand: structure, conduct, and performance. The Hague: Development Research Institute.

Shalit, H., and A. Schmitz. 1982. Farmland accumulation and prices. *American Journal of Agricultural Economics* 64(4): 709–710.

Shand, R. T. 1987. Income distribution in a dynamic rural sector: some evidence from Malaysia. *Economic Development and Cultural Change* 36(1): 35–50.

Shorrocks, A. F. 1983. The impact of income components on the distribution of family income. *Quarterly Journal of Economics* 98(2): 310–326.

Siamwalla, A., and S. Haykins. 1983. The world rice market structure: conduct and performance. Research Report No. 39. Washington, DC: International Food Policy Research Institute.

Siamwalla, A., and S. Setboonsarng. 1991. Thailand. In *The political economy of agricultural pricing policies*, Vol. 2, Asia, edited by Anne O. Krueger, Maurice Schiff, and Alberto Valdes. Baltimore: Johns Hopkins University Press.

Sinaga, R. S., and B. M. Sinaga. 1978. Comments on shares of farm earnings from rice production. In *Economic consequences of the new rice technology.* Los Baños: International Rice Research Institute.

Singh, I., L. Squire, and J. Strauss. 1986. *Agricultural household models: extensions, applications and policy.* Baltimore: Johns Hopkins University Press.

Singh, K. 1973. The impact of new agricultural technology on farm income distribution in the Aligarh District of Uttar Pradesh. *Indian Journal of Agricultural Economics* 28(2): 1–11.

Sriswasdilek, J. 1973. Thei yield performance and economic benefits of the high-yielding varieties in Chadi, Suphaburi, Thailand. M.S. Thesis, University of the Philippines at Los Baños.

Stiglitz, J.E. 1975. Incentive, risk sharing, and information: notes towards a theory of hierarchy. *Bell Journal of Economics* 6(2): 552–579.

Thapa, G. B. 1989. The impact of new agricultural technology on income distribution in the Nepalese Tarai. Ph.D. dissertation, Cornell University, Ithaca.

Thapa, G. B., K. Otsuka, and R. Barker. 1992. The effect of modern rice varieties and irrigation on household income distribution in Nepalese villages. *Agricultural Economics* 7(3/4): 245–265.

Timmer, C.P. 1989. Indonesia: transition from food importer to exporter. In *Food policy in Asia,* edited by Terry Sicular. Ithaca: Cornell University Press.

Tirasawat, P. 1985. Migration in Thailand: past and future. In *Urbanization and migration in ASEAN development,* edited by P. Hauser, D. Suits, and N. Ogawa. Tokyo: National Institute for Research Advancement.

Tjondronegoro, S.M.P., I. Soejono, and J. Hardjono. 1993. Rural poverty in Indonesia. In *Rural Poverty in Asia,* edited by M. G. Quibria and T. N. Srinivasan. Oxford: Oxford University Press.

United Nations. 1980. *1990 Revision of world population prospects.*

Upadhyaya, H. K. 1988. Labor market effect of modern rice technology and its implications on income distribution in Nepal. Ph.D. dissertation, University of the Philippines at Los Baños.

Upadhyaya, H. K., and G. B. Bhatta. 1989. A case study of the Lamage Irrigation System, Syangja. Applied Study Report No. 8. Pokhara, Nepal: Irrigation Management Center.

Upadhyaya, H. K., K. Otsuka, and C. C. David. 1990. Differential adoption of modern rice technology and regional wage differential in Nepal. *Journal of Development Studies* 26(3): 450–468.

Upadhyaya, H. K., C. C. David, G. B. Thapa, and K. Otsuka. 1993. Adoption and productivity impacts of modern rice varieties in Nepal. *Developing Economies* 31(1): 122–137.

Utami, W., and J. Ihalauw. 1973. Some consequences of small farm size. *Bulletin of Indonesian Economic Studies* 9(2): 46–56.

Uzawa, H. 1962. Production functions with constant elasticities of substitution. *Review of Economic Studies* 29(4): 291–299.

Verma, B. N., and D. W. Bromley. 1987. The political economy of farm size in India: the elusive quest. *Economic Development and Cultural Change* 35(4): 791–808.

Virmani, S. S., and I. B. Edwards. 1983. Current status and future prospects for breeding hybrid rice and wheat. *Advances in Agronomy* 36(1): 145–214.

Vyas, V. S. 1992. Elmhirst memorial lecture: Agrarian structure, environmental concerns, and rural poverty. *Sustainable agricultural development: the role of international cooperation,* edited by G. H. Peters and B. F. Stanton. Aldershot, England: Dartmouth.

Wangwacharakul, V. 1984. Direct and indirect impact of the cropping systems technology and irrigation in a community economy: the case of Oton and Tigbauan, Iloilo Province, Philippines. Ph.D. dissertation, University of the Philippines at Los Baños.

Warr, C.J.L., M. A. Quayum, and A. Orr. 1988. Agricultural resource use under natural hazards: deep water rice—Bangladesh. Research Report No. 3, Agricultural Economics Division. Dhaka: Bangladesh Rice Research Institute.

Watanabe, M. 1987. Economic development and interregional migration in Thailand. Tokyo: International Development Center of Japan. Mimeo.

Wattanutchariya, S. 1983. Economic analysis of the farm machinery industry and tractor contractor business in Thailand. In *Consequences of small-farm mechanization*. Los Baños: International Rice Research Institute and Agricultural Development Council.

Wharton, C. R. 1969. The Green Revolution: cornucopia or pandora's box. *Foreign Affairs.* 7(April): 464–476.

White, B. 1976. Population, involution and employment in rural Java. *Development and Change* 7(3): 267–290.

_____. 1979. Political aspects of poverty, income distribution and their measurement: Some examples from rural Java. *Development and Change* 10(1): 91–114.

World Bank (International Bank for Reconstruction and Development). 1986. *Thailand: towards a development strategy for full participation.* Washington, DC.

____. 1989. *World tables 1989/90.* Washington, DC.

Yadav, R. P. 1987. Agricultural research in Nepal: resource allocation, structure and incentives. IFPRI Research Report 62, Washington, DC: International Food Policy Research Institute.

Yadav, S. N., K. Otsuka, and C. C. David. 1992. Segmentation in rural financial markets: the case of Nepal. *World Development* 20(3): 423–436.

Yuan, L. 1985. *A concise course in hybrid rice.* Changsha: Hunan Science and Technology Press.

Zhu, R., ed. 1988. *Dangdai zhongguo de nongzuowuye* (The science of crops in modern China). Beijing: Social Science Press.

The Contributors

M. Mokaddem Akash is an assistant professor at the University of Dhaka, Bangladesh.

Violeta G. Cordova is an economist at the SPC-German Biological Control Project, Suva, Fiji.

Cristina David is a research fellow at the Philippine Institute for Development Studies, Philippines.

Mahabub Hossain is an agricultural economist at the International Rice Research Institute, Philippines.

Somporn Isvilanonda is an assistant professor at Kasetsart University, Thailand.

M. A. Jabbar is an economist at the Bangladesh Rice Research Institute, Bangladesh.

Tumari Jatileksono is an associate professor in the Faculty of Agriculture at Gadjah Mada University, Indonesia.

A. Kandaswamy is a director at the Centre for Agricultural and Rural Development Studies, Tamil Nadu Agricultural University, India.

Faisal Kasryno is a director general at the Agency for Agricultural Research and Development, Indonesia.

Justin Yifu Lin is a deputy director at the Department of Rural Economy Development Research Center, China.

Keijiro Otsuka is currently a visiting research fellow at the International Food Policy Research Institute, Washington, D.C.

P. Paramasivam is an assistant professor at the Centre for Agricultural and Rural Development Studies, Tamil Nadu Agricultural University, India.

M. Abul Quasem is an economist at the Bangladesh Institute of Development Studies, Bangladesh.

C. Ramasamy is a professor at the Centre for Agricultural and Rural Development Studies, Tamil Nadu Agricultural University, India.

Tahlim Sudaryanto is an agricultural economist at the Center for Agro-Socioeconomic Research, Indonesia.

Ganesh B. Thapa is a research specialist at Winrock International, Nepal.

Hari K. Upadhyaya is chairman of the Center for Environmental and Agricultural Research, Extension, and Development, Nepal.

Sarun Wattanutchariya is a professor at Kasetsart University, Thailand.

Index

About the Book

Two decades have passed since the introduction of modern rice varieties (MVs) and their accompanying technology in Asia. This volume looks at seven Asian countries with widely diverse production environments and agrarian and policy structures to determine to what extent the adoption of MVs only in the irrigated and the favorable rainfed-lowland areas has exacerbated inequalities in the distribution of income.

Refuting claims of Green Revolution critics, the contributors find that, when both direct and indirect effects of labor, land, and market adjustments are considered, differential adoption of MVs across environments did not significantly worsen income distribution. Instead, as MV adoption increased the demand for labor in the favorable areas, interregional migration from unfavorable areas took place, which mitigated potentially negative impacts by equalizing regional wages. Shifts to alternative farm crops or nonfarm employment, as well as enlargement of farm size in the unfavorable areas also contributed to the restoration of equity.